VOLUME 595

SEPTEMBER 2004

THE ANNALS

of The American Academy of Political
and Social Science

ROBERT W. PEARSON, *Executive Editor*
LAWRENCE W. SHERMAN, *Editor*

Being Here and Being There: Fieldwork Encounters and Ethnographic Discoveries

Special Editors of this Volume

ELIJAH ANDERSON
University of Pennsylvania

SCOTT N. BROOKS
University of California, Riverside

RAYMOND GUNN
University of Pennsylvania

NIKKI JONES
University of California, Santa Barbara

SAGE Publications Thousand Oaks · London · New Delhi

Origin and Purpose. The Academy was organized December 14, 1889, to promote the progress of political and social science, especially through publications and meetings. The Academy does not take sides in controverted questions, but seeks to gather and present reliable information to assist the public in forming an intelligent and accurate judgment.

Meetings. The Academy occasionally holds a meeting in the spring extending over two days.

Publications. THE ANNALS of The American Academy of Political and Social Science is the bimonthly publication of the Academy. Each issue contains articles on some prominent social or political problem, written at the invitation of the editors. Also, monographs are published from time to time, numbers of which are distributed to pertinent professional organizations. These volumes constitute important reference works on the topics with which they deal, and they are extensively cited by authorities throughout the United States and abroad. The papers presented at the meetings of the Academy are included in THE ANNALS.

Membership. Each member of the Academy receives THE ANNALS and may attend the meetings of the Academy. Membership is open only to individuals. Annual dues: $75.00 for the regular paperbound edition (clothbound, $113.00). For members outside the U.S.A., add $24.00 for shipping of your subscription. Members may also purchase single issues of THE ANNALS for $23.00 each (clothbound, $31.00). Student memberships are available for $49.00.

Subscriptions. THE ANNALS of The American Academy of Political and Social Science (ISSN 0002-7162) (J295) is published six times annually—in January, March, May, July, September, and November— by Sage Publications, 2455 Teller Road, Thousand Oaks, CA 91320. Telephone: (800) 818-SAGE (7243) and (805) 499-9774; FAX/Order line: (805) 499-0871; E-mail: journals@sagepub.com. Copyright © 2004 by The American Academy of Political and Social Science. Institutions may subscribe to THE ANNALS at the annual rate: $490.00 (clothbound, $554.00). Add $24.00 per year for subscriptions outside the U.S.A. Institutional rates for single issues: $95.00 each (clothbound, $106.00).

Periodicals postage paid at Thousand Oaks, California, and at additional mailing offices.

Single issues of THE ANNALS may be obtained by individuals who are not members of the Academy for $33.00 each (clothbound, $46.00). Single issues of THE ANNALS have proven to be excellent supplementary texts for classroom use. Direct inquiries regarding adoptions to THE ANNALS c/o Sage Publications (address below).

All correspondence concerning membership in the Academy, dues renewals, inquiries about membership status, and/or purchase of single issues of THE ANNALS should be sent to THE ANNALS c/o Sage Publications, 2455 Teller Road, Thousand Oaks, CA 91320. Telephone: (800) 818-SAGE (7243) and (805) 499-9774; FAX/Order line: (805) 499-0871. E-mail: journals@sagepub.com. *Please note that orders under $30 must be prepaid.* Sage affiliates in London and India will assist institutional subscribers abroad with regard to orders, claims, and inquiries for both subscriptions and single issues.

Printed on recycled, acid-free paper

THE ANNALS

Editorial Office: 3814 Walnut Street, Fels Institute for Government, University of Pennsylvania, Philadelphia, PA 19104-6197.

For information about membership° (individuals only) and subscriptions (institutions), address:
Sage Publications
2455 Teller Road
Thousand Oaks, CA 91320

Sage Production Staff: Joseph Riser and Paul Doebler

From India and South Asia, write to:
SAGE PUBLICATIONS INDIA Pvt Ltd
B-42 Panchsheel Enclave, P.O. Box 4109
New Delhi 110 017
INDIA

From Europe, the Middle East, and Africa, write to:
SAGE PUBLICATIONS LTD
1 Oliver's Yard, 55 City Road
London EC1Y 1SP
UNITED KINGDOM

°Please note that members of the Academy receive THE ANNALS with their membership.
International Standard Serial Number ISSN 0002-7162
International Standard Book Number ISBN 1-4129-1395-0 (Vol. 595, 2004 paper)
International Standard Book Number ISBN 1-4129-1394-2 (Vol. 595, 2004 cloth)
Manufactured in the United States of America. First printing, September 2004.

The articles appearing in *The Annals* are abstracted or indexed in Academic Abstracts, Academic Search, America: History and Life, Asia Pacific Database, Book Review Index, CAB Abstracts Database, Central Asia: Abstracts & Index, Communication Abstracts, Corporate ResourceNET, Criminal Justice Abstracts, Current Citations Express, Current Contents: Social & Behavioral Sciences, Documentation in Public Administration, e-JEL, EconLit, Expanded Academic Index, Guide to Social Science & Religion in Periodical Literature, Health Business FullTEXT, HealthSTAR FullTEXT, Historical Abstracts, International Bibliography of the Social Sciences, International Political Science Abstracts, ISI Basic Social Sciences Index, Journal of Economic Literature on CD, LEXIS-NEXIS, MasterFILE FullTEXT, Middle East: Abstracts & Index, North Africa: Abstracts & Index, PAIS International, Periodical Abstracts, Political Science Abstracts, Psychological Abstracts, PsycINFO, Sage Public Administration Abstracts, Social Science Source, Social Sciences Citation Index, Social Sciences Index Full Text, Social Services Abstracts, Social Work Abstracts, Sociological Abstracts, Southeast Asia: Abstracts & Index, Standard Periodical Directory (SPD), TOPICsearch, Wilson OmniFile V, and Wilson Social Sciences Index/Abstracts, and are available on microfilm from ProQuest, Ann Arbor, Michigan.

Information about membership rates, institutional subscriptions, and back issue prices may be found on the facing page.

Advertising. Current rates and specifications may be obtained by writing to *The Annals* Advertising and Promotion Manager at the Thousand Oaks office (address above).

Claims. Claims for undelivered copies must be made no later than six months following month of publication. The publisher will supply missing copies when losses have been sustained in transit and when the reserve stock will permit.

Change of Address. Six weeks' advance notice must be given when notifying of change of address to ensure proper identification. Please specify name of journal. POSTMASTER: Send address changes to: *The Annals* of The American Academy of Political and Social Science, c/o Sage Publications, 2455 Teller Road, Thousand Oaks, CA 91320.

OF THE AMERICAN ACADEMY OF
POLITICAL AND SOCIAL SCIENCE

Volume 595   September 2004

IN THIS ISSUE:

*Being Here and Being There:
Fieldwork Encounters and Ethnographic Discoveries*

Special Editors: ELIJAH ANDERSON
SCOTT N. BROOKS
RAYMOND GUNN
NIKKI JONES

Quick Read Synopsis

Preface

By
ELIJAH ANDERSON,
SCOTT N. BROOKS,
RAYMOND GUNN,
and
NIKKI JONES

These articles are gathered from the ethnography conference "Being Here and Being There: Fieldwork Encounters and Ethnographic Discoveries," which was held at the University of Pennsylvania in November 2003.

An ethnography fieldwork conference that was held at the University of California, Los Angeles, in May 2002, provided a rare opportunity for established scholars and graduate students to share their work and to socialize informally. Participants at the Penn conference explored further some of the projects, programs, and conversations from the California conference. In keeping with the previous conference, new and seasoned fieldworkers from various parts of the United States and the world came together to underscore the value of ethnographic work and also to seek new directions.

With these concerns in mind, conference participants discussed the social organization of urban life, culture, and the continuing significance of the city as a site for ethnographic studies. Seemingly, ethnographers are forever in search of ways to better get at these persistent issues: How do people live? How do they go about meeting the demands of life? How and why do they form their definitions of the situation? What do researchers know about these processes? How do we know what we know? and What is its significance? These are among the issues that were addressed over the course of the conference. There was ample opportunity for young scholars and veteran field researchers to come together in an intimate setting to bridge their work in ways that both take ethnography into the future and reestablish ties to their scholarly roots.

When the four of us met to discuss putting on an ethnography conference, we had no idea how much of a Herculean task it would be or how sat-

DOI: 10.1177/0002716204267846

isfying it would be for us individually and collectively. It seemed simple enough to get folks together who do ethnography; after all, what ethnographers do is "get with" people. Essentially, inviting friends over for a two-day dinner to share "stories" was what we envisioned and hoped for. Our friends came from far and wide. They came from many parts of the United States, as well as France, Finland, and England—and all had fascinating stories to share. We encouraged veteran fieldworkers to include their students in this wonderful enterprise as a way to make explicit the importance of mentoring as an integral part of ethnographic work.

Indeed, mentoring is a major theme that runs throughout the proceedings, and it is one of the threads that holds this volume together so well. Another thread is the ethnographer's passion for learning from others. In the pieces that follow, the reader will come away with a clear sense of the various ways ethnographers develop relationships with people in the field and learn from these people so as to conduct a systematic study of the culture of the people. In short, ethnography is about real life and how people go about meeting the demands of life.

One learns from this volume that as students of culture, ethnographers must possess curiosity, openness, and humility—three traits that are vital for "getting with" people.

We tend to be internally motivated to examine specific issues and people. We often find ourselves interacting with those whom others talk *about* but do not necessarily talk *to*. Sometimes, we are those people, a marginal status that we use to empower our observations and insights.

The insight gleaned is rich and poignant, seemingly perfect for social policy. But ethnography and social policy have a troubled marriage. The truths that are born of ethnographic work rarely fit neatly with the ways social policies are implemented. This tension plays itself out in a variety of ways—some more explicitly than others—but it is always present in ethnographic work.

This volume is unique, as far as we know, for bringing such a broad range of stories and researchers together. One might even wonder how they fit together; this is the point of gathering such work in a single source. The unity lies not so much in general themes, though they exist, but in the challenges and boons of fieldwork born out of "thick description" and examined experiences, which we were able to exchange at the conference. What lie before you are some of the "stories" that participants shared.

Introduction

By
ROBERT M. EMERSON

The articles collected in this volume were originally presented at the ethnography conference held at the University of Pennsylvania in November 2003. This conference was inspired, in part, by a similar conference held at the University of California, Los Angeles (UCLA), in May 2002, sponsored by UCLA's Department of Sociology and the LeRoy Neiman Center for the Study of American Society and Politics.

The UCLA conference was an informal affair, aimed at revisiting and reasserting the field-research traditions of the Chicago School and its emphasis on "bringing back the news" from unknown or misknown social worlds. Colleagues and friends involved in a variety of ethnographic projects were invited and encouraged to bring along their graduate students. Presentations were structured as "works in progress," highlighting evolving ideas and issues; the aim was not only to preserve the real-to-life "messiness" of the research process but also to inform colleagues of current projects and concerns, a recurrent problem in ethnographic work where data collection, analysis, and writing stretch out over time, often preventing peers from learning about what others are actually doing in the field. And efforts were made to strengthen and extend ethnographic networks

Robert M. Emerson is a professor of sociology at the University of California, Los Angeles. His publications on ethnographic and field-research methods include an edited a collection of readings on ethnography Contemporary Field Research: Perspective and Formulations *(Waveland Press, 2001, 2nd ed.),* Writing Ethnographic Fieldnotes *(coauthored with Rachel I. Fretz and Linda L. Shaw; University of Chicago Press, 1995), and recent articles in the* Handbook of Ethnography *(Sage, 2001) and* Inside Qualitative Research *(Sage, 2003). Substantively, his work uses qualitative methods to analyze the dynamics of interpersonal troubles and informal social control, as well as decision-making practices in formal institutions of social control, including juvenile courts, psychiatric emergency teams, public schools, and prosecutors' offices.*

DOI: 10.1177/0002716204268031

by making places for graduate students in both the formal presentations and the informal social occasions that marked the meetings.

The idea for the Pennsylvania conference emerged at UCLA when Elijah Anderson gathered during a break with three of his graduate students—Scott Brooks, Raymond Gunn, and Nikki Jones—and said something along the lines of, "We should do this at Penn." These students responded enthusiastically, insisting on being involved in all facets of conference organization. And indeed, on returning to Philadelphia, Anderson, Brooks, Gunn, and Jones began to meet on an almost weekly basis to plan the conference. While this planning process involved the inevitable nuts-and-bolts issues, it also provided occasions for wide-ranging discussions of such matters as the tenets and lineage of the Chicago School, W. E. B. Du Bois's place in that tradition, the changing nature of the city as a site for ethnographic study, and the impact of the changing economic structure on the daily life of the city. These discussions shaped the design and planning of conference sessions and hence the topics and issues addressed by the articles in this volume.

Neither conference attempted to represent all of ethnography: over the past several decades, ethnographic methods and sensitivities have spread widely, taking on divergent emphases and concerns and crossing a variety of disciplinary boundaries (Emerson 2001, vii-ix). Contemporary ethnography is too large, too diverse, and too contentious to be represented in its entirety in a single meeting or collection of articles. Rather, the conferences—and most of the articles from the University of Pennsylvania conference that are assembled here—reflect a distinctive approach to ethnography, an approach that seeks to engage, reassert, and reassess three recurring themes found in classic Chicago-style fieldwork.

First, ethnographers working in the Chicago tradition place a heavy emphasis on discovery. Emphasizing discovery assumes that field researchers make their distinctive contributions by identifying and analyzing new, unappreciated, or misappreciated processes that have important effects on social life. Ultimately, the defining element of ethnographic work in the Chicago School tradition is a focus on neither theory nor method. Rather, it is discovery in the sense of "bringing back the news" and, moreover, the process of discovery that sparks the theoretical creativity and methodological sensitivity of Chicago School field research.

A second defining element of the Chicago School tradition is what David Matza (1969) has characterized as "loyalty to the phenomenon." Guiding questions for researchers in this tradition are the following: What is happening out there? and How can we capture what is happening in our field notes and writings? Often, these elements are missing in projects that are described as ethnographic. Commonly, these projects rely first on theory and then, often to a lesser degree, on actual fieldwork. The resulting texts often tell us more about what particular theories suggest people are doing out there and less about what people are actually doing. These types of texts fail, as Mitchell Duneier would say, to "show us the people" and, as a result, are often flat and unconvincing.

Loyalty to the phenomenon does not require a "disloyalty" to theory; rather, one must balance theoretical concerns with a deep interest and sincere commitment to what the people we study are actually doing. As an example, those within the tradition would caution fieldworkers against simply framing a Provencal market as an instance of the sociology of contemporary "consumer culture" (see de La Pradelle 1996). The more revealing sociological question, and the question that is most true to the tradition, is rather, What are players in a Provencal market doing? A quality ethnographic text will not only vividly describe what the players in a Provencal market are doing but will also, through this description and the integration of original and relevant theory, instruct us on how the goings-on of a Provencal market speak to the larger phenomenon of the sociology of consumer culture.

A third element of the Chicago School is the collection of original data, as well as the collection of ethnographic data in original ways. This originality can spring from the choice of setting, the selection of people studied, or a particular angle taken in the field. For example, one can take an original angle by viewing a setting from the ground floor as opposed to from the position of people in power. Originality can also present itself in the way that researchers interact with and record evidence about the people they are studying. The constraints of fieldwork may make such attempts at originality difficult; as field researchers, we do not always have control over data-collection methods. Nonetheless, we should strive for originality and innovation.

These themes are evident in the pieces collected in this volume, which may be loosely divided into current, substantive fieldwork studies and discussions; and reflections on the history, processes, and contemporary issues confronting ethnographic research.

The first set of articles provides substantive and methodological ethnographic analyses of contemporary social life. Five of these articles are drawn on fieldwork carried out in Philadelphia. In "The Cosmopolitan Canopy," Elijah Anderson examines a variety of public-place settings and moments when people come together, hang out, look at, and occasionally interact with strangers without the sorts of distrustful wariness and distancing we often associate with public-place behavior. The key to understanding these moments and occasions, Anderson argues, lies in appreciating the practical "folk ethnography" that people engage in to make sense of and relate civilly with the diverse others they encounter at these times. Two studies examine fighting and violence among inner-city teenage girls. "Why Girls Fight: Female Youth Violence in the Inner City," by Cindy Ness finds that fighting is commonly reported among the girls she studied, who insist, just as with boys, that "holding your own" is an important skill in managing status and reputation in these poor, inner-city communities. In "'It's Not Where You Live, It's How You Live': How Young Women Negotiate Conflict and Violence in the Inner City," Nikki Jones explores differences in the ways in which teenage girls encounter and manage "disrespect," conflict, and violence in their everyday lives. Through two case studies, she contrasts a strategy that trades on a reputation for being a "fighter" with strategies for avoiding and defusing conflicts, noting that the young woman using this latter approach would still on occasion "have to fight," usually as the result of "loyalty links" to close friends. In "Inner-City 'Schoolboy' Life," Raymond Gunn contrasts his own socially expansive experience of growing up as an aspiring child actor in New York City with the ways in which promising, formerly academically motivated students may come to interact in hostile and antagonistic ways with school staff, leading to subsequent marginalization and exclusion from activities and programs intended to promote college admission. And finally, in "'Putting the Blessings on Him': Vouching and Basketball Status Work," Scott N. Brooks analyzes the processes of establishing status and credibility through which he gained entry to the activities of an elite Philadelphia high school basketball league. The key lay in the willingness of a former player and eminent coach to "vouch" for him, providing support and validation that borrowed from his own established status and identity.

Four articles provide ethnographic analyzes of contemporary social processes and phenomena in Europe. Heli Vaaranen's study of young males in Helsinki, who illegally and often dangerously race cars on weekend nights on public streets, roads, and highways, presents ethnographic materials from a very different urban and culture context. Vaaranen examines the subculture of these Finnish street racers, focusing on the class position and experiences of these youth, as well as the organization and emotional experiences of street racing. In "The Ethnography of Imagined Communities: The Cultural Production of Sikh Ethnicity in Britain," Kathleen D. Hall draws on her research on Sikh youth in the United Kingdom to argue that the ethnography of immigrant incorporation should move beyond an exclusive focus on local immigrant sites and activities to include consideration of the broader cultural politics of national identity and grounds for inclusion in the "nation." Two final substantive pieces examine aspects of social life in contemporary France. Octave Debary examines the history of a museum in a declining industrial town in France. Organizers of Le Creusot museum, housed in the castle residence of the former owners of a large iron- and steelworks, initially sought to develop an "ecomuseum" focusing on local industry and labor, but with the closing of the ironworks factory, they transformed it into an ordinary museum displaying exhibited objects. In "Paris Plage: 'The City Is Ours,'" Michele de La Pradelle and Emmanuelle Lallement analyze the creation, uses, and meanings of the Paris Plage, the thirty-foot-wide stretch of sand, palm trees, and deck chairs created on an expressway during the summer of 2003 along the bank of the Seine.

The second collection of articles in this volume provides a series of reflections on the history, methods, and current issues confronting ethnography. Tukufu Zuberi's "W. E. B. DuBois's Sociology: *The Philadelphia Negro* and Social Science" analyzes DuBois's community study as combining the social survey methods of Charles Booth and other researchers of the urban poor with a deep appreciation of the racially marginalized position of African Americans in Philadelphia at the end of the nineteenth century. In "Using the History of the Chicago Tradition of Sociology for Empirical Research," Jean-Michel Chapoulie urges avoiding "presentist" histories of social science to develop "full" histories that understand research findings "in the context of their time and look at production activities as well as institutional or other activities that accompany them" (p. 162). "Full histories" of the Chicago sociological tradition can promote and facilitate the controlled borrowing of prior sociological analyses to frame and guide fruitful empirical research in new and different social circumstances. Finally, Henri Peretz's "The Making of *Black Metropolis*" analyzes this classic ethnographic study of the South Side of Chicago written by St. Clair Drake and Horace Cayton and published in 1945. Peretz calls attention to the collective nature of the fieldwork and data collection, initiated as a Works Progress Administration project in 1935 with the collaboration of Cayton and anthropologist Lloyd Warner and carried out by a team of fieldworkers. The team fieldwork method produced the close documentation and diversity of themes that made *Black Metropolis* an exemplary ethnography of this African American community.

Three articles propose unorthodox expansions of ethnographic methods to previously neglected sites, processes, and issues. William Kornblum seeks to adapt and develop the methods of historical ethnography to describe the dynamics of race relations in the social worlds of jazz and blues as found in the roadhouses, clubs, and speakeasies of Chicago in 1924. In "Discovering Ink: A Mentor for an Historical Ethnography," he recounts his procedures for imaginatively reconstructing these worlds and their interactions by writing field notes based on primary sources, including contemporary accounts, autobiographies, recorded interviews, and oral histories. He ended up finding a retrospective "mentor," someone centrally involved in the jazz world of this era, in "race-record producer" Mayo "Ink" Williams. In "Beyond *Mysterium Tremendum*: Thoughts toward the Aesthetic Study of Religious Experience," Omar McRoberts seeks to move ethnographic studies of religion beyond the common primary focus on conversion to document the fieldworker's empathetic experience of a variety of more everyday, mundane religious activities. And Lawrence Sherman and Heather Strang elaborate a method for doing "experimental ethnography," specifying the place of qualitative data and analysis in an experimental design project on restorative justice in which the interactions of controlled contact between criminals and their victims are observed and recorded.

A final group of articles explores issues concerning the practice and place of ethnography in contemporary social worlds. In "The Liberty Bell: A Meditation on Labor, Freedom, and Culture," Paul Willis argues that human labor and cultural production have assumed new forms and meanings, challenging ethnographers to understand and represent new forms of cultural production and their implications. Charles Bosk and Raymond De Vries's "Bureaucracies of Mass Deception: Institutional Review Boards and the Ethics of Ethnographic Research" examines current tensions and disagreements around institutional review boards and efforts to develop "best-practice" guidelines for regulating ethnographic fieldwork. The article offers a series of practical suggestions for making the current system work better with and for qualitative researchers. The dialogue "On the Value of Ethnography: Sociology and Public Policy" incorporates a panel discussion extending an earlier e-mail exchange between Howard S. Becker and Herbert J. Gans on the social and political stance underlying Goffman's classic field research study *Asylums*: Is this study fundamentally an attempt to avoid conventional language and categories to develop a broadly comparative approach to oppressive institutions, or is it a more directly policy-relevant effort to "rehumanize" the mental patient? This issue serves as a point of departure for a broader consideration of the public and policy relevance of ethnographic research, including discussions by Diane Vaughan of NASA responses to her study of the Challenger launch decision with the recent Columbia disaster and by Katherine S. Newman on her work on poverty and downward mobility. Jean-Michel Chapoulie comments further on some of the often-neglected assumptions underlying these issues, including the presumed commitment of policy-making elites to improve the conditions of those at the bottom of the social scale and the ways in which the political priorities and time frames differ radically from those of ethnographers and other social scientists. Finally, in "On the Rhetoric and Politics of Ethnographic Methodology," Jack Katz argues that several critical issues easily can be masked in a debate between advocates of neutral and comparative analytic language and advocates of research cast in language that will be perceived as useful and relevant for assessing how power affects those it reaches. These critical issues are empirical matters: every ethnographer will define his or her position on each of these in each research project, whether self-consciously or sentimentally, and the stance taken will have major consequences for the demands of the research project. The Becker, Gans, Newman, and Vaughan discussion touches on three critical and practical issues: whether to mark policy or political relevance in textual language; how broadly and comparatively to frame the description of the substantive ethnographic research case; and which spatial and temporal dimensions of a social phenomenon should be included in its study.

The volume concludes with an overview by Renee Fox of recurrent issues and dilemmas that participant-observation fieldworkers confront.

References

de La Pradelle, Michele. 1996. *Les Vendredis de Carpentras: Faire son marche, en Provence ou ailleurs*. Paris: Fayard.

Emerson, Robert M., ed. 2001. *Contemporary field research: Perspectives and formulations*. Prospect Heights, IL: Waveland Press.

Matza, David. 1969. *Becoming deviant*. Englewood Cliffs, NJ: Prentice Hall.

The public spaces of the city are more racially, ethnically, and socially diverse than ever. Social distance and tension as expressed by wariness of strangers appear to be the order of the day. But the "cosmopolitan canopy" offers a respite and an opportunity for diverse peoples to come together to do their business and also to engage in "folk ethnography" that serves as a cognitive and cultural base on which people construct behavior in public.

Keywords: urban ethnography; cities; public space; race relations

The Cosmopolitan Canopy

By
ELIJAH ANDERSON

In 1938, Louis Wirth published "Urbanism as a Way of Life," based on his observations of city life and drawing on Georg Simmel's (1950) earlier work in Europe, "The Metropolis and Mental Life" (Spykman 1925). What mainly concerned Wirth were the qualities that for him defined the city, particularly the variables of size, density, and heterogeneity. Especially striking to him was people's "blasé" orientation as they traversed the urban spaces with an impersonal bearing that suggested an attitude of indifference.[1] In the sixty-five years since Wirth's groundbreaking formulations on urbanism, much has happened to big-city life. Of course, some conditions have remained constant, but many have changed profoundly. Strongly affected by the forces of industrialism, immigration, and globalism, the city of today is more racially, ethnically, and socially diverse than

Elijah Anderson is the Charles and William L. Day Distinguished Professor of the Social Sciences and a professor of sociology at the University of Pennsylvania. He is the author of A Place on the Corner: A Study of Black Street Corner Men *(2nd ed. with new preface and appendix, 2003),* Streetwise: Race, Class and Change in an Urban Community *(1990), and* Code of the Street: Decency, Violence, and the Moral Life of the Inner City *(1999). He is also director of the Philadelphia Ethnography Project at the University of Pennsylvania.*

NOTE: I would like to thank Randall Collins, Howard S. Becker, Jack Katz, and Christine Szczepanowski for helpful comments on this work.

DOI: 10.1177/0002716204266833

ever, with profound cleavages dividing one element from another and one social group from another (see Drake and Cayton 1945; Goffman 1963; Gans 1962; Suttles 1968; Jacobs 1961; Hall 1966; Sassen 2001; Duneier 1999; Wilson 1987, 1996; and Anderson 1990, 1999).

As the urban public spaces of big cities have become more riven by issues of race, poverty, and crime, much of what Wirth described as urbanites' blasé indifference seems to have given way to a pervasive wariness toward strangers, particularly anonymous black males (see Anderson 1990). In places such as bus stations, parking garages, and public streets and sidewalks, many pedestrians move about guardedly, dealing with strangers by employing elaborate facial and eye work, replete with smiles, nods, and gestures geared to carve out an impersonal but private zone for themselves. Increasingly, pedestrians are required to contend publicly with the casualties of modern urban society, not just the persistently poor who at times beg aggressively but also homeless people, street criminals, and the mentally disturbed. Fearful of crime, if threatened, many are prepared to defend themselves or to quickly summon help, if not from fellow pedestrians, then from the police. In navigating such spaces, people often divert their gazes, looking up, looking down, or looking away, and feign ignorance of the diverse mix of strangers they encounter. Defensively, they "look past" or "look through" the next person, distancing themselves from strangers and effectively consigning their counterparts to a form of social oblivion.

As anonymous pedestrians actively "see but don't see" one another, skin color often becomes a social border that deeply complicates public interactions; stereotypically, white skin color is associated with civility and trust, and black skin color is associated with danger and distrust—especially with regard to anonymous young males. Many ordinary pedestrians feel at ease with others they deem to be most like themselves; the more threatening the "other" is judged to be, the greater the distance displayed. Black strangers more often greet and otherwise acknowledge other strangers, particularly other blacks. But most other pedestrians seem simply to follow their noses, at times barely avoiding collisions with others. If they speak at all, they may utter a polite "excuse me" or "I'm sorry," and, if deemed appropriate, they scowl. In effect, people work to shape and guard their own public space.

Yet there remain numerous heterogeneous and densely populated bounded public spaces within cities that offer a respite from this wariness, settings where a diversity of people[2] can feel comfortable enough to relax their guard and go about their business more casually. A prime such location is Philadelphia's Reading Terminal Market. In this relatively busy, quasi-public setting, under a virtual *cosmopolitan canopy*,[3] people are encouraged to treat others with a certain level of civility or at least simply to behave themselves. Within this canopy are smaller ones or even spontaneous canopies, where instantaneous communities of diverse strangers emerge and materialize—the opportunities or openings provided by fascinating tidbits of eavesdropped (or overheard) conversation. Here, along the crowded aisle and eating places, visitors can relax and feel relatively safe and secure. Although they may still avoid prolonged eye contact or avert their glances to refrain from sending the "wrong" messages, people tend to positively acknowledge one another's existence in some measure. At times, strangers may approach one another to talk, to laugh, to joke, or to share a story here and there. Their trusting attitudes can be infectious, even spreading feelings of community across racial and ethnic lines.

Occupying a full city block in Center City Philadelphia, the Reading Terminal Market is composed of numerous shops, restaurants, and kiosks that offer an array of goods and services. It is a highly diverse setting wherein all kinds of people shop, eat, and stroll. Adjacent to the new convention center, it is centrally located among downtown office buildings and upscale condominiums but not far from white, working-class Kensington and black, North Philadelphia. The Terminal building itself, an enormous former train shed, has been part of Philadelphia for more than a century, since the days when trains arrived and departed through the space that became the market. In the 1990s, when the convention center complex was designed and built, the space for the market was kept more or less intact. Many long-time customers feared that it would become simply an upscale tourist attraction, a food court more than a market, but so far, the look of the place has more or less stayed the same, and it continues to draw residents from local neighborhoods, including professionals from Center City as well as Irish, Italian, Asian, and African Americans from Philadelphia's ethnic enclaves. Virtually all racial groups are well represented at Reading Terminal but not in even proportions. On average, about 35 percent of the people there are black, about 10 to 15 percent are Asian and other people of color, and the rest—somewhat more than half—are white, whether WASP or ethnic. The visual, impressionistic makeup of the place is that it is mostly white and middle-class with a healthy mixture of people of color.

The Terminal is a colorful place, full of hustle and bustle. Food is a major theme, and the smell of food is pervasive. The shops are bright and clean, and some are adorned with neon lights. Some of the craft shops have been carrying more expensive pieces aimed at tourists. But the grocery stalls still offer fresh produce and meat direct from Lancaster County farms, fish, seafood, and a wide array of fruits and vegetables; these stalls are interspersed with others selling flowers, health supplements, tea, coffee, spices, books, and crafts. A number of businesses are family owned. And Amish farm families are a strong historical presence in the market— their traditional dress adds an exotic element to the life of the marketplace. Their fresh produce, high-quality meats, and poultry are very inviting. Asian families are also well represented, selling all kinds of fresh fish and produce. Blacks own only a few businesses here, including an African crafts shop that sells masks, beads, and other adornments. Delilah's provides delicious African American cuisine, or "soul food." Other eateries, serving a great variety of tasty foods and drink, include a Thai place, an oyster bar, a French bakery, a Jewish bakery, a juice bar, a beer garden, and a cookie company, making the Terminal a particularly busy place at lunch time. Equally striking is the diversity of workers and the general comity with which they interact. For example, black stockmen work for the German butcher with apparent easygoing demeanor and attitude. Some of the white-owned businesses even have black cashiers, which would have been rare or nonexistent not too many years ago.

The customers, too, seem to be on their best behavior. People seem to be relaxed and are often seen interacting across the color line. Seeing a black woman with a walker wrestling with the heavy doors, two Irish men jump up from their meal at nearby Pearl's Oyster Bar to help her. The clientele at the many food counters represent various classes, races, and ethnicities. A black businessman can be seen talking on his cell phone. Hispanic construction workers are relaxing on their lunch break. This is a calm environment of equivalent, symmetrical relationships—a respite from the streets outside.

When diverse people are eating one another's food, . . . a social good is performed for those observing. As people become intimate through such shared experiences, certain barriers are prone to be broken.

And it has been this way for years. The Terminal is an institution in Philadelphia and has always been known as a place where anyone could expect civility. In the days when blacks never knew what treatment they would be given in public, they could come to the Terminal and know they would not be hassled.[4] The ambience has always been comfortable and inviting. Perhaps the focus on food is a reason for this, suggesting a kind of festival of ethnic foods. On any given day, one might see a Chinese woman eating pizza or a white businessman enjoying collard greens and fried chicken or an Italian family lunching on sushi. When diverse people are eating one another's food, strangers in the abstract can become somewhat more human and a social good is performed for those observing. As people become intimate through such shared experiences, certain barriers are prone to be broken. The many lunch counters also help encourage strangers to interact, as they rub elbows while eating. At certain counters in particular, there seems to be a norm of talking with strangers. One woman told me you cannot get people to shut up. The Terminal is a neutral space in which people who behave civilly, whatever their ethnicity, usually will not be scrutinized, as would likely happen in the ethnic neighborhoods of the city if an unknown person were to pass through. In those neighborhoods, such keen notice of strangers is the first line of defense,[5] but the Terminal is not defended in this manner.

Multiple sets of doors on three sides of the market are used from morning to late afternoon, six days a week. Upon entering from any side, one is met by shoppers, diners, and others here to stroll and take in the ambience. One encounters a varied assemblage under the Terminal's canopy: unobtrusive security guards, both black and white; retired people; teenagers who gather with their friends to hang out; twenty-somethings who come to meet members of the opposite sex; homeless people who gravitate to the market for shelter, food, and the unhindered use of public bathrooms; and business executives and workers from nearby office buildings who make up the lunch crowd. Wholesome sandwiches or healthful, full-plate lunches can be purchased at a reasonable price and consumed quickly on the premises or taken out. At one buffet, you can get a hot meal of collard greens, chicken, sausage, roast, and salad for around $8. Working people and retirees on fixed incomes take advantage of this bargain, at times meeting their friends for sociability.

By the back wall, near the restrooms, black shoeshine men work and socialize, keeping up with one another. They share personal stories and seem always ready for a good laugh. Italians, Jews, Asians, and blacks sit nearby, snacking on baked goods and coffee while enjoying melodious piano sounds played for tips. The municipal courthouse is within a short walk, and occasionally, people appear for lunch with "juror" stickers affixed to their clothing. There is always a scene to be part of and to observe here.

As indicated above, immediately under the canopy, people relax their guard—not completely, but they do look more directly at others as they observe the goings on and move about with a greater sense of security. As they stroll up and down the aisles, stopping at the various shops and kiosks within the Terminal, they experience other people, and they generally seem to trust what they see. There is usually little cause for alarm. As people stop and purchase items or just walk around, sometimes they greet one another, verbally or nonverbally; there is a feeling of being involved with the others present.

When taking a seat at a coffee bar or lunch counter, people feel they have something of a license to speak with others, and others have license to speak with them.[6] Strikingly, strangers engage in spontaneous conversation, getting to know one another as they do. Testing others, trying things out on them, people are maybe seeing whether those different from themselves are for real. They find that they are. People leave such encounters with a good feeling about the other, as though recognizing that they have experienced something profound, as they have—they have made human contact across the putative barriers of race, ethnicity, and other differences. Here, race and ethnicity appear salient but understated. The following field notes are germane:

It was around 11 a.m. on a warm but overcast Sunday morning in March when an African American buddy and I walked into the Down Home Diner, just inside the Reading Terminal Market. The place always seems to be crowded on Sunday mornings with a remarkable diversity of people, locals and out-of-towners, because the Terminal caters to both the convention center crowd and the people from Philadelphia neighborhoods. The crowd that morning buzzed with small talk, resulting in a low-level conversational din, a dull roar. The overall tone was friendly. We walked in, took our seats at the counter, perused the menu, and ordered. He requested ham and eggs, and I ordered pancakes, ham, and milk. We caught up with each other over coffee while waiting for our food, occasionally looking up and checking out the scene. After a few bites of my pancakes and a drink of my milk, I felt a tap on my shoulder. I looked up to see a red-faced Irishman about forty-five years old. "Who won the game last night?" he asked expectantly. Without missing a beat, I replied, "The Sixers, 98-79." I shot him a smile, and he said, "Thanks," and moved on.

I was struck by the way this man assumed he could approach me about the score of a ball game, in part because of the race issue but also because of his assumption that I am a sports fan. I felt that he probably would not have approached me out on the street. But here, because of the apparently friendly atmosphere prevailing, he felt he could make such a request and was likely to get an answer. Does he presume that because I am a black male, I might be especially interested in basketball, that I would have followed the Sixers game the previous evening, and that I would not mind sharing the score with him? He was somehow colluding with me as an individual but also as a Philadelphia sports fan. At least he expected that I would be agreeable, and in fact, I did not disappoint him. And again,

On Saturday, I was to meet Rae at the Down Home Diner at 10 a.m. for breakfast. I arrived at the Terminal at about ten to the hour and walked around the area. The Terminal was busy as usual, full of a diversity of people. Some seemed to be from the nearby convention center, where a trade show was in progress. Others looked more like residents of upscale areas of Center City and the suburbs, and from the local ethnic Irish, Italian, and black neighborhoods—there were also Asians from nearby Chinatown and other parts of the city. This was the typical mix, but Saturday morning at the Terminal is special.

On Saturdays, people seem especially relaxed, lazing about or doing their shopping in an unhurried way. The Down Home Diner was quite busy and crowded. There was a line of people waiting to be seated for the homemade pancakes, grits, eggs, sausages, and ham the place is known for—the smells wafting through the air, making people all the more hungry. The seating consists of four- and six-top tables, booths, and a counter for ten to twelve people.

I stood and waited for a bit, and when a seat at the counter became available, I took it. The stools are spaced quite close together, making for a certain coziness in which it is impossible not to literally rub shoulders with those seated on either side. As a result, upon sitting down, one is almost obliged to say "good morning" to his or her neighbor. The waitstaff is exclusively female and racially mixed, reflecting the diversity of the city. The kitchen is visible through the pass-through, and the cooks, who too are black as well as white, are busy. Now and then, a black dishwasher emerges to replenish the silverware or dish racks under the counter. The place hums, giving off the general impression of people busily going about their work, with few other concerns. Food is presented, dirty plates are cleared, money changes hands, and diners come and go.

While waiting for Rae, I ordered my coffee; it came quickly. In about five minutes, the stool next to mine became empty. I quickly covered it with my leather jacket and cap to reserve it. A white man of about forty was seated next to the empty chair. A few minutes passed, and then another white man emerged and asked, of no one in particular, if he could get breakfast here, revealing that he was new to the place. I answered, "Sure." He was really asking for the seat I was saving, which was the only available one. He stood there behind the seat and soon he asked me more directly, "Is this seat taken?" I said that I was saving it for someone and that she should be here soon. Feeling some pressure to order my food, when the waitress appeared, I asked for pancakes, bacon, and milk.

After taking my order, she looked over at the man standing up and asked if she could help him. "I'd like to order some breakfast, but he's saving the seat," he tattled, nodding at me, as if the waitress would make me remove my coat and give him the place. But the woman, a young Italian woman, simply looked at me, looked at the man, and moved on to another task, implicitly approving of my right to save the seat. After a few minutes, though, noting his frustration, I offered, "If she's not here in five minutes, you can have the seat." He nodded his acceptance. Then the man on the other side of the seat asked, "First date?" "No, no," I said. "It's not like that. I'm her professor." "Yeah, right," he replied, smiling.

Minutes passed and still no sign of Rae. So I removed my coat and offered the man the seat. "Thanks. If she comes, I'll move," he said. The waitress came over and he ordered eggs and oatmeal, and as my food arrived, he commented, "Those look good." "Yeah, the food is pretty good here," I replied as I ate. Soon, his food arrived, and he too began to eat. We sat there elbow to elbow, shoulder to shoulder. I gathered that he was not from Philadelphia, and I asked him outright where he was from. "I'm from Sacramento. I've got a booth over at the convention center and nobody's there to watch it." He was in town for an exhibition on farm implements and equipment, and he ran a manufacturing business. He noted how good his food was and how efficient the service was. He also mentioned the diversity of people here at the Terminal and that this situation was unusual for him, as he had little opportunity for this kind of interaction in Sacramento. Clearly, he was impressed. He revealed that he was from a pretty homogeneous background and that his water-skiing club was even more so. He told me that the club was white and male, including a couple of white supremacists, though he didn't share their views.

The man continued to tell me about his background, as I prompted him to talk about his work. It turned out that he employs a significant number of Mexicans in his business and that he is firmly in favor of allowing driver's licenses to illegal immigrants ("they get licenses and Social Security cards anyway on the black market, so we may as well regulate them ourselves"). Also, he says, his business would fold without them. "I would not hire a man of my own race—they ain't worth a shit!" he stated. As the conversation continued, he indicated that he assumed that I was not for Bush in the upcoming election, while betraying his own conservatism and support of Bush. He was concerned about terrorism. He worried about "a rise in UPS uniforms being sold on the Internet" and, looking around the Terminal, observed that the place was not protected and quite vulnerable to terrorist attack. Soon, he finished his breakfast, we said our goodbyes, and he left for his exhibition at the convention center.

What is so striking about this episode is that in this setting, a white man with white-supremacist friends is able to have a frank conversation with me, a black man, in which he reveals his own feelings about race and diversity. It is the ambience of Reading Terminal that one can go there and take leave of one's particularism, while showing a certain tolerance for others. The Down Home Diner can be viewed as a version of the cosmopolitan canopy under which opportunities are provided, at least situationally, to connect across ethnic and racial lines. Outside, in a more impersonal public space, there is little chance for such interaction; the man would not have approached me, and there would have been no opportunity for the exchange described above. Of course, at least an occasional tension crops up in any human group, and the Terminal is no exception. Rarely, racial and ethnic tension does indeed occur, perhaps in relation to people's ethnic origins and their working out of their sense of group position. More often, due to the apparent large store of comity and goodwill manifested here, tension remains on the individual level. People come to this neutral and cosmopolitan setting expecting diverse people to get along.

This cosmopolitan canopy that seems to spread over and affect relations within the general space called Reading Terminal Market can be divided into subzones that might be seen as the quasi-public impersonal and the more intimate zones, the former being off-putting and the latter socially more encouraging. In the more intimate settings within the canopy, such as at one of the numerous lunch counters, people often feel welcome and secure enough to relax, even to the point of engaging complete strangers in conversation. In these circumstances, people carry on their business but also engage in *folk ethnography* and formulate or find evidence for their *folk theories* about others with whom they share the public space.[7]

In Philadelphia, the Reading Terminal Market is but one of many such locations that may be viewed, conceptually at least, as existing under this kind of "cosmopolitan canopy"; other examples with a similar ambiance are Rittenhouse Square park, 30th Street Train Station, the Whole Foods Markets, the Italian Market, various fitness centers, hospital waiting rooms, the multiplex theater, indoor malls, and sporting venues, among other places.[7] Typically, under the canopy, within the exterior walls or within the prescribed street boundaries in the case of Rittenhouse Square—Philadelphia's premier public park—the atmosphere is usually calm and relatively pleasant, as a diverse mix of people go about their business, at times self-consciously on good or "downtown" behavior, working to "be nice" or civil to the next person they encounter. Here, they sit, eat, and walk, moving through the square, sometimes meeting new acquaintances or bumping into people they know.

The denizens return from time to time to conduct their business, while becoming more familiar with one another as well as with the social ambience of the place. In time, they come to "know" the "regular" people without ever having met them. A major theme is civility, and people are encouraged to behave civilly to one another; at times, they can be solicitous and extraordinarily helpful to complete strangers.

Such neutral social settings, which no one group expressly owns but all are encouraged to share, situated under this kind of protective umbrella, represent a special type of urban space, a peculiar zone that every visitor seems to recognize, appreciate, and enjoy.[9] Many visit not only for instrumental reasons—to have a meal or just to be "out and about"—but also for the experience of being among the social types they believe they are likely to find here. The ambience is decidedly "laid-back," and in navigating the quasi-public spaces here, there is little sense of obligation to the next person other than common civility. Visitors leave with the memory of a good experience and are likely to return another day, perhaps to relive an otherwise uneventful and pleasant experience.

As people engage others in these public settings, they can do what I call both practical and expressive folk ethnography. Simply put, cosmopolitan canopies are interesting places to engage in the fine art of "people watching," for "all kinds" of folk are represented. The curious will sometimes gawk at strangers, but most often, people are polite and, from a safe distance, watch others unobtrusively, if indirectly. Others may be reluctant at first, only to find themselves unavoidably overhearing conversations that pique their interest; then they eavesdrop and collect stories, which they may either repeat to friends or keep to themselves.

In the more quasi-public areas, it is common for people to publicly interact with complete strangers, exquisitely expressing themselves through face and eye work;

smiles and frowns are occasionally punctuated by a critical commentary of grunts and groans and outright talk. Through these various transactions, they legitimate a look here, discourage an advance there, and put "who they are" on public display. In time, their accumulating observations feed both prejudices and truths—affected by their own identities—about the others they encounter here.

With such frames in mind, they build on what they know, effectively "understanding" strangers they encounter and coming to "know" the public life of the canopy. They do all this with an eye to sorting out and making sense of one another, either for practical reasons or to satisfy a natural human curiosity. Later, among their friends, social peers, associates, people of their own ethnic communities, and others with whom they feel close enough, they share their observations, telling their stories and shaping them as they go.

> *[These] neutral social settings, which no one group expressly owns but all are encouraged to share, situated under this kind of protective umbrella, represent a special type of urban space, a peculiar zone that every visitor seems to recognize, appreciate, and enjoy.*

This complex process affects how they view and define this place and other interesting aspects of the city for their local social networks, while inspiring folk notions about "how people are" and "how things work." At Reading Terminal, for instance, they casually observe and perhaps ponder the "Jewish butcher," the "Amish farmer's stall," the "Asian fish counter," "the Italian bakery," or the "black shoeshine stand." The denizens learn to get along and deal effectively with life in this setting, all the while expressing their own identities with respect to others present.

While civility may rule and be taken for granted here, when people leave such zones, they may well be challenged in other ways that require different responses. The local neighborhoods from which they come and through which they must travel are publicly known for their racial and ethnic tensions. Because of this, the denizens of the most public spaces, spaces defined by civility as being within the cosmopolitan canopy, put an active, if unacknowledged, premium on up-close observations of others, including inadvertent eavesdropping and what are in effect informal studies of the local people. This kind of observation is never systematic or planned. And the collection of evidence as to what others are like is highly selective and might be seen as giving rise to or reinforcing persistent stereotypes, as well as uncovering unexpected truths about others they encounter.

In such urban social settings, passersby are often able and willing to sample sizable portions of other people's conversations. Such fragmentary data are like so many pieces of the jigsaw puzzle of social ambience or the ethnography of a given public place. People are inclined to fit these pieces together somehow, generally in a conscious manner with a grand design but also rather intuitively and inductively, creating a mental picture of the nature of the setting and of certain kinds of others. They may do this for no other reason than "to be in the know" or "not to make a fool of myself" in a given setting. They engage in folk ethnography to navigate uncertain terrain but also as naturally curious human beings inclined to make sense of their social habitat.

Naturally, a certain physical and social distance between people is common in the larger, more public settings such as Reading Terminal Market and Rittenhouse Square. And although the amount and quality of interaction are always a matter of person-to-person negotiation, numerous smaller quasi-public venues can be found all over the city where strangers coexist for a brief time with a kind of closeness bordering on intimacy. The more intimate the space, the more chance there is for up close "fieldwork," including direct and indirect observation and eavesdropping. Such places are important settings for diverse strangers to "learn" how to get along with one another, albeit at times superficially. The jazz bar Zanzibar Blue is an example of a setting that is both intimate and public.

After descending the steps off Broad Street down into Zanzibar Blue, one feels as though one has entered a dark inner sanctum, an underground world of live music, food, liquor, and a cosmopolitan mix of people who have in common a certain appreciation of jazz. On the left is a bar with a few people sitting around it, sipping their drinks, and nodding to the smooth beat wafting about and through space. As one's eyes slowly adjust to the gloom, little candlelit lamps suddenly become visible atop neat rows of four-top tables with bloodred tablecloths. One then encounters two hefty black bouncers in dark suits. They engage the visitor with small talk while checking him out to see what his business is, perhaps especially if he is a stranger dressed in dark clothes, though here everything has a dark hue.

Over in the corner sits a dark-skinned black man engaging his brown-skinned honey; his gold-rimmed glasses sparkle, capturing and reflecting the scarce light here. Nearer the bandstand, nine black women gather to honor a friend on her birthday—as becomes apparent later on when the waiter delivers a small cake with two candles on top. On the other side, facing the bandstand, another black couple enjoys their meal while waiting for tonight's sets to begin. The maitre d' shows another black man and me to a table, first a two-top but then a four-top that we accept more happily. We both order Delta catfish, Cokes, and bread to keep us until the meal arrives. We talk. More people slowly appear. A young, white, professional-looking couple sits behind us. In a while, to our right, another; and in fifteen minutes, still another. The place seems to be filling up, though it has a long way to go. This is Sunday night in downtown Philly. Our Cokes and bread arrive, and we sip and nibble and talk, taking in more of the scene, observing what is happening around us.

The band is now set up—a cool-looking white man on guitar, a black Muslim with a coofee [cap] on sax, a small brown-skinned man on drums, and the leader, a muscular, baldheaded black man, on bass. The leader opens with the usual introductions. To start the first set, he makes fun of straying black men and their family responsibilities while pleading for the audience not to be too judgmental—"give a brother some slack because he always comes home." Chuckles come from the audience, the blacks perhaps "getting it" more than the whites. The combo plays. Naturally, the sounds are smooth, melodious, stark, and loud. People go into conscious listening and watching mode, as they are here to see the show, and a show it is.

But a show is being put on not just by the combo but by the clientele themselves. The people observe one another, watching how this or that person reacts to the sounds. When a player works especially hard to bring out an unusual or seemingly difficult but appealing sound, the audience collectively agrees to give the player some recognition—applause, that is. And when the guitar player makes a sound not commonly associated with the guitar, members of the audience clap spontaneously—almost on cue. It is especially interesting when the blacks clap enthusiastically for the white player. Everyone notices. People here are aware of each other but at the same time anonymous. They feel a sense of community while they are here, and then they move on.

One might say that places like Zanzibar Blue are a salve for the hustle and bustle of more fraught urban experience. While the jazz club is a special experience,[10] with complete strangers participating in a collective entertainment and artistic production, intimate spaces of a different sort proliferate with the boom of the franchise business. More generally, they include the Starbuckses and McDonaldses of the world, places where complete strangers congregate and observe one another but may not feel as connected as people do at a jazz club. Through people watching and eavesdropping in a tight space, they may leave with strong impressions and stories of other people's lives, truncated and fleeting as they may be, which serve to shape their gossip, not simply about individuals but about the groups these strangers seem to represent.

In the outpatient waiting room of the local university hospital, among computer screens, alcoves, plastic chairs, coffee wagon, and reception desk, people have slowed down as they kill time waiting for the bureaucracy to go through its motions. This is an ideal setting in which to observe more relaxed, quasi-public race relations. What one observes is that while some people might like to group themselves with others who are of a similar race, here, people sit where they can and tend not to go to the extra trouble of such racial sorting. Still, people like to be comfortable.

On this particular day, there are about forty people intermittently seated in rows of cushioned chairs facing each other. The length of one side of the building is walled by a high and broad light-filled window looking out on a manicured courtyard. It is a somewhat busy setting, with diverse people moving to and fro doing their business. Staff people, who seem disproportionately African American, transport patients, equipment, and other materials. Every staff person is assumed to be engaged in critical work, a fact that garners certain respect, regardless of the worker's station, color, or perceived background.

Four no-nonsense, middle-aged black women handle paperwork at the various business windows, triaging outpatients. The patients are predominantly African American (about 70 percent), but whites (about 25 percent) and Asians and Latinos (about 5 percent) are being served as well. The black people, some of whom work for the university, are mostly poor to working class and from the nearby ghetto community, intermixed with a few middle-class people; the whites tend to be working to middle class as well. A younger black man and an older woman, who appears to be his mother, enter the setting and move slowly toward a couple of empty seats. Others present here, black as well as white, follow the couple with their eyes, momentarily, if inadvertently, making eye contact. They all take in the scene. A minor drama unfolds as the young man faces a seemingly difficult task of seating the heavy old woman. First, he relieves her of her bags and then helps her to remove her coat to make her comfortable, the object being to get her settled.

As this situation unfolds, a young, Irish, working-class man with stringy brown hair sitting in the next seat rises and offers assistance, which is soon shown to be unnecessary. But after seating his mother, the black man audibly thanks the young man anyway. The working-class white man nods. And things return to normal as people refocus their attention on their magazines, their children, or their partners. In this setting, actually quite a few older people are being helped by younger people who are more physically able and more capable of negotiating the hospital bureaucracy.

In a few minutes another scene develops. A rotund black man of about sixty-five in a motorized wheelchair, who has a hook for one hand, is clearly enjoying his conversation on his cell phone. He speaks at a voice level that allows many of those present to follow parts of his conversation. A few people are clearly annoyed by this, while others are perfectly tolerant in what is certainly a public place. It becomes clear that the man is speaking with a friend, apparently excited about the prospect of obtaining an artificial limb. Eyes follow the man as he moves across the room to be nearer the large window, perhaps for better reception on his cell phone. By the window, he continues his conversation, which is rather expansive, reflecting his cheerful mood.

When he finishes his phone call, he expertly moves back across the room, his *Daily News* jammed into the side of the wheelchair. People watch, and when he moves on, a few of the others there make knowing eye contact, whites and blacks alike. Over on the other side, the man strikes up a conversation with another heavyset black man of similar age, a person whom it is clear he does not know, and yet they talk rather intimately and loudly.

In this setting, the black people tend to be somewhat relaxed and at times even animated in their presentation of self (Goffman 1959). Most are of working-class status, but they outnumber the whites present. A perfunctory look might suggest that whites' attention is riveted on the blacks here, since this is a seemingly unique situation, but on close inspection, it is clear that people of both groups are curious and take this opportunity to observe each other closely. This is a relatively safe place, and people can look at others without feeling threatened, though some of the whites might feel somewhat awkward about being in the company of so many black people at one time.

Essentially, cosmopolitan canopies allow people of different backgrounds the chance to slow down and indulge themselves, observing, pondering, and in effect, doing their own folk ethnography, testing or substantiating stereotypes and prejudices or, rarely, acknowledging something fundamentally new about the other. Those observed may well become representatives of social types in the observers' minds and can be described afterward outside the setting as "this black guy," "this Jewish man," "this WASPy white guy," "this white dude"; a white person might say, "this black lady," or a black person might say to other black people, "this sister." An accretion of such shared observations made under the cosmopolitan canopies of the city becomes part of what people "know" about each other, a way they "make sense" of the more public world.[11]

The cosmopolitan canopy can also be mobile, as in the case of public transportation, which in Philadelphia is always a racial experience. Typically, black riders outnumber whites on buses and trolleys in downtown Philadelphia; there may be some racial tension, but most often, people are civil and polite, respecting one another's presumed social spaces. Such spaces can, of course, vary in level of neutrality—by time of day or night, by the specific individuals making use of them, or by subspaces within larger ones, such as the back of a big-city bus.

> Mei-Ling, a young Chinese graduate student, and her Chinese male friend got on the bus and unwittingly failed to respect the boundaries between blacks and whites—blacks typically congregating in the back of the bus and effectively claiming it as turf. Whites often stand rather than venture beyond a certain imaginary line. Vacant seats in the back remain so, and the whites stand for long periods. This situation is for all to see, white and black alike, and it informs the folk ethnography of everyday public transportation, particularly the city bus. Mei-Ling and her friend, however, walked right to the back of the bus and began to speak Chinese. After a point, their language got to be too much for one black woman, who responded with, "Don't ya'll be talking about me." Mei-Ling, surprised and confused, said, "We're not talking about you." Tension developed. One black man urged against arguing, but Mei-Ling stood her ground and kept speaking Chinese. Other black women smirked at one another, implicitly standing up for their counterpart, or at least enjoying the fracas. Finally, the woman put her fist in Mei-Lings's face and said bluntly, "Do you want a black fist?" At that point, the situation got to be too much for Mei-Ling, and she walked up to the driver and complained. The driver stopped the bus and asked her if the woman had actually hit her. Mei-Ling said no, whereupon the black woman came forward herself and told the driver, "I just told her to keep her voice down." The driver then told both women to apologize or he would call the police. The black woman did immediately apologize, but Mei-Ling's friend insisted that she had done nothing wrong, and Mei-Ling was left shaken by the incident. She says she never realized that the back of the bus belonged to anyone.

Most people, however, are civil and polite to one another, respecting the putative individual aura surrounding every person and defining the public conveyance as an utterly neutral space where people are generally on good behavior and will just leave other people be.

Equally important, public transportation reflects the class and racial compositions of Philadelphia neighborhoods, which, like many other big-city residential areas, remain racially segregated. Black and white urbanites alike may be put off by the anonymous "ghetto-looking" black male, but there has been some feeling that presently, due to terrorism perpetrated by Middle Eastern–looking men, a large black man is a welcome presence to some who were most prejudiced about black males.

The code of civility that defines the cosmopolitan canopy can break down in various ways on public transportation. People occasionally complain about seating or loud music and can be offended by one another. In particular, when race and gender come together in the presence of the anonymous black male, the ideals of civility and cosmopolitanism are severely tested. Observations on regional trains show that the anonymous black male is often the last person others will sit next to. Black men generally agree that they can ride the length of the train line seated alone, unless the train is crowded and seating is scarce. Black men of all social classes understand full well that they are avoided on public transportation. It is common knowledge among black men that they are stigmatized or degraded in public in this way, not just by whites but sometimes by blacks as well. The black male may "put white people off" just by virtue of being black, and the younger he is and the more "ghetto" he looks, the more distrust he engenders. This leads many to the working conception or folk belief that white people, protestations to the contrary, generally dislike black people, especially black males. White people are often put off by the black male, but there has been some feeling that presently, due to terrorism perpetrated by Middle Eastern–looking men, a large black man is a welcome presence to some who were most prejudiced about black males.

Essentially, cosmopolitan canopies allow people of different backgrounds the chance to slow down and indulge themselves, observing, pondering, and in effect, doing their own folk ethnography, testing or substantiating stereotypes and prejudices or, rarely, acknowledging something fundamentally new about the other.

As young black men talk among themselves, it seems as though each man has a story of police harassment or public discrimination, such as strangers not wanting to sit next to him or working to avoid him altogether. Whether true in an objective sense, it is too often believed true by the black male, leading him to develop his own sense of group position vis-à-vis the wider society, especially whites. In this respect, black men engage in folk ethnography, talking among themselves, comparing notes, and developing strategies for avoiding such arbitrary treatment and salvaging their self-respect.

At times, they may attempt to turn the tables. Deciding they would rather ride with a seat to themselves—which may well be in part a "sour-grapes" rationalization—they will sometimes puff themselves up and adopt an off-putting appearance, displaying looks geared to make others uptight and determined to avoid them. This approach stems from an understanding that the wider society (especially whites) wishes to avoid them, and they simply want to do it to the "other" first. Strikingly, other blacks will also sometimes seek to avoid anonymous young black males they are uncertain about, though blacks are usually more savvy about distinguishing those who pose an authentic threat from those who do not; familiar with black life, they are more capable of making finer distinctions than are their white counterparts.

In addition, some black men have taken to devising tests they use on whites who might face the prospect of sitting next to them. Typically, the test is employed in the following manner: After spotting an available seating area, including both an aisle and a window, the young man will move deliberately to the aisle seat, leaving the often more desirable window seat empty and requiring anyone wanting the seat to pass by him to get to it. He might sit with his legs sprawled or present a blank or sullen look on his face, making himself into an uninviting seat partner. His bet is that most whites will not want to cross the barrier he has set up, but if a white person is willing to rise to the occasion and request the seat and sit down, this person then passes the test. A white person willing to "run the gamut," as it were, may be judged acceptable. Some young black men report that they are taken by surprise when a white person does request the seat; then they may well engage the person in what conversation, albeit halting.

Conclusion

Under the cosmopolitan canopy, whether quasi-public or intimate, people seem to have some special need to observe the social setting closely; for many, people watching is a common pastime, and for some, it has risen to an art form. They check others out, practicing a form of folk ethnography, making sense of what they observe while reserving the right to be highly selective in their sources of evidence. The resulting understandings may in fact be as much about themselves as about the others they come to know—a factor that helps them to remain "folk" in the sense that Redfield (1947, 1956) defined—not urban or pre-urban, despite the city's ever-growing size, density, and truly mind-boggling diversity. This kind of exposure to a multitude of people engaging in everyday behavior often humanizes abstract strangers in the minds of these observers.

The existence of the canopy allows such people, whose reference point often remains their own social class or ethnic group, a chance to encounter others and so work toward a more cosmopolitan appreciation of difference. As canopies, the Reading Terminal, Rittenhouse Square, Thirtieth Street Station, the Whole Foods Market, and sporting events certainly do not provide identical social experience. But they do all provide an opportunity for diverse strangers to come together and be exposed to one another. In these circumstances, they have a chance to mix, observe one another, and become better acquainted with people they otherwise seldom observe up close.

As urbanites, they encounter people who are strangers to them, not just as individuals but also as representatives of groups they "know" only in the abstract. The canopy can thus be a profoundly humanizing experience. People in these places are also inclined to express common civility toward others. For instance, families with children in tow enable adults to model for their children, and their children to model for still others, including both children and grown-ups. Some parents use such a setting as a teaching tool, at times making a point of having their children respect people who are in some way different from themselves. And when people exposed to all this return to their own neighborhoods, they may do so with a more grounded knowledge of the other than was possible without such experience. In this way, the generations establish new social patterns and norms of tolerance, while encouraging everyday common civility, if not comity and goodwill, among the various groups that make up the city.

To be sure, people may develop new stereotypes or see fit to hold on to the ones they have previously formed. It is likely that they will opt to hold onto attitudes they are deeply invested in. Yet they will have been exposed to members of a heretofore unknown other (see Blumer 1958). If nothing more, through constant exposure, such environments can encourage common, everyday taken-for-granted civility toward others who are different from oneself.

As canopies proliferate, such neutral territories become an established element of the makeup of the city. Moving about through the major canopies such as the Terminal as well as the more intimate ones in restaurants and bars, people can have a sense of being out and about in a cosmopolitan setting. As they are exposed, others are exposed to them. And especially in the smaller settings, they can eavesdrop, look people over, and more closely observe people who are strange to them, whose behavior they previously could only imagine.

As the urban environment becomes increasingly diverse, the cosmopolitan canopy becomes ever more significant as a setting in which people of diverse backgrounds come together, mingle with strangers, and gain from their social experience a critical folk knowledge and social intelligence about others they define as different from themselves. In these circumstances, they may see profoundly what they have in common with other human being, regardless of their particularity. A model of civility is planted in such settings that may well have a chance to sprout elsewhere in the city. People are repeatedly exposed to the unfamiliar and thus have the opportunity to stretch themselves mentally, emotionally, and socially. The resulting folk ethnography serves as a cognitive and cultural base on which denizens are able to construct behavior in public. And often, though certainly not always, the end result is a growing social sophistication that allows diverse urban peoples to get along.

Notes

1. In Wirth's day, many wealthy people were concerned with moral contamination. Such people can be imagined strolling through the public spaces with their heads held high in an expression of disdain for those they considered beneath them. Today, the public issue more commonly is one of wariness and fear of crime.

2. Gans (1962) has described these urban types as "cosmopolites," "urban villagers," "the deprived," and "the trapped."

3. For a much earlier treatment of "cosmopolitans" and "locals" as a social types, see "Patterns of Influence: Local and Cosmopolitan Influentials," in Merton (1957).

4. Traditionally, in certain segregated neighborhoods, outsiders were kept at bay, and this has kept these neighborhoods relatively homogenous. Since the end of de jure segregation, this situation has been slowly changing. See Massey and Denton (1993).

5. See Suttles's discussion of "the defended neighborhood" in Suttles (1972, 21-43).

6. For an in-depth discussion of a similar phenomenon related to bar behavior, see Cavan (1966).

7. A distinction exists between Redfield's (1947) "folk society," which represents a "little tradition" in an enclosed folk setting, and the idea I am proposing of urban folk living in isolated ethnic communities within the context of the city (cf. Gans 1962). Philadelphia is quite an ethnic town, made up of neighborhoods that reflect its many ethnicities and that are rather particularistic. People from these neighborhoods carry along with them localized ideologies that tell them not only about their own situations but also about those of others. Some of these are clearly stereotypes they use in relating to others and in understanding how others relate to them. Yet this particularistic attitude is affected by class, education, and exposure to more cosmopolitan settings. So a tension forms between ethnic particularism and a more sophisticated understanding of diversity. When people leave their ethnic neighborhood or setting, it is imperative that they take on a more general perspective, especially as they move to more neutral territory where they encounter different kinds of people and the theme is one of general civility. It is in these settings that people can and do act civilly toward those who are different from themselves, even though it may be a challenge for them. Folk ideologies and orientation are challenged by the more sophisticated or tolerant signals of the more cosmopolitan situation. That is just the kind of place a cosmopolitan canopy is, and urban folk are challenged by the cosmopolitanism characteristic of these settings (cf. Wirth [1938] on urbanism and Hall [1966] on urban space and diversity).

8. Other places are different from Reading Terminal as well as from one another, but they are similar as settings where people can come together and experience diverse others—they are places where diversity seems to congregate. The Terminal is unusual, however, in the amount of conversation that occurs between strangers, especially strangers of different races and ethnicities.

9. For an example of a consciously constructed social setting of this type in Paris, France, see de la Pradelle and Lallement in this volume.

10. See Grazian (2003).

11. Similarly, see Lofland (1973), who approaches this theme from a different angle: "The cosmopolitan did not lose the capacity for knowing others personally. But he gained the capacity for knowing others only categorically" (p. 177).

References

Anderson, Elijah. 1990. *Streetwise: Race, class, and change in an urban community.* Chicago: University of Chicago Press.

———. 1999. *Code of the street: Decency, violence, and the moral life of the inner city.* New York: W. W. Norton.

Blumer, Herbert. 1958. Race prejudice as a sense of group position. *Pacific Sociological Review* 1:3-7.

Cavan, Sherri. 1966. *Liquor license.* Chicago: Aldine.

Drake, St. Clair, and Horace R. Cayton. 1945. *Black metropolis: A study of negro life in a northern city.* New York: Harper and Row.

Duneier, Mitchell. 1999. *Sidewalk.* New York: Farrar, Straus and Giroux.

Gans, Herbert. 1962. Suburbanism and urbanism as ways of life: A re-evaluation of definitions. In *Human behavior and social processes.* Boston: Houghton Mifflin.

Goffman, Erving. 1959. *The presentation of self in everyday life.* Garden City, NY: Doubleday.

———. 1963. *Behavior in public places.* Glencoe, IL: Free Press.

Grazian, David. 2003. *Blue Chicago: The search for authenticity in urban blues clubs.* Chicago: University of Chicago Press.

Hall, Edward T. 1966. *The hidden dimension.* New York: Doubleday.

Jacobs, Jane. 1961. *The death and life of great American cities.* New York: Random House.

Lofland, Lyn. 1973. *A world of strangers: Order and action in urban public space.* New York: Basic Books.

Massey, Douglas, and Nancy Denton. 1993. *American apartheid: Segregation and the making of the underclass.* Cambridge, MA: Harvard University Press.

Merton, Robert K. 1957. *Social theory and social structure.* New York: Free Press.

Redfield, Robert. 1947. The folk society. *American Journal of Sociology* 52:293-308.

———. 1956. The social organization of tradition. In *Peasant society/little community*. Chicago: University of Chicago Press.

Sassen, Saskia. 2001. *The global city: New York, London, Tokyo*. Princeton, NJ: Princeton University Press.

Simmel, Georg. 1950. The metropolis and mental life. In *The sociology of Georg Simmel*, edited by Kurt H. Wolff. Glencoe, IL: Free Press.

Spykman, J. Nicholas. 1925. *The social theory of Georg Simmel*. Chicago: University of Chicago Press.

Suttles, Gerald D. 1968. *The social order of the slum*. Chicago: University of Chicago Press.

———. 1972. *The social construction of communities*. Chicago: University of Chicago Press.

Wilson, William J. 1987. *The truly disadvantaged: The inner city, the underclass, and public policy*. Chicago: University of Chicago Press.

———. 1996. *When work disappears: The world of the new urban poor*. New York: Knopf.

Wirth, Louis. 1938. Urbanism as a way of life. *American Journal of Sociology* 44:1-24.

Why Girls Fight: Female Youth Violence in the Inner City

By
CINDY D. NESS

This article considers the resort to violence by inner-city female youth, including the external forces impinging on them. In addition to underscoring that girls actively pursue and enjoy physically dominating others, I argue that the incidence of violence by girls in low-income areas, particularly "street fighting," has been significantly underestimated in official statistics and generally by scholars. Engaging in violence was found to serve a number of functions for inner-city girls, similar to their male counterparts. Mothers were found to play an integral role in the anatomy of their daughters' use of violence. The article addresses the need to situate girls' violent behavior simultaneously on the level of individual psychology, on the cultural landscape of a neighborhood, and within the institutional framework that shapes both, in order to contextualize it properly. The article also considers how the method of ethnography is well suited to this end.

Keywords: female youth violence; inner city; ethnography; aggression

Although females who commit violence are no longer characterized as sexually anomalous, violent behavior by male and female juveniles routinely continues to be assigned different causal factors. This may reflect the belief that females are naturally aversive to inflicting harm (Tiger 1969; Tiger and Fox 1970), that they are socialized to that aversion (Block 1984; Steffensmeier and Allan 1991; Campbell 1993), that they inflict harm in small number as an approximation to male behavior (Adler 1975; Figueira-McDonough 1989; Rhodes and Fischer 1993), or that it brings needed attention

Cindy D. Ness is the director of programs at the Center on Terrorism and Public Safety at John Jay College of Criminal Justice and a practicing psychotherapist in New York City. Her research interests include urban and political violence committed by females and the structure of violence in inner-city communities. She is a former member of the Academic Advisory Council of the National Campaign Against Youth Violence. She is a Ph.D. candidate at Harvard University in human development and psychology and at the University of Pennsylvania in anthropology.

DOI: 10.1177/0002716204267176

to specific social, cultural, and economic circumstances associated with gender (Heidensohn 1985; Chilton and Datesman 1987; Chesney-Lind 1989, 1997; Gilfus 1992; Daly and Maher 1998). Despite their different premises, all of these accounts negate or at the very least offer little or no insight into girls as active agents of aggression.

This is not surprising because, unlike males, aggressive females have tradition-ally been seen as deviant, not only with regard to the code of penal law but to natu-ral law—that is, as an abomination to feminine nature (Lombroso and Ferraro 1895; Pollak 1950). In the first third of the twentieth century, Freud's (1905, 1925, 1931, 1933) characterization of normal female development as the relinquishing of active instinctual aims and the acceptance of passive ones decidedly cast female aggression as a move from the feminine to the masculine and served as the basis for many subsequent theories. As late as the 1980s, empirical literature typically reduced aggression to a single proposition: females internalize aggression, while males externalize it (i.e., Feshbach 1969; Whiting and Edwards 1973; Maccoby and Jacklin 1974; Hall 1978). It is only in the mid-1970s after feminist scholars began to question how social forces and cultural factors were involved in producing gender differences presumed to be natural (Baker-Miller 1976; Chodorow 1978; Gilligan 1982) that a more complex rendering of females who commit violence began to appear in the literature (Heidensohn 1985; Chilton and Datesman 1987; Belknap 1996; Chesney-Lind 1992, 1997). While some research—mostly on gangs—has recently been undertaken on the instrumental function of violence for adolescent girls, for example, as a source of protection and monetary gain (Camp-bell 1984; Brotherton 1996; Miller 2003), few studies have specifically contem-plated its value for girls as a source of pleasure, self-esteem, and cultural capital, factors that have readily been explored in connection with males (Bourgois 1995; Anderson 1999).

This article is based on a year of ethnographic fieldwork that I recently con-ducted in West and Northeast Philadelphia in which I set out to shed light on how low-income female adolescents experience causing physical harm and the mean-ing they assign to doing so, including what they see to be the external factors impinging on them. In addition to showing that these girls actively pursue and enjoy physically dominating others and take pleasure in inflicting pain and in emerging victorious, I argue that the incidence of violence by girls in low-income areas, particularly "street fighting," has been significantly underestimated.

The article also underscores the need to situate girls' violent behavior simulta-neously on the level of individual psychology, on the cultural landscape of a neigh-borhood, and within the institutional framework that shapes both in order to prop-erly contextualize it. It also considers how the method of ethnography is well suited to this end. Just as we cannot understand violence in urban neighborhoods without taking social complexity into account, neither can we understand it without taking into account an actor's psychological complexity and how these complexities lead an actor to perceive, and to operate in, the external world. In that ethnography, unlike other methods of inquiry, requires a researcher to immerse himself or her-self in another person's social world, it affords an extraordinary opportunity to witness phenomena on both a collective and an individual level. Yet despite its potential for revealing how collective meanings are held and revised individually, I contend that ethnography is seldom used in this way.

Girls' Violent Behavior in Statistical Context

To place my ethnographic data in context, I will start by offering a few statistics about female youth violence. According to the U.S. Department of Juvenile Justice, in the year 2000, girls accounted for 23 percent of juvenile arrests for aggravated assault nationwide, 31 percent of simple assaults, and 18 percent of the total violent crime index (Snyder 2003a). Considering the picture over time, longitudinal data reveal that the incidence of female juvenile violence has increased annually as a part of the total violent crime index since 1987 (Snyder 2003a, 2003b). To some extent, this trend line is an artifact of relatively low arrest rates for girls to begin with. That said, it is noteworthy that even though the juvenile violent crime rate has steadily declined since the mid-1990s for both males and females, the 2001 arrest rate for girls (112 per 100,000) remains 59 percent above its 1980 rate (70 per 100,000), while the 2001 rate for boys (471 per 100,000) is 20 percent below its 1980 rate (Office of Juvenile Justice and Delinquency Prevention, as adapted from Snyder 2003b).

Although the official statistics alone would be enough to suggest that a host of norms and a complex infrastructure of neighborhood culture and social institutions are involved in promoting the incidence and perpetuation of violence by girls, one must also keep in mind that arrest figures mask an even greater incidence of violent behavior as they reflect only the portion that comes to the attention of the justice system (Snyder 2003a, 2003b). According to the Bureau of Justice Statistics' National Crime Victimization Survey (2003), which, in an attempt to estimate unreported crime, has collected information on crimes suffered by individuals since 1973, fewer than half of the serious violent crimes by juveniles are reported to law enforcement.

Physical aggression that does not result in serious injury is even less likely to come to the attention of authorities. Lost to official statistics is the "ordinary" street fighting that represents the majority of violent behavior in impoverished neighborhoods. That female youths are far less likely to use and carry firearms than are their male counterparts (Center for the Study and Prevention of Violence 2004) greatly diminishes the visibility of their resort to violence. More often than not, however, scholars of youth violence cite official statistics without critically questioning their correspondence to facts on the ground. It is noteworthy as well that African American youth are typically overrepresented as perpetrators in the media, while their victimization is typically underrepresented, especially in comparison to white victims (Dorfman and Schiraldi 2001).

To investigate the meaning and social organization of the use of violence by girls, with a special emphasis on street fighting, I spent a year talking with girls, ranging in age from thirteen to seventeen, in a variety of settings: a public high school, an alternative high school for youth with behavioral problems, the adult criminal justice system where juveniles are directly filed for any assault with a deadly weapon, a residential placement center and boot camp, and a transitional alternative high school where girls leaving placement are sent before they can return to schools in their communities. To gain a window on the different levels of violence that girls participate in, as well as the impact the juvenile justice system has on their course, I decided it would be necessary to observe girls in relation to as much of the institutional infrastructure meant to deal with their violent behavior as possible. Of the eighty to one hundred girls with whom I had contact, I followed fifteen closely, two of whom I hung out with several days each week in their West Philadelphia neighborhood to better familiarize myself with their social world. Approximately 75 percent of the girls I spoke with were African American, 20 percent were of Hispanic origin, and 5 percent were Caucasian. Lastly, I spent numerous nights doing "ridealongs" in patrol cars in Northeast Philadelphia to observe police and female youths interacting.

Girls' Violent Behavior
in Sociocultural Context

As explanations for why girls resort to violence have largely centered on their maladjustment (Konopka 1966, 1976; Vedder and Somerville 1973; Campbell 1987; Armistead et al. 1992), it seems important to begin my discussion by underscoring that street fighting in low-income Philadelphia is a normative part of growing up for girls. Rather than being characteristic of only a small subset of girls who possess significant social and emotional deficits that leave them prone to delinquency, the use of violence by the girls I spoke with was decidedly commonplace. Indeed, even girls who had no contact with the juvenile justice system typically reported being in physical fights over the past year or, if they had not been, fighting more when they were younger. As one mother put it, when I asked her to introduce me to girls in her neighborhood who did not fight, "I don't know one girl who doesn't fight. At some point everyone fights." In fact, most of the girls I spoke with over the course of the year echoed her view, though there are important distinctions to be made among these girls with regard to the frequency and extent of the physical violence in which they engaged.

The reason fighting by girls is so commonplace in the neighborhoods I moved in can be explained only by taking into account larger social realities and local cultural norms; that is, by explaining how structural and cultural forces are involved in shaping behavior and feelings. Since female adolescent violence is often referred to as if it were a uniform phenomenon, without reference to a specific social setting or subgroup, it is all the more important to underscore here that issues of race and class are central to informing the instrumental value and symbolic meaning that violence holds for girls, as well as having profound implications for the nature of crime in the city. It is no coincidence that African American girls are three times as likely to be poor and three times as likely to be involved with the criminal justice system as white girls (Office of Juvenile Justice and Delinquency Prevention 2000)—poverty affords substantially different material, social, and cultural resources with which to negotiate one's life, a scenario that translates into multiple risk factors, many of them associated with the increased incidence of violence. Although few studies involve meaningfully sized female samples (Ingoldsby and Daniel 2002), there is good reason to presume that neighborhood effects related to failing institutions, dilapidated housing, high unemployment, poverty concentration, and crime, which operate to increase the likelihood of male juveniles' using violence (Wilson 1987; Furstenberg and Hughes 1997; Sampson, Raudenbush, and Earls, 1997), also increase the likelihood that female juveniles will resort to violence.

The cultural and social forces that inhibit physical aggression in middle-class girls do not operate to inhibit violence among the girls with whom I spent time.

The African American and Hispanic girls with whom I spoke typically saw themselves as closed out of white, middle-class America and abandoned by the failing institutions meant to serve them—the majority of students appeared to have disengaged from learning a long time ago in the schools through which I passed. Barring a few exceptions, girls thought that the authorities in their lives—their teachers, potential neighborhood employers, and the police—viewed them negatively or, in a word, as "ghetto." Exhibiting the anger and alienation that many poor urban girls experience daily, Aiesha asserts, "If a teacher gonna automatically think I'm stupid cause of the way I walk or talk—fuck her. I got nothing to say to her." With few prospects in the legal economy, the consequence to a girl's future for running afoul of the law, and in turn, the disincentive to abstain from doing so, is far less formidable in West and Northeast "Philly" than a middle-class neighborhood. Thus, it is no surprise that many of the girls I observed took a defiant and fatalistic attitude toward the delinquency charges brought against them. It is residential placement, and the loss of freedom it entails, that they mostly dread. Yet, while observations regarding the association between race, alienation, and violence have long existed in various literatures pertaining to males (Cloward and Olin 1960; Valentine 1968; Bourgois 1995; Devine 1996; Anderson 1990, 1999), as have ones regarding the association between violence and respect (Gilligan 1996; Anderson 1999), these issues have not been systematically explored in relation to girls who commit violence.

In addition, unlike middle-class girls who engage in physical fighting, girls who fight in West and Northeast Philly are not defying the feminine norms or other social expectations of their environs. Femininity as constructed by mainstream culture, while not rejected outright by low-income urban girls, is selectively appropriated alongside values that more closely fit their lives. The cultural and social forces that inhibit physical aggression in middle-class girls do not operate to inhibit violence among the girls with whom I spent time. Rather than being positively reinforced for demonstrating passivity, girls in West and Northeast Philly are socialized from a young age to stand up to anyone who disrespects them and to "hold their own."

A girl's mother typically plays a pivotal role in setting this process in motion. Just as it often falls on mothers as head of household to stand up to an outside challenge—girls' fathers rarely live at home—most mothers actively encourage their daughters early on to fight their own battles so that they will become similarly capable. In fact, both mothers and girls, in equal number, talk of the moment when a girl is told she must stand her ground in the streets or face her mother's wrath instead. This does not mean that most mothers want their daughters to fight; rather, they feel that their daughters must be able to defend themselves given the dangers that surround them on a daily basis. While fathers ordinarily do not discourage their daughters from fighting—they expect them to do what they have to do—they play far less of a role in influencing that process.

It is noteworthy that of the mothers I spoke with directly or heard about indirectly over the course of my study, nearly every one had a history of fighting when she was younger and about a third had yet to stop fighting altogether. Even those who had not had a fight in several years left the possibility of fighting open if it became "necessary," that is, if it came down to defending one's family or someone to whom they felt loyal—over and over, I heard mothers say that despite their best efforts, fighting was the language in which one sometimes had to communicate.

Lastly, while the analysis I offer suggests a particular sociocultural geography associated with the neighborhoods I frequented, it would be reductive to presume that class, race, or neighborhood presuppose a certain homogeneity where violence is concerned. Among the girls I talked with, the resort to violence ranged from minor street fighting to aggravated assault with a deadly weapon. Although we can learn much from the collective consideration of girls as a subgroup, and such insights are indispensable, individual life circumstances and the psychology of a girl are also central to understanding why a particular violent incident comes about. It is ultimately at the level of individual agency that the decision to take an action gets made. Being able to interact one-on-one with girls in my role as a participant observer made it possible for me to gain insight into the variation that existed within the same shared social and cultural setting. In essence, it is the larger sociocultural factors and cultural norms mentioned above, operating in concert with personal factors, that lowers the bar to girls' committing violence in West and Northeast Philly.

Girls' Violent Behavior
as Viewed from the Streets

Certainly, many of the fights that girls enter into are directly or indirectly tied to self-defense. Displaying force even in the absence of danger is a way for a girl to build a reputation that may help deter future attack. Although the risks associated with violence in poor urban enclaves are typically framed in terms of males, female youth must daily negotiate their safety on the very same streets. Being a good fighter is therefore of significant instrumental value to a girl. As Tamika explains, "If I seem like I'm scared to fight, some girl is gonna think she can mess with me all the time. I mean, even if I don't seem scared, she's gonna try me at some point till she knows how I am. She just better not go crying to anyone that I beat her the fuck up."

While the majority of girls I spoke with viewed fighting as a way to enhance their security rather than to jeopardize it, and most admitted taking great pleasure in beating up another girl without feeling remorse afterwards—"she got what was coming to her"—it is important to underscore that the inclination of girls to engage in violence exists on a continuum. For example, Tamika, a visibly angry girl with a long history of family difficulties, goes to far greater lengths than most of her peers to provoke a physical altercation. Adia, on the other hand, not one to hide from a confrontation, manages to avoid more fights than she enters into, both because she is generally easygoing by nature and because she is known for not being easily trifled with. It is this combination of popularity and reputation that saves girls from having to fight constantly. Through ethnographic observation, it was possible to hone in on the ways that the psychological and the sociocultural world of a girl came together and gain a window on how girls enacted their agencies within a shared cultural context. Such distinctions have enormous implication for understanding the production of violence in that they offer a more dimensional profile of the agency that comes into play.

Not every fight between girls in West and Northeast Philly, however, is related to issues of self-defense. As with boys (Anderson 1990, 1999), fighting for girls in poor urban neighborhoods provides a venue for identity enhancement. Girls look to fighting to make a statement about who they are. As Allie explains, "Fighting is about image. It's about showing you're no punk." In this way, to fight in West and Northeast Philly is part of carrying out girlhood—something that girls are expected to show themselves to be good at. This is not surprising as identity for the majority of these girls is negotiated on the street not in school or jobs, which are scarce.

The scenario portrayed above is especially the case for young female adolescents, ages thirteen to fifteen. Fighting in this age range has a quality of almost being instigated as a matter of sport. Similar to boys, it acts as a conduit for solidifying peer relations and for expressing youthful exuberance. Moreover, it serves as a kind of "proving ground" to exaggerate one's sense of invulnerability and fearlessness. As Allie notes, "Fighting is independence. I beat someone up if I feel like it." For Shayleen, it is a way to "feel better when things are stressing me out." Indeed, many girls seem to like the freedom they feel while fighting, though for some, "letting go" constitutes "losing control." As Samantha explains, "I get so hyped up, I black out. I don't care who gets hurt then. I don't even remember what happens afterwards." While these girls share a wide range of cultural understandings about enacting violence, the examples above illustrate how they appropriate them differentially, as well. These understandings then support different phenomenological experiences.

As long as a girl shows courage,
there is no shame in losing a fight.

Being a relatively good fighter also typically earns a girl a measure of status and respect on the street. Says Manuela, "When a fight is about to go down, everyone knows it. Go on the avenue. You run into so and so and fight. Even if you don't want to fight, to be popular you have to, so you just get it over with." As long as a girl shows courage, there is no shame in losing a fight. Far worse than losing a fight is to walk away from one. On the other hand, girls who better their opponents are rewarded with praise and adulation.

The contention that girls are looked upon favorably for fighting challenges the claim of several studies that aggressive girls manifest social and cognitive developmental deficits that renders them less popular (Talbott 1997; Henington et al. 1998). To the contrary, in West and Northeast Philly, I found that a girl's resorting to aggression often strengthened her peer ties. In addition, a girl's personal security is based on other girls' coming to her aid. As such, a girl who fights is generally seen as a valuable friend to have. As Allie relays about her best friend Natira, "that girl's my homie, she never gonna let anyone mess me up if she can help it and I'm the same with her." It is noteworthy that several girls keep a distance from other girls to avoid fighting. This has nothing to do with the issue of popularity, however. Rather, it reflects a generally held belief that most, if not all girls, are quick to involve themselves in "he-said, she-said" exchanges that end in fighting. Moreover, it speaks of a widespread view held by girls that girls cannot be trusted "because they always turn on you."

While male youths are commonly viewed in the public eye as resorting to violence more often than girls, girls on the streets of West and Northeast Philly are typically seen as willing to fight at a moment's notice—an observation strongly corroborated by teachers, the police, and treatment facility personnel with whom I spoke. Aiesha emphatically remarks, "You kidding me, girls be fighting more than boys do. They so emotional they'll fight over anything. Boys won't get into it over no he-said, she-said. They only gonna fight over something serious like money or drugs." Indeed, as fighting often turns deadly for boys due to the presence of guns, it follows that especially boys who sell drugs will be less inclined to fight over something minor. Frequently, as a girl moves into later adolescence and feels she has "less to prove," her interest in fighting shows signs of waning, too. Typically, the older girl with a stronger sense of confidence is more willing to walk away from a provocation as long as it remains in the verbal realm. As Aiesha says, "If she don't touch me she can say whatever the hell she wants."

Reasons Girls Fight

"Not liking the way a person looks at you" is the most frequently cited reason that younger girls give for why fights begin. Shayleen, who is currently in placement for aggravated assault, says, "If a girl looks at me the wrong way, I may hit her. I ain't gonna listen to no shit for too long." From the standpoint of an observer, what constitutes an insult or slight to a girl who is in the mood to fight can be almost imperceptible. That said, it is the real or imagined slight of a girl, thinking she is "better" than another girl, that makes for the combustible ingredient. Commenting about a girl who rubs her the wrong way, Tamika notes, "She be swishing her hips and acting all 'jo' [an exaggerated display to bring attention to oneself]. She just gets on my nerves." Allie expands, "If you are pretty, prettier than her, she feels insecure and you can always tell." Suggesting her own disinterest in what other girls think of her, Allie continues, "It's about status, you hate me, you make me."

The ire that a girl unleashes by calling attention to herself based on what she wears, how she carries herself, or the scene she makes in public is related to the perception that she "thinks she's special." One must wonder why a girl's attaching importance to herself inspires such animosity? Allie offers an explanation that begins to uncover the depth of jealousy and envy that exists among these teenage girls. "It's like, if another girl gets attention, she's taking it away from you. It's as if she's saying she's better than you. So you gonna knock her down a notch." Whereas middle-class girls negotiate jealousy and envy through what has been termed "relational aggression," given the host of social and cultural factors mentioned above, these same issues in West and Northeast Philly get staged and settled through force. Social aggression does not act as a substitute for physical aggression. Rather than conclude, however, that jealousy runs deeper in poor neighborhoods given their greater privations, I am inclined to believe that restrictions against girls' using violence in middle-class neighborhoods are more formidable than teenage jealousies themselves. The literature on relational aggression, which essentially is descriptive of middle-class girls, is testament to this (Jack 1999; Simmons 2002). Here, severe teasing, brutal gossip, and ostracizing are the order of the day, not physical aggression.

Other reasons that girls cite for fighting are insults to their mothers, loyalty, and pent-up rage. Like "being looked at the wrong way," the first two get invoked without much provocation. Victoria says, "I'm gonna hit someone if they disrespect my mom—if it weren't for my mom I wouldn't be here. It's worse than disrespecting me. Your mom is the highest because she raised you. She breaks her neck for you." Loyalty is in fact pledged to a wide range of associates, though sometimes only on a very temporary basis. The commitment by a girl "to watch someone's back" is built on intense feelings of belonging and pride that go far beyond the actual threat.

Far worse than losing a fight
is to walk away from one.

While such alliances serve as protection and as a deterrent to trouble, girls acknowledge that they fight to deal with pent-up rage. The depth of this anger, typically related to long-standing family problems and the accumulation of everyday pressures, varies from girl to girl. As Allie says, "I get mad thinking about my mother doing drugs when I was a kid and not being around, and sometimes it makes me feel like punching someone." Shayleen says, "Sometimes things feel like they get too much for me and I just need to let off steam. My mom used to beat me and she even burned me with cigarette butts a couple of times. I can't take it out on her so sometimes I get my anger out on the street." Although the case for many, not every girl reports a history of family abuse. Two of the fifteen girls I followed closely reported being sexually abused and five reported being physically abused. Treatment personnel, teachers, and police, however, typically portrayed girls as having more "issues" than boys and as presenting more angrily. Moreover, there was unanimous agreement among them that it was harder to break up girls' fights.

Lastly, while loath to admit it, girls frequently fight over boys. Even in the early stages of "talking" to a boy, a girl does not take kindly to another girl's getting too close. Although there is a shared understanding among girls that "messing with someone's man" is off limits, in practice, girls (and boys) move in on each other's romantic interests all the time. Whether the violation is real or imagined, the disrespect that a girl often perceives and then dishes out is enough to start two girls down a path to a physical confrontation. Suspicions run as high as they do, in part, because it is expected that most boys, especially those who sell drugs, will have sex with several girls. Roger explains, "You have to hold yourself a certain way to maintain a certain status."

Some of the biggest street battles start with two girls fighting about a boy. Competition over boys in low-income areas has an added economic ramification that raises the stakes beyond typical adolescent worries. Girls, for example, feel a need to protect their place as a boy's main girlfriend because that role often comes with spending money and other perks. This is certainly the case for a girl who is the "B.M.," that is, the "baby's mother"—the mother of a baby produced from a union with the boy. Even boys who do not deal drugs are looked to for incidentals. Interestingly, as no girl would admit to fighting over a boy, just as few boys would admit to coming to blows over a girl. It is important again to note here that while the above section attempts to summarize some of the major reasons that girls engage in street fighting and other forms of violence, it does not clarify the ways in which personal life history beyond these cultural values shapes a given girl's participation. In the end, to understand a girl's behavior, one must look at her idiosyncratic appropriation of cultural models contextualized in time and place.

What Actually Happens When Girls Fight

It is not fighting but fighting unfairly that gives a girl a bad reputation in West and Northeast Philly. Scratching, pulling hair, spitting, pinching, or biting in a fight is viewed negatively. Most girls go out of their way to communicate that they do not "fight like a girl." Tamika reveals, "I punched her in her face and then I banged her head against the ground. I only stopped cause someone pulled me off her." Shayleen confides, "I smashed her in the mouth with my fist cause she called me a punk." Of the many fights I witnessed over the course of a year, however, few went down as "cleanly" as girls suggested.

In reality, girls protect themselves in the midst of a fight any way they can. More than anything, how a fight progresses depends upon how equally matched girls are. Usually, a fight ends when onlookers deem that things have gone far enough—one girl is bleeding badly or is otherwise obviously overpowered. Oftentimes, whether winning or losing, girls do not want to stop and need to be restrained. Again, without exception, both male and female police officers report that they would rather break up fights between males any day of the week. Sergeant Palazzio explains, "Girls just won't let it go. You tell them you're gonna take them in and they get in your face and curse you out. You give a boy a chance to walk and he does." The phrase *girls gone wild* is commonly used by police, and by girls themselves, to describe this intensity and tenacity that girls exhibit in a fight.

Most girls report they like how it feels to hit another girl, though several acknowledge they often get nervous before a fight. Allie says, "I like the rush. I feel really hyped once I get going." Melissa adds, "I like seeing a girl get all messed up. You know, they start bleeding [*laughing*] and have to wipe their face." It is rare for a girl to say afterward that she feels sorry for hurting another girl. Zalika was somewhat annoyed when I asked her how she felt about hurting a girl so badly that the girl had to go to the hospital. She said, "Why you asking me this? I don't care. She came up to me for dumb stuff. If I didn't fight I'd get my ass kicked." Indeed, the sense that the surrounding world must be kept in check pervades the thinking of most people in West and Northeast Philadelphia. The moral reasoning that girls typically invoke to justify their actions and negate their culpability is "I do it to them or they do it to me."

Ethnography is particularly adept at accounting for shared social meanings and at portraying individual inner states given the intensive focus that participant observation makes possible.

Unlike boys, girls ordinarily take a negative view of fighting with weapons. To a girl, using a weapon suggests that she cannot defend herself with her own two hands. Most girls claim that they only carry a weapon if they suspect they are going to be "rolled on," that is, ambushed by several girls. When weapons are introduced into a fight, they are usually knives. It is common knowledge among youth that a girl with a knife is going to try to cut the face of another girl. Says Lakeesha, "This way she gonna see herself in the mirror everyday and remember what I did to her."

The reliance on peers, female relatives, and even one's mother to come to one's aid if outnumbered is an integral part of the anatomy of girls' fighting. Peers usually are first to expand a one-on-one fight into a wider circle of violence. The precipitant may be the perception of one party's crossing a line, an idle threat, or just a sense of heightened rage. To bring a fight to a girl's doorstep is viewed as a major sign of disrespect and often results in one's mother coming outside to fight. This "double-generational" dynamic whereby mother and daughter fight alongside one another is an important feature of fighting in West and Northeast Philly. While on a ride-along, I observed one such encounter where between twenty and thirty females squared off against each other. The police were called back three times—the first two times, they broke the altercation up and issued warnings. The third time they came back, they handcuffed a mother, daughter, aunt, and cousin and took them away in a paddy wagon.

It is noteworthy that this double-generational dynamic is unique to girls and their mothers with no corresponding parallel to boys and their fathers. Lakeesha's mother tells me, "I don't usually get in her business but if the fight isn't gonna come down fair, I can't not get involved. Anything can happen out there and you have to let people know you gonna protect your kid." To display the force at one's disposal is sometimes enough to deter an attack, though other times, it must be called upon to stave off what is believed to be further troubles (Anderson 1999). This identification and commitment that mothers have to their daughters' safety underscores a steadfast commitment, yet in practice, it can also encourage girls to escalate violence as they are virtually assured of reinforcements.

Lastly, although there is a considerable literature on how male youth in economically impoverished urban enclaves construct and affirm their masculinity through violence (Oliver 1993; Bourgois 1995; Anderson 1999), relatively little has been written about how girls in such neighborhoods negotiate their femininity while resorting to violence. From my own observation, though girls in West and Northeast Philly assert themselves aggressively, in many ways they still assume a traditional "feminine" role in their relations with boys. They spend a great deal of time on their appearance, often place the interests of boys above their own, and frequently relate to boys in a caretaking role. Little evidence suggests that girls view themselves as being any less feminine for resorting to violence or that boys perceive them that way either. As Allie notes, "I can be cute yet still mess some girl up if that's what I have to do." From the perspective of people living in West and Northeast Philly, violence is something undertaken by both males and females. The following excerpt presents a typical fight and the sequence that surrounds it.

Narrative of an Actual Fight

We are sitting on the stoop. Lakeesha and Candace are sharing a "blunt" that Lakeesha just rolled from the emptied cigar casing she bought at the "Chinese." The stoop abuts the side of a house, though the first level looks abandoned. It's a regular place to congregate. Lakeesha and Candace talk back and forth about Rashid and his girlfriend Marcea. "Did you see how she called him over? She be acting all 'jo.'" The girls dissolve into a cascade of laughter. This is the third straight night of such jokes. It is not clear to Candace whether she and Rashid are "talking." As they trade laughs, Rashid turns the corner and they wave him over. He helps himself to their blunt and when it's finished, he produces one from his pocket. As they get high, the parodying of Marcea continues.

Soon Marcea comes walking down the block with her girlfriends and sees Rashid sitting between the two. Marcea is clearly incensed over Rashid's proximity to Candace. She demands that Rashid come over to her, and Lakeesha and Candace erupt in laughter. Marcea is making a scene in the middle of the street but without approaching. It is Candace who is first to goad her to say something directly. In return, Marcea's friends egg her on, and within seconds, she is cursing in Candace's face. Candace stands up and the girls challenge each other to fight. Though verbal insults and pointed fingers are flying with the other girls holding shoes and handbags and pulling the two apart at critical moments, it is truly amazing that the two do not actually touch. Rashid in the midst of the chaos has disappeared. After a good five minutes of posturing, each labels the other a "punk," and the two groups disperse. But it is clear that the situation is not resolved. The question is when and where it will erupt next.

About an hour later, Marcea's mother and seven or eight females come to Candace's sister's house where Candace lives. The older women hanging out on Candace's block stand within striking distance should they be needed. Marcea's mother and Candace's sister exchange words, and at one point, Marcea's mother yells "just because I have my "keefah" on [religious garb] don't think I can't get ignorant with you." She makes it clear that Rashid is like her son and that Candace needs to stay away from him. Candace's sister, however, no longer wants to discuss the incident at hand. She confronts Marcea's mother about bringing the situation to her doorstep. Both women clearly lay out which boundaries cannot be crossed. This seems to be enough to end the matter for the evening.

Two days later, I learn that Lakeesha beat up Marcea because "she said stupid things so I punched her in her face." While Candace will fight to save face, hence all the showmanship, Lakeesha has more of a proclivity to fight particularly if she is already angry about something. The propensity to fight seems to run in her family, as only two days later, her mother Fazia ended up fighting a twenty-year-old woman who came to her house to accuse Lakeesha of "messing with her boyfriend." Incensed that the woman brought the fight to her door, Fazia "got in her face." The two began throwing punches with Fazia getting the better of the other woman. But even before the first punch was thrown, more than thirty people, mostly women, surrounded them. By the time the police came to break it up, many fights were going on. Fazia would not stop even after the police told her to. So the cops took her down to the station. She was issued a citation to appear in court two weeks later.

Conclusion

Violence by female adolescents in impoverished urban neighborhoods, particularly street fighting, has been significantly underestimated in official statistics. To understand why it is so commonplace in West and Northeast Philadelphia, one must consider the instrumental function it has for girls, including the measure of security it provides and the venue it offers for attaining a sense of mastery, status, and self-esteem in a social setting where legal opportunities for achievement are sorely limited. When girls who engage in violence are simply labeled delinquent, these functions go unnoticed. One must also consider that the incentive structure that normally inhibits aggression in middle-class girls is not in reach of most female adolescents in West and Northeast Philadelphia. Moreover, girls who engage in violence in West and Northeast Philadelphia are not viewed as defying feminine norms.

That social and cultural forces in West and Northeast Philadelphia produce a proclivity toward fighting in girls does not explain why that tendency is differentially taken up by girls or the ways in which these variations coexist among girls. Through presenting the views and experiences of several girls in their own words, this article has attempted to show that girls' street fighting is the product of a confluence of sociocultural and more individualized factors that are both tied to and go beyond the immediate performance of fighting (i.e., enhancing security, strengthening peer ties, degree of personal aggressiveness, extent of family problems, etc.). It is the interplay of social and cultural forces with individual factors that best explains the production of violent behavior.

Connecting structure with psychological experience, however, runs counter to tradition in the behavioral and social sciences. We have become accustomed rather to the rigid separation of objective realities—structures, laws, and systems of relationships seen as independent of individual desire and will—from subjective ones, that is, the meaning that individuals differentially ascribe to events. To bridge this all-too-common divide between individual and social causality, we need methodology that can capture the contours of social realities and trace their passage through the realm of personal experience—a methodology that is equally adept at focusing on one person's response to the surrounding world as taking heed of the fact that within the dynamics of a psychological moment, the structure of society also inheres.

As this article illustrates, ethnography is particularly adept at accounting for shared social meanings and at portraying individual inner states given the intensive focus that participant observation makes possible. The observation of variation that ethnography as a method can accommodate permits a researcher to highlight a range of reactions and competing outcomes and does not force him or her to promulgate the existence of only one local view, of one set of inferred meanings and emotions, and of a coherence of response that ordinarily defies intuition. Approaching ethnography from this perspective would allow for a more complex view of the multiple meanings that could emerge in the same situation, show meanings to be in a greater state of flux, and ultimately, serve to form a less caricatured view of the impact of social and cultural forces in a single social setting.

References

Adler, Freda. 1975. *Sisters in crime*. New York: McGraw-Hill.

Anderson, Elijah. 1990. *Streetwise: Race, class, and change in an urban community*. Chicago: University of Chicago Press.

———. 1999. *Code of the street: Decency, violence, and the moral life of the inner city*. New York: Norton.

Armistead, Lisa, M. Wierson, R. Forehand, and C. Frame. 1992. Psychopathology in incarcerated juvenile delinquents: Does it extend beyond externalizing problems? *Adolescence* 27 (106): 309-14.

Baker-Miller, Jean. 1976. *Toward a new psychology of women*. Boston: Beacon.

Belknap, Joanne. 1996. *The invisible woman: Gender, crime, & justice*. Belmont, MA: Wadsworth.

Block, Jeanne. 1984. *Sex role identity and ego development*. San Francisco: Jossey-Bass.

Bourgois, Phillipe. 1995. *In search of respect: Selling crack in El Barrio*. Cambridge, UK: Cambridge University Press.

Brotherton, David. 1996. Smartness, toughness, and autonomy. *Journal of Drug Issues* 26:261-77.

Bureau of Justice Statistics' National Crime Victimization Survey. 2003. *Comparing UCR and NCVS*. Bureau of Justice Statistics. Retrieved February 19, 2004 from http://www.ojp.usdoj.gov/bjs/.

Campbell, Anne. 1984. *The girls in the gang.* New York: Blackwell.

———. 1987. Self-definition by rejection: The case of gang girls. *Social Problems* 34 (5): 451-66.

———. 1993. *Men, women and aggression.* New York: Basic Books.

Center for the Study and Prevention of Violence. 2004. *CSPV fact sheet: Youth handgun violence.* Retrieved February 19, 2004 from http://www.colorado.edu/cspv/publications/factsheets/cspv/FS-006.html.

Chesney-Lind, Meda. 1989. Girls' crime and woman's place: Toward a feminist model of female delinquency. *Crime & Delinquency* 35:5-29.

———. 1992. *Girls, delinquency, and juvenile justice.* Pacific Grove, CA: Brooks/Cole.

———. 1997. *Female offender: Girls, women and crime.* Thousand Oaks, CA: Sage.

Chilton, Ronald, and Susan Datesman. 1987. Gender, race and crime: An analysis of urban trends, 1960-1980. *Gender & Society* 1 (2): 152-71.

Chodorow, Nancy. 1978. *The reproduction of mothering: Psychoanalysis and the sociology of gender.* Berkeley: University of California Press.

Cloward, Richard, and Lloyd Olin. 1960. *Delinquency and opportunity: A theory of delinquent gangs.* New York: Free Press.

Daly, Kathleen, and Lisa Maher, eds. 1998. *Criminology at the crossroads: Feminist readings in crime and justice.* New York: Oxford University Press.

Devine, John. 1996. *Maximum security: The culture of violence in inner-city schools.* Chicago: University of Chicago Press.

Dorfman, Lori, and Vincent Schiraldi. 2001. Off balance: Youth, race, & crime in the news. *Building Blocks for Youth.* Retrieved February 19, 2004 from http://www.buildingblocksforyouth.org/media/.

Feshbach, N. D. 1969. Sex differences in children's modes of aggressive responses towards outsiders. *Merrill-Palmer Quarterly* 15:249-58.

Figueira-McDonough, J. 1989. Community structure and female delinquency rates. *Youth & Society* 24:3-30.

Freud, Sigmund. 1905. Three essays on the theory of sexuality. In vol. 7 of *The standard edition of the complete psychological works of Sigmund Freud.* London: Hogarth Press.

———. 1925. Some psychical consequences of the anatomical distinctions between the sexes. In vol. 19 of *The standard edition of the complete psychological works of Sigmund Freud.* London: Hogarth Press.

———. 1931. Female sexuality. In vol. 21 of *The standard edition of the complete psychological works of Sigmund Freud.* London: Hogarth Press.

———. 1933. New introductory lectures on psychoanalysis. In vol. 22 of *The standard edition of the complete psychological works of Sigmund Freud.* London: Hogarth Press.

Furstenberg, Frank, and M. E. Hughes. 1997. The influence of neighborhoods on children's development: A theoretical perspective and research agenda. In vol. 2 of *Neighborhood poverty: Policy implications in studying neighborhoods*, edited by J. Brooks-Gunn, G. Duncan, and J. L. Aber. New York: Russell Sage.

Gilfus, Mary. 1992. From victims to survivors to offenders: Women's routes of entry and immersion in street crime. *Women and Criminal Justice* 4:63-89.

Gilligan, Carol. 1982. *In a different voice: Psychological theory and women's development.* Cambridge, MA: Harvard University Press.

Gilligan, James. 1996. *Violence: Our deadly epidemic and its causes.* New York: Grosset/Putnam.

Hall, Judith. 1978. Gender effects in decoding nonverbal cues. *Psychological Bulletin* 85:845-57.

Heidensohn, Francis. 1985. *Women and crime.* New York: New York University Press.

Henington, C., J. N. Hughes, T. A. Cavell, and B. Thompson. 1998. The role of relational aggression in identifying aggressive boys and girls. *Journal of School Psychology* 36:457-77.

Ingoldsby, Erin, and S. Daniel. 2002. Neighborhood contextual factors and early-starting antisocial pathways. *Clinical Child and Family Psychology Review* 5 (1): 21-55.

Jack, Dana, 1999. *Behind the mask: Destruction and creativity in women's aggression.* Cambridge, MA: Harvard University Press.

Konopka, Gisela. 1966. *The adolescent girl in conflict.* Englewood, NJ: Prentice Hall.

———. 1976. *Young girls: A portrait of adolescence.* Englewood, NJ: Prentice Hall.

Lombroso, Cesare, and William Ferraro. 1985. The female offender. London: T. Fisher Unwin.

Maccoby, E. E., and C. N. Jacklin. 1974. *The psychology of sex differences.* Palo Alto, CA: Stanford University Press.

Miller, Jody. 2003. *One of the guys: Girls, gangs and gender.* New York: Oxford University Press.

Office of Juvenile Justice and Delinquency Prevention. 2000. *Female delinquency cases, 1997.* Washington, DC: U.S. Department of Justice.

Oliver, William. 1993. *The violent social world of black men.* New York: Lexington Books.

Pollak, Otto. 1950. *The criminality of women.* Philadelphia: University of Pennsylvania Press.

Rhodes, Jean, and K. Fischer. 1993. Spanning the gender gap: Gender differences in delinquency among inner-city adolescents. *Adolescence* 28:879-89.

Sampson, Robert, Stephen Raudenbush, and Felton Earls. 1997. Neighborhoods and violent crime: A multi-level study of collective efficacy. *Science* 277:918-24.

Simmons, Rachel. 2002. *Odd girl out: The hidden culture of aggression in girls.* New York: Harcourt.

Snyder, Howard. 2003a. *Juvenile arrests 2000.* Washington, DC: Office of Juvenile Justice and Delinquency Prevention.

———. 2003b. *Juvenile arrests 2001.* Washington, DC: Office of Juvenile Justice and Delinquency Prevention.

Steffensmeier, Darrell, and E. Allan. 1991. Gender, age, and crime. In *Criminology: A contemporary hand-book,* edited by J. F. Sheley, 67-93. Belmont, CA: Wadsworth.

Talbott, Elizabeth. 1997. Reflecting on antisocial girls and the study of their development: Researchers' views. *Exceptionality* 7:267-72.

Tiger, Lionel. 1969. *Men in groups.* New York: Random House.

Tiger, Lionel, and Robin Fox. 1970. *The imperial animal.* New York: Holt, Rinehart & Winston.

Valentine, Charles. 1968. *Culture of poverty: Critique and counterproposals.* Chicago: University of Chicago Press.

Vedder, Clyde, and Dora Somerville. 1973. *The delinquent girl.* Springfield, IL: Charles C Thomas.

Whiting, Bea, and C. Edwards. 1973. A cross-cultural analysis of sex differences in the behavior of children aged 3-11. *Journal of Social Psychology* 91:171-88.

Wilson, William Julius. 1987. *Truly disadvantaged: The inner city, the underclass, and public policy.* Chicago: University of Chicago Press.

To navigate inner-city neighborhoods, young women, though reluctant at times, are often encouraged to become known as able fighters for their own protection. Among peers, one's reputation, once established, is an important social resource. The following narratives illustrate how two young women negotiate the context of violence they confront in their everyday lives.

Keywords: violence; youth; urban ethnography; violence in women; female offenders

"It's Not Where You Live, It's How You Live": How Young Women Negotiate Conflict and Violence in the Inner City

By
NIKKI JONES

S everal years ago, I was invited to work as an ethnographer for a city-hospital-based violence-intervention project—the Violence Reduction Program (VRP). The project serves youth aged twelve to twenty-four who present in the hospital's emergency room as a result of an intentionally violent incident, excluding domestic violence and child abuse. All of the young women and men in the project are purposely drawn from neighborhoods in the south, west, and southwest sections of a large northeastern city. Many of these neighborhoods are, as a consequence of patterns of racial segregation within the city, predominantly African American, and in turn, almost the entire population of young women and men in the violence-intervention project are African American youth.

Known drug markets operate within many of the neighborhoods, and residents can often quickly recall stories of violence associated with the salience of the neighborhood drug economy. While there is often a visible police presence in the neighborhood, many residents are reluctant to believe that the police are there to protect them.[1] Large orange "condemned" signs announcing that houses are being reclaimed by the city serve as visible markers of distress on individual blocks. On many of these blocks, trash accumulates in empty lots where aban-

Nikki Jones earned her Ph.D. in sociology and criminology at the University of Pennsylvania. She is an assistant professor at the University of California, Santa Barbara.

DOI: 10.1177/0002716204267394

doned homes once stood. Seasonal signs of poverty and distress are less obvious: some homes are warmed by small box heaters on the coldest winter days and cooled with simple box fans during the hottest summer months. Additional signs of distress include what parents and students often refer to as "out of control" neighborhood schools. School counselors, who will often insist that there are "good kids" in the school, will also occasionally use war analogies to describe their day-to-day attempts to counsel youth. It is inside these schools and within these neighborhoods that young women and men are most likely to experience the violent incidents that lead to emergency-room visits—and their subsequent entrance into the violence-intervention project.[2]

Once they enroll in the violence-intervention project, a random sample of youth is assigned to receive intervention from a team of transitional counselors who, over the course of several months, visit the young people in their homes, offer referrals, and provide mentoring in an attempt to reduce the risk of subsequent violence. My primary role as a researcher was to qualitatively document this intervention process. My curiosity quickly extended beyond the process of intervention and into the lived experience of the young people who came through the hospital doors. I became especially interested in the experiences of young women and girls in the project.

In service of my curiosity, I began to ask the team of transitional counselors about girls and young women very early in the research process. On one of my very first days, I sat down and had a conversation with Tracey. She is an African American woman who was, at that time, twenty years old and a recent graduate of the same public city high school that some of the youth she now counseled attended. Tracey still lives in one of the inner-city neighborhoods included in the VRP's target area; she could even walk to some home visits. During this conversation, which took place in one of the hospital's conference rooms, I asked Tracey whether there were girls in the project. She said that there were. In fact, at that time, her entire caseload was made up of girls. Most of the girls, she told me, entered the emergency room with cuts or bruises from fights at school. The following is an excerpt from that conversation:

"What are they fighting about?" I asked.
"About being disrespected—that's about it," she replied.
"Being disrespected?"
"Yeah."
"So how's that look? What does that mean?" I asked.
"I don't know . . . they're always saying, like, 'nobody talks to me like that' and all. And I'm like, 'yeah, but would you rather die over something somebody said?'"
"Do they see death as a real risk?" I asked her.
"No, no. They just see getting beat up and getting laughed at, that's all. And I try to tell them that life is too short to just do stupid stuff. You can't argue over dumb stuff. I don't expect you to go to school and not fight anymore because that would just be too unreal. I was like, 'but time will tell.' I don't know. I don't know. I don't know. Just crazy. I'm like okay, ya'll were fighting because she said your sneakers were ugly—okay . . . and [*laughs*] where does the argument start at?"

"Do they answer you? Do they tell you where the argument starts?"
"Yeah, they were, like, she said my sneakers were ugly, and I said this, and then she said
    this, and next thing you know this girl said this and we just all started fighting."

This early conversation with Tracey (and similar conversations during the course of the project) struck me for several reasons. First, descriptions of fights like the ones Tracey described are most commonly associated with fights between boys in inner-city high schools and neighborhoods. The social impetus for such violence has been described in detail in Elijah Anderson's ethnography of "the moral code of inner-city life." Specifically, in *Code of the Street*, Anderson (1999) defines "the code" as a set of "informal rules of behavior organized around a desperate search for respect that governs public social relations, especially violence among so many residents [of the inner-city], particularly young men and women" (p. 10). Anderson highlights especially the relationship between masculinity, respect, and the use of violence, writing that "many inner-city young men in particular crave respect to such a degree that they will risk their lives to attain and maintain it" (p. 75). While Anderson's work emphasizes the relationship between masculinity and the code, Tracey's claim that young women are fighting "about being disrespected—that's about it" suggests that the code (i.e., the relationship between respect and violence in the inner city) is not necessarily gender specific. Furthermore, Tracey's admission, "I don't expect you to go to school and not fight anymore because that would just be too unreal," suggested to me that "girl fights" in this setting are not an anomaly but rather a real daily possibility. Girls and young women can and do fight.[3] As I continued to develop this project, I began to consider the following questions: What is the context of violence in the lives of young women in the inner city? How do young women negotiate conflict and violence? What are the consequences of these processes of negotiation?

To respond to this guiding set of research questions, I relied on my work with the VRP, which introduced me to scores of young women and men who were injured and who, in some cases, had injured others during violent incidents. I spent my first year and a half in the field riding along on home visits with intervention counsel-ors.[4] After I spent a year and a half observing home visits, informally interviewing both young women and men injured in violent incidents and transitional counsel-ors, I began to conduct one-on-one, in-depth interviews with young women and men in the project. Some of these young people I was meeting for the first time, while others I had met during the course of the previous year. In addition to these interviews and visits, all of which took place in the neighborhoods and homes of the young people in the project, I engaged in extended conversations with grandmoth-ers, mothers, sisters, brothers, cousins, and friends of the young people. I also sys-tematically observed interactions in the spaces and places that were significant (as revealed during this initial period of fieldwork) in the lives of these young people. These spaces included trolley cars and buses, a neighborhood high school nick-named "the Prison on the Hill," the city's family and criminal court, and various correctional facilities in the area.[5]

Girls Fight

Through this multilayered fieldwork experience, I have come to find, first, that girls do fight. Girls are not isolated from many forms of violence that men also experience in the inner-city setting. Furthermore, within the inner-city setting, girls, like their male counterparts, realize through observation and experience that violence is a potential tool to mediate the physical vulnerability they may experience in their everyday lives. Some young women, equipped with a history of fighting and winning, are invested in developing and maintaining a reputation as a

---

[A reputation as a "fighter"] is an important social resource because it can provide young women with a sense of security and confidence with which they can navigate their neighborhoods and school environments.

"fighter." This reputation is an important social resource because it can provide young women with a sense of security and confidence with which they can navigate their neighborhoods and school environments. Other young women, who are less invested in an identity as a fighter, will find ways to negotiate their way out of potential conflicts, with varying degrees of success. The following narratives, the first belonging to Terrie, a self-identified "violent person," and the second to Danielle, a young woman who has fought but is not a fighter, highlight the context in which young women negotiate potential conflicts and violence. In addition, these narratives demonstrate the various strategies young women consider and select to negotiate the neighborhood and school setting. Ultimately, these narratives illustrate young women's instrumental use of violence in the inner-city setting.

"Ain't I a Violent Person?": Terrie's Story

Terrie is seventeen years old and was just completing her junior year at a local public high school when we first met. She stands about 5 feet 8 inches and weighs about 165 pounds. She lives in an older row home with members of her immediate and extended family including her mother, her mother's fiancée, her Uncle Slim, and a collection of real and adopted sisters. Terrie has not seen her biological father, who is currently serving time in one of the state's prisons, in years. However, the man she terms her "real" father (her mother's ex-boyfriend), who Terrie believes "chose" to be her father (a lineage that she defines as far more significant), remains a stable presence in her life. During the day, Terrie is charged with taking care of her little sisters. Terrie's mother, who Terrie says is like her best friend, works two jobs and is home just two nights of the week. In addition to the role of caretaker that Terrie occupies within the home, she is often seen as a counselor for most of the younger kids in the neighborhood, who often come to her with questions and concerns.

Terrie's neighborhood is only blocks from the invisible yet well-known "cut-off point" that extends around the university area where I began most of my days in the field. A somewhat integrated neighborhood populated with working-class African American families and university students is bounded by a walking bridge that crosses over a set of regional railroad tracks. Quite literally on the other side of the tracks is Terrie's neighborhood, populated by a mix of residents whose income levels range from little to none to steady; often, the homes these residents inhabit share a wall with abandoned or condemned houses. Drug dealers, teenagers, and grandmothers share the space within the neighborhood boundary. At the end of the block is a house that is a center for a variety of illegal hustles, including drug selling and arbitrary violence. On the opposite end of Terrie's block is a corner that is a center of open-air drug trafficking and thus the locus of much of the violent activity that occurs in the neighborhood. Terrie can quickly recall several young men who have been shot on the corner in recent years, including her own cousin. She explains to me that whenever she walks by the corner all the guys say "Hi" to her. "See," she explains, "they all know me."

A Violent Person?

Everybody knows Terrie because, after living in the neighborhood for fifteen years, she has built a reputation as what she defines as a "violent person." As Terrie explains to me over a series of conversations, the fights she gets into serve in some way to protect this reputation and the authority and respect that enable her to navigate the neighborhood and school setting. The stage for her fights is often the public high school. Terrie explains to me in detail the fight that landed her in the emergency room.

She tells me that it was early one morning when she was approached by her cousin who informed her that another young woman was "stepping to her"—instigating a potential physical conflict. Terrie's cousin believed that she would likely end up in a physical battle with this young woman unless someone intervened, and this is why she came to Terrie.

Terrie tracked down the young woman who was "stepping" to her cousin, talked to her, and they agreed, Terrie says, to "squash it." Terrie explained very simply that if the young woman stepped to Terrie's cousin, she would have to step to Terrie. At this moment, the argument ended, according to Terrie, on the strength of her intervention. Later in the day, however, Terrie's cousin came back to her and told her that this young woman had stepped to her again. Terrie recognized this as a direct violation of the agreement she had reached with this young woman earlier in the day. It was, Terrie explains, "supposed to be squashed." According to Terrie, such a flagrant violation of their agreement had become a public sign of disrespect toward her. Terrie was essentially being "called out" and would now have to choose a response. She chose to publicly challenge the young woman.

Terrie catches up with the young woman in the hallway; they are surrounded by other young people who tend to gather at the scene of any potential fight. As Terrie turns to say something to a friend of hers, Terrie's cousin spots the young woman doing what young women do when they are preparing for a fight: she has taken off her wig and wrapped a scarf around her head to prevent the hair pulling that sometimes happens during the course of a fair one gone wild. "She's about to hit you!" someone calls out from the crowd. Recognizing that she will soon be at a disadvantage if she does not strike first, Terrie turns around and punches the young woman in the face. As additional punches are thrown the young woman bites down on Terrie's hand. Terrie grabs the young woman's head with her other hand and uses her body weight to bang the other woman's head into a vending machine until the blood from the woman's face is spilling into the open wound on Terrie's hand. School security guards finally reach the center of the fight and break it up. Terrie is quickly suspended and goes home more concerned about how she is going to deal with her mother's response to her suspension than her obviously injured hand. Terrie continues to ignore the gash on her hand until it has doubled in size as the result of an infection. Terrie finally visits the emergency room and has her infected wound cleaned and stitched back together.

Trading on Violence

Terrie gets something other than an infected wound from this fight. First, she has taken on a challenger and won in front of an audience. Her reputation as a fighter, as someone not to be bothered, is left intact. She is still a violent person. And she can now go on doing the things she does, walking the halls in school or the streets in her neighborhood, as someone whom "everybody knows" and respects. She can also continue to do the other things she does at her high school, including attending her advanced-placement classes. Terrie attended a course for gifted students at a local university over the summer, and she is now making plans to attend college. She plans to be the first in her family to graduate from high school and go to college.[6]

Terrie's use of violence to facilitate her mobility through both her neighborhood and her school is just one of the ways that Terrie can trade on her prowess and the reputation that is associated with it. Terrie can also trade on her reputation as a fighter in other ways; for example, she can come to the aid of people she sees as vulnerable. A year after the fight described in the previous section, Terrie stumbles upon the following scene: two young women are stopped in the hallway facing another young woman, most likely a very frightened freshman. It is clear to Terrie that the two girls are about to "roll on" (attack without much prior notice) this young woman, which, according to Terrie, "just wasn't fair." So Terrie steps in and asks what is going on. The young women says, "Well, I think she has a big mouth." Terrie responds that maybe *she* has a big mouth. Then she makes clear to the young women that this freshman is her "cousin," and she "doesn't want anyone to mess with her."[7] The two young women walk off in a huff, the freshman is relieved, and Terrie feels good about herself. Since this showdown, Terrie's newly minted cousin, acutely aware of the protection she received from her association with

---

[By intervening in a potential conflict], Terrie has tested and validated her reputation once again without having to actually fight.

Terrie, has repeatedly thanked Terrie for coming to her aid. She also continues to trade on this association as she makes her own way through the school. Terrie explains that whenever she sees her "cousin" in the crowded halls of the high school she yells out, "Hey Terrie!" loud enough for everyone to hear. Terrie laughs as she tells me this story. Terrie always says "Hi" back but, she confides, "still has no idea what that little girl's name is."

Ultimately, the girl's name does not matter. The purpose of Terrie's intervention is really twofold. First, Terrie clearly derives a sense of power and self-confidence from intervening in an unfair situation and making it right simply on the strength of her own reputation. Perhaps most important, however, Terrie has tested and validated her reputation once again without having to actually fight and thus has avoided the threat of suspension or expulsion, which allows her to continue her other activities in the school, including continuing to pursue her goal of graduating and going to college.[8]

"It's Not Where You Live"

The strategies used by young women to negotiate conflict and violence are illuminated by examining not only the stories of those with well-established reputations as fighters, such as Terrie, but also of those who have not established such reputations. One example of such a person is Danielle, who would rather do anything but fight. She is a slim, brown-skinned young woman who recently graduated from one of the city's public high schools. While in high school, she was on the track team and performed well enough in her classes to enroll in a small, predominantly white university hours outside of the city, one that by her own account, is worlds away from her inner-city home. While she enjoyed her experience with college life, Danielle left school in the middle of her freshman year, after discovering that she was several weeks pregnant. Her baby's father, Jimmy, attended the same university on a partial athletic scholarship, but he too dropped out and returned to the inner-city neighborhood across town from Danielle's. Jimmy calls and visits Danielle often, and while Danielle is excited about "making a family," as Jimmy often promises, she has also had to confront her regret about being "back here" in the project apartment where she grew up. "When I left," she tells me, "I didn't plan on coming back except for holidays and stuff like that."

Danielle now spends most of her days in the eleventh-floor apartment she shares with her mother and two brothers, one nine and the other an eleven-month-old. Danielle's grandmother and grandfather live several floors below, and Danielle visits often. This family unit, along with her Christian faith, provides Danielle with a relatively stable support system that she often uses to insulate herself from various forms of conflict. While much of Danielle's time is spent imagining what life will be like when her baby arrives, our series of conversations about life in the projects and her direct and indirect experiences with violence highlighted for me the complicated backdrop of violence that informs the everyday lives of young women who grow up in distressed inner-city neighborhoods.

Violence as the Backdrop of Everyday Life

During our first visit, I ask Danielle how she likes living in the projects.

> "It could be better," she responded, "without the drugs and all, the violence that go on, like cops and stuff and the fire alarms be going off in the middle of the night, like 3:00 or 4:00 in the morning, because some kid pulled the alarm. . . . And, you know, crackheads that be in the building and stuff like that knock on your door asking for stuff. . . . It could be better."

The projects where Danielle lives, like many housing projects around the country, are now in transition. These changes, which redistribute complex residents to different areas in the city, have tangibly affected the environment in Danielle's home, as residents from the northside projects, the eastside projects, and Danielle's complex are required to share space after years of conflict. As a result, Danielle tells me, there have been a lot more fights in the complex this past summer.

Danielle's most personal and still most memorable experience with violence occurred during her early teen years when she was dating Jamal, a young man who she inadvertently learned was also a local drug dealer after greeting him with a hug and finding a gun tucked in his waistband. Danielle became quite upset when she found the gun and began to yell at Jamal, who asked her to just let him explain. Jamal went on to explain his strained relationship with his mother, how Danielle was the first woman to ever express love for him, and how she was the first woman that he ever cared about.

Against her better judgment, Danielle continued to date Jamal and, while doing so, encouraged him to make some changes. For example, she got him to constrain his selling to less hard drugs—"weed," for example—instead of crack. Still, dating a drug dealer, Danielle confides, was difficult and included restraints on their mobility within the neighborhood. She explains what this was like: "it was hard, like, we couldn't go anywhere, to the movies or anything because he was selling and you never knew when someone who was looking for him would find him." While visiting her boyfriend on the block one day, Danielle quickly learned that dating a drug dealer was not just potentially dangerous but actually dangerous. The following is an excerpt from my conversation with Danielle:

> Well, one day I wanted to go see him on the block. I wanted to see him because I hadn't seen him in a few days and my cousin was with me and she wanted to see her boyfriend, too. But Jamal told me never to come to the corner when he was working. But my cousin and I went to see them and we walked up to him and my cousin's boyfriend. The next thing I remember is this black car with tinted windows pulling up to the corner. As I'm talking to my boyfriend and she is talking to her boyfriend the next thing I see is a gun pointed at my cousin's head. I'm like frozen. The guy with the gun is asking my cousin's boyfriend where his $700 is. He keeps saying, "Where my money!" After, like, forever, my boyfriend reaches into his pocket and pulls out a thick wad, *thick*, he pulls out $900 and gives it to the guy. He's like, "Here it is and here's an extra $200. Just take it."

Danielle tells me that the guy with the gun took the money, got back into the black car, and pulled away. After the young men left the corner, Danielle's cousin collapsed and Danielle attempted to revive her and regain her own composure. While some young women are undoubtedly attracted by the lifestyle that some drug dealers can afford, for women like Danielle, the risk of danger associated with dating a drug dealer is not worth the energy or the effort. For Danielle, the experience described above was enough for her to refuse to date Jamal or any other drug dealer in the future. Her constraint on this particular type of social relationship is just one of the ways she chooses to negotiate a potentially violent setting.

"It's How You Live"

While Danielle agrees that much of project life is characterized, fairly or unfairly, by the types of experiences I have described, she is also able to reflect positively on how she has lived out her own life within this context; "I'm blessed," she tells me, "I really am." She continues, "Some people will use living in the projects as an excuse but not me. It's not where you live, it's how you live." It is to a certain degree how Danielle lived that helped her to make it through almost her entire nineteen years without a fight. Danielle was particularly adept at mediating potential fights in school before they reached the point of a fistfight or worse.

Danielle is able to identify at least three strategies that she used to negotiate potential conflicts in the school setting. First, Danielle was careful in the way she presented herself. For example, she did not exhibit a demeanor that indicated "she had a point to prove," as some young women do, and in fact, Danielle did not feel like she did have a point to prove or a reputation as a fighter that she needed to protect. Second, because Danielle had no point to prove, she did not feel compelled to meet every challenge with a challenge—that is, every bump with a bump. When a potential conflict did arise, Danielle was quick to activate her networks of authority. Danielle sums up these two strategies when I ask her how she avoided getting into a fight:

> Not saying nothing. If people, like, call me names or push me or something I just brush it off. Something like that. Or go to someone, like, I talk to a teacher. I was always talking to a teacher [*laughs*]. I'm scared, I'm a punk [*laughs*]. Little punk.

Danielle also tried to talk out potential conflicts before they escalated into a public battle. For example, she once approached a young woman who had been "talking about her" after school, away from the eyes of an audience. Cutting through the tough front this young woman presented, Danielle simply explained to her "you don't even know me." The two talked briefly, and the next day, the young woman told her friends that Danielle was "okay." And that was it.

Despite the energy Danielle exerted to avoid potential conflicts each day, she did end up in a fight once. One of the common ways that young women who are not fighters get involved in fights is through their "loyalty links." The strength of these loyalty links is often designated by the given status of a young woman's relationship to other young women. At least two status positions exist: "friend" indicates a strong link and "associate" indicates a weaker link. It is commonly assumed that young women should fight for a friend but are not necessarily required to fight for an associate. So one of the ways that young women insulate themselves from potential conflicts is by limiting the strength of their social relationships with other young women.

Loyalty Links

Danielle explains to me how her loyalty link to her best friend resulted in her being in her first and only fight in nineteen years. She tells me that a group of girls had been threatening her best friend who, at the time, lived with Danielle and her family in their project apartment. This group of girls repeatedly threatened to "get" her best friend after school. Danielle was very concerned about this because, as she explains, "It's my best friend and I don't want nobody to hurt her." As Danielle and her friend began to walk home from the high school to the projects, the group of young women followed, making it clear that they wanted to fight. During the walk, the young women continued to test Danielle and her friend. Danielle explains,

> And we were walking and they were following her, calling her names, telling her that you better watch your back "B" or fight me now, just sayin' stuff. So we got in front of [the local hospital] and I said, "Katrina, drop your bags," 'cause they're behind me and they're coming closer, and I dropped my bags. Just to make sure that nobody not tryin' to jump her.

Even though Danielle had never been in a fight before, she was aware of how to handle such a situation. She explains that you cannot keep walking with your back turned or you might get "jumped." Danielle had also done what many young

---

One of the ways that young women insulate themselves from potential conflicts is by limiting the strength of their social relationships with other young women.

---

women do when a fight is imminent; she called ahead to her mother who then met them halfway home. When Danielle's mom arrived on the scene, she was prepared to do her part to make sure that the fight did not get out of hand, despite the fact that she was several months pregnant. Danielle continues,

> So my mom was there and everything like that. And Katrina got into the street—and this was something—they was about to swing and fight each other. And I, my mom was there and I was there, so we can make sure that nobody don't interfere with their fight. You know, make sure it's not a blood bath or nothing like that, you know, make sure . . . 'cause sometimes you got to fight, not fight, but get into that type battle to let them know that I'm not scared of you and you can't keep harassing me thinking that it's okay.

Once Katrina and the young woman she squared off with began to fight, Danielle was quickly moved from being a bystander to a participant when another young woman punched her in the face. Danielle explains,

> I was there, like, just watching everything and then before I knew it I got snuck. . . . I got, somebody came and pulled my hair and hit me in the eye. So I'm, [I] can't see. I'm like, "what's going on?" I'm tripping over the curb, fallin' on the ground, hit my back on the curb and everything like that and I'm on the ground and I'm getting like this girl beat-

ing on me and stuff and I'm, like, "who is this?" I couldn't really see 'cause my eye got
hit and I'm trying to see who this is and me and her fighting and everything.

Danielle eventually regained her composure and moved from receiving punches
to landing some punches herself:

> So I flip her over and I finally get my sight back and we fighting because she hittin' me, I'm
> hittin' her and everything. Then she get up and I run after her 'cause I'm real angry. I
> want to like hurt this girl because she hit me for no reason. So I go up to her [and] me
> and her fightin' and then they ran . . . and we was, like, "Come back and finish! Don't
> run now because you getting your butt kicked!" So they left and we got in the car and
> came home. My eye was black. I was seeing stars [laughs].

While this fight did not convert Danielle into a fighter, she does confide in me
that she felt good when she went to school the next day. She felt confident that she
could handle herself. She was not, after all, "a punk." Since this fight, Danielle's
best friend has moved down South with her family. Danielle did not have any additional problems with the young women she fought. She has continued to engage in
strategies to negotiate conflict before it can escalate. For example, when she ran
into the girls, she would make an attempt to avoid walking by them or speaking
directly to them.

If not for her loyalty link to her best friend, Danielle may have made it through
her entire high school career, as some young women undoubtedly do, without ever
getting into a fight. If that would have happened, however, it would be a result not
of luck or even because Danielle is "blessed" but, as is demonstrated above, of her
investment in negotiating potential threats of interpersonal conflict before they
reach the point of a violent battle. In her neighborhood, Danielle restricted her
social network to a few friends and a tight-knit family who had a strong relationship
with the church. At home, Danielle chose to spend most of her time in her apartment, to avoid being involved in her neighbor's "petty" arguments that could
quickly escalate into fights. In school, Danielle sought to address perceived conflicts by talking with other young women or, when that was not a sufficient remedy,
by seeking the help of other authority figures whom she could trust. Danielle's only
direct involvement in a fight stemmed from her strong allegiance to Katrina, her
best friend. Not willing to let someone "just hurt her," Danielle realized that the
two of them would have to meet the challenge presented by the group of young
women who were following them home. She realized this herself, she prepared for
it, and when she had to, she fought.

Conclusion

In distressed inner-city neighborhoods young women like Danielle and Terrie
come of age against a backdrop of real and potential violence. This remains true
despite the decline of the types of violence that characterized the nation's inner cities during the late 1980s and early 1990s. Often, young women in distressed inner-

city neighborhoods are encouraged to both be and become known as able fighters for their own protection. The utility of such a reputation is demonstrated in Terrie's narrative. A self-identified violent person, Terrie is known and respected by both the drug dealers and the grandmothers on her block. Being known in this way allows Terrie a certain degree of security and mobility in her neighborhood and school setting. To maintain this reputation and its benefits, Terrie must at times fight, and she does so when necessary. Young women without a known reputation as an able fighter must still account for the violence that exists beneath the surface of everyday life. As demonstrated in Danielle's narrative, while she is not a fighter, she still exerts quite a bit of energy negotiating potential conflicts with a remarkable degree of success. The narratives of Terrie and Danielle, and other young women like them, encourage us to reconsider current conversations about "violent girls" that tend to pathologize young (predominantly African American) women who use violence while ignoring the structural and cultural context within which young women negotiate conflict and violence and the variety of strategies they use to do so. For young women in distressed inner-city neighborhoods, being able to fight and being known as a fighter are at times the most reliable social resources available to them in their everyday lives.

Notes

1. In my own fieldwork, I have found much support for this theme, which Elijah Anderson explores in detail in *Code of the Street* (1999). Regarding the relationship between the police and many inner-city residents, Anderson writes, "The police, for instance, are most often viewed as representing the dominant white society and not caring to protect inner-city residents." See also "Going Straight: The Story of a Young Inner-city Ex-convict" (Anderson 2001, 136).

2. See Massey and Denton's *American Apartheid* (1994) for a discussion of the consequences of concentrated poverty. For a discussion of how the interaction of "structure" and "culture" influence crime and victimization in distressed inner-city neighborhoods, see Lauritsen and Sampson's "Minorities, Crime, and Criminal Justice" (1998, 65-70) and Sampson and Wilson's "Toward a Theory of Race, Crime, and Urban Inequality" (1995).

3. My own fieldwork suggests that despite the decline in the violence that characterized the inner city in the late 1980s and early 1990s, many young men and women still rely on the "code of the street" as a useful framework in which to consider potential threats of violence and its consequences. This research complements the work of Anderson by examining how *young women* experience the threat of violence and, in turn, work "the code" to mediate those threats.

4. During this time, I developed a close relationship with two women who grew up in the same inner-city neighborhoods where they now worked for the Violence Reduction Program: Stephanie, who was the intervention team coordinator, and Tracey, the intervention counselor I described earlier who evolved into a "key informant" in the field.

5. Anderson defines a staging area as "hangouts where a wide mix of people gather for various reasons. It is here that campaigns for respect are most often waged" (Anderson 1999, 77). During visits to the homes of young women and men in the project, fostered initially by Tracey, and then in my own observations of public transportation scenes during key times of the day, I discovered the trolley as an additional staging area for youth of high school age.

6. It is important to note that while the use of violence can ensure a degree of respect, freedom, and protection, for some young women like Terrie and those she deems worthy, this same reputation is essentially meaningless in the face of other threats young women face, particularly the threat of sexual assault. For example, during a visit to her boyfriend's neighborhood, Terrie took a walk to the corner store. After she entered

the store, the owner proceeded to lock the front door, trapping Terrie inside. But he was then interrupted by a customer knocking on the locked glass door. When he returned to the front door and unlocked it, Terrie slipped out. She was clearly shaken by the experience but eventually calmed herself down enough to talk with her boyfriend about what she considered a potential sexual assault. She told me that her boyfriend wanted to go to the store to "see" this man, but Terrie forbade him to do so. "If I wanted someone to shoot him," she explained to me, "I'd get my brothers." This brief example demonstrates that despite Terrie's physical strength and her strong reputation as a fighter, she is less capable of challenging certain forms of violence. I pursue this theme in greater detail in my dissertation *Girls Fight: Understanding the Context of Violence in the Lives of African American Inner City Girls*.

7. The adoption of fictive kin has been discussed in classic ethnographic studies including Elijah Anderson's *A Place on the Corner* (1976).

8. One would be incorrect to conclude that Terrie is essentially a violent person. Erving Goffman's discussion of the presentation of self in everyday life is helpful in considering the role of the self to the "performance" in which Terrie is so deeply invested (Goffman 1959). Goffman writes, "A correctly staged and performed scene leads the audience to impute a self to a performed character, but this imputation—this self—*is a product of a scene that comes off, and is not a cause of it*. The self, then, as a performed character is not an organic thing that has a specific location, whose fundamental fate is to be born, to mature and to die; it is a dramatic effect arising diffusely from a scene that is presented, and the characteristic issue, the crucial concern, is whether it will be credited or discredited" (Goffman 1959, 253; emphasis added). Goffman's explanation encourages us to consider the present analysis not as a study of violent girls per se but rather as a study of how young women and girls use violence to mediate potential threats of violence in their everyday lives.

References

Anderson, Elijah. 1976. *A place on the corner*. Chicago: University of Chicago Press.

———. 1999. *Code of the street: Decency, violence and the moral life of the inner city*. New York: W.W. Norton.

———. 2001. Going straight: The story of a young inner-city ex-convict. *Punishment and Society* 3 (1): 135-52.

Goffman, E. 1959. *The presentation of self in everyday life*. New York: Doubleday.

Lauritsen, Janet L., and Robert J. Sampson. 1998. Minorities, crime, and criminal justice. In *The handbook of crime and punishment*, edited by Michael Tonry. Oxford: Oxford University Press.

Massey, D. S., and N. A. Denton 1994. *American apartheid: Segregation and the making of the underclass*. Cambridge, MA: Harvard University Press.

Sampson, Robert J., and William Julius Wilson. 1995. Toward a theory of race, crime, and urban inequality. In *Crime and inequality*, edited by John Hagan and Ruth Peterson. Palo Alto, CA: Stanford University Press.

Inner-City "Schoolboy" Life

By
RAYMOND GUNN

Academically oriented young males, or "schoolboys," who reside in inner-city communities are often required to choose between their home and their school and are at risk of becoming alienated from either community, with far-reaching and dire consequences. The two cultures are often mutually antagonistic, and most students are severely challenged when trying to maintain a balance. The author uses relevant insights from his own childhood to approach his ongoing research with African American male students in a college preparatory magnet high school in Philadelphia.

Keywords: urban ethnography; race relations; inner-city school; status mobility

Academically oriented young black males from low-resource urban communities almost invariably face a quandary: on one hand, they must convince their peers in the neighborhood that they are as masculine as the rest of them; on the other hand, they must convince school personnel that they are different from the rest, which requires them to efface any vestiges of the hypermasculine behavior that carries so much currency in their home community. Very early on, these students must decide upon a strategy that will help them to achieve some kind of balance between their life at home and at school. The strategies "schoolboys"[1] employ are unique to individual personalities and backgrounds, as I will show, but the desired outcomes are the same. The schoolboy's aim is to let other males in the neighborhood know that he is like them—even if he does not do all the things they do—and thus, they should not "mess" with him. The schoolboy also intends to communicate to school personnel in powerful positions

Raymond Gunn is a Ph.D. candidate in sociology and education at the University of Pennsylvania

NOTE: I would like to thank Elijah Anderson, University of Pennsylvania, Department of Sociology, for his mentorship and encouragement on this project, specifically, and on my research, generally.

DOI: 10.1177/0002716204267404

that he is not the same as his peers, to convince personnel to give him the "benefit of the doubt." It is a difficult balance to strike, and most schoolboys are unsuccessful in their attempts. The result is that one side offers strong peer relations within a group that is marginalized by the damaging stereotypes the larger society holds of it, while the other side holds greater incorporation into the larger society at the expense of satisfying relations with peers at home.

I will first offer two examples from my own childhood of schoolboys who were fairly successful at achieving this delicate balance. In the latter part of the article, I will offer two examples of schoolboys from my current research who are less successful at achieving a balance between home (or community) and school.

Much research has been done on the pitfalls that plague inner-city communities in which the subjects of this article are likely to live. It is because of these pitfalls that life on the big-city streets is lived very differently from life in other parts of the country. Countless boys in these communities are deprived of meeting their potential because they are routed by circumstances that are largely beyond their control. Anderson (1990) shows that it takes quite a lot of forethought for the denizens of such communities to merely go up and down the street. One learns and adapts to a certain "code of the street" (Anderson 1999), which is largely the result of the severely weakened ties between the community and the rules of civil law. For young males on these streets, proof of one's masculinity becomes pressing at a very early age. Usually, teens try to establish their masculinity through certain sports like basketball, through entertainment like gangsta rap, through a variety of money-making ventures—be they in the legal or illegal economy—or through violence. It is unlikely that one's academic success is going to help one to establish a masculine identity in such communities. The behaviors that one generally must engage in to achieve academic success are not those that will send telegraphic messages that one is not to be trifled with to other males in the area or in similar areas.

To be academically successful, one must usually attend school regularly, carry around a knapsack laden with books, spend hours completing assignments—often in isolation—and be an active member of the school community, a community that has demonstrated in numerous ways that it is hostile to urban African American young males.[2] To avoid persecution, these students must develop certain strategies that allow them to negotiate two separate and hostile worlds: home and school. To illustrate how this is done, I examine my own and my friend James's schooling experiences as African American boys who had academic aspirations but who were from a low-resource urban community. What I want to suggest is that these young people are put in a unique position in which they must make conscious, deliberate decisions about their lives at home and at school that will likely have far-reaching ramifications on their educational outcomes.

In my working-class Bronx neighborhood in the 1970s, masculinity was measured by three primary factors: how "nice" one was with "the hands" (how well one could fight), one's "rap" (how well one could get girls to be romantically interested), and how good one's "moves on the court" were (how well one could play basketball, particularly with finesse). Adolescent males who chose to excel in school either remained indoors or lived elsewhere. There were a few of us who attempted to balance the two worlds, and we met with varying degrees of success. Some tried to master a particular aspect of basketball, such as the jump shot, and became dependable members of a team. Others mastered the street art of "snappin'," or riotous jokes about the perceived defects of another's physical or personality characteristics and/or family members (e.g., "Yo' mama so black she was marked absent in night school").[3] Or, like my friend James and I, the rest of us had to show that we could "handle" ourselves in a variety of ways when the situation called for it. Thus, we had to be prepared to demonstrate at any given moment that we had nice enough hands to defend ourselves should someone come along to test us. Even if we did not win the fight, we had to show that we were no "punk" and were not afraid to stand up to anyone who challenged us. We also had to know how to play ball well enough not to embarrass ourselves on the court. And we had to be sure to be seen displaying our "rappin'" skills in some public place where others could see us in a tête-à-tête with a pretty young lady.

The adolescent terrain for males in my neighborhood, such as it was, was full of social land mines. One false step and the consequences were dire. My older brother Harold taught James and me how to box and defend ourselves. We both became nice enough with our hands to earn a reputation for not being someone to trifle with. James and I put in an inordinate amount of time and energy practicing basketball, though neither of us liked it very much. James became a dependable blocker of shots; I mastered the free throw and had something of a talent for the jump shot. Being more handsome than I, James had lots of girls who wanted him to rap to them. I, on the other hand, used what little charms I had to keep a few girls interested, though admittedly I have had my share of feminine rebuffs.

In hindsight, I am in awe of James's prodigious discipline. Despite the almost daily tests of masculinity, James graduated near the top of our class of more than six hundred students. I was far less disciplined and relied more heavily on what I believed at the time to be my natural intellectual gifts. Still, I managed to graduate in the top 10 percent of the class.

For some reason, which I am still trying to figure out, James and I never thought it was an option to fall on one side of the fence or the other. That is, it never occurred to us that we could exclusively embrace the academic life or the street life. An exclusive embrace of the academic life in our neighborhood meant a life of isolation and/or being the target of ridicule and interpersonal violence. An exclusive embrace of the street life meant a life of short-term gratification that inevitably led to a dead end. Neither was acceptable to us, so we chose to do a balancing act that required far more energy and mental agility than either of the other two options. We were exhausted by the time of high school graduation, but we were joyous too because we both had been accepted to universities far away, both physically and socially, from our Bronx neighborhood that we planned to leave and never look back upon again.

Of course, we did look back. How could we not? Our childhood and adolescent experiences in that Bronx neighborhood shaped us in numerous and incontrovertible ways. In fact, they laid the foundation for who we would become and for what we wanted out of life. Although our life paths have taken us to places far, far away from those tough Bronx streets, when James and I meet as adults, we invariably look back at our childhood, taking inventory of what became of our battle-weary friends and schoolmates and wondering why our own lives turned out so differently. Many of our friends died or were sent to prison during the drug-crazed 1980s. Others trained for soon-to-be-obsolete manufacturing jobs and became mired in unstable relationships. A few went on to college, but most never got beyond the remedial classes that many colleges started to offer in the 1970s to accommodate high school graduates who clearly had never learned basic reading, writing, and math skills. A handful of us, though, managed to have some success in college and even to pursue advanced degrees. But James and I are never quite sure how it happened.

Notions of exceptionalism strike us as inadequate. We can both rattle off at least a dozen of our peers who were far more charismatic, intelligent, and agile than we and who had a host of other excellent qualities. Our families were clearly not any different from those of our peers. We had our share of alcoholism, domestic violence, underemployment and unemployment mixed in seamlessly with familial love, trips south to visit relatives, and holiday gatherings. Snappin' on one's friend's family was usually safe territory because everybody's family was fair game. We all had skeletons in our closet with the door wide open for anyone to see. There was that one thing, however, that James and I could point to that steered us toward a different trajectory than the one our friends were on. At the age of ten, James and I embarked on careers as child actors.

For us, this turn of fate came about through Mr. Warren, my Nana's husband. Short and pudgy with a thick head of salt-and-pepper hair and a bushy mustache, Mr. Warren appeared as far removed from the glamorous life of show business as one could imagine. What few people knew about Mr. Warren was that he was a magnificent basso. When not working as a building superintendent, Mr. Warren could be found showcasing his talent in nightclubs around Manhattan. He would respond to ads in *Show Business* and *Variety*, newspapers that cater to performing artists, which held vague promises of showcases where theatrical agents and managers went to discover new talent. Mr. Warren's wonderful voice was never discovered.

Mr. Warren, who had married my Nana long before I was born, was always very kindly toward me—letting me beat him at checkers, sitting on floor with me to play marbles, taking me for long walks in the neighborhood. I never recall his ever being exasperated with me no matter how many times I asked him to repeat one of his card tricks. On the contrary, he seemed to enjoy my childish antics and would exclaim to my Nana, "Honey, that boy is full of personality!" to which my Nana would answer, "He sure is that!"

So it was Mr. Warren who used his connections to get me an interview with a theatrical manager for children. Peggy Bramson's office was high up in an impressive building on Fifty-Seventh Street and Broadway. My twelve-year-old sister accompanied me to the after-school appointment on the subway from the Bronx to Midtown Manhattan.

Valerie was in her first year of junior high school, and she had learned to put her considerable artistic talent to use by copying to near perfection the monthly train passes her school issued to children who lived too far from the school to walk. There had been many a gleeful afternoon when Valerie and I escaped our older brother Harold's watchful eye and traveled illicitly through the bowels of the city rather than stay at home to do our homework and household chores. But on this occasion, we had permission from our parents to ride the subway, and thanks to my sister's dubious talent, we were able to use the money our mother had given us for tokens and an emergency to buy soda and chips instead for the long ride into the city.

The adolescent terrain for males in my neighborhood, such as it was, was full of social land mines. One false step and the consequences were dire.

We took the subway to Columbus Circle and made our way to 250 West Fifty-Seventh Street. We walked down the long corridor until we came to a door with the nameplate of "Peggy Bramson, Talent Manager." My sister opened the door to a cubicle of an office with three chairs and a receptionist's desk, a file cabinet, and a glass end table with several gossip magazines and clothing catalogs piled atop it. The pretty, young, white receptionist was on the phone as we entered and motioned for us to have a seat. She soon hung up and asked how she could help us. I spoke up, "I'm here to see Miss Bramson." I wanted to sound important, imperious in the way that I imagined a star was expected to sound.

"I see," said the receptionist. "And may I have your name, please?"

"Raymond Gunn," I announced. "This is my sister, Valerie," I said as I gestured with my hand to my entourage.

"Oh, I see. And are you both here to see Peg?"

"No, just me. My sister only came with me." The receptionist checked her appointment book for my name, circled it when she found it in the book, and said that Peg was in with someone else but would be right with me as soon as she was done. My sister had picked up a Sears catalog, and I sat swinging my legs in the chair and looking at the pictures of smiling kids' faces on the office wall. I was sure that I had seen some of the kids on television or in magazines. I was impressed. It was not long before the closed door to Peg's office swung open.

As the little girl she had been meeting with was reunited with her mother, Peg turned toward me, smiled, stuck out her hand, and said, "You must be Raymond, right?"

"Right!" I said.

"Do you prefer Raymond or Ray?"

"Raymond," I answered. I thought Raymond sounded more professional.

"Then Raymond it is. And who is this?" Peg stuck out her hand to my sister, who answered shyly, "Valerie. I'm his sister."

"Oh, well, nice to meet you, Valerie. I just want to finish up with these nice people and I will be right with you. Okay?"

Both Valerie and I said okay. Peg turned around and went into her office where the mother and child waited. I was so excited about the possibility of my becoming a star that I could no longer stay seated. Billy Preston's "Outta Space" popped into my head, and before I knew it, I had made the little space between the reception-ist's desk and the chairs my own little dance floor. My feet seemed possessed like those of the young girl in "The Red Shoes." I was sliding and camel-walking and James Browning all over the floor. The receptionist started to clap and laugh, which only egged me on further. My sister made a few feeble attempts to get me to sit down and keep still but finally gave up. I attempted a spin that I had once seen James Brown do at the Apollo Theater in Harlem, and just as I was approaching the 180 degree mark, the door to Peg's office opened, causing me to lose my balance and almost stumble into the little girl's mother. I caught myself in time, but when I looked up at the woman's face, I could see that she was in no mood to be bumped into by the likes of me. I hurried back to my seat as the little girl giggled behind her mother's leg.

"What's going on out here?" Peg asked, smiling.

"Oh, Raymond here was just showing me some of the latest dance moves," the receptionist said. "Thanks! I'll try them out tonight," she winked.

I chuckled as I imagined her trying to do my dance moves.

Peg said goodbye to the mother and the little girl and then called me into her office.

Once in the office, Peg and I chatted about things that I liked to do besides danc-ing—my favorite subjects in school, how many best friends I had, what games I liked to play, and so on. She insisted that I call her "Peg" as opposed to "Miss Bramson," as I was brought up to do with adults who were strangers. Strangers were "Miss" (it did not matter if they were married) or "Mr." and last name. Famil-iar adults were "Miss" or "Mr." and first name, as in "Miss Martha" or "Mr. Joe." Our parents taught us that it was disrespectful for a child to address an adult by a name without the handle.

Yet here was this white woman, who looked as if she could have been one of my teachers, insisting that I call her "Peg." It made me feel very adult, and I cozied up to the idea quickly. "Well, Peg," I answered in response to her question of why I wanted to be an actor. "I always wanted to be in commercials when I was little. I used to run to the TV any time a commercial came on and sing the songs. And when they went off I went back to playing with my blocks."

I had not really remembered doing any such thing, but I had heard my mother tell it to so many people that I appropriated it as my own memory. I hoped that I sounded like those precocious child stars who appear on talk shows and who everyone finds irresistible. Peg threw her head back and coughed out a laugh. I had done it. I slipped into my role as child star and fielded Peg's questions with the ease of a veteran performer.

After a short while, Peg tamped out her lipstick-stained cigarette in an ashtray littered with lipstick-stained butts, swiveled her chair around to a file cabinet within arm's reach in her tiny office, and pulled out two legal-size sheets of paper with a lot of small writing on them. She opened the office door and called my sister in to explain that it was very important that our parents read, signed, and returned the form to her. She indicated with an X where one of our parents needed to sign.

With a hand on the top of my head, Peg ushered my sister and me to the door. I said "so long" to the receptionist who again thanked me generously for showing her my dance moves. I looked at the 8 x 10 photos of all the smiling children on Peg's wall and knew that one day soon I would be among them. I was bursting with feelings of goodwill toward all, and I wanted nothing more than to wrap my arms around Peg's waist and give her a tight squeeze of thanks for recognizing my star quality. Nevertheless, I managed some self-restraint and instead held out my hand, "Thank you for taking the time to see me." I remembered what Mr. Warren told me to say if I wanted people in the "business" to take me seriously. She took my hand and thanked me for coming in with my busy school schedule and all.

"Peg?"

"Yes?"

"Can I tell my friend James to call you, too?"

"Sure. Have him do that."

If I was to be a star, I reasoned, why not be a star with my best friend? And so began our careers in show business.

❊   ❊   ❊

The seventeenth-century political philosopher Thomas Hobbes (1651/1986) described human life as "nasty, brutish, and short." There can be no better words to sum up my career as a child actor, the details of which I will reserve for a different article. Suffice it to say here that my ego received a relentless thrashing at a time when one is most vulnerable—the preadolescent and adolescent years.

Over the next several years, James and I convinced our parents to spend hundreds of dollars on professional headshots that we had to carry with us to every audition. As growing boys, our physical appearance changed rapidly, and our pictures needed to be updated frequently to keep pace. Acne became a horrific problem. I was convinced that every new pimple would cost me a role in a commercial. By the age of fourteen, we could legally hold summer employment, and whatever money we made went toward making ourselves more employable as actors. Acting classes, professional resume writers, acne ointments, photographs, train fare to get to auditions, and clothes, clothes, clothes. We constantly tailored our wardrobe to approximate that of the children we encountered in auditions who were getting parts in commercials that evaded James and me. Button-down shirt, crewneck wool sweater, khaki slacks or Levi jeans, sneakers of no particular brand, slightly worn—this was the uniform worn by all the successful child actors we met in auditions. Very suburban, very upper middle class. The only thing that James and I could not allow ourselves to copy were the sneakers. In our neighborhood, the kind of sneakers one wore was of the utmost importance. Acceptable brands were Pro-Keds, Converse, Adidas, and Puma. Anything else was called "Skips," the etymology of which I am unsure, but I suspect that it had something to do with the images of little white kids skipping down clean suburban streets. This was just plain corny to the kids in my neighborhood, and anybody suspected of subscribing to such corn could be the target of relentless ridicule and even violence. The condition of one's sneakers was also utterly important. Sneakers were to be kept clean at all times. A single smudge could make one the butt of jokes at a snappin' party, as one's family could be considered too poor to afford new sneakers or, even worse, too unsanitary to care about the state of one's belongings. Many a teenager scrubbed their sneakers clean with a toothbrush and hung them outside their window to dry overnight so as to avoid the mordant commentary of their peers on the playground or in the schoolyard the next day.

While James and I succeeded in making ourselves passable to our peers in school and in the neighborhood, there did not seem to be anything we could do to gain favorable attention from the New York casting directors. We never got anything for which we had auditioned. I once landed a commercial for a fast-food restaurant chain but had not auditioned. Peg simply called me and told me to report to a certain location. It was not until I had arrived at the location that I discovered I was there for a shoot and not an audition. It was a two-day shoot, spanning several hours each day. At $60 an hour, I was quite pleased with my check when it arrived in the mail a couple of weeks later.

That commercial turned out to be my one and only paid acting gig, and I never even saw the commercial air. By our senior year in high school, James and I had had it. It was on the set of a movie in Riverside Park in Manhattan that we had come to a decision. We were both chosen to be extras in a movie about gang violence in New York. Again, neither of us had to audition for the roles; we were simply chosen based on our photographs. We were to be members of a gang whose leader was a white actor by the name of Michael Beck. Both James and I thought the premise of the movie ridiculous on two basic counts. First, we had never heard of an integrated gang of black, white, Asian, and Latino members. We knew that truly tough gangs came from the city's poorer communities, which were anything but racially integrated. Blacks had their gangs and Puerto Ricans had theirs. I had been chased many times by Italian gangs wielding bottles and bats as I crossed Little Italy to get to and from junior high school, so I knew that there were white gangs. And, while I had never seen an Asian gang, I had heard that Chinatown housed some fairly treacherous ones. My folk theory told me that if there were such an aberration as a racially integrated gang, it could only originate in middle-class communities like

Stuyvesant Town or Roosevelt Island.[4] Moreover, if such gangs existed, they were very unlikely to be taken seriously as tough. Second, our gang leader in the movie was a blonde Hollywood actor who did not look as if he could lead a gang out of a paper bag. James and I had auditioned for many roles for street urchins, but each time we lost out to actors who knew about as much of life on the hard New York City streets as James and I knew of the country clubs in Scarsdale, New York. At least, that was how the actors presented themselves at the auditions. After some time, it finally dawned on us that the casting directors did not want actors who were from the streets but actors who were decidedly not of the streets playing characters who were from the streets. A big difference, we learned, but perhaps not quickly enough.

[From our brief acting careers, we learned]
a host of intangible things one did to
communicate to others that
one belonged.

At seventeen, James and I had become jaded New York actors. As we sat around for hours in the cold in our gang outfits of torn denim and bandanas, we made a pact to each other: if we did not get our big break by the end of that summer, we were going to forget about our dreams of acting and go off to college where we would focus on our studies. At the end of the day's shooting, James and I turned in our wardrobes and went home. We did not report for a second day of shooting, and our big break did not come along by the end of that summer. We never even got paid for a day's work, and in our disgust with the "business," we did not even protest it. James went off to Syracuse University and I to the State University of New York at Buffalo, leaving our childhood dreams of a career in show business packed away in the boxes and crates that held the other items we felt we would never again need as we embarked on a new phase of our lives.

As "nasty, brutish, and short" as our acting careers were, in hindsight, I realize that we did not walk away from the experience empty-handed. James and I had learned some tangible skills that were transferable to other areas of our lives, such as resume writing and interviewing skills. We also learned some less tangible and arguably more important skills. We learned much earlier than most of our peers about presentation of self.[5] It was not so much that we learned of its importance—almost all teenagers know that—rather, it was more that we were keenly aware of its mutability. We knew how important it was to adapt one's self to the specific surroundings. This involved not only such things as the way one enunciated certain words but also the topics of conversation one chose; not only the vocabulary one used but also the way one constructed the sentences; not only the clothes one wore but also the way one held one's body in those clothes. It was a host of intangible things one did to communicate to others that one belonged. By going out for countless auditions in powerful office buildings on Madison and Park Avenues, by taking acting classes with children from the Upper West Side and Montclair, New Jersey, and by having to engage in small talk with adults and children whose points of reference were far different from our own, James and I walked away from this experience with firsthand knowledge of questions of great sociological concerns about race, class, and presentation, as well as about social reproduction and achievement, and of how all of these forces interact with one another to affect individual outcomes.

While we had miserably unsuccessful acting careers, James and I had school careers that were far more successful than those of our peers in part, I believe, because of our interactions in this other world that we would not have had access to if we had not pursued acting careers as children. The comfort we developed in talking to—and charming—middle-class adults held us in good stead with our teachers. Both James and I became quite chummy with many of our teachers in high school. Mr. P., our ninth-grade social studies teacher, for example, had an ironic sense of humor that often fell on deaf ears with students. But James and I got it, and what was more, we appreciated it. We often engaged in playful banter with Mr. P., and it was not long before we had clearly become his favorite students. Even as seniors, when we had long since left his class behind, Mr. P. sought James and me out to give us advice on colleges. The same was true of Miss O'Rourke and Mrs. Steinfeld, our eleventh-grade math and English teachers, respectively. They adored us not only because we were good students—after all, they had other good students—but also because they could talk to us in a way that they could talk to very few other students in their classes. Conversely, I believe that the friendly relations we shared with many of our teachers further supported the image we had of being good students. Students who could manage this type of relationship with adults in powerful positions in school were often rewarded with real, if not shadowy, perquisites. Because our teachers felt that they knew James and me and liked us as well-rounded individuals, they were much more inclined to give us the benefit of the doubt on our exams and papers. On more than one occasion, a teacher has indicated to me in some way that I was taking the wrong approach in solving a problem on an exam or that I had not quite responded appropriately to an essay prompt. At times like these, I would have the opportunity to look over my work and make the necessary changes under the watchful eye of my teacher/friend.

My experiences were not unusual among a small circle of students in my high school. Very few of us were at the top of our class because of the sheer power of our scholastic brilliance. More than likely, we were the students who had come to be the teachers' and administrators' favorites. I believe that James and I accomplished this through our experiences as child actors. How other students managed these relationships with the adults in the school, I cannot say with any degree of certainty.

I do know that we all had adults in powerful positions in the school who could and would advocate for us in a variety of ways. Moreover, we high-achieving students cultivated these relationships with certain adults in the school. For example, to be given the benefit of the doubt on exams and papers, I had to demonstrate in some way that I was interested in the teacher's subject matter. One strategy I used to great effect was to establish early in the school year that I wanted to use the course material to help me to work out some larger question that I had about the world, which I would suggest was keeping me up at night. Teachers often find irresistible those students who show enthusiasm for their course material. After putting in some extra work in the beginning of the semester, the student can gradually slack off as the school year progresses because the teacher is ready to give him the benefit of the doubt. The student at this point finds himself in a position to negotiate assignments with the teacher, and sometimes, even class attendance can be up for negotiation. It is a kind of seduction that many high-achieving students and the adults in their schools engage in but that often goes unspoken.

❊ ❊ ❊

While I did not have a well-thought-out research agenda when I ended up on the front steps of MHS,[6] I did have unresolved questions incubating in my subconscious about my own academic achievement, which in many ways placed me on a particular research path. Thus, like Anderson (2003), my choice of a site was not entirely by chance.[7] My research agenda might have been vague, but I was clear about the type of environment I wanted to conduct it in and the types of participants I wanted to be in it. I knew that I wanted a high school that had a selective admissions policy based on academic performance, standardized test scores, teacher or counselor recommendations, and behavior marks. In choosing such a site, I knew that I would be put in touch with African American male students who by these conventional standards had already been designated as high-achieving students. These students too would come from various parts of Philadelphia, allowing me access to high-achieving students who came from the many low-income sections of town.

I happened upon MHS while working on a research project for a professor, which required me to visit several high schools in Philadelphia. I immediately liked the school, I think, because the administrative staff did not seem to immediately *dis*like me, as the staff at the other schools I had visited seemed to. At other schools, I was almost invariably treated shabbily by the staff: I was ignored, condescended to, forgotten about, rushed out, you name it. It was clear that my presence as part of a research staff was not welcomed. Contrarily, at MHS, the principal, assistant principal, and counselor all found time not only to meet with me but also to accommodate the needs of the research project on which I was working.

The more I visited the school, the more interested I became in it. One of the first things to strike me about the school was the diversity of the student body, yet the diversity was different from what I had come to expect at a school with a high academic reputation. It was not a majority white population; rather, it was a majority black and brown population. With fewer than six hundred students, MHS had about a 50 percent African American population. Whites comprised about 25 percent of the student body, Asians and Latinos together accounted for another 20 percent, with the remaining student body described as "other."

After my yearlong stint on the research project, I maintained relations with some of the administrators at MHS, especially the counselor, and would periodically go back there over the next two years to do small projects to meet various course requirements, as well as to volunteer. I believe fervently in giving back to communities in which I conduct research, and as a volunteer, I lent my talents to the school community in a number of ways.

All of my activities at MHS put me in close touch with a handful of very high-achieving kids, and I formed a good rapport with them. Three of these students are African American males, two of whom are ranked fourth and seventh, respectively, in a class of approximately 120 students. It is Tre'Vaughn, the higher ranked student, to whom I will now turn my attention.

A senior at MHS, Tre'Vaughn is a highly intelligent, self-possessed young man. He does not so much walk through the narrow corridors of the school as he strides. His broad shoulders and long legs—which he has put to good use on the school's track team—seem to compel his classmates to clear a path for him. He is unquestionably the big man on campus. Although he is involved in a number of school projects and has a circle of close friends at school, Tre'Vaughn gives one the sense that he is forever guarded and is most comfortable when alone.

More than anything, Tre'Vaughn wants to attend a top-tier university, especially one of the Ivy League institutions. He is determined to make his mark on the world, and he believes that the best way to do that is to earn advanced degrees from prestigious institutions of higher learning. His parents separated several years ago, and he and his younger sister, who suffers from cerebral palsy, live with their mother in a low-resource section of North Philadelphia. Although he sees and talks to his father regularly, their relationship is strained. Tre'Vaughn believes that his father does not really take the time to understand him and that his father might be a little in awe of Tre'Vaughn's academic achievements and aspirations. Tre'Vaughn is, however, very close to his mother and sister, and he feels very protective of them. In fact, until a year ago, he had severely limited his college choices because he did not want to be away from his family. He had intended to apply only to colleges and universities in the Philadelphia area, with his sights set firmly on the University of Pennsylvania, one of the eight Ivy League schools. However, once his sterling academic record drew the attention of many colleges and universities from across the country, which then began sending him information, Tre'Vaughn began to have second thoughts about his decision to limit his options. Through frequent conversations with me, the counselor, and his mother, who convinced Tre'Vaughn that he should do what was best for him, he widened his college search to as far north as Rhode Island and as far south as Washington, D.C.

Tre'Vaughn gets along best with the adults at school. Mrs. O, the head counselor at MHS, said, "I like talking to Tre'Vaughn. He doesn't just talk off the top of his head like these other kids do. He's very thoughtful. And you can talk to him about a lot of different things." His friendships with his peers, however, are not always so smooth. His closest friends are three other students who are highly ranked: a Nigerian American girl who is ranked number one, a white male who is the second-ranked student, and an African American girl who is the sixth-ranked student in the senior class. He is also close friends with another African American male in his class who is ranked in the bottom half of the class.

In his North Philadelphia neighborhood, Tre'Vaughn says that he does not associate with any of the people there. "Those guys aren't about anything. They just want to hang out on the street or in front of buildings. I don't have time for that,"

It would appear that diversity is a double-edged sword at schools like MHS, whereby in the effort to attract students from a range of racial, ethnic, and socioeconomic backgrounds, these schools also succeed in flattening difference among the students.

---

he says dismissively. When I ask if the guys in the neighborhood ever challenge him, he replies, "Nah. Those guys don't mess with me." When I ask how he manages to avoid conflict with them, he responds, "I don't know. I guess it's the way I carry myself. Like, I'll say 'hi' to them and whatnot, but I sort of let them know, I guess with body language or what have you, that I'm not going to be hanging out with them. Like, they give me respect and I give them respect."

One of Tre'Vaughn's college-application essays is instructive on the tension he experiences as a schoolboy:

> I have been a high achiever all of my life. The dull, lackluster world of mediocrity has never suited my multifaceted personality. My ambitious nature sets me apart from most young people and the fact that I am an African-American male makes me even more of a rarity because of debilitating generalizations. Unfortunately, my unique situation has left me with the burden of being resented by my peers because of their own strict racial characterizations and stereotypes.
>
> I believe that the manner in which I present myself is very important. Therefore, I take pride in my speech, conduct, dress and academic pursuits. I do not feel a need to express myself in the slang terms that many of my peers subscribe to. . . . My style of dress, like my use of language, suggests that I am drawn to presenting myself in a way that many would describe as mature and professional. . . . However, too many of my peers are of a different

opinion. They say that I am trying to set myself apart from them, that I am trying to be something that I am not, that I am trying to be—in a word—*White*.

To me, Blackness has always been an expansive word, not the limiting term that so many of my peers seem to want to box me into. Our divergent opinions, sadly, have led to some discomforting encounters. One example that comes to mind occurred when I was inducted into the National Honor Society. As I stood on stage to receive the honor, a friend of mine later told me that he had commented that it was a shame that I was the only "brother" to join. To that, another one of my classmates, an African-American male, responded that I didn't count as a "brother." In this person's opinion, I had taken on the persona of a White person and, in effect, had succeeded in inflicting a kind of indignity onto the Black race. [December 2003]

Tre'Vaughn's essay offers a glimpse into the inner world of schoolboys, which is often fraught with conflicting loyalties—loyalty to themselves as individuals, on one hand, which is a value that school culture places at high esteem. On the other hand, they espouse loyalty to their community, to which the school culture often has a distant, even hostile, relationship. Tre'Vaughn expresses this conflict quite articulately in the same essay: "I and people like my disparaging classmates are forever engaged in an ironic tug-of-war, in which I perceive myself as working hard to help lift a people and they perceive me as working hard to distance myself from them as a people." Tre'Vaughn sees himself as being in a unique position to disabuse mainstream society of the stereotypes it holds of young, urban, African American males, even if it means sacrificing his friendships with other young, urban, African American males. It is a heavy burden to bear.

One day at MHS, as I was sitting in the counselor's office waiting for her to return, Raheim, an African American senior, stopped by looking for Mrs. O. I explained that she stepped out and would be right back, and I invited him to wait. We began to chat about what I did in the school, and I asked him why our paths had never crossed. He shook his head, "They don't invite me to nothin' in this school." I asked what he meant by that. "Like, that's why I came here [the counselor's office]. I heard that there was a trip to Ursinus College but that only ten students could go. I wanted to put my name on the list, but I know Mrs. O ain't gonna let me go."

We chatted some more:

> "Yo, like, who you workin' with here?"
> "You mean, like, which students I'm working with?"
> "Yeah."
> I rattled off the names of four African American males that I had come to work closely with, including Tre'Vaughn's.
> "Check it, I ain't got nothin' but love for those brothas, but if you only talk to them, you're gonna know only about one MHS. But there's two MHS's: One for them and one for me and the fellas like me! They get everything; and they don't be givin' us jack here."

I could see Mrs. O approaching the office and I knew that my conversation with Raheim would have to come to an end. I asked him if he would be willing to show me this other MHS and introduce me to his friends. He agreed just as Mrs. O walked in. He asked Mrs. O about the trip to Ursinus, and sure enough, he was denied. Mrs. O said that it was because he had not turned in his permission slip on time and that all the spots were taken. He argued that he had just found out about the trip, but Mrs. O eyed him keenly and countered that the flyer had been posted right outside her office for two weeks. Raheim let out a loud sigh, shook his head, and walked out of Mrs. O's office. He had not been given the benefit of the doubt.

Since that day, Raheim and I have been meeting once, sometimes twice, a week. It has not been easy. He often arrives to our meetings so late that we have only five to ten minutes left to talk before the bell rings to end the period. Slowly, though, Raheim is introducing me to this other MHS, the one that I cannot have access to through the administrators or the teachers or through the high-achieving African American male students like Tre'Vaughn with whom I had been working closely.

It is important for me to keep in mind that at one time, Raheim and his "fellas" were considered high-achieving students. They would have had to be high achieving to be accepted to MHS. But, along the way, something has changed; they are no longer thought of in this way, and I wonder how they think of themselves.

Raheim and his fellas often walk through the school corridors in groups of four or five. They are big guys and take up a lot of room. On winter days, their puffy jackets and oversized clothes make them look even bigger. The perpetual scowls on their faces make them that much more expansive—yet my meetings with them are always cordial. They are polite, they readily grin boyishly, they ask my advice about colleges, and they offer me insights to their world at MHS—a world that is apart from any of the other students at the school. They have invited me to their home communities, and I plan to take them up on the offer in the near future.

The strategies that Raheim and his fellas employ have activated something in the MHS culture that effectively relegates them to a position in which they are frequently at odds with the adults in powerful positions in the school. The antagonistic relationships between these students and the adults have a direct impact on the educational outcomes of the students. It is these students who are routinely sent from MHS to their neighborhood high school, which is almost invariably mired in the problems that plague most comprehensive urban high schools—low resources, poor facilities, unqualified teachers, uninspired curricula, and so on. Tre'Vaughn's strategies, on the other hand, have placed him in good favor with the adult power brokers of MHS, which will likely lead to an Ivy League education. Both boys— Raheim and Tre'Vaughn—have had to make decisions early in their young lives that promise to have far-reaching repercussions on their educational outcomes, and both boys have had to make serious sacrifices because of these decisions, ones that they could not avoid making.

※ ※ ※

For young black males, a life on the streets is becoming increasingly risky. When I graduated from high school in 1978, the prison population in the United States stood at approximately 300,000. Today, the prison population has hit the 2 million mark, with more than a quarter of the inmates being black males between the ages twenty and thirty-nine (Duster 1995; Randall 2003; U.S. Department of Justice

2002a). Black males between ages eighteen and twenty-four are almost ten times more likely than white males of the same age to be the victims of homicide (U.S. Department of Justice 2002b).

Moreover, the increasingly globalized economy, with its persistent erosion of job opportunities in urban centers and its demand for highly skilled labor, has made higher education more urgent than it has ever been. Yet low-income, urban, African Americans males are becoming more and more segregated in pockets of major cities across the country that are bereft of the most basic resources. As social services are cut, job opportunities erased, and family structures redefined, African American males are caught in the crosshairs.

Unlike most other high school students in America, the urban black male student must reckon with the demands of hypermasculine images of young, urban black males that get wrapped up in a package of violence, sex, drugs, alcohol, and prison—all of which ultimately militate directly against academic success. Thus, my research asks the question: are magnet schools and programs—long considered the "way out" for poor, high-achieving urban kids—positioned sufficiently to address the unique concerns that African American males from low-resource neighborhoods bring with them?

Although I continue to collect data at MHS and therefore am loath to make conclusions, my research would suggest that a large part of the answer to the question above might be found, ironically, in the way MHS and all magnet schools and programs practice diversity, a cornerstone principle in the school's mission. It would appear that diversity is a double-edged sword at schools like MHS. In the effort to attract students from a range of racial, ethnic, and socioeconomic backgrounds, these schools also succeed in flattening difference among the students. The emphasis on treating everyone the same has made MHS ill equipped to understand the unique choices that their African American male students must make and the impact these choices have on their academic performance. I want to offer for consideration, therefore, that many black male students, like Raheim, either drop out or graduate at or near the bottom of their classes. In either case, these students, who had shown such academic promise earlier in their school career, are now placed at risk of being absorbed by a life on the street and away from mainstream society. The very few academically successful black male students at the school, like Tre'Vaughn, have felt the need to harden to their community lest they ruin their chances for upward social mobility. As the high-achieving students become more incorporated into the wider society, the fear is that they will forever turn their backs on the communities from which they came, which are in desperate need of the skills that such students will acquire on their way up the social ladder. Although it was difficult in the 1970s, James and I were able to strike a balance between high academic achievement and strong relations in our community. As inner-city communities become more isolated, the balance between home community and school community may become less and less an option for young black males.

Notes

1. I borrow this term from A. A. Ferguson (2001), who talks about "schoolboys" in relation to "trouble-makers" among African American male middle-school students.

2. There are many reports that show that black male students are disciplined more often and more severely in school than other students for the same or lesser infractions. One of the most revealing studies is Foster's (1995) survey of educators' and noneducators' perceptions of black males.

3. I attribute this snap to the comedian Chris Rock.

4. These are sections of Manhattan reserved for middle-class housing.

5. This is a reference to Erving Goffman's (1959) classic study of how middle-class Americans behave in social situations and the way they are perceived.

6. This is not the real name of the school.

7. In the twenty-fifth-anniversary edition of Anderson's classic ethnographic study of a neighborhood bar in an African American section of Chicago, he talks about how he found his field site: "As I began my field-work, I had no definite idea where the research would lead, nor where each possible direction might take me. In part, this open-ended approach was a conscious act; in part it was a sensible and natural way to proceed" (Anderson 1978/2004, 237).

References

Anderson, E. 1990. *Streetwise: Race, class, and change in an urban community*. Chicago: University of Chicago Press.

———. 1999. *Code of the street: Decency, violence, and the moral life of the inner city*. New York: W. W. Norton.

———. 2003. *A place on the corner*. 2nd ed. Chicago: Chicago University Press.

Duster, T. 1995. The new crisis of legitimacy in controls, prisons, and legal structures. *The American Sociologist* 26 (1): 20-29.

Ferguson, A. A. 2001. *Bad boys: Public schooling in the making of black masculinity*. Ann Arbor: University of Michigan Press.

Foster, H. L. 1995. Educators' and non-educators' perceptions of black males: A survey. *Journal of African American Men* 1:37–70.

Goffman, E. 1959. *The presentation of self in everyday life*. New York: Doubleday.

Hobbes, T. 1651/1986. *Leviathan*. Middlesex, UK: Penguin.

Randall, K. 2003, April 10. US population—over 2 million—hits new record: 12 percent of black men in 20s and 30s incarcerated. *World Socialist Website*. Retrieved May 18, 2004 from http://www.wsws.org/articles/2003/apr2003/pris-a10.shtml.

U.S. Department of Justice Bureau of Justice Statistics. 2002a. *Demographic trends in correctional population by race*. Retrieved May 18, 2004 from http://www.ojp.usdoj.gov/bjs/glance/tables/cpracetab.htm.

———. 2002b. *Homicide trends in the U.S.* Retrieved May 18, 2004 from http://www.ojp.usdoj.gov/bjs/homicide/tables/varstab.htm.

"Putting the Blessings on Him": Vouching and Basketball Status Work

SCOTT N. BROOKS

While being a basketball player is an important identity for kids, it is also an abiding interest for some black men in Philadelphia. Identity is a collective action, created through group interaction and made public through interaction in which friends "vouch" for each other. The criteria for social position and having high social status do not always transfer across social spaces; rather, the space and those who interact in it negotiate and determine which social traits are salient and of high status. This article examines two different types of basketball identity or status—direct and borrowed identity—and explores the way in which those identities are created and used in negotiating group membership and social interaction.

Keywords: identity; status; vouching; direct identity; borrowed identity

S uppose this is the case: identity is a social and collective process, bound up in a group's shared ideas of personality types, status, and concomitant behavior. One's identity, then, is not simply what she or he claims but, more to the point, what others claim it to be. In this way, an individual does not have a single identity but at least as many identities as the number of groups to which he or she is a member.[1] How a person is seen by others has real implications for social relations; people act toward others based upon an interpretive process that determines meaning and prescriptions for action.[2] Still, identity is not static; it is in a state of flux to be worked out through one's social interaction with others.[3]

For some black men in Philadelphia who play basketball or are associated with players and the game, self-identity is as much about whom one knows and how one is perceived by others in terms of status and identity as it is about how an individual views himself. At the same time, one's

Scott N. Brooks is an assistant professor of sociology at the University of California, Riverside. Professor Brooks's academic interests include urban sociology, race and ethnic relations, and the sociology of sport. He resides in Riverside with his wife, Kara, and their two sons, Kenan Scott and Clay Ali.

DOI: 10.1177/0002716204266593

ANNALS, *AAPSS*, 595, September 2004

basketball identity is rooted in a larger structure of relations fitted to one's network and social relations. For these men, basketball is a social institution, and they are basketball players because basketball is considered a significant social activity in their social world and within a certain network.

Identity, as it is used here, is a set of social labels or categories, generally held by some group, that define a personality type[4] and suggest a certain person's values and behavior.[5] Identity is presented by individuals who are attempting to fit their actions to notions of what some role is and who are acted upon by others.[6] Status is the position that one has in a group based upon one's identity. Because both status and identity guide interaction and the way in which individuals present themselves to others and are responded to by others, the terms will be used interchangeably throughout.

In the Field

As an ethnographer who strives to become an observing participant in a research setting, I enter the field with the hope of evolving from being an outsider to being an insider. It is sometimes an emotional moment and most often a gratifying one, when a researcher realizes that he or she has become an insider, even if only partially or temporarily. The idea for this writing was that I would share an ethnographic discovery—some idea or conflict gained through a fieldwork encounter—that might illustrate how fieldwork leads inductively to some theoretical development. As such, this article is a product of my own self-scrutiny and observation of people who are close to me; in this way, it represents the process of "getting in," effectively an important "status passage"[7] for me in which I was able to gain the trust of my research subjects and become a member of the social world that I was researching.

For three years, I have had the privilege of studying a number of young black men, their families, and black adult males active in Philadelphia basketball. My ethnography is a study of masculinity, status, and mobility in the inner city; it specifically addresses the issue of why young men play basketball and explores what happens when they play, practice, and engage in basketball as a pastime. In this article, my concern is only with representing how my own identity and status were negotiated and what this might suggest about status, identity, and interaction.

I have spent my three years in the field as a coach in an "elite" basketball league. It is considered an elite league for a few reasons. First, the league is not for everyone; it is predominantly made up of players who have been selected to play for their schools. Second, the league is an advanced league requiring that players have a certain knowledge about basketball, such as how to play man-to-man defense. Finally, the league has a history in that many former and current professional basketball players were members.

I have been an assistant coach for an "old head," Chuck, who has coached South Philadelphia's basketball team for more than thirty years. He was a prominent young basketball player in Philadelphia and was a member of the first-team All-

Stars of Philadelphia's Public High School League. Plus, he played against and with some of Philadelphia's legendary players. He considers himself and is considered by others to be a great former basketball player. He has spent a significant amount of time playing, refereeing, and coaching. Although he has won and lost games, he has mostly proven himself by establishing a social identity as a basketball player.

Through my association with Chuck and the league, I have come to view identity in two ways: as "direct" identity, which was exemplified by Chuck, and as "borrowed" identity, which will be illustrated below.

Vouching

As part of the collective action of friends, persons "vouch" for each other, making claims to outsiders of how "good"—that is, adept at basketball—a person is. Vouching is a routine part of being a friend or associate. It may provide protection, when among outsiders, for a person who may not be very good. Vouching may only work, however, if the friend is thought to be a credible source, usually because the friend is known to be a good player. In this way, association validated through the vouching of personal identity tells a researcher about a group's social organization—its norms, values, and order.

Among the men and young men whom I have come to know in my ethnographic study, identity vouching is an important mechanism because it identifies how people interact with others and how individuals present themselves and are presented by others.

My status

I am a basketball player or a ballplayer or what some might call a "baller"—this is how I think of myself. I am often asked if I play or played basketball because I am 6 feet 4 ½ inches tall, black, and male. I am in my early thirties as well, so I suppose I may still claim to be young. All of these characteristics—height, race, and gender—match stereotypes of basketball players. Undoubtedly, being asked by others if I play basketball adds to my sense of being a ballplayer. Therefore, I am not simply a ballplayer because I like basketball or think that at one particular time I was pretty good but also because others see me as being a ballplayer. But when I entered the world of Philadelphia basketball, I was not seen as a ballplayer simply because of my physical attributes, namely, race and height. Instead, my identity as it relates to basketball has been created via associations with others who are known and accepted as creditable among folks that I have come to know in Philadelphia. My identity and status are attached to Chuck's status and the status of a professional basketball player whom I knew as a child. Below is an excerpt from my field notes that describes how Chuck introduced me to his network and how I began to work out an identity through borrowed status.

Chuck bragged about the fact that when I was with him "I was good" [accepted]—that everyone immediately accepted me because of his status. And everyone seemed interested to meet me. They would look over at me, during or after they greeted him, and all had warm smiles and shook my hand.

During a conversation early on in our relationship, Chuck had said to me, "You know what's strange, Scott? Nobody even asked if you could gig [play basketball], and you look like a ballplayer. If they had asked you I would have told them that you could f—k them up and that you was a monster."

Chuck sometimes introduced me as, "My man Scott who is at Penn," when we were outside of basketball spaces. But when he wanted to impress people in his network or who were considered basketball players, former or current, he would mention that I was from Oakland and that I was real tight with Jason Kidd, a current professional basketball player from my hometown. "This is my man Scott. He from Oakland and you know who he lived right next door to? You'll never guess . . . Jason Kidd. That's right. That was his neighbor."

Reflecting on the above discussion, I realized that Chuck showed me how to tell that two people were friends. Chuck's introductions not only served to establish an identity for me but also showed that he and I had a relationship. He told me that he would have told people that I could play basketball well, if they had asked, even though he had never seen me play. The fact that he knew or appeared to know personal information about me gave the impression to members of the network to whom I was introduced that Chuck and I were close. He was willing to be a sponsor for me to others or, as Chuck and others say at the league, to "put his blessings on me." Vouching for my ability, whether the ability was real or not, was a way of showing closeness. He was "speaking for me" just as he and members of his informal network spoke for each other, reciting statistics, achievements, and memorable events of the other to validate his basketball identity.

Moreover, Chuck claimed that I was "good" when I was with him, implying that I was accepted because of his social position and credibility. In this way, friends are those who vouch for one another, that is, those who are willing to risk losing some respect or status by putting their reputations on the line to bolster a friend's status. This bolstering is necessary when the friend is thought to be unable to prove himself on his own or has not proven himself at that time.

By vouching for me and by employing his own credibility to ensure that I was accepted by others, Chuck demonstrated that it was necessary for me to be accepted by others and also indicated that acceptance could come by way of borrowed identity. I also borrowed identity from my hometown and from Jason Kidd. Oakland had status, at least in Chuck's eyes, because it is the hometown of a number of professional basketball players and, particularly, of Jason Kidd, who is a perennial all-star.[8] I came by my identity via borrowed status—essentially, via the collective action of people working together. My status was tied to knowing someone who was respected, but this alone was not enough to confer status. I had to be operating in a social setting with others for whom this would be important and relevant to our interaction and presentation of selves. I presented to Chuck the information that I was from Oakland and knew Jason Kidd, and Chuck accepted the presentation, at least tentatively, to facilitate sociability. In turn, he would present me to others based upon my association. In this way, Chuck and those to whom he introduced me engaged in a group action in which I was defined as someone who knew Jason Kidd. However, there was a risk: that I might not be who I said I was or that I did not know Jason and was not from Oakland. If Chuck or his network discovered that I had falsified my identity or alleged connections, I would surely lose face and Chuck might be ridiculed for being gullible. My presentation of self would be invalidated, and the nascent identity and status I had gained would be lost.

Fortunately, my association with Jason Kidd was verified one evening when Chuck attended a Sixers (Philadelphia's professional basketball team) game and was able to meet and speak with Jason in person.[9] The next day, during announcements at the basketball league, Chuck told the kids about his meeting Jason Kidd.

Hey, I just wanted to tell you about our league and one of our special guys that helps us run this league. You see this man? [*He pointed to me and beckoned for me to stand up.*] He come all the way across the country to help you. That's right. He from Oakland, California, and he come all the way here and got with me and said "I want to help kids in Philadelphia. What can I do?" So I told him that he could get with us in the league and my man has been here ever since. He's a great guy, wanting to help you kids.

Plus, I just went to the Sixers game last night. To see them play the New Jersey Nets, who is playing real good right now. They [the Nets] the best in the East because they got one of the best basketball players in the league. You all don't know what I'm talking about because you think just because a guy can dribble 'round they back and through they legs or dunk the ball, they a great basketball player. But that's not it. A great basketball player is one that can do EVERYTHING. If you need them to score, they do that. If you need them to pass, they do that. They play tough D [defense]. They do everything. They do whatever it takes to win. Well now, you [the kids] call that a throwback [old-style] guy, when it's really just a basketball player. But the Nets got that kind of a player now and it's made them worlds better. They used to be on the bottom and now they on the top. Who am I talking about? [*A few kids raised their hands and he called on one of them. The first kid called upon answered the question correctly and Chuck continued.*]

That's right, Jason Kidd. So I go up to the guy, right. I am on the floor with the players, 'cause they know who I am. I'm the GURU. And I introduce myself to Mr. Kidd.

I say, "How are you doing? Your team looking pretty good, since you got here. I'd like to congratulate you on having a good season so far. My name is Chuck Green and I am with the world famous Sammy Hall League, the greatest basketball league in the WORLD for young folks. And down there is a guy that I have gotten very close to that says he knows you."

He [Jason] says, "who?"

And I say, "Scott Brooks."

And you know what he did? He immediately broke into a smile and he said, "Scott Brooks. Scott Brooks is the greatest guy in the world!"

"The greatest guy in the world," he said. That's the biggest compliment you can say about a man. That's the kind of people that you got trying to help you. Hey man, if Jason Kidd think that about this man, then how else can you think of him?

My initial identity was borrowed from Chuck's and Jason's statuses, and neither was my own. Chuck introduced me as, "This is my partner, Scott. He from Oakland and grew up right around the corner from Jason Kidd," which he had verified. He also identified me as "his partner." In these ways, I was not simply Scott—I was Scott via an association with Chuck and Jason. And the associative nature of my identity changed with the context and the people to whom Chuck introduced me. When we entered a jewelry store on the fringe of Jewelry Row in Center City Philadelphia, he introduced me to a woman and her son who ran the store. "This is my partner, Scott. He is a very bright man, very bright. He is getting his doctorate from Penn and is a terrific guy. I am teaching him all about Philadelphia basketball." In this context, I gave him respectability by being a graduate student at an Ivy League university rather than by knowing a famous basketball player or by being a player.

In basketball settings and in jewelry stores, Chuck was essentially fitting his actions to the specific situation. With basketball guys or men who valued basketball and were part of some network where ability served as a criterion for membership, I was introduced as knowing Jason and being from Oakland. The jewelry store owner and her son seemed to be solidly middle class, so for Chuck to present me as nearly a Ph.D. was impressive and even status enhancing for him.

Friends are those who vouch for one another, that is, those who are willing to risk losing some respect or status by putting their reputations on the line to bolster a friend's status.

Furthermore, Chuck illustrated his acceptance of me when he explained that he would have vouched for my playing ability had he been asked, even though he had never seen me play. Chuck would have vouched for me and given me status by claiming that I was a player and one that could beat others. This illustrated that ability or perceived ability was important for membership, although ability did not have to be proven. At the same time, it made a great deal of difference who delivered the message. Not just anyone could make a statement with credibility; for example, if I had made a statement about my own ability, it would not have had the same impact as a statement made by Chuck.[10] He was legitimate because of his membership and status. This was due to his basketball identity as a basketball guru and legendary player. However, my identity and status began to change with personal experiences in the network.

My borrowed status from Chuck enabled me to become an assistant coach in the league and to develop contacts and relationships with other members of the informal network and the formal Sammy Hall network.[11] While adults volunteered time to the league, becoming a coach was not guaranteed and Chuck's staff was chosen from the informal network. My selection as an assistant coach to Chuck solidified my membership because it meant that I not only had a relationship with him but also had inherited a relationship with others in the group. When Chuck offered me the position as his assistant, he told me that he had asked the other guys and that they thought I was okay. I had become someone associated with basketball, someone who it could be said knew something about the game or had a deep connection with people who knew something. But even though I thought of myself as a baller, I was not one to them. I had gained a position as a member of the informal network due to the strength of association that I had with others and then began forming personal bonds.

Membership afforded me introductions to people outside the league, such as former players who may have made it to the professional ranks or into coaching. Eventually, I earned my own status with the "old head" network, although I was still connected with Chuck, because I was committed to the program and spent a great deal of time in the league.

My place became more established when our team won a league championship. Chuck and I coached a team to a championship title, and this gained me status outside of the informal network as a coach. Immediately after winning the championship, I was approached by other coaches and called "coach." Winning increased my visibility greatly and allowed me to gain a direct identity. I was now known as a winning coach and had gained personal credibility; I was asked questions about certain players, and I was asked to coach in other leagues and on an all-star team.

Ability was not key to my gaining membership; rather, it was my association with Chuck, or borrowed status, and the role that I had come to play, which perhaps then enabled others to make certain presumptions about my past ability. To my knowledge, Chuck never had to vouch for my ability, and I was rarely asked to speak about my own playing history, so my ability was either presumed or unimportant or both.

However, I do not want to convey the notion that my status or identity was easily established or confirmed all at once. Rather, gaining status is a process and is always a work in progress. Chuck did not simply accept my story of being a friend to Jason Kidd and being from Oakland; instead, he confirmed it. In early interactions with me, he demonstrated deference in accepting my presentation of self, but this did not mean that others had to respect or accept my presentation. My status was validated through Chuck's status and position, and it would have been a threat to others to question it publicly, especially after Chuck confirmed my status personally. Another example of my status negotiation should illustrate how such status was constantly being negotiated and yet was still not equal to Chuck's.

Although I was Chuck's assistant coach, I often coached games alone, acting as the head coach when he was absent. Chuck had a penchant for showing up when he felt like it, and of course, he could do so with little consequence because of his status. Chuck often said, "This is MY league. I helped build it and I got just as much say as Sammy [the league's namesake and president]."

I was coaching a game in which the score was close but my team was behind—and increasingly so. It was right after halftime, and I was hoping to close the lead when TD, the league's coordinator and Chuck's former assistant coach, yelled to me from the stands.

TD told me to put my other players in, that is, to play the kids who had not played yet. But we were losing and these kids were not my best players. I looked up at him and nodded affirmatively but did not put in the other kids as substitutes. I was hoping that my best players would make the game close and even pull ahead in the second half so that I could then play the players of lesser ability. My strategy was to put in lesser players when the game's outcome was not an issue, when we were either winning by a margin that could not be erased or losing by such a margin. After a short bit, he yelled to me again, "Scotty, get 'em in." I started to say something but did not finish my sentence because I was frustrated and did not want to say something I might regret. I wanted to keep my best players in and did not want to do as TD requested.

TD was a big man, around 6 feet 6 inches tall and 260 pounds, known for being a "big" man, meaning that he played either the center or the power forward positions where an individual must be aggressive and strong to grab rebounds and score. Chuck and others said that TD could dominate games and outplay many guys that were much taller than he, but a knee injury ended his basketball career, and he struggled with depression. Chuck helped TD get a job as a probation officer and fooled him into coaching youth basketball in the Sammy Hall League. Chuck explained that he asked TD to do him a favor and coach a team because he would be late in arriving for the game. Chuck did not show and expected that TD would coach the team. Chuck did this a few more times, sometimes showing up after halftime, and TD was hooked; he became invested in working with kids and coached with Chuck for twenty years before becoming the chief coordinator for all the league's activities.

League rules stated that each player on a team was to play; there was no guaranteed time allotment, as there is in many youth leagues, but coaches were to strive for giving each kid at least five minutes of playing time. This was a norm set to appease parents. After all, parents paid a league fee for their kids to play, and the fee was essentially a deposit for their children's participation in public—playing only at practices would not suffice. The league rules served as a contract obligating coaches to play kids whose parents had paid a fee and expected that their children would play. By not playing some kids when TD said, I was violating the league's contract with parents.

To my surprise and embarrassment, TD came down from the stands and confronted me. He asked me why I had not put the substitutes into the game after he had told me to do so. I felt like a child responding to a parent. Not only was TD a bigger and taller man than I, but he was also a teacher to me. As Chuck's former assistant, he felt obliged to befriend me because, in a sense, I had inherited his position. In this instance, I was being disrespectful to him and to the league by violating the contract, and I had also failed to defer to him as an older man and teacher. My disobedience was a threat to both of us; he could not let me defy him in public. My defiance could have been read as a signal that I did not really respect him, or it could have been an indication that the respect I had shown him previously was simply ceremonial.

I responded to TD's questioning and told him that I did not put in the substitutes because I was trying to win the game. He referenced the league rule, to which I responded, "But Chuck doesn't always play all the guys." He quickly shot back, "But you ain't Chuck. You ain't THAT guy." I was brought back to the reality in which I was engaged, to its social order, and to my position in the network.

"You're right," I said. "That's all you have to say." I then turned to my players and said, "Derrick, Tommy, Jay, get in."

Gaining status is a process and is always a work in progress.

I was embarrassed for forgetting my position and for disrespecting TD. I was operating under a different definition of the situation than TD was: I felt that I did not have to play some players because Chuck did not when he coached. But I was able to see the situation from TD's point of view when he reminded me of my position. I was able to revise my own version of the social norms precisely because I believed and understood what TD was saying. It was clear to me that I had not gained Chuck's status in the network. To hold onto my erroneous definition of the situation would have been disrespectful to the league's informal network, as well as to Chuck and TD. I could not bend the rules, although they were bent for me on occasion, because I did not have the status.

TD tried to ease my embarrassment and said, "You don't have to put them in for long, but you have to play them. And if you had put them in when I told you you'd be all right. If you wait, you're *not* going to play them! Play them early and then get your guys [the better players] back in and you might have a chance to win."

His advice showed that he interpreted my temporary lack of deference as a sign that I was not attempting to disrespect him; I was still learning how to coach and how the status order operated. I accepted his interpretation by quickly relenting and telling him he was right. In deference, my tone was apologetic and self-effacing. I appreciated his coaching me, but my shoulders shrank a little. Embarrassment set in as I thought of how it must have looked for TD to descend from the stands and confront me in the middle of the game. I did not understand that he was teaching me how to coach and to play substitute players at the same time that he was enforcing a league rule. He had confirmed our teacher-pupil relationship by reading my disobedience as mere ignorance.

He returned to the bleachers and yelled to me again, "Scotty, you can take 'em out in three minutes." I nodded again, this time fully intending to listen. After only two minutes elapsed on the game clock, the opposing team widened the lead by scoring a few baskets and TD yelled to me, "Put 'em back in now." We lost, but I had been put in my place. The definition of the situation was restored: Chuck was "the man" and could violate certain rules, TD was the legitimate enforcer of the rules, and I had not earned a status level that afforded me the right to deviate without negative repercussions.

This experience highlighted the social order and how individuals operated; there were implicit rules and codes to follow, and status was not settled but continually worked on in different circumstances.

Conclusion

The discussion above represents an ethnographic discovery gleaned on my journey into Philadelphia basketball that reveals identity for black men in a Philadelphia basketball network as social and as the result of collective action. I have presented three primary research findings: first, there are at least two kinds of social identity in action, which I have referred to as direct identity and borrowed identity. Researchers need to consider these types of identity, to examine what types of identity an individual may choose to deploy, and to explore the process through which this identity is negotiated—that is, individuals may say one thing but may actually be viewed in quite a different fashion by the group of which they are a part.[12] Second, identity is fluid and a work in progress. Finally, borrowed rather than direct identity—who is connected to whom and in what ways—may not really tell a researcher much about an individual's ability but more about the social organization of a group. In ethnographic fieldwork, particularly during the early stages, we are not always sure of what things mean immediately, but in time, through diligence, taking the role of the other, and careful attention to the social processes of everyday life, we often come to provocative understandings, which not only inform us about those we study but also tell us something profoundly about ourselves.

Notes

1. This idea of individuals' having multiple selves is basic to role-identity theory.

2. See Blumer (1969, 2) for his three premises of symbolic interaction.

3. See Anderson (1976) and Katz (2002, 255-78).

4. Hughes (1928) wrote about personality types as "the classification of persons into types according to their behavior" (p. 755).

5. Shared symbols, notions, and definitions of situations or culture are key to social interaction. Blumer (1969) says that we live in a world of symbols, and it is this shared culture that enables people to interact with understanding. Everyone may not have the exact same definitions, interpretations, or understandings, but they are similar enough to allow for communication and coherent lines of action.

6. Goffman (1959) claims that individuals present their "self" to others and are treated in accordance with how others perceive them, accepting or rejecting their presentations of self. How individuals fit their actions is based upon the idea or image that they are trying to convey to others. Mead (1934) talks about people's being objects to themselves, meaning that people are able to look at themselves and their actions from the view of others. This enables people to fit their actions to what they think would be convincing to and in line with others' ideas of who they are. Blumer (1969) adds that the objectified self is a social process, an interpre-

tive one. Individuals define and interpret the response of others and then respond in a manner based upon their developed meaning and goals.

7. See Glaser and Strauss (1971).

8. Sometimes, Chuck would also mention that other players were from my hometown, like Gary Payton, to bolster my identity. It suggested that I came from a basketball city, similar to how he and his friends thought of Philadelphia as a basketball city. The idea of a basketball city is that it produces good basketball players, namely, professional players.

9. Chuck attends Sixers' games at least a couple times a year because of his wife's kinship with Wilt Chamberlain. Wilt was such a legendary player for the Sixers that family members are invited to games to celebrate the anniversaries of some of his historical basketball achievements, such as scoring 100 points in a single game.

10. Goffman (1967) wrote that people could not give themselves deference and that deference was a function of social interaction.

11. As W. F. Whyte (1943) says, "As long as I was with Doc and vouched for by him, no one asked me who I was or what I was doing." Moreover, Anderson (1976) talks about "going for cousins" with Herman and how this gave Anderson status and a solid footing in the hierarchy at Jelly's.

12. Anderson (1976) wrote of this with regard to wineheads and hoodlums who claimed to be regulars and men of stable means when they were not thought to be so by other men, particularly those men who were regulars.

References

Anderson, Elijah. 1976. *A place on the corner*. Chicago: University of Chicago Press.

Blumer, Herbert. 1969. *Symbolic interactionism*. Berkeley: University of California Press.

Glaser, Barney, and Anselm Strauss. 1971. *Status passage*. Chicago: Aldine-Atherton.

Goffman, Erving. 1959. *Presentation of self in everyday life*. New York: Doubleday/Anchor Books.

———. 1967. *Interaction ritual*. New York: Doubleday/Anchor Books.

Hughes, Everett C. 1928. Personality types and the division of labor. *The American Journal of Sociology* 33:754-68.

Katz, Jack. 2002. Start here: Social ontology and research strategy. *Theoretical Criminology* 6 (3): 255-78.

Mead, George Herbert. 1934. *The mind, self, and society*. Chicago: University of Chicago Press.

Whyte, William F. 1943. *Street corner society*. Chicago: University of Chicago Press.

The Emotional Experience of Class: Interpreting Working-Class Kids' Street Racing in Helsinki

By
HELI VAARANEN

Reproduction of social class through culture has puzzled social scientists especially in the Nordic, advanced welfare states where social equality has been the official policy of governments for most of the postwar period. In the following article, I address this issue through the emotional experience of class that culminates in the weekend excesses of youths and even the street-racing scenes of Helsinki. Based on ethnographic fieldwork with eighteen- to twenty-four-year-old male street racers of Helsinki, I argue that stagnant class locations build on stunted ambition and feelings of injustice. The cultural performances and camaraderie of these like-minded racers support these youths' public, carefree identities and subcultural careers. Instead of resisting exclusion, they conform to it, celebrating "a room of his own" where shared risk, craftsmanship, driving skill, and disregard of education prevail.

Keywords: street racing; emotional experience; cultural performance; subculture; class

Every year, thousands of Finnish young adults, fresh driver's license holders, are introduced into the social order of a motorsports-loving nation through street-racing and car-oriented lifestyles.[1] These young boys and a few girls take pride in the victories of Finnish racing stars by vicariously celebrating the winners, calling themselves by the names of race champions.[2]

Intoxicated eighteen- to twenty-year-old males with lower education dominate the accident statistics of the young,[3] thus confirming the myth of the Finnish working-class, car-oriented, drink-loving masculinity. According to the Central Organization for Traffic Safety of Finland (report, August 12, 2003; period of study, 1998 to 2002), an average of 84 young people between fifteen and twenty-four years of age were killed while 2,500 were injured per year. Weekends, especially Saturday nights in the summertime, were accident-prone times. Dur-

Ms. Heli Vaaranen, Ph.D., is a research fellow in the Department of Sociology, University of Helsinki, Finland.

DOI: 10.1177/0002716204267494

ing weekend nights, young people take to the streets, roads, and highways, often in groups, to have fun and to travel between cities in their cars to meet people. More than 75 percent of youths killed in road accidents between 1998 and 2002 were young men.

My research was initiated when I became interested in the driving culture and the emotional and factual experience behind these seemingly senseless sacrifices. I had to ask what these young men were sacrificing their lives for. Was it for modernity? The car industry or masculinity? Success in motor sports? What about the speeding youth groups and lone riders: did they not want to stay alive? Why should these young men meet their deaths on the roads in times of peace?

In Great Britain, Beatrix Campbell (1993, 29-47) described joyriding as a conflict between youths and the city.[4] I agreed but also witnessed the complex engagement of *Resistance through Rituals* (Hall and Jefferson 1976) and meaning of style (Hebdige 1979) within youth subcultures. Accordingly, I came to understand these youths' car-oriented *Crimes of Style* (Ferrell 1993) as an identity construction, and following the thinking of Douglas Foley (1990) in *Learning Capitalist Culture*, I came to realize the role of sociality and cultural performance in social reproduction.

In literature concerning subcultures, I missed the unveiling of the emotional experience of subculture membership. In the field, I learned that the youths' emotional experience concerned the micropolitics of social class and the feelings of inequality that lead to a thirst for balancing counterexperiences. I needed to know how these feelings were born and how the street-racing boys searched for redemption. I needed to know how these youths saw themselves. What did they think of their school years and present lives? Where did they come from? What did they dream of? What did their parents say to it all?

My research perspective was encouraged by Mike Presdee (2001, 163), who believes that researchers should make sense of marginalized groups, starting with their emotional and material experiences. On the following pages, I argue that the emotional experience of class builds on stunted ambition, stagnant class locations, and feelings of injustice, lived through the racer's exclusion from access to competition in commercial culture. I argue that this exclusion of the working class is socially reproduced as an emotional experience even when official structures speak for the social equality of a Nordic, advanced welfare state. For young people, reproduction of the emotional experience of class takes place in the cultural performances, that is, in weekend excesses including street racing.

Inspired by Jeff Ferrell and Mark S. Hamm (1998, introduction), who urged ethnographers to get down to the immediacy of crime in search for a Weberian understanding, I took a fieldwork journey deep into the subculture of street racing in Helsinki. Through ethnography and "edgework"[5] in car chases and street races, I participated in the street racers' world. The research data include fieldwork diaries most intensively from the fall, winter, and spring of 1999 to 2000, involving interviews; participant observation; notes from meetings with street racers, their girlfriends, and family members; and notes of participation during weekends in street-racing cars. Follow-up interviews and participant observation were conducted up until the end of 2002.

The films *The Fast and the Furious* (2001) and *2 Fast 2 Furious* (2003) portray fictional street racing in Los Angeles; nevertheless, they reveal some important differences between the street-racing scenes of Helsinki and Los Angeles. The Helsinki street racers rarely fought with their fists. They proved their worth with cars. They were unathletic and skinny, with the delicate but oily hands of a pianist or a car mechanic. The Helsinki racers did not race for money since money was their

---

The street-racing youth used their cultural performance to create nighttime counterexperiences for their daytime experiences of lost opportunities.

---

most limited resource. They avoided verbal challenges and, out of loyalty, let others maintain their privacy. However, in both the Helsinki and the Los Angeles street-racing subcultures, a car-oriented masculinity involved communication through manual skills and horsepower. The street racers build a social community with reciprocal relations and a sense of belonging as noted in a previous study by Vaaranen and Wieloch (2002). As the street-racing boys felt socially and materially incompetent to enter the challenges of the bigger world, they focused on their peers and after-hours lives on the streets and at the cruising club.

As I joined these rides as an ethnographer and a former street-racing girl, I understood the joys of street racing. Successful street-racing nights were truly enjoyable. They were spontaneous, creative, and filled with laughter and excitement. Under this surface was fear, craziness, destruction, and "mechanic violence" with threatening ways of driving. Indeed, my street-racing fieldwork was like living in the "unscripted drama" (Presdee 2000, 139) of a motion picture. I did not miss seeing films or reading fiction; my real life among the racers was more exciting than any ready-made entertainment. I saw the boys getting hyped up by the speed, the crowds, and the race. Every night the young drivers went racing, they received an intoxicating natural high.[6] In the street-racing boys' eyes, I was a woman almost twice their age, a joker, and a curious "doc-to-be." I was there to make these youths visible and to address the political and social problems they faced.

The street-racing youth used their cultural performance to create nighttime counterexperiences for their daytime experiences of lost opportunities. This counterexperience became "a room of his own," it defined a street racer's masculine identity, and it functioned as a coping strategy to fight exclusion. Ironically, the "room of his own" owed to class solidarity, and it only sealed all exits out of this subculture. Instead of resisting exclusion, the young street racers of Helsinki conformed to it, fighting for respect but celebrating this space where shared risk, craftsmanship, driving skill, and disregard of education prevailed.

Nipe: A Street-Racing Lad

Nipe was eighteen when we met and the kid brother of my neighbor. He loved his life on the weekends and was proud of what he was doing with cars. When I met Nipe, he was bored with vocational school. Later, he poorly tolerated his job. He was a handsome Finn, tall and slim with blonde hair and large blue eyes. He had an impudent smile, especially when talking about the past weekend's encounters with girls and out-of-town cruisers. He chain-smoked and talked endlessly about cars. He was the most talkative of the otherwise quiet boys, and I liked listening to him. At night, the crowds embraced him as a street racer and as one of the fastest behind the wheel. I regarded him the most accountable of the cruising club[7] boys, so I rode with him the most. Like him, his pals Miro, Kallu, Kaide, Mika, and Hume were boys with a passion for the motorcar and speed. These young men wore jeans and shirts. They were often clean-cut and shaven, thus making a distinction from the Amcar crowd. The cruising club boys liked leather jackets and boots but thought of them as unnecessary and directed all their finances to cars and to fancy, up-to-date Nokia cell phones instead.

Nipe drove a black, matte-painted Opel Ascona 1978 (Figure 1). "It's all engine and nothing else," Miro admired the vehicle. Although Nipe's focus on the streets was fast driving, he relied on others for modifying. The cruising club boys who were mainly interested in engines did not bother to paint their cars but competed with modifying skills instead. Some created a dark impression with slow cruising and black-only decoration of their cars. They rode with men only and sometimes wore sunglasses through the night. Others had red-velvet interiors in their aged Toyota Corollas of the early 1980s to speak for the sexual maturity of the young drivers. In many of the boys' cars, music functioned as an erotic invitation to young women, promising everlasting and tireless sexual energy.[8] The cars, with their noise, style, and speed were an endless resource for stirring attention. On the other hand, a car in poor shape was likely to give a more profound, bodily experience of speed, and it was supposed to get the driver and passengers to the edge easier and faster.[9] As Dick Hebdige pointed out in 1979, the need of privacy was now replaced by a craving to be noticed. With cars, attention could be gathered throughout the social spectrum of viewers and subculture members on the streets. There seemed to be something for everyone. A young racer could pick up girls and show off with a worn-out, twenty-year-old BMW when the car was remodified by hand.[10] With this style, he offended others and created aggression. This style of crudeness, throbbing low-bass music, vulgarity, a signal of danger, and a thousand variations of these coalesced in an audiovisual style I call "rough bravado."

FIGURE 1
1978 OPEL ASCONA IN THE CLUB GARAGE

SOURCE: Photograph taken with author's camera.

This style meant resistance against the bourgeois ways of consumption. Middle-class youths could expect a contribution from parents when purchasing the first car of their own, but for working-class boys, buying a car with their own money was a source of pride as well as a sign of independence and maturity. The style of rough bravado—created by aged, self-modified, loud, and crude-looking cars that some-times were called "toilets" and "rats"—was an attack against what these racers perceived as effeminate and weak car orientation. Young men who understood little of motorcars were considered "weird, and possibly a little stupid" by the street racers, and this message was sent forward through an audiovisual style on the streets. Furthermore, this rough style was to impress and to scare "nerds" and "old people"—men over thirty-five in prestigious cars. The racers did not hesitate to show these fellow traffickers the international finger sign, to call them homosexual, and to display the willing young women in their back seat, saying, "We have got something they don't. They've lost their youth."

Helsinki Case of School Failure

Finland is an exceedingly education-oriented nation. Following the loss of community membership through urbanization and the rise of high-tech working culture, the status of both skilled and semiskilled manual work has fallen dramatically. On the job, Hume told me, he was nonverbally put in his place. He told me that he might as well have been transparent. When I asked the other boys about their work, they grew even quieter than usual and talked of it as if it were prostitution: "It's only for the money." It seemed that during the day, on the construction sites and in the factories where these boys worked, they got no respect but could only count on each other and the racing scene to provide for their basic need of recognition. When I met one of the older club racers, Pede, for lunch by the construction site where he worked as a handyman, I remember thinking "what a proud personality in such a stained, blue overall." He looked at me as if he were a prisoner inside his work clothes.

These youths' battles for social recognition through weekend excesses created a sense of failure that reflected even on the families of the street racers, who called their sons "quitters." This portrays the general mentality of the nation: the assumption that the state has done its best; the failure is your own. I was, however, convinced that this "failure" had not been caused by the boys' lack of intelligence. The boys had voluntarily produced conditions in which they could get by as easily as possible, even when this resulted in being ruled as a class, similar to the condition of the working-class kids in England, noted by Willis (1977). What the Helsinki kids calculated they would get in return for selling themselves short was a careless youth with plenty of time to indulge in sexual affairs and lots of hanging about without worries about exams or about parents' reactions. Parents, according to the boys, "didn't care" or "had given up complaining long ago."

Within the street racers' families, parents helped in practical matters but, on the other hand, took pride in the early independence of their offspring. It even happened that mothers and daughters, fathers and sons went out together to clubs to drink and to try to find sexual partners, usually as a favor to the older generation. Although the youths clearly (and proudly) led self-supporting lives from their late teens or early twenties, the parents together, or separately when divorced, helped in moving and provided small cash loans. They lent their vehicles and gave rides. They arranged for a bottle of hard liquor when needed and made dinner for their hungry offspring. As a counterfavor, Nipe, Miro, Kallu, and the other boys of the cruising club were at their parents' disposal for similar tasks. Accordingly, they functioned as sober designated drivers for their parents who were, often separately, spending the night on the town drinking. The parent-youth relationship was reciprocal and often loving. This love was expressed without words, without showing affection, or without, for example, making an effort to keep their kids in school.[11] This "you have your own life now" lesson in survival, with the parents' utterance to "do with your life whatever you want," expressed the admiration of self-reliance within the working-class family.

At school, the cruising club boys did not do their homework. They resented taking foreign-language courses and did not get along with authorities. Some had begun drinking through the last years of comprehensive school. Some killed time, only waiting to get to drive motor scooters in the woods afterward. In their opinion, school had been a waste. At school, the Finnish working-class kids strove for a reputation whether it was bad or good. For example, when Kallu was called a "drunkard" and Miro plain "crazy" by their school mates, the boys proudly carried these labels that were given with admiration of their rough bravado that had begun already at school. This clearly distinguished them from other—in their view—useless categories of young men, such as nerds. Nerds made them nervous even then, and later, during their street-racing years, the cruising club used to challenge and race nerds, who were judged by their appearance and the makes of their cars. The racers used to beat them every time, as the cruising club boys took these encounters as if racing for their lives.

One reason for [these street racers'] stunted ambitions was that wanting too much seemed an act of disloyalty toward one's own group and class.

"I don't understand how the hell you could afford studying for six years," Kallu kept wondering, when we met at a gas station for a coffee. I looked at his hands that were covered with small cuts and bruises. I wondered quietly how long his body could afford the drinking and the frequent minor injuries he suffered at the construction site. At twenty-one, he already suffered from nicotine addiction, badly shaking hands, tinnitus, bad teeth, and an arm he could not rotate normally, resulting not from a racing accident but from a close call on the job. The boys, however, took pride in these symptoms that progressively made them look older, more mature, and like "real men," often disregarding the state-subsidized dental and medical care.

When I asked them about their transition to vocational school or about early participation in the labor force, many of the street-racing boys described relief. Life had gotten easier when they no longer had to go to school. Some were pleased at the opportunity for a state-subsidized vocational education that some of them completed. I could not help wondering at this since the boys were street smart. They managed the gray market of their car sales well. A majority of them held steady jobs. They had decent rental apartments, and many of them had loving girlfriends at home. They hustled this n' that, making money on the side. They worked overtime a lot. I felt they could easily have used this street smartness to get ahead at school had they wanted to. But they did not. Like Willis's working-class kids, they were headed for blue-collar occupations from their early years onward. They certainly escaped the grayness of office-corridor culture and the impossible prospect of sitting in one room all day. But what worried me was their disregard for health, safety, and future aspirations. They were literally "just living one day at a time," or sometimes, "a minute at a time,"[12] endlessly testing their courage and pushing the edge of daring and skill a little further. As noted earlier (Vaaranen and Wieloch 2002), this seemed to speed their way toward only two possible outcomes: dead-end jobs or death by car accident.

Conflict between Class Interests and Individual Pursuits

Although Thornton and Gelder suggested in 1997 that subcultural capital serves as a boundary marker to other groups, I wondered to what extent such boundary markers ever were necessary. For example, class and economic boundaries were already internalized by these street racers, needing no emphasis. The working-class kids, who enjoyed the advanced welfare security of a Nordic social democracy, still could not escape the universal "hidden injuries of class" that Richard Sennett and Jonathan Cobb discussed in 1972. For these boys, such injuries were the constant fear of unemployment and loss of benefits on the job. These everyday life worries excelled any fears of bodily harm in speeding.

After some years at work, schooling became more attractive. While drunk, Miro often expressed a desire to "do paperwork like you," and the other boys expressed a wish to go back to night school. "I could easily do it," they said, but they did not. One reason for stunted ambitions was that wanting too much seemed an act of disloyalty toward one's own group and class. The class solidarity of these youths was solid once they had closed the doors of the high school. By then, and despite some aspirations that came and went with drunkenness, these youths felt that their horizon of expectation was set forever. This mentality of giving up the struggle was typical of many everyday situations where a little endurance and planning would have been profitable. These stunted ambitions of class made it impossible to see alternatives and ways out of situations that to me seemed unbearable. For instance, on the construction site where Hume worked, the older workers drank on the job. This caused problems even for the younger fellows. There was a hierarchy that was difficult to go up against. You had to choose your side. For example, Hume once told me, "The older guys make me drink at work. I can't say no. What would they think of me? I'm new there. They start with beer already in the morning." He could not think of a solution, except to consent. The powerlessness of these boys in the workplace and the hostility and indifference in their workday environment made them withdrawn there and almost mute. In daytime Helsinki, respect was hard to gain for a young man, if he was materially dispossessed, stigmatized by youth, attracted to getting drunk in public, and lacked the executive look and education. For the boys of the racing scene, their experience of class was an emotional experience of inequality and lost opportunities. This emotional experience resulted in a constant search for a counterexperience, which pushed them only further down the path of speeding tickets, car crashes, court appearances, and trouble.

Sometimes, the economic struggle to live better took curious paths. When Miro won 8,000 euros in the lottery, I expected him to make some improvements in his life, or the lives of his girlfriend or his child. Instead, he went on a three-day drinking spree with the boys.[13] Miro was not happy when he told me about his drinking. Despite the jolly memories of goofing off around town, staying awake all night, and taking numerous cab rides, he seemed to be saying that life was a game he just could not win. He just could not do the right thing with the money, so he partied it all away. There was no revolution in sight.

Within the street-racing culture, the position of a woman was more traditional than elsewhere in a society that is proud of its gender equality.

After work, the club boys told me, they ate a cold meal if the girlfriend was away. Then, they surfed the Internet to find car parts and skimmed through pornography sites. I thought of the hopes of the working class's uniting through radical Internet communication and action. The young intellectuals of Europe had done it, in the form of L'attac, for example. But I could not picture the cruising club boys becoming writers and union activists or forming political-pressure organizations through their laptops. It seemed to me that this was to remain a neo-Marxian dream as long as boys like these did not want to bother. "What does it matter what you do eight hours of your day?" they said. I anticipated the Internet's making little change in the class formations of its users. The racing boys' actual lives started at 5 p.m., when they came home from work, and they were not letting anything, not even class struggle, get in the way of their leisure excesses.

But even the nighttime victories on the streets could not lessen the importance of these boys' daytime experience in society. For example, Nipe often told me that the police harassed him for being young.[14] He suffered from being young, since it seemed enough to make him vulnerable for harassment in traffic and also on the job. Being stigmatized for his most valued resource during the day, his youth, he directed his struggle for dignity into the night and into the weekend. On the streets, it was payback time. The street-racing youths went into this micro-level collective action of payback time by manifesting their youth, their desirability, their subcultural capital, and their "erlebnis." This manifestation was a necessity for them to save their sanity, since their class location, age, occupational role, and gen-

FIGURE 2
STREET RACERS CHANGING A TIRE

SOURCE: Photograph taken with author's camera.

der were constantly run over by the economic and symbolic power of the dominant structures. Such dominant structures were the unemployment office, the boss, the manager, the poorly managed economy, a payment reminder, a crashed car, a broken lamppost, a pursuing cop car, an angered girlfriend, and a crying mother. Things were not under control. This social disempowerment made every performance on the streets into a search for respect and a struggle fought with motorcars. The struggle needed a stage, and the streets were it (Figure 2).

By the age of eighteen, the street-racing youths got their driver's licenses. Exceedingly, through rally racing events, car shows, and street racing, the boys were introduced to commercial culture. Now, it was money that counted. Although these working-class kids found themselves unable to compete directly in the commercial culture, they did it indirectly. They learned to enter the commercial culture with what they had, even when it meant making a mockery of oneself, using the leftovers of car industry. But doing it with humor meant also doing it with pride. The engineering that economically concentrated on the engine left the rest of the vehicle subject to cosmetic engineering with stickers, animal-skin-imitation seat covers, and furniture spray paint (Vaaranen and Wieloch 2002). I have even seen cars put together with package tape. These cars exhibited a sexist worldview. When the boys were pleased with their cars, the cars were referred to as a "she," "the babe," and "the whore" and then made into sex machines with maximal music equipment, roaring engines, and erotic interiors.[15] Also, this created a nighttime counterexperience for the subordinate, emotional experience of class.[16] The young viewers were captivated and astonished by this bravado, thus adding to the reputation of the car club with stories and eyewitness accounts.

At night, the street racers possessed the symbolic capital of being real men, superior to any other social strata of the streets. But despite group solidarity, and being among friends, even these real men had to fight for their social order on the masculine ladder. Although group solidarity was a requirement for the cruising club membership, it nevertheless left space for interpersonal problem solving. This problem solving was accomplished through driving. On the street corner, the cruising club boys connected competition in risk and skill with honorable masculinity. This competition against one another, against the clock, and against unknown racers on the streets was a zero-sum game. If one lost respect, somebody else gained it and partied it publicly.[17] I saw the boys' constant quest for honesty, loyalty, camaraderie, and support strengthen some public identities and break others. Those who held on to these common principles had the clubs' support, which immaterially ensured the well-being of both the boys and their cars.

The struggle for respect was an emotional one. Like Bourgois (1995) pointed out, a quest for respect had turned into a fear of disrespect. Nipe's eyes glittered when he described how he took over another racer or beat a standing record. I also saw him grow quiet when a person he knew died or was injured in street racing. But the dead drivers always had respect; they had left with their boots on. After such an accident, Nipe came back in two months, recovered, to the street corner as if nothing had happened, to continue his subcultural lifestyle. The struggle for respect was a collective one, and the club did not approve of nonappearance of its members. "We are together, but alone," the young racers said, underlining the collective task of "doing reputation" for the car club with their own risk.

The cruising club boys had gone to school together, although not in the same grade. Later, Nipe and Kallu went on to vocational school together, after which they participated in mandatory military service. (Only Nipe, of all the cruising club boys, did not feign injury or unexplained back pain and thus completed the required minimum-length service of six months.) Later, Nipe and Kallu worked side by side at a construction company as technicians, whereas Miro washed windows. Hume and Sepe worked in a chocolate factory, and Mika in a brewery. To them, these occupations offered an insufficient living standard, which was a constant source of harm, though keeping in mind that often the boys' greatest expense was paying fines for traffic violations.

In Finland, the media and the society define street racers by their lack of economic worth and future prospects.[18] At night, the boys turned these categories upside down and made economic security and education shameful, effeminate, and a threat to freedom. The American working-class icon Bruce Springsteen captured this when he sang, "Some men just give up and start dyin' a little, piece by piece. Me, I come home and wash up, and go racing in the street."

This conflict between daytime and nighttime identities became a blazing battle-field and an adventure. The boys wanted "to show them" and "to get them" with their tricks in traffic. In this joyful battle, they risked being killed in action. Yet free-dom and youth were theirs.

Indeed, the Helsinki street racers fought not only against their experience of subordination but also against adulthood, which they dreaded as a continuum of senseless nights: the picture of oneself, night after night, lying on the living-room couch, sipping beer, and watching TV.

Street-Racing "Babes"

The car club boys named street racing "target-oriented public relations," the targets being young women. Within the boys' battles for status, having a steady girl-friend, a "babe" ready for a relationship, or a "loose chick," that is, an available young woman riding in the car, was regarded subordinate to the status of street rac-ing and car ownership yet almost equal in respect.

Although sex was an important motivation for street racing, most boys favored long-term relationships and were (relatively) able to adjust to monogamy, moti-vated by not only shared rent and warm meals but also affection. This affection was not expressed with words or by touching in public, except for an occasional stroke of a cheek, yet there was tenderness in the boys' voices when they talked of their girlfriends, forgiving them for scratching the wheel rims on curbs or for breaking the rear light when reversing: "I need to get to the garage. Ninni crushed the rear light, come and look at this," Nipe said when he asked me to look at the damage his girlfriend had done to one of his cars, a BMW–86. "The concrete bollard was put in a stupid place."

Within the street-racing culture, the position of a woman was more traditional than elsewhere in a society that is proud of its gender equality.[19] The babes, girl-friends, and loose chicks of the Helsinki street-racing scene did not dress or act provocatively as, for example, the fantasy girls of *The Fast and The Furious* (2000) and *2 Fast 2 Furious* (2003). Instead, they expressed modesty and timidity in their clothes and makeup. When riding in cars, girlfriends were silent, while the young men talked. If a young woman did not obey these unspoken rules when sober, she probably was not dating anyone in the club but was a loose chick on her own. Often these loose chicks attracted attention acting boyish and driving around with an atti-tude, which often resulted in minor accidents. Here is Sari's example of "driving with the right attitude." Sari was eighteen years old and worked for a gardening company:

> Once there was this guy, he walked up to me and chatted this n' that. Then he said: "Hey, your car is nice. What kind of an engine does it have" and blah blah. I told him it's a one point six, but he didn't believe me. I said "Let's go and I'll show you. Then you'll shake shit out of your pants." He sat in the car. He went all white! He was OK when I drove cool in the beginning, but then when we came to some smaller dirt roads where I've driven on with my bike, I really let go and pushed the gas pedal. The car almost tumbled over in a curve

since it was, yeah, it was winter then, and slippery. So I made cool turns with the hand brake and all, at full speed. When we got to the highway I drove some 140, 150 kilometers per hour. See, I'm just like that. If someone doubts me, I just want to show them.

The guy didn't say anything the whole time. "Yeah, your car moves all right," he said then. (Fieldwork notes, August 1999)

By the roadside, young women watched and cheered as young men were in control of the noise, music, movement, safety, and atmosphere of the racing event. The hypnotized gaze of the young women watching, with their desire to go for rides and wave at the passing cars, made me think of their futures. I thought of their bodies being controlled, used, possessed, and owned by their lovers and husbands for reproduction and by their children for the "thankless chores"[20] of upkeep. Now, the young men displayed their freedom and domination, and the young women were loving it, inviting it, ready for subordination, and thus, manifesting the failure of feminist politics to reach working-class women.

Although sexual affairs were an important motivation for the out-of-town cruises of the club, the boys favored long-term relationships. Still, after breaking up with a girl, a new companion was easy to find for a young racer with a car, a status, and a cruising club membership. Nipe said that when cruising to another town to race, like to the town of Lahti, 100 kilometers north of Helsinki ("a street-racer's dream, no cops!"), he got to spend the night with a different girl every time. Sex was frequently used among men in their fight over status. Even the most competent street-racing boys respected a fellow who knew his way around women.

Closing All Exits

In his book, Mike Presdee questioned whether joyriding was, in the eyes of the public, a senseless act in a world based on material acquisition (Presdee 2000, 151). To answer Mike Presdee's question, street racing was a must for these boys, a necessity, and an act with sense and a reason.

Miro: We like to play in traffic. There you get those best moments of surprise. You never know what's gonna happen. You never know whom you're gonna take on.
Vaaranen: The best moments of surprise?
Nipe: It's in traffic where the best action is.
Miro: The best encounters, yeah.
Nipe: Exciting moments when you yourself don't know which way to turn, what to do.
Miro: That's right. And I'm better [at driving] than Vatanen and Mikkola [Finnish racing champions] put together. Haven't had too many accidents. Last summer I drove off the road and the car rolled over twice. That wasn't my fault either.

By investing their bodies in risk and self-destruction and by gaining extreme experiences and thrills in traffic, the boys conformed to and reproduced their own deadly culture. One late night when drinking beer, Kallu sent me the following cell-phone text message: "I thought here that, maybe one reason why young people race. Would be that when things aren't going your way and you feel you're losing in life and then when you win something on the streets, it makes you feel better . . . understand?" Thus, the street-racing boys surrounded themselves with challenge, noise, speed, and continuous action as if the hurt of lost opportunities only could be forgotten when gaining a reputation, inhaling a cigarette, drinking beer, driving fast, or making love. Through an intensive, tireless search for activity and "action," these young racers amputated the desire in themselves to be on the consuming side of the commercial culture.

The emotional experience of class reinforced camaraderie and cultural performances but weakened the relation to the bigger world.

Those responsible for the dangerous street-racing acts were not the irresponsible car industry or failed parenthood. Neither was it the street-racing boys' failure at school. It was not the boys who had failed at school; the school had failed them. The Finnish education system had failed to impress on them why an effort to pursue education would be profitable. In a country that spends 7.8 percent of its GNP on the public educational system and one that is among the leading countries in the PISA (Programme for International Student Assessment) study regarding learning results in literacy, mathematics, and science, these were the lost boys (OECD 2000). Perhaps the education system presented its agenda as an alternative to what the boys desired.

I came to understand the object of their desire after having gotten many answers like "I don't know" and "I can't say." It was as if I had asked the boys to describe how they knew they were in love or why they loved a particular girl. As Mike Presdee writes, "Enjoyment, desire and pleasure are important features of social life and in some way they are both transposed into cultural forms and emanate from them" (Presdee 2000, 5). For the cruising club boys, the object of their desire was immediate satisfaction. The one producing this was not a woman but a motor car, worthy of investment. "Cars are more trustworthy [than women]," Mika says. "I mean, you can have someone whining there at home, but the garage is a man's world. . . . And when you have invested thousands of hours of work to those cars, that's what you want to talk about and think over with your pals. In the end, when you know what it is that the guys value, women don't matter. . . . They do belong here, though." This desire to cultivate one's skills in male companionship and to test the car and oneself in a race was built into these boys' age, gender, and orientation. Their passion for speed, then, found its fulfillment in morbid fear and fascination, joy and desire that threw the riders into challenge. The car was the primary daydream of the boys: a Madonna in the kitchen and a hooker in bed. The boys caressed their cars in the garage, speaking to them and of them gently. And in public, they gave hell to their cars, driving them violently. This masculine desire and its fulfillment on the streets became a "room of his own." Nothing else but a fast car could be this obedient and give the right kind of satisfaction. Building on Presdee's note on enjoyment, street racing was an embodiment of a masculine desire to control, to admire, to caress, to own, to challenge, to remodel, and to use in a fight against other men in a race. The race, then, became a male joie de vivre, a sweet escape. It became a saturnalia of driving, drinking, and car erotics.

The tragedy of the "room of his own," however, was that it closed all exits from the subculture. The emotional experience of class reinforced camaraderie and cultural performances but weakened the relation to the bigger world. Upward mobility was desired but not carried out, however close and within reach it was. This realization accelerated the boys' way to self-destruction. It promoted the street-racing crimes of passion, leaving behind death and injury: the human sacrifice of the modern age. As Miro told me, "This is my life and I do with it what I want. If I'm going to die, I'd rather die in a car driving at 300 kilometers an hour going off a highway."

Notes

1. Street racing in Finland is called both *kortteliralli*, which literally translates "cruising-around-the-block," and *kaahailu*, which translates as "speeding." To cover both of these local expressions and to further emphasize illegal driving competition and time tracking, I chose to use the notion of street racing. See Vaaranen and Wieloch (2002) for a more thorough description of the Finnish street-racing customs.

2. Some names of international formula-one racing champions or runners-up are Mika Häkkinen and Kimi Räikkönen, and in rally racing, Tommi Mäkinen, Ari Vatanen, Hannu Mikkola, and Juha Kankkunen.

3. See Salmi and Summala (1998).

4. Joyriding can be defined as a pleasurable ride, as a ride with a stolen vehicle, or as driving a car without the owner's permission. Street racing, on the other hand, is not defined as a word or a notion by any of the main dictionaries. According to Internet sites, films, and literature, *street racing* means racing for excitement, status, or money in self-modified cars, in illegal places, and at unpredictable times. According to my Helsinki fieldwork, street racers do not steal cars but value ownership. The cruising club boys called car thieves "punks who don't deserve respect" and "kids who needed to be taught a lesson." When the car was all they owned, this ownership became celebrated to a point where touching or leaning on others' cars was not a wise thing to do at club garages or informal car shows. For example, the racers protected this ownership by warning me often not to touch the vehicles unless I was buying. "Don't touch!" they would say in an informal car show, even if I were only walking about and just looking.

5. The notion of "edgework" is from Stephen Lyng's article "Dangerous Methods: Risk Taking and the Research Process" in Ferrell and Hamm's edited collection *Ethnography at the Edge* (1998). Starting from the winter of 1999, I applied this notion of edgework into my fieldwork, thus participating in speeding experiences as a driver and a passenger. Before that, I observed these youths as a roadside viewer and a regular visitor at their meeting places. This change of method from fieldwork in meeting places to extreme experiences in these youths' cars generated a flow of information I would not have been able to obtain otherwise.

6. Although they frequently drink beer and hard liquor, these youths did not use other narcotics. They despised drug users, calling them "losers." This may have been as much an economic as a moral choice, but I even saw it as a part of a struggle for honorable, Finnish masculinity that despises weakness.

7. The boys founded a cruising club where they modified and engineered their cars. Their rented club garage was located thirty minutes from downtown Helsinki.

8. There is more about this in Vaaranen and Wieloch (2002, 49).

9. Stephen Lyng (1998) found this characteristic also in individuals involved in extreme mountain climbing and rock climbing. "A common pattern among risk takers is to increase the risk of dangerous activities artificially by incapacitating themselves in various ways," Lyng (1990, 861) borrows from his main report "Edgework."

10. See Vaaranen and Wieloch's (2002, 48-50) discussion on music equipment in street-racing cars.

11. This "practical parenthood" reminded me of the work of feminist author Audre Lorde (quoted in Clough 1994, 98) who pointed out that sometimes survival is the best gift a parent can give his or her offspring and that sometimes tenderness gets lost in the process.

12. A Finnish sociologist Matti Kortteinen (1982, 1992) suggests that the Finnish, blue-collar working ethos differs from the Protestant ethos of capitalism, accounted for by Max Weber. Whereas Weber accentuated how the sacrifice of the Protestant ethos of capitalism is both hard work and withdrawal from consumption, according to Kortteinen, the Finnish working ethos sacrifices the health of the worker. Kortteinen continues that a Finnish worker takes pride in surviving hard work and rough conditions. Ironically, the offspring of the working class still renounces a way out through higher education. Despite the state's efforts for the past thirty years to ensure social equality in education for all, middle-class youth take part in university education at a rate four times that of youth with working-class backgrounds (Nevala 1999).

13. Within the Finnish drinking tradition, one does not just start out to have a few for jollification and sometimes slip unintentionally into inebriety. Rather, men, women, and youth set out to drink for a night or for a few days in a row during holidays or trips, calling the experience a *putki*: an experience of a timeless flow in a "tunnel" of intoxication. To name another example, in Russian tradition, there is *zapoji*, a period of drinking that may last for several weeks or even months, whereas the Finnish putki normally lasts only a few days or a week or two.

14. Nipe kept thoughtfully reminding me how old I was (I was thirty-six when we met) and how that would protect me from police harassment in traffic.

15. The erotic interiors were composed of red-velvet linings, cushions, blackened back windows, and curtains. I even heard a boy say to another that he wants to paint his car with the colors of female sexual organs. Young women who were concerned about their reputations were unwilling to step into these cars, but just as many were drawn to them. Even the boys who were not transparent about their cars as tools in sexual seduction blackened the rear windows, possibly to make a nest for their late-night dates. The boys' popularity among girls did not depend as much on the make and decoration of the car as on the reputation and social skills of the boys.

16. A similar counterexperience, in a form of collective action, was found behind the scenes where illegal cruising clubs worked to engineer the fastest cars possible (keeping in mind that some of these cars were twenty-year-old European cars and aged American Fords at their best). This production house, the club garage, was as a collective responsible for the street performance of the club members.

17. Philippe Bourgois's (1995) "In Search of Respect: Selling Crack in El Barrio" may make an interesting comparison for the reader of another search for respect, also clouded by a culturally reproduced, stunted ambition.

18. For example, when I asked around in pubs, looking for the ideal type of youths "with a heavy foot on the gas pedal," racing fans used to be surprised that I would want to meet such individuals. "Oh, those shitheads?" they said in disbelief. "Oh yes," I reassured them, "Those shitheads." I was not willing to make the distinction that what I wanted was a "social critic, a rebel, even a revolutionary." I borrowed this description from Laurie Tailor and Stanley Cohen's (1976, xii) preface to the first edition of their book *Escape Attempts: The Theory and Practice of Resistance to Everyday Life*. Taylor and Cohen suggest that the ideal type of a deviant acts to fight against the repression of the surrounding world.

19. To name a few examples of gender equality, the president Tarja Halonen is a woman and so is the mayor of Helsinki. Finland has had two secretaries of defense who were women, and 37 percent of the members of the parliament are women. This year, almost half of the cabinet members are women.

20. This follows the thoughts of June Jordan (quoted in Clough 1994, 98).

References

2 Fast 2 Furious. 2003. Film. Hollywood, CA: Universal Studios.

Bourgois, Philippe. 1995. *In search of respect: Selling crack in El Barrio*. Cambridge, UK: Cambridge University Press.

Campbell, Beatrix. 1993. *Goliath: Britain's dangerous places*. London: Methuen.

Central Organization for Traffic Safety Finland. 2003. A review of road accident statistics, 1998-2002. Report, August 12.

Clough, Patricia Ticineto. 1994. *Feminist thought*. Oxford, UK: Blackwell.

Cohen, Stanley, and Laurie Taylor. 1976. *Escape attempts: The theory and practice of resistance to everyday life*. New York: Penguin.

The Fast and the Furious. 2001. Film. Hollywood, CA: Universal Studios.

Ferrell, Jeff. 1993. *Crimes of style: Urban graffiti and the politics of criminality*. New York: Garland.

Ferrell, Jeff, and Mark S. Hamm. 1998. *Ethnography at the edge: Crime, deviance and field research*. Boston: Northeastern University Press.

Foley, Douglas. 1990. *Learning capitalist culture: Deep in the heart of Tejas*. Philadelphia: University of Pennsylvania Press.

Hall, Start, and Tony Jefferson, eds. 1976. *Resistance through rituals: Youth subcultures in post war Britain*. London: Hutchinson.

Hebdige, Dick. 1979. *Subculture: The meaning of style*. London: Methuen.

Kortteinen, Matti. 1982. *Lähiö: Tutkimus elämäntapojen muutoksesta* [The suburb: A study in the social change of everyday life]. Porvoo, Finland: WSOY.

———. 1992. *Kunnian kenttä: Suomalainen palkkatyö kulttuurisena muotona* [The fields of honor: Finnish wage labor as a cultural construction]. Hämeenlinna, Finland: Hanki ja jää.

Lyng, Stephen. 1990. Edgework. *American Journal of Sociology* 95 (4): 851-86.

———. 1998. Dangerous methods: Risk taking and the research process. In *Ethnography at the edge: Crime, deviance and field research*, edited by Jeff Ferrell and Mark S. Hamm. Boston: Northeastern University Press.

Nevala, Arto. 1999. *Korkeakoulutuksen kasvu, lohkoutuminen ja eriarvoisuus Suomessa* [The growth, division and unequality of university education]. Joensuu, Finland: University of Joensuu.

Organisation for Economic Co-operation and Development (OECD). 2000. *Programme for International Student Assessment*. Retrieved June 6, 2004 from http://www.pisa.oecd.org/knowledge/home/intro.htm.

Presdee, Mike. 2000. *Cultural criminology and the carnival of crime*. New York: Routledge.

Salmi, Helinä, and Heikki Summala. 1998. *Nuorten kovavauhtiset liikenneonnettomuudet 1996-1998* [Youths' speeding accidents 1996-1998]. Helsinki, Finland: Ministry of Traffic.

Sennett, Richard, and Jonathan Cobb. 1972. *The hidden injuries of class*. New York: Vintage.

Thornton, Sarah, and Ken Gelder. 1997. *The subculture reader*. New York: Routledge.

Vaaranen, Heli, and Neil Wieloch. 2002. Car crashes and dead end careers: Leisure pursuits of the Finnish subculture of "kortteliralli" street racing. *YOUNG. Nordic Journal of Youth Research* 10, no. 1. Retrieved June 6, 2004 from http://www.valt.helsinki.fi/staff/hvaarane/kortteliralli.pdf.

Willis, Paul. 1977. *Learning to labor: How working class kids get working class jobs*. Hampshire, UK: Gower.

The Ethnography of Imagined Communities: The Cultural Production of Sikh Ethnicity in Britain

By
KATHLEEN D. HALL

A shift in ethnographic vantage point from an exclusive
focus on everyday worlds to the broader historical and
cultural processes in which these worlds are embedded
brings to light forms of politics that challenge traditional
ways of understanding immigrant incorporation in modern nation-states. The author argues that the cultural
politics of immigration and citizenship in the global era
require this shift in ethnographic perspective.
Multisited ethnography enables researchers to illuminate the more complex cultural processes of nation formation and the contradictory and, at times, incommensurate forms of cultural politics within which immigrants
are made and make themselves as citizens. Viewing
immigration from the perspective of nation formation,
moreover, brings into question the explanatory power
and political implications of traditional assimilation
models of immigrant incorporation.

Keywords: immigration; nation formation; race; Sikh
ethnicity; cultural production

The problem of world history appears in a new
light. At its core is no longer the evolution and
devolution of world systems, but the tense,
ongoing interaction of forces promoting global
integration and forces recreating local autonomy. This is not a struggle for or against global
integration itself, but rather a struggle over the
terms of that integration. . . . At the center of
this study is the question of who, or what, controls and defines the identity of individuals,
social groups, nations and cultures.
—Bright and Geyer (1987, 69-70)

Ethnographers have been entering the everyday worlds of immigrants and their children for
nearly a century to learn about the process of
becoming American. We have studied immigration by "being there," that is, by engaging in
ethnographic encounters in the places where

*Kathleen D. Hall is an associate professor of education
and anthropology at the University of Pennsylvania. She
is the author of* Lives in Translation: Sikh Youth as British
Citizens. *Her research interests focus on South Asian
transnational migration and the cultural politics of citizenship in the United Kingdom and the United States.*

DOI: 10.1177/0002716204266950

immigrants and their children live their everyday lives. Numerous classic ethnographies have been produced, yet studying immigration ethnographically could still be considered paradoxical. For while ethnographers traditionally attend to localized everyday experience, immigrant incorporation involves the interplay of transnational, national, and local processes.

Although questions of scale are hardly new to ethnography, the dilemma has reemerged quite powerfully as ethnographers have turned to study globalization (Burawoy 2000; Perry and Maurer 2003; Hall 1999) and "cultural flows" that move across time, space, or levels of social scale (Appadurai 1991, 1996; Comaroff and Comaroff 2003). Inspired by developments in culture theory as well, anthropologists in particular are turning away from traditional concerns with people in places and from place-based notions of "the field" (Gupta and Ferguson 1997). The localized field is being replaced by what George Marcus (1998) refers to as a "multisited research imaginary," focusing on the circulation of discourse, the production of social imaginaries, and the forging of transnational networks across levels of scale and connecting people across time and space. For anthropologists, the challenges of doing ethnography now center on questions of scale and, concomitantly, on questioning scalarity itself (Tsing 2000).

In my contribution to this volume on ethnographic encounters, I consider how multisited ethnography might bring to light cultural dynamics that are critical to the immigrant experience but seldom addressed in traditional sociological research on immigrant incorporation. While recent sociological work on immigrant incorporation increasingly emphasizes multiscale factors (Portes and Zhou 1993), the immigrant experience continues to be framed in terms of assimilation and acculturation.[1] *Culture*, in these analyses, is defined as the beliefs, values, identities, and traditions that individuals and groups possess and, as they acculturate, choose to retain or to leave behind. Defined in this way, cultural analyses remain focused on the level of subjective meanings or group practices and seldom consider broader processes of national-identity formation and its relationship to immigrant incorporation and cultural change.

It is curious that questions of nationalism and of the making of nationalist identities have largely been absent from much of the sociological literature on becoming American. Nationalism has been a taken-for-granted and, hence, largely undertheorized backdrop for analyzing assimilation and acculturation. It is "the host society" to which immigrants adapt and "American culture"—however heterogeneous—to which they eventually acculturate. The nation—the boundaries of which imply the very terms of distinction between migrant and immigrant—is reified as an enduring context within which the immigrant experience takes place. This reification of the nation and of nationalism limits our ability to explain fully the cultural dynamics of immigrant incorporation.

What is needed, I argue, is a multisited ethnographic analysis of how national boundaries and ethnic identities are created, circulated, debated, and contested across social contexts and levels of scale.[2] Ethnographic research should consider not only how immigrants are incorporated but also how "incorporation regimes" themselves are culturally produced (Soysal 1994). Turning to issues of nation building directs our ethnographic attention to cultural politics in the public sphere where immigrant statuses are defined and debated, citizen rights and responsibilities invoked, structural inequalities challenged, and cultural identifications created—to the cultural processes in which immigrants are made and make themselves as citizens and new national imaginaries, eventually, are envisioned (Anderson 1983/1991).

Before developing this argument further, however, I first consider how issues of culture and scale are addressed in the segmented-assimilation model. I then highlight elements of an approach developed in my own ethnographic work concerned with how second-generation, working-class Sikhs are becoming middle-class British citizens.

The Assimilation Paradigm

For generations, sociological studies of immigration in America—ethnographic as well as survey research—have been framed in terms of a classic narrative of migration and social incorporation.[3] The immigrant experience has been narrated as a journey, as Lisa Lowe (1996) puts it, from "foreign strangeness to assimilation to citizenship." Immigrants, it is assumed, become Americans through linear and irreversible stages of cultural "acculturation" and social "assimilation" into the host society. While typologies differ in the attention given to distinctive dimensions of or routes to assimilation, they share a common assumption that acculturation and assimilation are inevitable and necessary to promote and protect the broader social good.[4]

Over the past fifteen years, studies influenced by developments in the new economic sociology (Guillen et al. 2002) have moved beyond single-dimension models of "straight-line" assimilation and acculturation to explain the different levels of educational and economic success among immigrant populations. The development of a multidimensional model of segmented assimilation has been central to this advancement (Portes and Zhou 1993; Portes and Rumbaut 2001). In the 1990s, Alejandro Portes, Rubén G. Rumbaut, and colleagues completed The Children of Immigrants Longitudinal Study (CILS), a multifaceted survey of the educational performance and social, cultural, and psychological adaptation of the children of immigrants in American. Analyses of these longitudinal data have made substantial contributions to both the empirical knowledge base and the theoretical formulations of processes of segmented assimilation (see, particularly, Portes and Rumbaut 2001; Rumbaut and Portes 2001).

Contrary to models of the past, the segmented-assimilation theory stresses heterogeneity, within both the immigrant population and the host society itself. New immigrants (post-1965) can be distinguished, the authors argue, along three dimensions critical to second-generation adaptation: (1) individual features or human capital, influenced by educational background, occupational skills, financial resources, and facility with the English language; (2) the host society's reception of immigrant populations, particularly in relation to governmental policies, popular attitudes, and the presence of coethnic populations; and (3) the composition of immigrant families (Portes and Rumbaut 2001, 46). The model stresses the interplay between background factors, intergenerational patterns, and external obstacles. Each stage in the assimilation process involves dynamics that occur across levels of social scale. Acculturation is "conditioned" by background structural "variables," such as parents' human capital, the mode of incorporation that a group experiences, and family composition. This produces different intergenerational patterns of acculturation or cultural learning, processes typified by either "dissonance" between the cultural orientations of the first and second generation, "consonance" (learning across generations takes place at about the same pace), or "selective acculturation" among both generations (partial retention of home language and norms).

For anthropologists, the challenges of doing ethnography now center on questions of scale and, concomitantly, on questioning scalarity itself.

As Portes and Rumbaut (2001) argue, "The central question is not whether the second generation will assimilate to U.S. society but to what segment of that society it will assimilate" (p. 55). Their analytic framework isolates three "external obstacles" or challenges to the second generation's educational attainment and future career success, including the following: racial discrimination, labor market barriers (deindustrialization and progressive inequality in the labor market), and inner-city marginalization and the consequent influence on youth of what Portes and Rumbaut call "inner city subcultures" (p. 55). Parental factors, modes of incorporation, family contexts, and intergenerational acculturation are all related to ways the second generation confronts these barriers and to the resources the second generation brings to these encounters. Segmented assimilation, then, results from a form of "cumulative causation," or the "progressive narrowing of options for action brought about by the accumulation of past decisions and events" (Rumbaut and Portes 2001, 312). Cumulative causation works across distinct paths where initial characteristics and the reception of newly arrived immigrants facilitate or prevent the future access of the second generation to key moral and material resources. This access, the authors conclude, or the lack thereof, determines the probabilities of a successful path to social mobility or to "downward assimilation" (Rumbaut and Portes 2001, 312).

The segmented-assimilation model provides rich insight into the structural dimensions of immigrant incorporation. Qualitative case studies designed in accordance with this framework have also directed attention to some of the cultural aspects of segmented assimilation. Many of these studies, influenced by the new economic sociology, emphasize how networks and social-capital resources influence interpretations of opportunities as well as life choices (Fernández-Kelly and Schauffler 1994, 670). Using data largely generated from interviews, culture is addressed in these case studies at the level of subjective meanings. Waters (1994), for example, describes "individual variation in the identities, perceptions and opinions" of adolescent, second-generation West Indian and Haitian Americans in New York City. She then groups their racial and ethnic identities into a typology that includes three different orientations of being American: "identifying as Americans, identifying as ethnic Americans with some distancing from black Americans, or maintaining an immigrant identity that does not reckon with American racial and ethnic categories" (Waters 1994, 802). Similarly, Fernández-Kelly and Schauffler (1994) compare the meaning of assimilation and of ethnic identity for individual children from five immigrant groups: Haitians, Vietnamese, Cubans, Nicaraguans, and Mexicans. Analyses such as these tell us a great deal about how people make sense of their lives but little about how classificatory schemes are produced, circulate, and organize social practice.

To avoid the classic fallacy of separating structural from cultural processes, researchers must pay more attention to how structural factors are shaped by the cultural logics of particular classificatory systems—systems that are expressed, debated, and continually transformed across domains within the public sphere of nation-states.[5] How do structural forces work through cultural forms to configure social organizational relations, and how do people subjectively experience these forces and formulate understandings of themselves and of others?

Immigrants become citizens through processes of social incorporation—processes that include the formation of social ties with the host society—traditionally referred to as "assimilation." But whether and how peoples come to be viewed as "assimilatable" is informed, in part, by broader processes of cultural change associated with the symbolic creation of "the nation" as an imagined community. Imagining the nation and defining the basis of national belonging involve a dual process of delineating boundaries of inclusion and of exclusion. National imaginaries, in this sense, are never simply given and never fixed or enduring. Notions of national belonging and, in turn, national identities and citizenship statuses are continually redefined, negotiated, and debated as they come to be articulated within different forms of nationalist discourse.

The ongoing project of nation formation entails complex and multiple forms of cultural politics, which play out across a number of sites within the public sphere of democratic, capitalist nations—in law and policy, education, and the media, as well as in face-to-face interactions in families and ethnic communities. In the context of these cultural politics, "immigrants" are produced as subjects, multiple types of subjects associated with distinctive "minority" statuses that classify those so defined in racial, ethnic, religious, linguistic, generational, and gendered terms. It is here, I argue, that identities and subjectivities are made, here, within the varied forms of cultural production at work within the public sphere.

The cultural politics of nation formation is the battlefield upon which immigrants and their children fight for inclusion and to shift the boundaries of belonging. Citizens, in other words, are not simply made but actively participate in making themselves. As Lisa Lowe (1996) explains, immigration experiences are a matter of immigrant acts, the interplay between structural forces that act upon immigrant peoples—defining them in relation to particular ascribed or imposed minority statuses—and the acts of immigrants themselves, through which individuals fashion their own forms of self and collective identities, create particular lifestyles, and pave future life paths. The complexity of their social and cultural worlds necessarily involves individuals in processes of cultural translation—everyday acts of interpretation, negotiation, and situational performance. I turn now to illustrate these dynamics through a discussion of Sikh immigration and British nation formation.

Sikhs as British Citizens

Sikhs as a people are associated historically with Sikhism, a modern religion that traces its origin to the birth of the first Sikh guru, Guru Nanak, in 1469. Their homeland is the Punjab, a state in northern India. Most of their historic shrines are found in the territory on either side of the border separating India from Pakistan, an area that was, prior to partition, considered part of Punjab. Over the past 150 years, their travels and relocations have created a Sikh diaspora that stretches across the globe. Many among this first generation to grow up in Britain were born to upwardly mobile families and to parents who reached adulthood in the villages of Punjab or in the racially divided cities of colonial East Africa. They migrated to Britain from the Punjab during the 1950s and 1960s and from East Africa during the late 1960s and early 1970s.

The ethnographic study of Sikh immigration, I argue, must be located within a broader analysis of the making of a multiracial, postcolonial British nation. In the years that have transpired since the beginning of the end of the British Empire, the colonial ties between ruler and subject have been transformed into "race relations" between purportedly "equal citizens." The migration of ex-colonial subjects of color to the imperial motherland in the aftermath of empire represents a final chapter in the history of British colonialism, a chapter that one group of sociologists, in their book on British race relations, provocatively titled *The Empire Strikes Back* (Centre for Contemporary Cultural Studies 1982).

The story of Britain after empire is one of a nation's struggling to come to terms with itself as a multiracial society as its ex-colonial citizens of color challenge the basis of national identity and fight their battles to truly belong. Yet immigration has hardly been the only force to test the nation's foundations. Economic globalization, European political unification, and the establishment of a Scottish parliament and a Welsh assembly have undermined Britain's political sovereignty. A cherished sense of the cultural "purity" of "Britishness" has become part of the nation's sacred past, available now largely in commodity form as "heritage" sold to tourists. This, however, is hardly Britain's destiny alone. In this era of identity politics, contests over culture and claims to rights based on the principles of cultural recognition are testing the modern ideal of the culturally unified nation throughout the democratic

---

The cultural politics of nation formation is the battlefield upon which immigrants and their children fight for inclusion and to shift the boundaries of belonging.

---

world. While the politics of plural publics challenge the nation-state from within, the forces of global capitalism increasingly defy these boundaries from beyond. Immigration in general, and the education and mobility experiences of immigrant children more specifically, must be considered in relation to these dynamic tensions of nation formation within the global era.

The postwar British public sphere has been a contested terrain on which the politics of cultural pluralism and of social incorporation have configured the possibilities and the limitations of citizenship and national belonging. Immigrant incorporation is negotiated across shifting fields of power and cultural politics in the public sphere, where collective identities, social statuses, and cultural subjectivities are produced in law and policy, education, and the media. Sikh immigrants and their children become citizens in relation to what Yasemin Soysal (1994) calls an "incorporation regime," the processes through which host societies come to define, to delineate, and therein, to produce collective identities and statuses that configure the possibilities and the limitations of citizenship and national belonging.

The process of defining political statuses and determining minority rights is a matter of heated political, legal, and policy debate; yet these statuses, when designated, invoke identities, inscribe social positions, and confer privileges that are officially recognized, legitimated, and accepted by the state and its institutions. Legal discourse and social policies, in other words, constitute group identities and statuses and, in the way these are constituted, forge the terrain upon which rights and resources can be claimed and contested (Benhabib 1999, 298). These minority statuses become the vehicles through which citizens engage in the politics of recognition to claim rights and to assert social needs.

Successive nationality and immigration laws enacted in Britain in the years since World War II and the passage of the British Nationality Act of 1948 chronicle a progressive narrowing of notions of British belonging from the expansionist vision of empire (which joined all British subjects in an allegiance to the monarch, granting them full privileges and protection, including the right to enter the United Kingdom) to the current exclusionary practices of the postcolonial British nation. The legal status of British nationality has been transformed through these acts from a concept of belonging founded upon connections of subjecthood within the British Empire to a notion of nationality based upon what is defined as "a genuine connection" to Britain through a "natural bond" of kinship and culture. The passage of increasingly restrictive nationality and immigration legislation has articulated an ideology of national belonging, delineated national boundaries, and determined new criteria for who could qualify as a citizen. Through defining national identity, however implicitly, in racial terms, the law has positioned Britain's citizens of color outside these boundaries of national belonging.

As the government sought to control entry to the nation through increasingly rigid immigration controls, other laws were passed in the 1970s aimed at bringing about the harmonious "integration" of those who had already arrived. Under the auspices of the Race Relations Acts, legal statuses have been constructed that protect and provide special rights to groups who meet particular status criteria. These criteria have been defined and further refined within legal deliberations over cases that have been brought before the court. Within these deliberations, particular peoples have been recognized, and thereby produced, as "racial" or "ethnic" groups.

British Sikhs are subject to a range of political discourses and legal acts that grant them distinctive types of minority statuses. Their status as immigrants or citizens has evolved in the passage of Britain's increasingly restrictive nationality and immigration acts. Their status as a racial or an ethnic minority has been constructed in discrimination cases fought under the auspices of the three British Race Relations Acts, passed in 1965, 1968, and 1976. Numerous court battles have ensued to determine whether particular peoples qualify for protection under the law as racial or as ethnic groups. In *Mandla v. Dowell Lee* (over whether a student in a private school had the right to wear a turban with his uniform), decided in the House of Lords in 1982, it was concluded that, in Lord Templeman's words, "the evidence of the origins and history of the Sikhs . . . disclosed that the Sikhs are more than a religion and a culture. . . . The Sikhs are more than a religious sect, they are almost a race and almost a nation." While lacking in precision, the judgment clarified that the civil rights of Sikhs were protected under the auspices of the Race Relations Acts.

Legal discourse constitutes minority statuses in efforts to determine who belongs to a nation and to protect the rights of those who do. These forms of political discourse designate minority status on ethnic reductionist terms—terms that assume a homology between a community and a culture. These essentialist constructs, in contradictory fashion, provide the basis for challenging discrimination while defining the boundaries of national belonging in racial terms. Yet processes of social incorporation are not shaped only within the designation of legal statuses and the provision of particular rights. They are founded upon and informed by visions of national unity—visions that provide the rationale for different types of integration efforts. What is assumed to preserve the social fabric of a nation or, contrastively, to tear it apart? and How are cultural differences imagined to contribute to either of these social ends?

The politics of difference in culturally plural nations brings into focus a fundamental contradiction inherent in modern liberal democracies: How can nation-states protect the moral community of the nation while accommodating the diverse and sometimes conflicting cultural beliefs and practices of members of its citizenry? What has been referred to as "the challenge of multiculturalism and the politics of recognition" (Gutmann 1992) strikes at the heart of some of the central presuppositions of liberal democracy. It has stimulated a great deal of debate about the relationship between individual and collective rights, the fundamental basis of forms of civic solidarity, the value of different modes of social integration, and the legitimacy of minority cultural rights to financial support and legal protection for their languages and practices, particularly in the field of education.

What Nancy Fraser has characterized as "the eclipse of a socialist imaginary centered on terms such as 'interest,' 'exploitation,' and 'redistribution'" has brought to light a new political imaginary—a politics founded in notions of "identity," "difference," "cultural domination," and "resistance" (Fraser 1997, 11). Social-justice discourse, which in the past had privileged class and socioeconomic inequities, has been reconfigured, informing politics that now target cultural domination—forms of disadvantage and disrespect, misrecognition and social exclusion rooted in attributions of difference. This emphasis on cultural injustice, in the words of Charles Taylor (1992), assumes that

> nonrecognition or misrecognition . . . can be a form of oppression, imprisoning someone in a false, distorted, reduced mode of being. Beyond simply lack of respect, it can inflict a grievous wound, saddling people with crippling self-hatred. Due recognition is not just a courtesy but a vital human need. (p. 25)

Across this political terrain, "cultural recognition has displaced socioeconomic redistribution as the remedy for injustice and the goal of political struggle" (Taylor 1992, 11). The political discourse of cultural recognition differentiates people into "members of discrete ethnic, linguistic, and other cultural groups" in need of "public recognition and preservation of particular cultural identities" (Gutmann 1992, 9). Within this political imaginary, subordinate peoples gain the power to claim rights on the basis of cultural, religious, or linguistic authenticity in conflicts ranging from battles over indigenous land rights to contests over language education policies (Turner 1994).

The 1980s in Britain, as in other Western industrial nations, witnessed the expansion of liberal politics of recognition galvanized in the name of "multicultural" principles. The rise of the politics of recognition, in Britain as elsewhere, both challenged the traditional hegemony of the culturally homogeneous nation and prompted the invocation of objectified cultural and linguistic forms in arguments for awareness and valuation of the linguistic and cultural practices of ethnic others. The cultural politics of education in Britain has produced quite distinctive positions concerning education's role in forging national unity, bringing about social integration, and furthering social justice. At the heart of these debates is a classic tension between positions that privilege efforts to nurture national solidarity and provide for the "common good" and those aimed at protecting individual (and group) rights to practice different cultural traditions. These debates, in turn, configure additional statuses for those who, like British Sikhs, find their culture and language objectified within educational discourse about difference.

Essentialist constructs . . . provide the basis for challenging discrimination while defining the boundaries of national belonging in racial terms.

Sikhs have found themselves positioned as culturally and linguistically different—as bilingual or bicultural—within education policies aiming to increase educational equity. But citizenship rights and national responsibilities obviously are not simply articulated or negotiated at the level of top-down policy making or legislative actions. To understand the dynamic nature of processes of social incorporation, one must examine how groups so defined as "ethnic" or "racial" or "immigrants" make claims and assert their rights as citizens.

A campaign organized by Sikh parents at a school that was a site of my ethnographic research provided a rich case of this type of citizen action. The parents organized to demand that their heritage language, Punjabi, be taught as part of the school's modern language curriculum. In campaigns such as this one, which I do not have the space to consider here, immigrant parents instrumentally make use of what political theorist Nancy Fraser (1989) refers to as "the politics of needs interpretation" to assert their rights. Legal-rights discourse provides an avenue for minorities to make claims against the state; it creates opportunities for groups to assert their interests under the cloak of liberalism's principles of fairness and equity for "all."

The paradox of cultural pluralism in nation-states is central to debates over imagined future nations and corresponding visions for immigrant incorporation. These challenges will not be easily resolved. Policies infused with tropes like "education for all" and "unity in diversity" cannot resolve the contradictions at the heart of the politics of difference. Contests over culture, discourses of difference, and politics of identity will continue to test traditional notions of the homogeneous national "social order" as the forces of capitalism deepen relations of inequality on a global scale. The paradox of pluralism in democratic nations is no longer simply a national concern as issues of social integration are influenced by structural inequities grounded increasingly in the workings of global political and economic relations as well as the influence of policies and legislation originating in supranational political bodies, for example, in Britain's case, the migration policies of the European Union. Questions of immigrant incorporation, in this way, increasingly imply transnational politics and cultural dynamics.

Conclusion

In exploring the ethnography of immigrant incorporation, I have chosen to focus on a key dimension in the making of immigrants into citizens—the cultural politics of nation formation. Many more cultural processes are obviously at work in the lives of second-generation British Sikhs: the role that the media play in the making and circulation of national, religious, and ethnic representations and political imaginaries; the often-contradictory role of schooling; the movement of youth between cultural worlds in their families, peer groups, and ethnic communal associations; and the cultural influences that connect and circulate across transnational diaspora networks.[6]

The Sikh youth that I worked with in my ethnographic study in Leeds, England, imagine their futures in relation to numerous possible identities, potential communal ties, and alternative life paths. Their sense of self is molded by contradictory cultural influences in contrasting social settings and transmitted through multiple forms of media. In their homes, at the Sikh temple (or *gurdwara*), and in religious education classes in British schools, "their culture," "their heritage," and "their religion" are represented in different forms and are talked about and interpreted in distinctive ways. As members of a global South Asian diaspora, their sense of what it means to be "Asian," "Indian," or "Sikh" is shaped not only by culture learning at home or at school but by ideas and images, film narratives, and artistic forms circulating across networks linking Leeds, Vancouver, New York, and Amritsar (the sacred center for Sikhs in Punjab). As teenagers in a capitalist culture, British Sikhs also consume youth culture commodities providing myriad cultural styles and subcultural orientations to use in creating adolescent identities.

I chose to focus primarily on the role of nation formation and cultural politics in the public sphere because in so doing, I was able to bring into relief cultural processes that underlie assumptions about assimilation and immigrant incorporation. A shift in ethnographic vantage point from focusing exclusively on everyday worlds to focusing on the broader historical and cultural processes in which these worlds are embedded brings to light forms of politics that challenge traditional ways of approaching the immigrant experience in modern nation-states. While a number of sociologists continue to argue for the value of assimilation and acculturation models for explaining immigrant incorporation, viewing immigration from the perspective of nation formation brings into question the explanatory power of these models and highlights the political implications of viewing immigration through these lenses. Contrary to the type of ethnographic analysis I have briefly described, assimilation and acculturation models leave unquestioned the nationalist projects in which assumptions about integration come to be produced as well as challenged. Assimilation models take as self-evident "the mainstream" social order into which immigrants and their children will, over time, eventually fit—to different degrees and in distinctive class positions—and, through their efforts, will also contribute to transforming. In the words of Alba and Nee (1997),

> Whatever the deficiencies of earlier formulations and applications of assimilation, we hold that this social science concept offers the best way to understand and describe the integration into the mainstream experienced across generations by many individuals and ethnic groups. (p. 827)

Shifting the question to how the mainstream or the nation comes to be imagined troubles the social reproductive emphasis implicit in assimilation and accommodation analyses. Understanding the cultural politics of immigration and citizenship in the global era requires this kind of shift. Multisited ethnography enables researchers to illuminate the more complex cultural processes of nation formation and the contradictory and, at times, incommensurate forms of cultural politics within which immigrants are made and make themselves as citizens. The path from foreign strangeness to citizenship is paved by cultural dynamics that work through different axes of power and across levels of scale.

Notes

1. Milton Gordon's (1964) model of assimilation, of course, was also multidimensional.

2. My approach to studying immigration draws from a range of developments in anthropology and cultural studies, in particular Aihwa Ong (1999a, 1999b, 2003), on the anthropology of citizenship; George Marcus (1998), on multisited ethnography; and Paul Willis's (1977, 2000) contributions to linking ethnography and cultural studies. While the move to combine forms of cultural analyses or to conduct multisited or multiscale ethnography is hardly new, my aim here is to demonstrate its particular utility for studies of immigrant incorporation.

3. See Morawska (1994), Alba and Nee (1997), DeWind and Kasinitz (1997), Gans (1997, 1999), Portes (1997), Zhou (1997), and other articles in a special edition of the *International Migration Review* (1997, vol. 31, no. 4), titled *Immigrant Adaptations and Native-born Responses in the Making of Americans*, for insightful discussions of the history, current state, and future directions of assimilation theory in the field of immigration research.

4. The theoretical frameworks for migration research vary widely across the disciplines. I engage in this article with one among many theoretical approaches to the study of migration, the assimilationist paradigm, which, over the years, has informed both ethnographic and survey research. I consider this paradigm in particular because of the key role it has played in research into cultural change among members of the second generation, the central focus of my own ethnographic work (e.g., Gibson 1988; Portes 1997; Portes and

Rumbaut 2001; Rumbaut and Portes 2001). For an overview of the wider range of theoretical approaches to migration across the disciplines, see Caroline B. Brettell and James F. Hollifield's edited volume *Migration Theory: Talking across Disciplines* (2000).

5. Zolberg's (1989) work on the role of the state in the control of migration flows is obviously related to the processes discussed here. I am arguing, however, that such state-level analyses would benefit from considering not simply the political forces promoting immigration or the politics of legislation or policy making but the cultural aspects of the laws and policies themselves and what they tell us about how national identities and immigrant statuses are imagined in and produced through these discourses. In this sense, my work builds upon Brubaker's (1996) important work on nationalism.

6. In my book *Lives in Translation: Sikh Youth as British Citizens* (2002), I develop a theoretical framework that focuses on each of these forms of cultural production as well as others that I found to be influencing the process of becoming British and middle class among the young people with whom I worked.

References

Alba, Richard, and Victor Nee. 1997. Rethinking assimilation theory for a new era of immigration. *International Migration Review* 31 (4): 826-74.

Anderson, Benedict. 1983/1991. *Imagined communities: Reflections on the origin and spread of nationalism.* New York: Verso.

Appadurai, Arjun. 1991. Global ethnoscapes: Notes and queries for a transnational anthropology. In *Recapturing anthropology*, edited by Richard G. Fox. Santa Fe, NM: School of American Research Press.

———. 1996. *Modernity at large.* Minneapolis: University of Minnesota Press.

Benhabib, Seyla. 1999. Civil society and the politics of identity and difference in a global context. In *Diversity and its discontents: Cultural conflict and common ground in contemporary American society*, edited by Neil J. Smelser and Jeffrey Alexander. Princeton, NJ: Princeton University Press.

Brettell, Caroline B., and James F. Hollifield, eds. 2000. *Migration theory: Talking across disciplines.* New York: Routledge.

Bright, Charles, and Michael Geyer. 1987. For a unified history of the world in the twentieth century. *Radical History Review* 39:69-91.

Brubaker, Rogers. 1996. *Nationalism reframed: Nationhood and the national question in the new Europe.* Cambridge, UK: Cambridge University Press.

Burawoy, Michael. 2000. *Global ethnography: Forces, connections, and imaginations in a postmodern world.* Berkeley: University of California Press.

Centre for Contemporary Cultural Studies. 1982. *The empire strikes back.* London: Hutchison.

Comaroff, Jean, and John Comaroff. 2003. Ethnography on an awkward scale: Postcolonial anthropology and the violence of abstraction. *Ethnography* 4 (2): 147-79.

DeWind, Josh, and Philip Kasinitz. 1997. Everything old is new again? Processes and theories of immigrant incorporation. *International Migration Review* 31 (4): 1096-111.

Fernández-Kelly, Patricia M., and Richard Schauffler. 1994. Divided fates: Immigrant children in a restructured U.S. economy. *International Migration Review* 28 (4): 662-89.

Fraser, Nancy. 1989. Struggle over needs. In *Unruly practices: Power, discourse, and gender in contemporary social theory.* Minneapolis: University of Minnesota Press.

———. 1997. From redistribution to recognition? Dilemmas of justice in a "postsocialist" age. In *Justice interruptus: Critical reflections on the "postsocialist" condition.* New York: Routledge.

Gans, Herbert J. 1997. Toward a reconciliation of "assimilation" and "pluralism": The interplay of acculturation and ethnic retention. *International Migration Review* 31 (4): 875-92.

———. 1999. Filling in some holes: Six areas of needed immigration research. *American Behavioral Scientist* 42 (9): 1302-13.

Gibson, Margaret A. 1988. *Accommodation without assimilation: Sikh immigrants in an American high school.* Ithaca, NY: Cornell University Press.

Gordon, Milton. 1964. *Assimilation in American life.* New York: Oxford University Press.

Guillen, Mauro, Randall Collins, Paula England, and Marshall Meyer, eds. 2002. *The new economic sociology: Developments in an emerging field*. New York: Russell Sage.

Gupta, Akhil, and James Ferguson, eds. 1997. *Anthropological locations: Boundaries and grounds of a field science*. Berkeley: University of California Press.

Gutmann, Amy. 1992. Introduction to *Multiculturalism and "the politics of recognition,"* by Charles Taylor. Princeton, NJ: Princeton University Press.

Hall, Kathleen D. 1999. Understanding educational processes in an era of globalization. In *Improving educational research*, edited by Ellen Lagemann and Lee Shulman. San Francisco: Jossey-Bass.

———. 2002. *Lives in translation: Sikh youth as British citizens*. Philadelphia: University of Pennsylvania Press.

Lowe, Lisa. 1996. *Immigrant acts: On Asian American cultural politics*. Durham, NC: Duke University Press.

Marcus, George E. 1998. *Ethnography through thick and thin*. Princeton, NJ: Princeton University Press.

Morawska, Eva. 1994. In defense of the assimilation model. *Journal of American Ethnic History* 13:76-87.

Ong, Aihwa. 1999a. Cultural citizenship as subject making: Immigrants negotiate racial and cultural boundaries in the United States. In *Race, Identity and Citizenship: A Reader*, edited by Rodolfo D. Torres, Louis F. Miron, and Jonathan Xavier Inda. Oxford, UK: Blackwell.

———. 1999b. *Flexible citizenship: The cultural logics of transnationality*. Durham, NC: Duke University Press.

———. 2003. *Buddha is hiding: Refugees, citizenship, the new America*. Berkeley: University of California Press.

Perry, Richard Warren, and Bill Maurer, eds. 2003. *Globalization under construction: Governmentality, law and identity*. Minneapolis: University of Minnesota Press.

Portes, Alejandro. 1997. Immigration theory for a new century: Some problems and opportunities. *International Migration Review* 31 (4): 799-825.

Portes, Alejandro, and Rubén G. Rumbaut. 2001. *Legacies: The story of the immigrant second generation*. Berkeley: University of California Press.

Portes, Alejandro, and Min Zhou. 1993. The new second generation: Segmented assimilation and its variants. *The Annals of the American Academy of Political and Social Sciences* 530:74-96.

Rumbaut, Rubén G., and Alejandro Portes, eds. 2001. *Ethnicities: Children of immigrants in America*. Berkeley: University of California Press.

Soysal, Yasemin Nuhoglu. 1994. *Limits of citizenship: Migrants and postnational membership in Europe*. Chicago: University of Chicago Press.

Taylor, Charles. 1992. *Multiculturalism and "the politics of recognition."* Princeton, NJ: Princeton University Press.

Tsing, Anna. 2000. The global situation. *Cultural Anthropology* 15 (3): 327-64.

Turner, Terence. 1994. Anthropology and multiculturalism: What is anthropology that multiculturalists should be mindful of it? In *Multiculturalism: A critical reader*, edited by David Theo Goldberg. Cambridge, MA: Blackwell.

Waters, Mary C. 1994. Ethnic and racial identities of second-generation black immigrants in New York City. *International Migration Review* 28 (4): 795-820.

Willis, Paul. 1977. *Learning to labor*. New York: Columbia University Press.

———. 2000. *The ethnographic imagination*. Cambridge, UK: Polity Press.

Zhou, Min. 1997. Segmented assimilation: Issues, controversies, and recent research on the new second generation. *International Migration Review* 31 (4): 975-1008.

Zolberg, A. R. 1989. The next waves: Migration theory for a changing world. *International Migration Review* 20 (2): 151-69.

Deindustrialization and Museumification: From Exhibited Memory to Forgotten History

By
OCTAVE DEBARY

This ethnographic study of the creation of a museum in Le Creusot (France) provides an analysis of the heritage industry that emerged in the wake of the demise of a family company around which the town was built. This museum was a reaction to the passing of an age when industrial and urban environments were intrinsically linked. Through this description of how the past is collected and recollected in a museum, this article attempts to determine if this duty of remembrance is not, to a certain extent, a strategy of forgetfulness. Is cultural regeneration—the staging of history fading into oblivion—our society's sole response to industrial regeneration?

Keywords: ecomuseum; industry; Le Creusot (France); memory; museum

In the dead of night, you could hear hissing noises, gasping moans and terrible rumblings. Julien was increasingly apprehensive:

"What do we have here, Monsieur Gertal? Some great tragedy seems to be taking place."

"No, little Julien. Ahead of us lies Le Creusot, the biggest factory in France and perhaps even in the whole of Europe."

—Bruno (1877/1970, 109)[1]

Did Le Creusot give birth to the "class war" or to the "biggest factory in the whole of Europe"? From its creation in 1780 and the arrival of the Schneider family—the new ironmasters—in 1836, the local industry was applauded and vilified in equal measure.

Octave Debary is an anthropologist, Doctor (Ph.D.) of the Ecole des Hautes Etudes Sociales de Paris, member of the LAHIC laboratory (Laboratory of Anthropology and History of Cultural Institutions, CNRS). His research, which deals with the transformation of history into a heritage industry through contemporary museography, draws upon the anthropology of politics, institutions, and memory. He has written several articles on this subject for New York University, for the Musée d'Ethnographie of Neuchâtel in Switzerland, and for L'Homme et Publics & Musées in France. This article takes up some aspects of his recently published thesis La Fin du Creusot ou l'Art d'Accommoder les Restes (2002, Paris, CTHS Press).

DOI: 10.1177/0002716204266630

ANNALS, *AAPSS*, 595, September 2004

"Should Le Creusot be seen as a *capitalist fiefdom* which was stifled by its own feudalism? Or was it an example of successful paternalism?" (Perrot quoted in Catalogue de l'Exposition 1995, 306). Which of these two different stories should one write?

The question was turned on its head at the beginning of the 1970s. The death of Charles Schneider (1960) announced the onset of industrial decline and the departure of his family, which had presided over the destiny of the most famous industrial town in France for four generations. It was the end of a period of history during which there had been a merger between town and industry; it also marked the end of employment. With the advent of postindustrial modernity, the story of the town's past started coinciding with its epitaph: industrial history, which was now living on borrowed time, tried to delay the inevitable outcome Scheherazade-fashion by telling its own story.

The modernity of culture condemns history to celebrate what it once was and therefore no longer is. The passing of time needs a rite of passage: old industrial activities are turned into scientific curios worthy of a final discourse. We recognize their beauty, we grant them the right to be exhibited for the last time, and finally, we give them their own resting place: a museum. This article outlines some of the practical and theoretical conclusions drawn from my extensive fieldwork in Le Creusot (Debary 2002a, 2002b). My research is an attempt to study museums from an anthropological point of view. More specifically, it is a meditation on the time we devote to exhibiting the past in order to forget it. Through the analysis of a historical watershed (the deindustrialization of a town) and the emergence of the heritage industry that accompanied it, I try to determine why culture and history are fascinated by the loss of their frame of reference: the passing of time. My approach runs counter to the historiographic work on "memorial sites" (*lieux de mémoire*) spearheaded by Pierre Nora (1996) in France. Memory is not the equivalent ("in lieu of") of history. History becomes memory through a process of reconstruction of the past (a past that is redefined, forgotten, and sometimes denied) not through mere transmission. I posit an alternative hypothesis concerning the relation between history and memory. Pursuing the idea that the past is recalled in order to be forgotten, I attempt to understand how willful amnesia lies at the heart of these so-called memorial sites.

Schneider: A Family, a Company, or a Town?

Located in central eastern France, Le Creusot is renowned for its industrial past. The creation of this town, as well as its expansion over more than 150 years, was due to a family concern that organized the entire urban space around its factories. In 1836, the Schneiders became owners of a village (which then counted a mere 800 inhabitants) where they located what was to become one of the biggest factories in nineteenth-century Europe. For four generations—until 1960—the fate of this factory and therefore of the town (which at one point counted almost 15,000 workers out of 30,000 inhabitants) would be determined by this family. On

October 21, 1836, the Schneider brothers (Eugène and Adolphe) launched a company whose destiny was legally bound up with that of the family. Eugène Schneider explained that "the legal status of the company was chosen in order to create a family business" (quoted in De la Broise and Torres 1996, 22).

In Le Creusot, the development of the iron and steel industry was linked to the transformation of iron into finished goods: the company operated as an "integrated plant" where extraction was followed by the transformation of metals and the production of mechanical constructions. Through its ironworks and steelworks, the Schneider factories produced railway tracks, bridges, locomotives, and weapons. The originality of Schneider & Cie was the way in which its production system was organized. The Schneiders settled in the middle of nowhere and built everything—including schools and hospitals—from scratch. The central production unit was safeguarded by the organization and control of its external parameters: Schneider hospitals with Schneider maternity wards, Schneider schools, houses,

---

The modernity of culture condemns history to celebrate what it once was and therefore no longer is.

---

stadiums, and old people's homes—even the churches belonged to them! The Schneiders' omnipotence also took the shape of a series of monuments dotted around town: each family member had his own statue and a church named after him. The Schneiders moved into a castle in the center of town, which was surrounded by a seventy-nine-acre park overlooking the factories. They also controlled the local political scene. When the Schneiders themselves were not mayors or members of Parliament, those positions were filled by friends or people who worked for the Schneiders. Historians have defined this system as a form of "industrial paternalism." In the same way, Le Creusot could be described as a "factory-cum-town" because of the overlapping productive and urban spaces. But this expression does not do justice to the town's highly original identity. Le Creusot had no urban center; the center was occupied by the factories themselves. Around them, the town possessed a pluricentrality with the development of autonomous neighborhoods, which all had their own churches, schools, parks, and sports infrastructures. The Schneiders erected public buildings that connected the different neighborhoods (Frey 1986, 273). The Schneiders' housing policy enabled them to control local urbanism while allowing locals to become owner-occupiers. Does the name *Schneider* refer to a family, a company, or a town? In 1856, five thousand signatories of a petition called for the town to be renamed "Schneiderville."

The accidental death of the last ironmaster, Charles Schneider (who slipped on his yacht in Saint-Tropez), heralded the demise of this family capitalism. The absence of male heirs (Charles Schneider had two daughters, Dominique and Catherine) led to the breakup of the company's capital. Without a family member at the helm of the group, Le Creusot's industrial policy changed radically. In 1970, the new management decided to sell off the company's nonindustrial assets, which had been the cornerstone of the Schneiders' paternalism. The schools, houses, churches, and stadiums were all sold to the town overnight. The castle—which until then had been the Schneiders' official residence protected by a six-meter-high wall and guards in uniform—also became municipal property. The local press underlined the fact that "this architectural jewel with its surrounding gardens" was now "in the public domain!" History was being unveiled for the first time because this had always been a private space hidden away.

The local inhabitants inherited the Schneider dynasty's power base. Its sheer size caused acute embarrassment to the new owners. The town hall was reluctant to move into this highly charged symbol of industrial power. Henri Graffare, who was a member of the local authority team at the time, explained, "It never occurred to us that the factories would be separated from the castle. We had no plans what-soever; you can't do just anything with this sort of place. It was quite natural that we shouldn't know what to do with it" (personal interview, 1998). How could the local authority reconcile the history of this family power base with its new municipal dimension? After examining several projects, they decided to conserve the castle and turn it into a museum.

A Museum Project

The mayor chose not to put a local figure in charge of the project. Marcel Evrard, a museographer and art collector, thus became the first curator. Evrard was eager to involve politicians, industrialists, and trade unionists in the running of the museum, but as it turned out, nobody wished to move in or be associated with the staging of a chapter in history that was still being written at the time. Evrard also had to deal with another tricky problem. Charles Schneider's widow and daughters still lived in the castle and had no intention of leaving. After a whole year of negotiations, Marcel Evrard moved in and the Schneiders moved out.[2] But the castle was a residence not a gallery; its transformation into a museum began in 1972. Since Mme Schneider had taken the furniture and all her personal belong-ings with her, the new museum was left with nothing to exhibit and had to redefine its project. The impossibility of opening a conventional museum led to the emer-gence of a new type of museum that was dubbed "ecomuseum" (*écomusée*) in France. It would soon become the international symbol of a new form of community-based museography.

In 1970, Le Creusot redefined its administrative identity through the creation of the "Urban Community (Communauté Urbaine) of Creusot-Montceau-Les-Mines," a redrawing of territorial boundaries that brought together sixteen districts and some 120,000 inhabitants. The museum of Le Creusot would take this new administrative area as its frame of reference. Its remit, which was now far more comprehensive, was to accompany the economic and social transformation of the Communauté Urbaine. Hugues de Varine, the then director of the International Council of Museums (ICOM), who took part in the launch of the project at Evrard's request, explained, "We decided that it would be based on two things: the end of paternalism (how do you move from paternalism to modernity?) and the creation of an instrument that would assist the birth of the Communauté Urbaine" (personal interview, 1999). The museum would thus be a political instrument. Hugues de Varine, who belonged to the international movement of redefinition of the role and principles of museums, which flowered in the early 1970s, was one of the driving forces behind this local cultural policy (Desvallées 1994, 15-39).

The new museum was seen as a revolutionary weapon and as a means of development for the population: "To achieve this, we need a revolution at the museum. The museum must be decolonized culturally" (Varine [1969] quoted in Desvallées 1994, 58). The theme of decolonization, which was then very much in vogue, was extended to museums. In the context of a museum, the liberation of people meant the liberation of objects. The first stage of the revolution in Le Creusot was the extension of the museum to the entire Communauté Urbaine: "The building is replaced by the area which is that of a community" (Varine [1979] quoted in Desvallées 1994, 70). As early as 1973, Varine claimed that "the whole community forms a living museum with permanent visitors. In fact, there are no visitors in this museum, only inhabitants" (Varine 1973/1991, 37). Objects were recruited in similar fashion: "Any object, piece of furniture or building within the confines of the Communauté is the moral property of the museum—this new notion of 'cultural' property has nothing to do with that of 'legal' property" (Varine 1973/1991, 42). Through this "moral" abolition of private property, the local "population" became the nominal, theoretical owners of the museum. The revolution had to be embodied, fleshed out, and acted out: the population would thus be recruited to the cause by the museum's most fervent militants. These new converts formed the museum's local power base. Marcel Evrard (the museum's future curator) was more concerned with art than with politics. The museum project started distinguishing itself from an ordinary museum by taking industry as the object of its study and by confronting this world of labor with that of art (as a creative process and generator of social practices). The liberation of objects—through Evrard's aesthetics or Varine's politics—became an instrument of the liberation of humanity.

If the new museum was to be a means of revolution, a revolution had to take place in the museum. The project was presented as a museum of a radically new kind because of its revolutionary pretensions and its ambition to provide a framework of local and even national regeneration. But could it still be described as a museum? The verdict fell in May 1972. Varine and Evrard unveiled their project during a conference organized by the ICOM: "I explained that we wanted to create a territorial museum without collections" (Varine, personal interview, 1999). Jean Châtelain, the director of *Musées de France* (Museums of France) who attended this conference, soon gave his answer: "Jean Châtelain got a bit angry and told me that it couldn't be described as a museum if there were no collections" (Varine, personal interview, 1999). Since they were not allowed to use the word *museum*, the creators of the project turned to a new and radical form of museology that enabled them to move away from the traditional concept of museums and gave them a scientific guarantee. The impossible museum of Le Creusot was thus renamed an "ecomuseum"—a word coined in France in 1971 to describe the open-air ecological museums created in former farming areas transformed into nature reserves for tourists. The definition of these ecomuseums (which were not dependent on the Ministry of Culture but on the newly created Ministry of the Environment) was extremely vague, which enabled the museum of Le Creusot to join their ranks and become the Ecomuseum of the Communauté Urbaine of Creusot-Montceau-Les-Mines. This Ecomuseum was described as an open-air museum without walls or collections, which was built around the local population.

The new museology had no historical artifacts to put on display, but it found much better: talking objects.

The new museum of Le Creusot inaugurated the transformation of industrial history according to the rural model (nature reserves with their ecological ecomuseums). In this instance, the Communauté Urbaine stood in for the nature reserve, and its past was studied like nature in the other ecomuseums. The use of a discourse borrowed from the ecological heritage industry made it possible to hide the fact that Le Creusot was dealing with transforming industrial history into museum exhibits. This would never actually be said openly. The organizers of the museum claimed that they were talking about ecology and not the local industry.[3]

In the early 1970s, this local industry was in the process of being restructured following the dismantling of the paternalist system on which it had always been based, but nobody equated the birth of the Ecomuseum with the death of industry. The process of "cultural" reappropriation of history was to start with a visit of the former ironmasters' residence. Few people, however, dared to actually go in. Maurice Camus, who used to work at one of the Schneider plants, explained, "For us, the castle was the Schneiders', it was still haunted by their presence over four generations. In 1970 nobody wanted to go there, including me! It's hardly surprising when you think that it used to be protected by railings, guards and cannons aimed at the street. . . . It's not so much that we were scared, it's just that we'd been used to glancing at the castle quickly as we walked by when we were kids" (personal interview, 1999).

Pierre Balland, a former metal worker at a Schneider plant, explained how the park and its trees still bore the stigma of the employers' presence: "Eugène Schneider was a real tyrant. He used to put marks on the branches of the trees that he wanted to cut. But nobody was allowed to touch them, it was *his* park. Although none of this had anything to do with industry. This is why the locals—the true *Creusotins*—were scared stiff to go into the bosses' castle" (personal interview, 1998).

Considering these circumstances, it is hardly surprising that one of the very first exhibitions (the third that ran from July to November 1973) was based on the theme of "Trees: From Prehistoric to Modern Times." Before turning the castle into a permanent museum, a few temporary exhibitions were held to encourage the locals to transcend their fear of the castle. The history of trees was such a pretext. The inhabitants were invited to discover a park that just happened to be that of the Schneiders' castle. The trees were labeled to identify them. A room, on the first floor of the castle, was devoted to the presentation of the different varieties of trees. A local paper, *Le Progrès*, was thus able to explain that "the park is ideally-suited to this kind of presentation" (July 13, 1973). Every effort was made to turn the former ironmasters' private residence into an ordinary dwelling. *Le Bien Public*, another local paper, wrote—without a trace of irony—that "the park surrounding the castle is an ideal introduction to an exhibition devoted to trees" (August 14-15, 1973). Nobody wanted to acknowledge that the exhibition marked the inauguration of the museum. Among the exhibits, you could find the "Schneiders' tree of Life"—the family tree of the dynasty that used to live in the castle. Jean-Jacques Badet, who belonged to the Ecomuseum, noticed that "some people were more attracted by the castle itself than by the exhibitions. They asked where the furniture was, what the bedrooms looked like" (personal interview, 1999).

The development of the Ecomuseum was based on substituting the preservation of nature for that of industry. Marcel Evrard stated, "We never really took ourselves as an ecomuseum" (personal interview, 1999). Ecology was used as an excuse for a form of genre-bending museography, which led to a great deal of confusion. A member of the Ecomuseum explains that "there was a permanent crisis going on. We devoted endless meetings trying to define what the museum stood for. What did 'Eco' mean? We faced a permanent identity crisis" (personal interview, 1999).

From the Impossible Museum to the Ecomuseum

The fact that it was well-nigh impossible to create a conventional museum in Le Creusot was made up for by a series of "pretext actions" as the Ecomuseum management called them. These exhibitions (like the aforementioned one devoted to trees) were held throughout the Communauté Urbaine. The organizers of the Ecomuseum were denied the traditional working methods and even the status of an ordinary museum, but they responded with creative initiatives. Nothing was fixed, at first, since the museum was almost totally devoid of objects. Instead of collecting objects, the Ecomuseum collected the people who were likely to bring relevant artifacts and talk about them. The inhabitants of Le Creusot took part in the creation of their own museography. Between 1973 and 1975, exhibitions were held throughout the Communauté Urbaine. Gradually, "satellite" museums were created in every one of the sixteen districts. The empty castle and the Le Creusot site in general were used to chronicle the activities of this devolved museum. In 1974, a permanent exhibition was inaugurated at the castle, telling the story of the entire region. The exhibition stood in for the absent family without ever mentioning its members or factories.

The Ecomuseum, this museum without walls, was in a rather contradictory position: the castle was presented as part of the heritage industry as it used to be the Schneiders' residence, but the plants that the family once ran were still working. Le Creusot was exhibiting its factories as a sign of a past that was still alive. The popularity of the Ecomuseum was due, in part, to the numerous meeting opportunities it offered. Visitors were able to discover what was about to disappear. Short of a conventional exhibition on local industry, you could catch the live show by visiting the town and the factories that had not yet been closed down. Besides trying to involve the local population in its activities, the Ecomuseum quickly started to express its opposition to industrial paternalism. The Ecomuseum became famous for criticizing the industrial world. The various events it organized (exhibitions, international conferences, publications, research programs, and visits) were perceived as revolutionary. Le Creusot became a magnet for academics and artists. A comprehensive list of all these visitors would include several hundred names. Le Creusot became a fashionable place to hold cultural or political meetings and to be seen. As museologist Kenneth Hudson would later put it, the Ecomuseum became a "religion" with "its prophets, martyrs and reforms" (Hudson 1992, 27), adding that "museologists the world over started making a pilgrimage to Le Creusot" (Hudson 1996, 61).

Marcel Evrard's charisma, combined with his talent for mobilizing and forming efficient research teams, enabled the Ecomuseum to become a reference point in the world of museums. Academics saw the town as a history book and the local workers as exhibits. The new museology had no historical artifacts to put on display, but it found much better: talking objects. Evrard's team members also became the objects of their own studies to the point of displaying themselves as exhibits. All those who were involved in the daily running of the Ecomuseum, and who were exhibited at conferences or in the offices, gradually became actors in their own plays. This is how history came to repeat itself. According to one of his employees, Marcel Evrard "started reproducing the very paternalism he had been studying in social movements." The spectacle of the downfall of paternalism was staged at the castle, but the Schneider trial proved so successful that it led, paradoxically, to its rebirth. As another employee confided, "Evrard was able to unite all the different strands of opposition to paternalism, but paradoxically enough he also created a very paternalistic structure" (personal interview, 1999).

Between 1983 and 1984, the conflict between Evrard, the new symbol of cultural paternalism, and his employees reached its climax. The government had no other option but to intervene. The choice was simple: either Evrard left or the Ecomuseum would have to disappear. The Ministry of Culture finally decided that Evrard had to go and that the Ecomuseum would become a more conventional type of museum. The fate of the local industry closely followed that of the museum: the Schneider factories went bankrupt and closed down the same year; paternalism and its factories disappeared at the same time as the Ecomuseum. This is hardly

Museums tell the story, and so,
the past can become a memory.

surprising given that the Ecomuseum was created to accompany the disappearance of the town's industry by transforming the downfall of paternalism into a spectacle. The Ecomuseum became a countercultural model at a time when politicians were looking for a way to make up for the decline of industry.

After 1985, a whole new story began. Le Creusot now really belonged to history and a museum was needed to store it away. The impossible museum of the 1970s began its metamorphosis. The reform of the Ecomuseum involved turning the castle into an ordinary museum. A few years later, in 1990, the idea of putting on a Schneider exhibition was floated. Displaying the deceased had always been on the agenda, but it was impossible without a corpse or any objects to show off. The new curator of the museum organized the exhibition in collaboration with Charles Schneider's daughter. The objects that had left the castle at the beginning of the 1970s were returned to where they belonged. They were arranged and displayed by Dominique Schneider, the new exhibition designer.[4]

There were 27,400 visitors out of a total population of 28,900 inhabitants. As if to pay a final tribute to history, the museum was visited by the equivalent of the town's entire population! This marked the end of a long wait: the return of the Schneiders and their belongings to Le Creusot. That twenty-five years had to pass before an exhibition devoted to the Schneider family could be organized is highly significant. The Schneiders had become exhibits in a museum—objects symbolizing a past history that could now be disposed of. Museums tell the story, and so, the past can become a memory. The passing of a generation was therefore necessary before history could select the objects it wanted to exhibit for all eternity. The museum played an important part in the mourning process, which followed the demise of the local industry. Today, this funeral rite is complete. I became aware of this when I decided to follow visitors around the museum—to analyze their behavior—and had to wait for more than two hours before anybody showed up. This may be the museum's real success: it has succeeded in becoming useless and deserted. The museum ended up being abandoned in turn, leaving only the objects behind as sole keepers of the remains of history.

From Exhibited Memory
to Forgotten History

The theaters of memory are laid out like exhumation tables, and the operation of the heritage industry consists in preserving the leftovers that cannot be sacrificed. The burial of Le Creusot's industry took almost thirty years. The museum accompanied the dismantling of the paternalist production system. The museum, located in the ironmasters' former residence (the château de la Verrerie), became the object of this story. The rise and fall of the Schneiders' local paternalism was reenacted in this living museum, which attracted scores of artists and researchers. Once this story had been told—once it was truly over—the objects of bygone days (belonging to the Schneiders) returned to the château, which turned into a run-of-the-mill museum. The cultural revolution that took place at the museum of Le Creusot constantly reenacted past social struggles. While waiting for the return of the Schneiders' objects, the impossible museum of local class war kept looking for its own.

Cultural inexorability takes place within a ritual that transforms leftovers into garbage. Class war became a warehouse, a garbage dump for dead objects and stories. The "museum rites" were supposed to keep the living alive. In a first stage, the actors of this story were called upon as witnesses before becoming the spectators of their own exhibition. The time devoted to exhibiting the past masked the time it took to forget it. Memories turn into images and can be contemplated like curios, cultural—perhaps even touristic—daydreams. If museum culture originates in this fascination with loss, it also serves as a consolation. It is this culture that leads to the appeasement of a restored memory. But can the memory of Le Creusot be appeased?

As Paul Ricœur showed (2000), there is a tension in the link between memory and history. Memory, like museums, is not history regained and authenticated. Quite the contrary, in fact, memory contains its "other," a space filled with uncertainty that is oblivion. One can only remember because one has first forgotten: every memory implies a prior process of forgetting. The difference between a pacified memory and one that has been falsified lies at the heart of this problem. Beyond this lies the ethical and political issue of defining what characterizes a fair recollection or a fair memory: how does a society treat its past?

The work of memory takes place within different modes of history (*régimes d'historicité*), to use François Hartog's (2003) expression. In museums, memories are transformed into exhibited objects. The historian Philippe Braunstein (2003, 10) wondered if human suffering could really be an object of historical study: this question should be extended to the sphere of museums. What types of museums and what types of objects can tell the story of the past? Whether history can be reduced to an object or not, one must recognize that the historiographic process transforms absence into the past by separating experience from history. This process lies at the heart of a human science that turns history into a tale of separation and even of death (De Certeau 1975/2002, 138-42). From this point of view, the history of the Ecomuseum of Le Creusot is the tale of the impossible return of the past, of the quest for an object that can neither be found nor exhibited: class war. The impossibility of reducing human experience to an object is the mirror image of the impossible reconciliation of discordant times: how can one say that the past is indeed past if one has not yet mourned its passing?

According to Hannah Arendt (1968/1993) and François Hartog (2003), this unspeakable threshold marks the birth of history. Both consider the same extract from Homer's *Odyssey* as a poetic paradigm of the first historical tale. When Ulysses asks the poet Demodocos to sing the story of the Trojan war and its hero, Ulysses "finds himself in the testing position of having to listen to his exploits recounted in the third person" (Hartog 2003, 63). How does Ulysses react upon becoming the witness of his own story? He breaks down and cries. His tears are not due to the fear of death but to this experience of alienation that we could call the discovery of historicity. How does one apprehend one's own past in its past dimension? Ulysses's response—his incapacity to respond—are symbolized by his tears. The tears of Ulysses are the tears of memory. His return is the utopian voyage that endows the present with meaning.

Notes

1. Written by Augustine Fouillée under the pseudonym G. Bruno (a reference to the Italian philosopher Giordano Bruno), *Le Tour de France par Deux Enfants* (1877/1970) tells the tale of two orphaned brothers who travel throughout France. Subtitled *Devoir et Patrie* (duty and homeland), it was used for many years as an instrument of Republican propaganda.

2. Marcel Evrard sent many letters (between February 12, 1971, and January 20, 1972) to the mayor of Le Creusot asking to "invite" Madame Schneider to leave the castle with her furniture (Ecomuseum's archives).

3. Hugues de Varine claimed that "if we had been recognized as a museum we would never have called ourselves an ecomuseum. I was forced to compile a totally fictitious dossier for the Ministry of Environment justifying the ecological dimension of the project of Le Creusot" (personal interview, 1999).

4. The exhibition was first held at the Musée d'Orsay, from February 27 to May 21, 1995; it then transferred to the Ecomuseum of Le Creusot (June 23 to November 30, 1995). It is now a permanent exhibition at Le Creusot.

References

Arendt, Hannah. 1968/1993. *Between past and future: Eight exercises in political thought*. New York: Penguin Books.

Braunstein, Philippe. 2003. *Travail et entreprise au Moyen Âge*. Brussels: De Boeck.

Bruno, G. 1877/1970. *Le Tour de France par deux enfants*. Paris: Belin.

Catalogue de l'exposition. 1995. *Les Schneider, Le Creusot: Une famille, une entreprise, une ville (1836-1960)*. Paris: Fayard.

Debary, Octave. 2002a. *La fin du Creusot ou l'art d'accommoder les restes*. Paris: Comité des Travaux Historiques et Scientifiques, Ministère de la Recherche.

———. 2002b. *Restes d'une visite au musée*. Text and photographs. Published with the support of the Musée d'Ethnographie of Neuchâtel (Switzerland) and the Maison des Sciences de l'Homme (Paris).

De Certeau, Michel. 1975/2002. *L'écriture de l'histoire*. Paris: Gallimard.

De la Broise, Tristan, and François Torres. 1996. *Schneider, l'Histoire en force*. Paris: Monza.

Desvallées, André, ed. 1994. *Vagues, une anthologie de la nouvelle muséologie*. Vol. 2. Mâcon, France: Mnes.

Frey, Jean-Pierre. 1986. *La ville industrielle et ses urbanités, La distinction ouvriers-employés. Le Creusot 1870-1930*. Brussels: Mardaga.

Hartog, François. 2003. *Régimes d'historicité, Présentisme et expériences du temps*. Paris: Le Seuil.

Hudson, Kenneth. 1992. The dream and the reality. *Museums journal* 175:27-31.

———. 1996. Presentation in *From Burgundy to Bergslagen—The growth and development of the Ecomuseum concept during 25 years*. Papers presented at the international seminar, Riksutställningar, Stockholm, in collaboration with Bergslagens ekomuseum, dac.

Nora, Pierre. 1996. From *lieux de mémoire* to realms of memory. In *Rethinking the French past: Realms of memory*, edited by P. Nora. New York: Columbia University Press.

Ricœur, Paul. 2000. *La mémoire, l'histoire, l'oubli*. Paris: Le Seuil.

Varine, Hugues. 1973/1991. *L'initiative communautaire*. Mâcon, France: Mnes.

Paris Plage: "The City Is Ours"

In 2003, for the second year running, the Paris municipality entrusted a young theater designer with the transformation of one stretch of the banks of the Seine River—normally congested with heavy traffic—into an open space evocative of the seaside. Paris in August is therefore Paris by the seaside. The objective of our study is to examine the entire operation, from the moment the political decision was taken by the municipality to the many and varied activities of all those who participated. Through this study, we attempt to highlight the different forms of material and symbolic (re)creation of Paris being undertaken today. We show that in a situation such as this, a reflection on the fieldwork undertaken and the production of ethnographic knowledge is in fact the key factor in the analysis.

Keywords: Paris; public space; urban performance; political event; social relationships; anthropological description

By
MICHÈLE
DE LA PRADELLE
and
EMMANUELLE
LALLEMENT

In response to Elijah Anderson's invitation, we conducted an investigation of an event that was special for Parisians and made the headlines in France and elsewhere last summer: *Paris Plage*, which means Paris Beach. This was an appropriate site to show the social processes at work in the making of a contemporary city that

Michèle de La Pradelle, anthropologist, is directeur d'études at Ecole des Hautes Etudes en Sciences Sociales of Paris. Her research area covers the city (the making of urban worlds), the market exchanges, and the social relations to objects. She initiated the "Anthropology of the city, of exchanges and of objects research group." She published many research works on these subjects, in particular Les vendredis de Carpentras *(Faire son marché en Provence ou ailleurs [Price of the French Academy], Fayard, 1997). This book will be published by the University of Chicago Press.*

Emmanuelle Lallement is an assistant professor at the University of Paris 4–Sorbonne. As an anthropologist, she specialized in the field of exchanges and trading spaces and completed a Ph.D. thesis on the Parisian neighborhood Barbès and the representation of multiculturalism in the city at the Ecole des Hautes Etudes en Sciences Sociales in Paris. She is a member of the "Anthropology of the city, of exchanges and of objects research team."

DOI: 10.1177/0002716204267195

involve the interplay of many actors, those who conceive and manage the city as well as those who live there.

What is Paris Plage? In the heart of Paris, below the quays of the Seine, listed as part of the world heritage by the UNESCO, between the Pont des Arts bridge and Île St. Louis, runs the Georges Pompidou expressway, the main artery crossing Paris from east to west since 1967, which is usually overrun with cars. Between July 20 and August 17, 2003, for the second consecutive year, it was closed to traffic. In the 30-foot-wide road thus freed, the concrete and security rails were replaced by plants (mostly palm trees), parasols, hammocks, deckchairs, two sandy "beaches" along with two lawns, beach cabins, refreshment stands, restaurants, and several activity centers: a "pétanque" area (this is the French version of *bocce*), a climbing wall, a roller-skating track, and a trampoline. Passersby strolled down an asphalt central path. On the pavement next to the water, people in various states of undress relaxed on deckchairs. Others, mostly in bathing suits, lay on towels spread out on the sand between the road and the quay wall. On every bridge from the Pont des Arts at the Louvre end to the Sully bridge toward Bastille, people lean over to observe the scene.

What may seem to be a promenade or a sort of seaside beachfront, the kind found in French resorts from Deauville to Nice, is actually a completely artificial operation, resulting from the actions of a great many actors with different abilities and with a variety of interests.

First of all, Paris Plage is a political act, conceived and implemented by the new socialist Mayor Bertrand Delanoë and his public relations officers, intended to symbolize his politics.

The presentation of Paris Plage to the press was therefore a big event. We were there. In the city hall reception rooms, with their red velvet, gilded chairs, and Baccarat crystal chandeliers, Delanoë, surrounded by the entire municipal team, set the tone: "My goal is to give the riverside back to Parisians. It's a feasible dream. Paris Plage will be a nice hangout at which people, with their differences, will mingle. It is a philosophy of the city, a poetic time for sharing and brotherhood." Ridding the riverside expressway of traffic made it look like a seaside, thus "giving it back to people out for a stroll, a bike ride, or roller skating." It was open to all Parisians and, more generally, to "Franciliens"—residents of the greater Paris metropolitan area—people from the poorer suburbs "who never leave on vacation," as well as to tourists "in a popular, festive, civic-minded and convivial spirit." In its press release, city hall announced that Paris Plage would offer the pleasures of a free vacation and enable everyone "to take possession of public space and to experience city life differently." It also touted the across-the-board involvement in the project, including public service agencies and private companies whose participation was presented not so much as a form of sponsorship as support for the implementation of a novel urban policy that should be everyone's business.

The socialist mayor, Bertrand Delanoë, was elected in 2001 following an electoral campaign sometimes called "the battle of Paris." The key phrase in his platform was "to give Paris back to the Parisians," meaning that Paris would no longer be appropriated by the privileged but would belong to everyone. Delanoë's Paris is embodied both in great festive get-togethers and in the values of neighborhood life, with the city seen as a collection of villages. The administration's most outstanding operation might be the construction of 120 kilometers of bicycle paths. Or it might be Paris Plage.

Paris Plage is also the work of a scenography agency, which specializes in staging public events. After all, how do you make a Paris Plage? Delanoë gave the project to a team composed of young scenographers and two sociologists, who had proven their worth in creating the twenty-first-century pavilion at the Hanover World Fair in 2000. Jean-Christophe Choblet, who heads the group, explained, "The idea is to give new life to public places. In this case we will turn the banks of the Seine into a public place."

The key phrase in [the mayor's] platform was "to give Paris back to the Parisians," meaning that Paris would no longer be appropriated by the privileged but would belong to everyone.

The two sociologists of the team, Roger Perrinjacquet and Ursula Paravicini, are very committed to what present-day France calls urban renewal. They became the theoreticians of the operation, following their evaluation of its first edition in 2001. Starting from the observation that the density of social life, commerce, and entertainment is declining in modern European cities (Paris is increasingly less populated because its high real estate prices force the middle classes out to the suburbs), they called for a rehabilitation of urban life around the idea of a cross-cultural society, the appropriation of collective space by residents, and women's access to public space. This gave Paris Plage its conceptual framework.

Choblet provided a shape for this "alternative use of the city." He went to work "to serve an idea," as he put it, and took that idea literally. "After a week of seclusion in southern France, we came up with a very simple project. We took a beach: what are its symbols? Some ordinary things: sun, sand, wind, people in bathing suits, vacationing," said Choblet. His idea was to "tell a story"—the story of the beach—so that the project would not be confused with a riverside improvement operation. With this in mind, he wrote a storyboard, as if for a film. He said he was staging a theatrical event by "setting up dramas" and by creating an atmosphere, with three thousand tons of sand, rolls of sod, dozens of potted Mediterranean plants, blue and white striped beach cabins, teak furniture, and large parasols, to "bring out attitudes."

The graphic designers and scenographers designed a series of sequences, proposals for such activities as sports, play, festivities, and relaxation. Each element was conceived independently ("every piece of furniture was designed for the circumstance"). Still, the idea was to create an organized whole, to make the three kilometers of Paris Plage a coherent, unified space. All these facilities, side by side, were meant to reflect a vacation day by the seaside. People would follow the movement and intensity of the sun as they strolled around the area: early morning taï chi at the Pont des Arts, sunbathing and beach games at the Pont Notre Dame, refreshments and picnics at noon near city hall, a nap across from Île St. Louis, and a drink at the open-air cafe in the evening at Sully Morland. They would distribute a map all around town to guide visitors, which would also be reproduced on large panels at entrances to the quays.

The promoters also produced a logo. This design, found everywhere from the signposts along the path to the T-shirts, caps, and other souvenirs created for the occasion, publicized Paris Plage and turned it into an event almost like the 1998 World Championship. But these various setups and elements were also unified by the color blue (blue banners on the lampposts illuminated the Seine at night, along with the blue beach cabins and deckchairs), as well as the pervasive presence of plants and banners along the path, fluttering in the wind blowing along the Seine.

If we take the planners' statements seriously, they did not confine themselves to organizing a functional space, in which users relax, and some leisure-time activities. They were conceiving and creating a "project." They intended to make a work, an œuvre, not a work of art but certainly an original creation. And they hired a lawyer and actively worked to gain recognition and protection of Paris Plage as a collective work.

But Paris Plage was also the result of the actions of the visitors, without whom it would be a mere stage set. And people—three million this year—really did go there and thus brought Paris Plage into existence, from dawn to dark, despite the heat spell, for its duration. The banks of the Seine were visited by people of all ages and all social types: Parisians, suburbanites, visitors from the provinces, vacationing foreigners. Parisians tended to meet there on evenings, around a picnic, while young people went roller skating, women with children stayed near the sandbox, and office workers met over their sandwiches at noon; yet people from these various groups intermingled (Figure 1). At the Monoprix refreshment stand, one might find a couple of young actors, a woman working at the town hall of Montigny-les-Cormeilles (one of the last suburbs to have kept its communist mayor) with her son who wanted to try the climbing wall, tourists from New York who had read about the event in the press, and saleswomen from the nearby Samaritaine department store, all at the same table.

Thus, this place in the middle of Paris gave a vision of an unusual diversity, otherwise found only in such places as the subway or at events like the street music festival. Businessmen in three-piece suits rushing from one appointment to

FIGURE 1
PICNIC BY NIGHT

another would cross paths with a handful of kids from the suburbs sauntering along in small groups "to watch the girls in bathing suits"; elderly people sitting on the sides, as they would in a park, commenting on everything; and whole families settling on the sand with their picnic baskets, towels, and beach toys.

Everyone did as he or she liked, taking advantage of the many activities available and the different types of movement allowed. Joggers, roller skaters, and bicycle riders wove in and out among the strollers. People wandered idly. Some loitered around the message board, then left to look for some shade toward Sully, where the willows bend over the Seine, or under the tunnel at *Pont d'Arcole*, slowing down for a minute at Pont Marie to listen to an opera singer, who had come to test the acoustics of the vault and who was soon replaced by a rap group. Mothers left their children with the youth club monitor and settled down in a deck chair. Children built sandcastles under the watchful eye of a group leader (Figure 2). Some kids patiently waited their turn at the climbing wall, a mock rock set up along the wall of the quay. Napping was legitimate at the Plage, and so was the writing workshop. You could also choose between volleyball and reading a paperback from the little lending library. In fact, people browsed, wandering from workshop to workshop, most simply passing by, looking around more or less attentively.

FIGURE 2
CHILDREN'S SANDCASTLE CONTEST

Clearly, one could go to Paris Plage to do all these things, but most of all, people went there "to have a look": to see whether things really were the way the newspapers said, whether the pictures were telling the truth, whether the spectacle announced was really happening. Cognition comes before recognition in this sort of production. The pleasure here was that of verification, of tasting the joys of recognition (Augé 1997, 24), of attending a spectacle, and of being part of it. What made the evening picnic so attractive was that one could tranquilly check out what was happening around one's own little territory, watching the neighbors and sauntering passersby. Everyone gladly participated, smiling into the cameras of amateur photographers and ostentatiously holding up a bottle of Bordeaux or a birthday cake. The spectacle offered the tourists on the *bateaux Mouche* boats sailing along the Seine a new, a more unusual show than the facades of the homes on Île St. Louis that light up as they go by.

People also became part of the event, like everyone who crossed the Pont Neuf wrapped up by Christo[1] in 1985, they were well aware that they had no more responsibility in the affair than Fabrice at Waterloo, but knowing how important his work was in the history of art, they could tell themselves that they had been eyewitnesses to a "historic" moment (Millet 1997). Being there, even fleetingly, just to take a look, was what made Paris Plage exist, and people knew it. Everyone knew it would be a failure if only a few onlookers straggled by. And, in fact, what you heard everywhere was the expression "the human tidal wave." "I came for the first Sunday, when it opened, you couldn't even move. I gave up," explained Marine, a young woman who preferred to go there on weekdays for bike rides. People reveled in the idea that finding a hammock was a feat: "If you move ever so slightly, people come running, like when they're looking for a parking spot," said Gaël jokingly, an off-and-on actor come to spend the day writing the dialogues of her latest play in the shade of a willow.

Participating in Paris Plage also meant commenting on it. The operation existed through discourse about it—contained in official speeches and the mass media—the discourse of those who resist as well as of the enthusiasts, of people who were there and those who were not. Whether they came to play pétanque or just to see what was up, visitors all participated in at least one activity, at some point: talking about what was happening. People constantly measured the phenomenon and assessed the situation. "They thought of everything, even the drinking fountain"; "They brought in more sand than last year"; "The planning is very good, it's very well organized"; "They've put in more deck chairs." When we questioned people, but not only then, the main subject of conversation was Paris Plage. Everyone had something to say, even if they occasionally expressed reservations, like Sophie, who said, "The sceno[graphy] is really poor, there are holes, empty places along the path. And that pseudo-Roman walk with its oleanders and potted phoenixes, really, it looks like a big flower shop." Of all the activities that made up Paris Plage, commenting was surely the most widespread. Some people never put on a bathing suit, but everyone expressed an opinion. Some judged the quality of the services, others became connoisseurs, comparing this year to the previous edition, making comparisons with other recreational facilities (parks or vacation places), or assessing the aesthetics. Delphine, a business school student, had made a date with a friend who was doing an internship in a production company there. They were about to lunch together—she had her salad and green apple, he had his ham sandwich and chocolate éclair. They liked the crowd, they said, and the "popular feel" that made the operation successful, in their opinion. Others were like Lucie, a retiree, who admitted that she "has a problem with all that exposed flesh: old people, ugly people, just about anything," but at the same time, she was very interested in the restaurant menu, with its fish menu "for her" and its meat menu "for him": she thought that was "really neat."

In the last analysis, beyond the variety of practices and the impression of freedom conveyed by this diversity, were not people simply doing what they had been told to do? They walked on the asphalt and lay down on the sand. No one played pétanque outside of the place reserved for it or took the chairs out of their assigned area. People did not bring their own chairs, and they returned their books to the library. They not only obeyed the rules but also behaved well. Even the scenographers were amazed at how little damage the facilities suffered and by the near absence of thefts and aggressive behavior. And, like a leitmotif, they reminded us that women felt safe and did not hesitate to lie on the sand in their bathing suits.

In short, as designer Matali Crasset told us, commenting an interview she had given to *Zurban*, a cultural magazine, as we picnicked at Paris Plage: "The visitors understand the message, so they react by doing it: sunbathing, reading. It's incredible! A pinch of sand, two pieces of wood, and people start playing pétanque." The impression of obedient, civic-minded participation is even more striking since the police were quite discrete and there were no obvious forms of control, which took the form here of lessons given by monitors, eager to share their know-how, and supervision by young facilitators who looked like everyone else.

Beyond the variety of practices and the impression of freedom conveyed by this diversity, were not people simply doing what they had been told to do? . . . They not only obeyed the rules but also behaved well.

If we take what people said and did at Paris Plage seriously, it is clear that they did what was expected of them, what had been planned. They treated the event as an organized attraction that provided a number of activities. Furthermore, they knew that it was a theatrical production. There was no simulacrum but rather a game, identified and accepted as such. Everyone saw it as the mayor's political move, as perhaps even a symbolic action, which was in fact his objective, as a small group of city hall employees, contemplating the scene during their break, said enthusiastically, "Ah, our mayor is great." Even those who belittled Paris Plage saw it as a political strategy. The Right said, "That's Delanoë amusing the folks," but some people on the Left also said, "Politically, that sort of demagogy is horrible."

In the end, it was a world where everything happened as planned. Paris Plage did become the public space that the project had hoped it would (de La Pradelle 1997, 2000). Through their various operations, the different actors made the quays not only an open, shared place for collective activities (Figure 3) but also a public space[2] since people not only coexisted and did the same things side by side but also acted "publicly": they treated each other as coparticipants in a public scene (Lallement 1999). If a public life of sorts came into existence, it was because Paris Plage was a fleeting event, allowing people to have different social relations from those governing ordinary life; because it took place on a site that usually belongs to no one in particular and has no social status; and because there was free access, so that people did not feel like consumers.

FIGURE 3
THE QUAYS DURING PARIS PLAGE

The emergence of such a social space requires one prerequisite. Paris Plage worked so well because everyone agreed on one goal: to divert the bank of the Seine from its original function for a definite period, by carrying on all these activities in a place usually filled with passing cars.

All the actors, from those in charge of the operation to those it was designed for, participated in the playful, slightly rebellious transfiguration of the space. The pleasure came from appearing to break the rules, and the efficiency of the entire scheme rested on an implicit, overall agreement to participate in this diversion and thus to produce a fleeting moment of social enchantment. The highway became a stage, as if in a theater. And on that stage, people played at "being at the beach."

Clearly, the sea was absent from this beach scene. In fact, no one was fooled. People knew they were not at the seaside, and no one would think of going swimming in the Seine or taking the subway in a bathing suit, any more than returning home draped in a simple pareo, as if one were in Saint Tropez (Urbain 1995). Paris has the Seine, not the sea. And the absence of the sea was, precisely, the prerequisite for Paris Plage; the efficiency of the operation rested on exactly that. Paris Plage was successful because everyone accepted the absence of this fundamental

The Paris Plage project worked so well because everyone agreed on one goal.

element, the sea. Had the sea actually been present, nothing would have worked. The reversal would have been impossible. With the sea present, Paris Plage really would have been a beach like any other beach, and people would simply have used it. Because the sea was not there, the project was not simply another urban development scheme, and the work of the scenographers created an artistic production and not a landscaped promenade. They could not just "cut and paste" an image of the beach. They copied nothing.[3] The beach they created was more than perfect. It had everything: hammocks and also deck chairs, lines of perfectly blue banners, and even sand. But the sand was so clean and fine that it had to come from a civil engineering company and not from a real beach or from the French coasts—so many of which are filthy as the result of oil spills. And the beach-resort scene was outrageously overstaged. Its designers' catchphrase was *sensory immersion*, again precisely because the sea was missing. The oversupply of elements meant to suggest seawater (atomizers, aquatic course, showers, as if for rinsing oneself after a swim) were there to create an atmosphere and to elicit sensations, but again, they certainly emphasized the sea's absence.

Because the sea was not there, people were not simply users or spectators but the main levers of the scheme, themselves the actors and authors of Paris Plage.

Everyone was participating in an event whose concept was precisely to make the absent sea be present. With the sea gone, the event became a performance. People were invited to play in a fictional beach, like a piece of performance art whose idea is to make a beach in a place that is not a beach, turning the spectators into per-formers (see Goldberg 2001).

We finally understood the logic involved when we looked at the way we did our fieldwork and saw how people reacted to us—as elsewhere, how accessed knowl-edge reveals the social processes at work. We were struck, throughout our investi-gation, by this: we wanted to take pictures of Paris Plage, to add to our field notes. We usually find it difficult, even uncomfortable, to photograph in the field. But in this case, everyone agreed to be photographed: families and couples, even close up, even when they were scantily dressed. We could not have done this on a real beach or in a Paris park. On the beach in Deauville, or in the Tuileries gardens, you are dealing with Monsieur and Madame Dupont or Durand, who are real people. At Paris Plage, you are seeing the actors of Paris Plage, a status that effectively puts each individual's identification between parentheses. So they are not photo-graphed as individuals but as "Paris Plagers."

So a beach scene is performed, in a place that cannot be the sea: we are in Paris. By creating something that cannot be in Paris—a beach—the city is brought into being, in a sublimated form, by conjuring up what, by definition, it cannot be. Paris Plage also functioned like some works of art, "machines for making the world visi-ble," which do not withdraw from it but "send us double-quick back into reality," as psychoanalyst Gérard Wacjman (1998) put it.

Paris Plage also seemed to act as an actualization—in this case, of the city. A mock beach in Paris sets up a special city, a new Paris that is not a simple juxtaposi-tion of neighborhoods and segregated spaces but a "good-natured, convivial" Paris: a city where "every place would belong to everyone." This is what its creators meant by "for the people." In this respect, it is important that Paris Plage happen in the heart of the city and in a neutral place.

Along the lines of "the city belongs to us," we can imagine that all sorts of places, even the most unexpected and unusual ones, might be taken over, hinting at the possibility of a Paris in which we would not be passive residents, spectators of a city as museum or scenery, but rather, we would be its artisans, treating it as raw mate-rial out of which we might fashion new social relations.[4]

Paris Plage was thus one of those places not devoted to culture but taken over by it in a deliberately ephemeral way, playing, for that reason, a central role in produc-ing a new Paris, a city about which people would talk endlessly: they would be its specialists, in a sense. With Paris Plage, where everyone photographed everyone, where people commented on what others were doing, and came "to see" what was going on, we had the beginnings of a city composed of sociologists and specialists of urban life. It was successful because it exhibited the possibility of a city authored by everyone. By that very fact, it created the means of its own transformation, even if just for one summer.

So thanks to the twofold absence that Paris Plage created—absence of the city and absence of the sea—the old May '68 refrain of "under the pavement, the beach" was replayed, along with a new 2003 tune, "under the sand, the city."

Notes

1. "Une façon d'innover est de jouer sur le paradoxe de la durée et de l'éphémère en transformant un monument en événement. Comme l'a souvent fait Christo, avec ses emballages. Soustrait à son invisibilité ordinaire et à la grisaille du temps historique, le monument 'emballé' regagne une visibilité et une brillante actualité, mais pour peu de temps" (Hartog 2003, 174).

2. About the production, by some different actors, of a public space, see de La Pradelle (2001).

3. About the concept of copy, see Deleuze (1968).

4. See the studies made by the group "Anthropology of the city, of exchanges and of objects" of Michèle de La Pradelle, Ecole des Hautes Etudes en Sciences Sociales, Paris. See also the works of Emmanuelle Lallement (2000, forthcoming) about the social relations in a popular and commercial neighborhood.

References

Augé, Marc. 1997. *L'impossible voyage: Le tourisme et ses images*. Paris: Rivages Poche/Petite Bibliothèque, Payot.

de La Pradelle, Michèle. 1997. *Les vendredis de Carpentras: Faire son marché en Provence ou ailleurs*. Paris: Fayard.

———. 2000. La ville des anthropologies. In *La ville et l'urbain, l'état des savoirs*, edited by Thierry Paquot. Paris: éditions La Découverte, collection L'état des savoirs.

———. 2001. Espaces publics, espaces marchands: Du marché forain au centre commercial. In *Réinventer le sens de la ville: Les espaces publics à l'heure globale*, edited by Cynthia Ghorra Gobin. Paris: L'Harmattan.

Deleuze, Gilles. 1968. *Difference et répétition*. Paris: PUF.

Goldberg, Rose Lee. 2001. *Performance art: From futurism to the present*. London: Thames and Hudson.

Hartog, François. 2003. *Régimes d'historicité: Présentisme et experiences du temps*. Paris: Editions du Seuil.

Lallement, Emmanuelle. 1999. *Au marché des différences Barbès ou la mise en scène d'une société multiculturelle: Ethnologie d'un espace marchand parisien*. Ph.D. dissertation in anthropology and ethnography, under the direction of Jean Bazin, Ecole des Hautes Etudes en Sciences Sociales, Paris.

———. 2000. Barbès: D'un quartier arabe à un marché de toutes les differences. In vol. 37 of *Annuaire de l'Afrique du Nord*. Paris: CNRS Editions.

———. Forthcoming. DeTati à Barbès: Au bonheur des differences. *Ethnologie Française*.

Millet, Catherine. 1997. *L'art contemporain*. Paris: Flammarion.

Urbain, Jean Didier. 1995. *Sur la plage*. Paris: Payot.

Wacjman, Gérard. 1998. *L'objet du siècle*. Paris: Verdier, collection Philia.

W. E. B.
Du Bois's
Sociology:
The
Philadelphia
Negro and
Social Science

By
TUKUFU ZUBERI

The author addresses how, as a scholar, W. E. B. Du Bois transcended disciplinary boundaries and genre by providing answers to questions of racial colonialism and enslavement, the role of theory in social change, and the role of race in the dehumanization of the African, to name only a few. Here, the author offers a critical review of Du Bois's application of sociology to the study of the African diaspora in America in *The Philadelphia Negro: A Social Study*. The article gives an overview of Du Bois's sociological research as historical, statistical, demographic, and cultural in nature—the type of research that, Du Bois demanded, must lead to social action.

Keywords: W. E. B. Du Bois; *The Philadelphia Negro;* African Americans; racism; sociology

I was going to study the facts, any and all facts, concerning the American Negro and his plight, and by measurement and comparison and research, work up to any valid generalizations which I could. I entered this primarily with the utilitarian object of reform and uplift; but nevertheless, I wanted to do the work with scientific accuracy. Thus, in my own sociology, because of firm belief in a changing racial group, I easily grasped the idea of a changing developing society rather than a fixed social structure.
— W. E. B. Du Bois, *The Autobiography of W. E. B. Du Bois* (1968)

As W. E. B. Du Bois notes, both race and society change, and thus, to study society is to study social change. To study race is to study racial change. My own work and life as a scholar—a sociologist—have always unfolded under the shadow of the work of W. E. Burghardt Du Bois. Like Du Bois, my work is an attempt to understand humanity, to make the world a better place, and to do so by fostering a better under-

Tukufu Zuberi is a professor of sociology at the University of Pennsylvania. He is the director of the Center for Africana Studies and appears on the PBS show History Detectives.

DOI: 10.1177/0002716204267535

standing of society. My writings have asked what does it mean to be human? What does it mean to be civilized? What does it mean to be different? I have attempted to address these questions in the context of the crisis of civilization, and in the process, I have had to come to critical terms with the work and research of Professor Du Bois. Du Bois's work elevated the conversation about civic life and institutions that maintain the lifestyle and psyche of everyday citizens. He elevated the conversation beyond the racial barbarism that marred such discussions during his life. He was, however, influenced by the prevailing prejudices of the racial context of his age and place in what might be called the crisis of modern European civilization in its most advanced form in the United States.

We have often been blessed with individuals who, by their personality, intelligence, and efforts to better our world, leave an indelible mark on each and every one of us. The restructuring of the color line has been distinguished by such persons: David Walker, Sojourner Truth, Harriet Tubman, Frederick Douglass, Martin Delany, John Brown, Alexander Crummell, Anna Julia Cooper, Marcus Garvey, Malcolm X, and Nelson Mandela.

In this distinguished company of activist scholars stands Du Bois. As a scholar, he transcended disciplinary boundaries and genre. His contributions to our understanding of the questions of racial colonialism, racial enslavement, the African question, the role of theory in social change, and the role of race in the dehumanization of the African and the diaspora population have been surpassed by few and serve as a model.

Du Bois challenged the world, the nation, universities, and scholars to set out on an academic and activist journey. At the end of the twentieth century, Du Bois's blueprint is as vital, as relevant, and as inspirational as it was at the start. In this article, I provide a critical review of Du Bois's application of sociology to the study of the African diaspora in America in *The Philadelphia Negro: A Social Study.*

Du Bois's sociology is historical, statistical, demographic, and cultural. In "The Study of the Negro Problems," published in 1898 in *The Annals of the American Academy of Political and Social Science*, Du Bois wrote,

> It is not *one* problem, but rather a plexus of social problems, some new, some old, some simple, some complex; and these problems have their one bond of unity in the act that they group themselves about those Africans whom two centuries of slave-trading brought into the land.

For Du Bois, "a social problem is ever a relation between conditions and action, and as conditions and actions vary and change from group to group from time to time and from place to place, so social problems change, develop and grow." Thus, he placed the study of the African diaspora in America into two categories: the study of African Americans as a social group and the study of their peculiar social environment. As Du Bois himself recognized, these two categories are difficult to separate in practice.

Du Bois rejected the eugenic and racist grand theorizing that dominated social research at the turn of the century. He advanced the need for statistical methods in social research; however, he entered this discussion by questioning social statistics. In discussing the credibility of the results of his study, he wrote the following:

> The best available methods of sociological research are at present so liable to inaccuracies that the careful student discloses the results of individual research with diffidence; he knows that they are liable to error from seemingly ineradicable faults of the statistical method. (Du Bois 1899, 2-3)

Here, Du Bois provides a rather astute description of social statistics at the turn of the twentieth century. *The Philadelphia Negro* is Du Bois's model application of the ideas he outlined in "The Study of the Negro Problems." He was a pioneer in the pursuit of using statistics in social science in the United States, especially during the formative years between 1894 and 1910. Originally published in 1899, *The Philadelphia Negro* was the first scientific study of race.

As Du Bois himself recognized, [the study of African Americans as a social group and the study of their peculiar social environment] are difficult to separate in practice.

For Du Bois, observations of human action were essential for understanding and changing society. Du Bois's sociological work shows clear signs of influence by Gustav von Schmoller and Adolph Wagner—Du Bois's German economic professors—and by the statistical work of Charles Booth, who studied the working class of London, England. Du Bois's method of social observation consequently was based heavily on statistics that he used to advocate social change. As a consequence, Du Bois's work is consistent with the perspectives of Adolphe Quetelet (the Belgian statistician who lived between 1796 and 1874) and Emile Durkheim (the early-twentieth-century French sociologist). Like Quetelet and Durkheim, Du Bois viewed groups as entities with collective traits that could be statistically described. Du Bois added to these methods his desire to advance the status of the African American community.

Du Bois's book "revealed the Negro group as a symptom, not a cause, as a striving, palpitating group, and not an inert, sick body of crime; as a long historic development and not a transient occurrence." And in his effort to combat the justifications for racial hierarchy that dominated discussions about society, he extended this research to other communities in Virginia and Georgia and to the United States as a nation. Between 1898 and 1904, the U.S. Department of Labor financed and published four other studies by Du Bois modeled after *The Philadelphia Negro*. In addition, Du Bois served as the chair of the sociology department at Atlanta University between 1897 and 1915, and during this period, he and his students and colleagues produced more than nineteen studies and reports of African American life. In one way or another, these studies were all modeled on *The Philadelphia Negro*.

Philadelphia had the largest northern concentration of African Americans—45,000—in a nineteenth-century, modern city. Unlike Charles Booth in London who had fifteen assistants, Du Bois worked alone and was not wealthy or part of the Settlement movement of his Hull House sponsors. The Philadelphia branch of the College Settlement Association, the driving force behind the effort to have Du Bois write the book, was a welfare organization with affiliations at the Wharton School of the University of Pennsylvania. The association wanted Du Bois's research to support its political reform agenda, which included its moral reforms. This arrangement put Du Bois in the position of reporting on Philadelphia's African community as an outside observer, to an outside agency with a preestablished political agenda. He was very much aware of his outside status, of the distance this intellectual orientation placed between him and the community, and of the tensions that accompanied that distance; however, he was not able to separate his analysis from the moral agenda of his benefactors.

He noted in *The Autobiography of W. E. B. Du Bois* (1968), "The colored people of Philadelphia received me with no open arms. They had a natural dislike to being studied like a strange species." The very nature of his investigation presented the objects of his study—the African community of Philadelphia—as a "strange species" from which he would gain information for the College Settlement Association. Yet the community did not fancy itself as an "other" in need of a great intellectual savior; indeed, there was an obvious tension between Du Bois and the city's Negro elite. In the end, Du Bois interpreted the community's aloof reception of him as an indication that he "did not know so much" about his "own people." "First of all I became painfully aware that merely being born in a group, does not necessarily make one possessed of complete knowledge concerning it. I had learned far more from Philadelphia Negroes than I had taught them concerning the Negro Problem." Yet he maintained that his book did serve a positive purpose.

Du Bois's community study focused on the social dynamics of the African American community of Philadelphia. Unlike Booth, his study centered on what might be done to understand and solve the community's social problems rather than on the examination of a social problem like poverty. Du Bois did study poverty, but African American poverty was not the object of his study. The object of Du Bois's study was the African American community of Philadelphia.

Usually, social scientists fail to reflect on how their values affect their research, but Du Bois considered these matters as he wrote about the significance of *The Philadelphia Negro*: "We must study, we must investigate, we must attempt to solve; and the utmost that the world can demand is, not lack of human interest and moral conviction, but rather the heart-quality of fairness, and an earnest desire for the truth despite its possible unpleasantness." In the tradition of most social science, Du Bois created and defined "those Africans whom two centuries of slave-trading brought into" Philadelphia.

Du Bois's analysis presented two pictures. In one view, the problems of African Americans resulted from enslavement and capitalism within the United States; in the other, the problems stemmed from African Americans' moral failings and include a lack of integration into the "greatest of the world's civilizations." Consistent with the College Settlement Association's agenda, Du Bois sought to explain the African Americans' plight from a moral perspective that accepted a peculiar and mainstream, or Eurocentric, view of civilization. He attributed this lack of integration to a lack of culture among African Americans and the lack of empathy on the part of white America. This lack of culture, he argued, resulted from racial exclusion. He suggested the need for more assimilation with European American traditions. He suggests that assimilation would lead the Philadelphia Negro to civilization and make him or her more acceptable to the white community.

By focusing on how Du Bois interpreted his results, we place his writing within a social context. Du Bois's legacy extended beyond the difficulties he encountered reconciling his cultural preoccupations with his statistical results. He confronted related dilemmas as he faced his findings, dilemmas having to do with the place and mission of an antiracist scholar primarily influenced by European traditions of scholarship and thinking. Du Bois bequeathed these dilemmas, best described as racial ambivalence, to the generations that followed him.

Unfortunately, the field of sociology did not appreciate Du Bois's model of investigation. *The Philadelphia Negro* was not seen as a theoretical text; at best, sociologists saw it as a historical example. Du Bois was never offered a professorial appointment in a major "mainstream" university department; the University of Pennsylvania grudgingly extended him the title of "assistant in sociology" for the duration of his study of the Seventh Ward.

Du Bois had shown the uniqueness of the African experience in the urban United States. He described the illogical nature and historic impact of racism and argued in an eloquent voice that it was a mistake to consider the problems of the African American population as parallel to those of European immigrants. However, these insights were in large part ignored by American sociologists. In the tradition of the Chicago School and its early, pre-1940s research on urban conditions in the United States, most scholars confounded race, in the sense of distinctions of color, with ethnicity, in the sense of immigrant status. They interpreted—and many continue to interpret—the urban plight of African Americans as comparable to the challenges European immigrants faced in adjusting to American life. For European newcomers, the problem—and, in a sense, the solution—could be summed up in the word *assimilation*. But assimilation was a solution to something quite different from the problems posed to a formerly enslaved population held in contempt and pity by Americans of European origin.

In fact, Du Bois argued that European immigration prevented the early advancement of the African American population in Philadelphia. Because of racial hierarchy, Du Bois observed, "No differences of social condition allowed any Negro to escape from the group, although such escape was continually the rule among Irish, Germans, and other whites." European immigrants could assimilate through economic advance, but the African American remained racially marginalized and segregated regardless of economic standing. This situation prevailed well into the 1940s and was observed by St. Clair Drake and Horace R. Cayton who noted that "upper-class Negroes do experience discrimination and race prejudice in the form of inconveniences, annoyances, and psychic wounding. Exclusive shops and restaurants discourage or refuse their patronage. They cannot buy homes in most of the better residential neighborhoods, and in others they can do so only after protest, violence, and court fights" (Drake and Cayton 1945/1993, 551).

[Du Bois] described the illogical nature and historic impact of racism and argued in an eloquent voice that it was a mistake to consider the problems of the African American population as parallel to those of European immigrants.

Du Bois's *The Philadelphia Negro* sought a balance between exploring the problems of a racial hierarchy and explaining the often-uncivilized behavior of the victims of this hierarchy. Although he saw structural and behavioral problems as related, Du Bois was often apologetic in his appreciation of the cultural and historical distinctiveness of the African American population. He shrouded his discussion of African American oppression with admonitions and moralizing about their behavior.

Du Bois found himself in a particular scholarly bind. The moralistic tone of *The Philadelphia Negro*, especially toward the behavior of working-class and lower-class African Americans, served to legitimate European American moral criteria. In so doing, it may have helped Du Bois get the ear of some European American scholars. But whether Du Bois consciously intended his moralizing as a tactic to gain such a hearing, it came at a cost.

Du Bois produced a mass of data, but his problem came in how he interpreted these data. And this problem continued to appear in other studies that depended on the collection and analysis of large data sets. Drake and Cayton's *Black Metropolis: A Study of Negro Life in a Northern City* (1945/1993) and Gunnar Myrdal's *An American Dilemma: The Negro Problem and Modern Democracy* (1969) are two of the most well-known examples.

Du Bois's dilemma is familiar to scholars' today. As a pioneer social scientist, he may have been among the first to discover that for African American intellectuals, participation in the academy restricts one's voice. Often, African American intellectuals conduct their research within an academy that marginalizes what they write and say. They are in some respects part of the larger academy yet remain separate and marginalized within it. This condition influences their intellectual production. Seeking to articulate a message that will help change the condition of African Americans, they write to an audience that is primarily composed of the "white world." The audience, demanding a certain type of language and viewing the world from a distinct Eurocentric position, becomes an obstacle to expression. For while African Americans and European Americans share space, time, and many aspects of culture, they share these things in a contested context, a context they describe in different voices. African American intellectuals are caught in the dilemma of needing to talk to two audiences—their own "people" and the academy—in these different voices at the same time.

Above all, to talk in the voice that is comfortable for the academic and public audiences, African American intellectuals tend to speak of themselves as different—as the "other." They study their people through the Euro-American eyes and with a Euro-American voice. Like Du Bois in *The Philadelphia Negro*, they speak in ways that demonstrate the dilemma of conducting research on race. African American intellectuals spend most of their time talking to their European American colleagues as these colleagues can offer legitimacy. But becoming immersed in this academic world and accepting it as the way to understand reality may blunt the impulse toward contributing to fundamental social change. Carter G. Woodson described the dynamic in his classic book *The Mis-Education of the Negro*:

> No systematic effort toward change has been possible, for, taught the same economics, history, philosophy, literature and religion which have established the present code of morals, the Negro's mind has been brought under the control of his oppressor. The problem of holding the Negro down, therefore, is easily solved. When you control a man's thinking you do not have to worry about his actions. You do not have to tell him not to stand here or go yonder. He will find his "proper place" and will stay in it. (Woodson 1993, xiii)

For Woodson, the prevailing prejudices of the racial context biased African American scholars and forced them to assume a moral position that could not foster positive change for African Americans. From Woodson's perspective, the contempt and pity expressed by the European American academy influenced the research of African American scholars who shared their European colleagues' "code of morals." African American scholars sought to find their, and their subjects', "proper place" within the social structure as it existed. In this context, the sociology of Du Bois was limited by the voice in which it was articulated. Du Bois discussed his findings through the Victorian morality of his day.

It may seem unusual to describe Du Bois in such terms; he did go on to become one of the premier African American activists of the twentieth century and an eloquent advocate of radical social change. However, even his radical perspectives were primarily influenced by the biases of the nineteenth-century European traditions. An African American savant, Du Bois confronted the paradox that the historical and social factors that racially oppressed his people were a "twice-told tale" that was growing old with his European American audience and patrons. Yet he was intellectually committed to presenting this tale to them in a language they understood. Even in that language, the book must have startled these readers, given the extent to which it broke with the racial and intellectual orthodoxies of its day. *The Philadelphia Negro* showed Du Bois as one of the first scholars to pursue issues of race, class, and social structure in the analysis of African American life. Because most scholars at the time accepted the tenets of white supremacy, Du Bois's antiracist assumptions contrasted strongly with mainstream sociological research and the views of the general European American public. In rejecting biological explanations of African American poverty and political powerlessness, the book emphasized the importance of historical, structural, and cultural factors. In its conclusion, Du Bois argued that protesting the impact of racism was essential to the African American's future, "but he must never forget that he protests because those things hinder his own efforts, and that those efforts are the key to his future." Du Bois's analysis provided a systematic exposition of African American political exclusion and economic marginalization.

It is, however, how Du Bois handled the issue of culture that makes his historical and structural interpretations problematic. Culture is not separate from everyday life or economic activity. On the contrary, culture is about these things. Culture comprises the imaginary world of what is seen as possible and the way in which we organize our social space and social relationships that dominate our everyday lives. Yet Du Bois judged African American cultural behavior in moral terms—and in terms of Eurocentric morals at that. This is not to suggest that he should have glorified crime among the poor. We might have learned more, however, if he had presented African American responses to racial oppression and capitalist society from a perspective sensitive to the oppressed—by contextualizing those responses, as he did later in his more Marxist text *Black Reconstruction in America* that was written in 1935. Instead, in *The Philadelphia Negro*, Du Bois viewed African American behavior from the lens of the elite class. In particular, he advocated the cultural behaviors of those African Americans who had most embraced the cultural values of the European "aristocracy." He revealed much about his expectations for this class in recording his dismay at its ambivalence toward the mass of African Americans:

> They teach the masses to a small extent, mingle with them but little, do not largely hire their labor. Instead then of social classes held together by strong ties of mutual interest we have in the case of the Negroes, classes who have much to keep them apart, and only community of blood and color prejudice to bind them together. If the Negroes were by themselves either a strong aristocratic system or a dictatorship would for the present prevail. With, however, democracy thus prematurely thrust upon them, the first impulse of the best, the wisest and richest is to segregate themselves from the mass. (Du Bois 1899, 317)

What is it that Du Bois would have had the elite Negroes of Philadelphia "teach the masses"? Du Bois assumed that the elite served the essential role of "buffering" the impact of living in a racially stratified society. He suggested that this class could provide an example to keep alive the perception of African American assimilation of European American family and employment norms. In his view, the elite's steady employment and family stability could serve as a norm for lower-class behavior. Yet the African American elite failed to play the role of a responsible leadership; in fact, it viewed the African American masses with the same contempt expressed by the European American population.

Du Bois's view of the elite as a buffer to racial hierarchy has been a consistent theme among major sociologists, from E. Franklin Frazier to William Julius Wilson. Both of these scholars echo Du Bois in looking to the African American middle class to provide guidance for the less well-off; they also echo his disappointment at that class's limitations in its appointed task. In his classic study, *Black Bourgeoisie: The Rise of a New Middle Class in the United States*, Frazier argued that

> because of its struggle to gain acceptance by whites, the black bourgeoisie has failed to play the role of a responsible elite in the Negro community. *Many individuals among the first generation of educated Negroes, who were the products of missionary education, had a sense of responsibility toward the Negro masses and identified themselves with the struggles of the masses to overcome the handicaps of ignorance and poverty.* Their influence over the masses was limited, to be sure—not, however, because of any lack of devotion on their part, but because of the control exercised by the white community. Nevertheless, they occupied a dignified position within the Negro community and were respected. (Frazier 1957, 193-94)

In this passage, Frazier maintained that African Americans had suffered a loss of the bonds that once held the community together. Wilson expresses a similar sense of loss regarding the "modern" African American middle class:

> Whereas today's black middle-class professionals no longer tend to live in ghetto neighborhoods and have moved increasingly into mainstream occupations outside the black community, the black middle-class professionals of the 1940s and 1950s (doctors, teachers, lawyers, social workers, ministers) lived in higher income neighborhoods of the ghetto and serviced the black community. (Wilson 1987, 7)

The irony here is important. Du Bois, Frazier, and Wilson alike view the disorder within the African American community as a breakdown in its moral order. Critical to their arguments is the notion of the moral decay of the poor, whose numbers are always rising, and the potential role of the African American middle class as a savior class. All three look back nostalgically to a golden age when this middle class is presumed to have played that role, maintaining the social ties that held the African American inner city together. Yet Frazier holds up as an example the very generation Du Bois scolded for failure to "teach the masses," and Wilson, in turn, praises the postwar middle class that Frazier found so wanting. The reader may be forgiven for wondering at the continuing pursuit of this elusive golden age of the African American middle class, particularly when one scholar's golden age is another's disappointing present. This, in turn, may lead one to question the assignment Du Bois, Frazier, and Wilson seem to have handed the middle class, namely, that it save the African American community from itself.

Du Bois's recipe for change in *The Philadelphia Negro* rested on a misguided hope. In the "Final Word" that concludes the book; he advocated inclusion for African Americans—an inclusion led by their middle class. "In their efforts for the uplifting of the Negro the people of Philadelphia must recognize the existence of the better class of Negroes and must gain their active aid and co-operation by generous and polite conduct." He did not, however, envision the need for a social transformation—for inclusion is not transformation. Surprisingly, like Booker T. Washington, Du Bois here offered a solution to the race problem that suggested that African Americans accept the behavioral norms and necessities of the status quo. This is an important aspect of Du Bois because although he observed the racial hierarchy of American society, his solution at this time did not go beyond the simple solution of assimilation.

African American intellectuals are caught in the dilemma of needing to talk to two audiences— their own "people" and the academy—in these different voices at the same time.

Like Washington, Du Bois called on African Americans to change themselves into an acceptable group within the confines of the normative structures that dominated American elite bourgeois culture. As subsequent history has shown, however, inclusion in that culture has not transformed its racist nature nor forestalled its legacy of racial conflict and capitalistic exploitation. In fact, African American elites, like those described in *The Philadelphia Negro*, have tended to hold the African American "masses" in contempt. Inclusion turned out to be an escape for the "aristocracy of the Negro," an escape that resulted not in acceptance but in a kind of invisibility. Du Bois's words of the 1890s still resonate today: "The colored people are seldom judged by their best classes, and often the very existence of classes among them is ignored."

Ultimately, the Du Bois of *The Philadelphia Negro* analyzed the structural and behavioral aspects of African American oppression from a Eurocentric perspective, arguing for an end to white racism within a cultural context where African Americans would become more "white." He held that white racism denied African Americans access to resources, political power, and the avenues to becoming culturally white: assimilation. Du Bois did not critique the "dominant morals and assumptions" of American society as such. Rather, he challenged the white racism that prevented full African American participation within the context of the existing social relations. He suggested that social inclusion was essential to improve the African American social status.

> If in the heyday of the greatest of the world's civilizations, it is possible for one people ruthlessly to steal another, to drag them helpless across the water, to enslave them, to debauch them, and then slowly to murder them by economic and social exclusion until they disappear from the face of the earth—if the consummation of such a crime be possible in the twentieth century, then our civilization is vain, and the republic is a mockery and a farce.

In the final analysis, *The Philadelphia Negro* sought no more than to remove the barriers to assimilation while maintaining the socioeconomic status quo. Du Bois suggested that the problem was African American access to the civilization not a change in that civilization.

I may disagree with Du Bois's ideas about how to solve the "Philadelphia Negro" problem. Du Bois's conclusions include a critique of racism; however, he does not adequately critique American society, a social order that a century after he began his study of the Seventh Ward, remains rooted in distinctions of race and class. Upon self-reflection, Du Bois himself noted that at this point in his intellectual development, his research agenda "was weak on its economic side." He argued, "The program ought to have been. . . . The Economic Development of the American Negro Slave; on this central thread all other subjects would have been strung." However, his Marxist critique was almost as narrow as his dreams of assimilation. Yet none can deny his intellectual vitality despite being on the margins of the academy, nor can we ignore his intellectual relevance within society. Du Bois not only suggested a course of research; he demanded that this research lead to social action. His cultural orientation may have been prudish and conservative, but his insurgent intellectual activities still challenge us to make our social science relevant to social transformation. And the reality of social transformation is captured only in our efforts to understand and create the future of civilization; we have already lived its past.

References

Drake, St. Clair, and Horace R. Cayton. 1945/1993. *Black metropolis: A study of Negro life in a northern city*. Chicago: University of Chicago Press.

Du Bois, W. E. B. 1898. The study of Negro problems. *The Annals of the American Academy of Political and Social Science* 11 (1): 1-23.

———. 1899. *The Philadelphia negro: A social study*. Philadelphia: University of Pennsylvania Press.

———. 1935. *Black reconstruction in America*. New York: Harcourt, Brace.

———. 1968. *The autobiography of W. E. B. Du Bois: A soliloquy on viewing my life from the last decades of its first century*. New York: International Publishers.

Frazier, E. Franklin. 1957. *Black bourgeoisie: The rise of a new middle class in the United States*. New York: Collier Books.

Myrdal, Gunnar. 1969. *An American Dilemma: The Negro problem and modern democracy*. New York: HarperCollins.

Wilson, William Julius. 1987. *The truly disadvantaged: The inner city, the underclass, and public policy*. Chicago: University of Chicago Press.

Woodson, Carter G. 1993. *The mis-education of the Negro*. Washington, DC: Associated Publishers.

Using the History of the Chicago Tradition of Sociology for Empirical Research

By
JEAN-MICHEL
CHAPOULIE

What use is literature about past research in social sciences to people carrying out empirical research in sociology? More generally, other than the celebration of academic ancestors, what is the point of a history of research in social sciences? How should we conceive this history if it is to be useful? This article develops the possible contributions that a nonpresentist history (following the model of *histoire à part entière* of Lucien Febvre) of the social sciences can make to research in these disciplines. The article analyzes the various obstacles that prevented, for more than fifty years, the introduction of the Chicago sociological tradition into French sociology and the changes that led, after 1980, to an increasing interest in an ethnographic approach in France.

Keywords: history of social sciences; Chicago tradition in sociology; conceptualization in social sciences

To understand the present, you have to get out of it.

—Emile Durkheim, *Année sociologique*
(1899, v; preface to vol. 2)

A *Chicago industry* (to paraphrase one of Henrika Kuklick's expressions)—a collection of publications of a more or less historical nature devoted to the sociology produced by the sociology department of the University of Chicago (Kuklick 1999)—began around 1970, with the new edition of Robert Faris's book *Chicago Sociology, 1920-1932* (1967/1970). Beginning in the 1980s, these publications became numerous in the English-speaking world and elsewhere as well. A reader published in 1997, which contains

Jean-Michel Chapoulie has done field research on secondary school professors (Les professeurs de l'enseignement secondaire: Un métier de classe moyenne, *Presses de la Maison des Sciences de l'Homme, 1987*), *historical research on the development of schooling in France since 1800* (Les collèges du peuple, *with J.-P. Briand, Editions du CNRS, 1992*), *and a historical book about Chicago sociology* (La tradition sociologique de Chicago, 1892-1961, *Éditions du Seuil, 2001*). *He is currently a professor of sociology at the University of Paris 1 (Panthéon Sorbonne).*

DOI: 10.1177/0002716204266686

forty-six articles—only a small fraction of the available accounts, analyses of a clearly historical intention, and varied reflections on the work of Chicago sociologists—provides us with a first idea of the scale of the literature:[1] thus, the expression *Chicago industry* is not out of place. I contributed an article to this literature in 1973, a second in 1984, and then several others (Chapoulie 1973, 1984). In 2001, I published a book about Chicago sociologists during the period 1892 to 1961 (Chapoulie 2001b).

What use is this literature to people carrying out empirical research in sociology? More generally, other than the celebration of academic ancestors, what is the point of a history of research in social sciences? How should we conceive this history if it is to be useful? The first two questions are put bluntly, but it is clear that a lot of sociological writing is intended less to be read than to contribute to the promotion of the author's career. In the following article, I will leave aside the institutional uses of literature on past sociological research and will concentrate on the possible contributions the history of the social sciences can make to research in these disciplines. I will begin with some examples borrowed from the descendants of the Chicago tradition in France and in the United States.

The Chicago Tradition

First, a word about the historical object I call the "Chicago tradition" in sociology. We know that a sociology department was opened in 1892 at the University of Chicago, the second to bear this name in an American university. It was not until 1918, with the publication of *The Polish Peasant in Europe and America*, that it became known as a department where important research was done. In the following years, the main model for sociological research in the United States was the work carried out in and around this department. After 1935, when Robert Park (who inspired most of this research) retired and left Chicago, the reputation of the department suffered somewhat, even though some of Park's former students, who had returned to teach at the university, did research and guided the work of another generation of students. These studies focused on the topics studied earlier, such as cities and ethnic-group relations, but also on such new themes as work and social movements. Between 1940 and 1955, a new generation of sociologists was thus trained. Some of their analyses became well known toward the end of the sixties, mainly those based on an ethnographic approach. As Andrew Abbott recently reminded us, the term *Chicago School*, applied to the research done between 1920 and 1935, is a construction of the 1950s. A new label, "Second Chicago School," has recently been coined for the work done between 1940 and 1955 (Abbott 1999; Fine 1955). The works we describe with these labels are not homogenous, and the relations between the three generations principally concerned—that of Thomas and Park; that of Hughes, Blumer, Wirth, and Franklin Frazier; that of Becker, Goffman, and Gusfield, to go through them quickly—are complex. It seems more apt to me to use the term *Chicago tradition*, which suggests that there are intellectual relations between the works of these different periods, than the term *Chi-*

cago School. It is empirically inexact to describe these works by referring to a school of thought built up around a few principles. What connects these works is only a kind of "family resemblance." What separates them is as interesting as what unites them. Remember that the researchers of the second and third generations were in contact with strong personalities who had almost nothing in common with the pragmatist current to which we can link Park and Blumer; I am thinking of William Ogburn for the second generation and Lloyd Warner for the third. It is the concrete historical object made up of these groups of researchers that I call the "Chicago tradition in sociology" or "Chicago sociology." One of the inheritances credited to Chicago sociology is urban ethnography—research based on an ethnographic approach to American society—but there are, and were, others such as urban ecology.[2]

What did these researchers accomplish? The very first generation, that of the founders Albion Small and Charles Henderson, established sociology as a new discipline at the University of Chicago; they trained a significant number of those who became the first professors of sociology in other universities. I will leave these institutional contributions aside and concentrate on the normal works of sociologists: social science texts based on research data. The generation of Park and Thomas, as they guided the work of the next generation, elaborated general schemes of analysis made up of elements taken from many sources and defined a way of studying the contemporary world, with characteristic forms of data and a characteristic style of research reporting. The last generation, whose career is ongoing today, introduced different ways of studying the world, mainly using an ethnographic approach but keeping, to a certain extent, some of the intellectual heritage of the previous generations.

French Sociology and the Chicago Tradition: A Belated Meeting

I will begin with a detour via French sociology, which, by concentrating on the Chicago tradition in the past few years, lets us sketch a partial but empirically based picture of the uses of the history of sociology by empirical research.

Before 1970, a few French researchers had read some of the works of the Chicago sociologists carefully and had discussed them, but the French researchers did not convince their colleagues of the importance of these studies, and their presentations of these works had almost no consequences. From the mid-1980s on, however, references to the Chicago tradition appear frequently in French sociological writing. Indeed, we find many references to certain works of the Chicago tradition in current French research, and some young researchers cite these works as a model and a source of inspiration for their own studies. The translation of several "classic" texts by the Chicago sociologists is another indication: part of the Park and Burgess reader *The City* in 1979; several of Goffman's works, beginning in 1967; Becker's *Outsiders* in 1985, followed by four more of his books; a collection of

Hughes's essays in 1996; Nels Anderson's *The Hobo* in 1993, followed by two partial translations of *The Polish Peasant in Europe and America*; and several books by Anselm Strauss.

French sociologists' belated interest in Chicago sociology can be related to important changes in the definition of sociology in France that occurred during the 1970s and 1980s. (1) During the 1970s, university research units stopped doing sample surveys and their accompanying statistical analysis, an activity that had put them under the exclusive authority of such state organizations as INSEE (the French National Institute of Economic and Statistical Information), INED

French sociologists' belated interest in Chicago sociology can be related to important changes in the definition of sociology in France that occurred during the 1970s and 1980s.

(French National Institute of Demographic Studies), and so on, which alone had the means to carry out such work. These organizations have indeed welcomed sociologists who wanted to join forces with them. (2) With the abandonment of French national planning from 1945 to 1970, the financing of research depended less on the state than it had in the past. The building of the European Community (EC) and the 1983 decentralization laws ensured other means of financing, through EC institutions and local authorities. But EC, the towns, and the regions were not so concerned with the results of national surveys. Instead, some were interested in comparisons within Europe; others wanted precise knowledge about limited geographical areas. (3) The intellectual situation of the social sciences during the 1980s was marked by a profound rupture with the previous period. Sociology was less directly confronted with a scientific model borrowed from the experimental sciences, which took statistical analysis as a guarantee of "being scientific." And conceptual schemes linked to analyses of social inequalities lost their appeal due to sociopolitical reasons that I will not detail here. At the same time, public debates on unemployment and conflicts in certain working-class areas made it evident that immigration had produced a new heterogeneity in the French population, which in turn gave birth to what were seen as "communities in the making." We can note the similarity to the United States of the 1920s.

The ethnographic or semiethnographic survey (based on interviews), until then considered not very scientific, thus became an acceptable and appropriate approach for the types of surveys that could be financed. The analyses of the Chicago researchers, notably, the third generation, offered models of data gathering and conceptualization compatible with an ethnographic approach, which earlier French research, seldom based on this approach, had not. The Chicago tradition has especially led French researchers to pay attention to the subjective dimension of behavior and to situational dynamics. Chicago sociology could also provide a sort of label: as a supposed connoisseur, I have, on several occasions, been asked to join a Ph.D. examining committee to confirm that certain pieces of research were good examples of the Chicago ethnographic approach. (It often seemed to me that this was not so, but this is certainly less true today than in 1990, when Jean-Pierre Briand and I [1991] systematically examined the ethnographic research carried out in France. Now, good ethnographic research has been published on such aspects of French society as hospitals, the police, drugs, behavior in working-class areas, etc.) However, French researchers have not paid much attention to the work of Chicago researchers in the field of ethnic relations; this topic appeared only recently in French sociology and seems to lack conceptual organization.

This example from France shows how earlier analyses can, long after their publications, inspire research in a social situation completely different from the one in which they were born. The case of research on race and culture relations also suggests that there are sometimes obstacles specific to the borrowing, even when this might have seemed useful.

This introduction of Chicago analyses into French sociology obviously resulted from the reading of both the classic works of the tradition and the literature that makes up the Chicago industry. Indeed, for a reader who does not know the context of the period and of the United States, an accurate understanding of these works, for the better part so deeply anchored in the context of their time and of their country, could not be immediate.

It is the same for understanding works carried out in a previous period, even within a national tradition. As Herbert Gans (1992) and many others have pointed out, sociological amnesia is a chronic phenomena that leads to the frequent repetition of previous analyses. It has proven difficult to effectively pass down not only the results of earlier research but also abstract (theoretical) schemes of analysis, as well as research expertise and experiences. The history of earlier research is the only instrument capable of curing this amnesia, which is also found in the other social sciences. Historical knowledge is even more essential when it comes to avoiding the obstacles created by differences of national culture.

So how can we write the history of social science to improve communication between today's researchers and the works and expertise of their disciplinary past?

Presentist History and
Standard History of Social Sciences

The transmission of knowledge in the social sciences requires a history that explains earlier works in the context of their production and circulation. Such a history, which gives access to the categories of thought, judgment, and action of those who produced the earlier work, lets its readers understand the overall social experience of those authors, clarifies the relations between their analyses and the debates of their time, and sheds light on the relations between their analyses and those of their predecessors, rivals, and allies. Such a history challenges one of the elements of the professional ideology of sociologists: the belief that you can separate the abstract schemes elaborated by sociological research from their context of production. (I do not accept this idea, nor do most historians.)

You could not, until the early 1980s, find such analyses in the histories of sociology or of the social sciences. Works in these fields, with rare exceptions, consisted of analyses of ideas about the social world, their main subject matter consisting of a sort of Pantheon of sociological works (including many works written without any reference to sociology). These histories were based on the critical analysis of texts, the standard technique of literary and philosophical studies. At best, the author proposed a summary historical contextualization of the works or of their authors. And the inspiration of such history was always presentist and fundamentally normative: the questions it asked were suggested by the controversies of the moment, especially those relevant to the particular position in the discipline of the person writing the history. Such histories were analyzed with current categories, and judgments were made according to the norms of the social sciences of the time.

This type of history—often presented as "theory" in sociology—is still with us today. Part of the Chicago industry has such an orientation.[3] This approach is important in teaching sociology in the United States and in France.[4] Besides constituting, as many have noted, the core of the culture of a discipline fragmented into specialties that are not closely related, this type of history conveys essential elements of sociologists' professional ideology, one of which is the conviction that abstract schemes are the principal element of social science analyses, and the related conviction that works can be reduced to a small number of abstract schemes. Another element of sociological ideology deals with relations of "influence" between works and authors, which many of these analyses desperately try to establish.

Another type of history of social science has developed over the past thirty or so years, which uses different sources and different approaches and asks different questions.[5] These analyses adopt the point of view and the approaches applied by historians of any object: they try to understand products of research in the context of their time and look at production activities as well as institutional or other activities that accompany them; they aim to objectify norms of judgment and do not apply today's criteria to works of the past. In short, these analyses are what Lucien Febvre calls "full history." Febvre himself provided a model for the analysis of cultural works in *Le Problème de l'Incroyance au XVIe Siècle* (*The Problem of Unbelief in the 16th Century* 1968). Some recent studies of the history of American social science follow this model: for Chicago sociology, for example, the books by Jennifer Platt (1996), Martin Bulmer (1984), and James Carey (1975). The history of ideas is neither the only nor the main object: research techniques and approaches; debates, public or internal to social science; and institutions and the activities that support them, including academic rivalries and the financing of research, all get equal attention.

Today, the two types of historical analysis distinguished here coexist, almost without controversy. Moreover, to my knowledge, there has been no attempt to clearly formulate the program of a "full" history of social science. Those who write this type of history limit themselves to criticizing presentist biases.[6] But it is not always easy to distinguish between full history and presentist history: the projection of today's categories onto the past is the kind of error no historical study can be sure of escaping. Furthermore, explicit or implicit judgments, made according to unspecified criteria, inevitably threaten histories of social science because those producing are part of the universe they are studying, which makes objective work difficult.

The peaceful coexistence of these two types of history creates problems because they do not serve the same purposes. Presentist histories of social science are used to defend the professional ideologies of academic disciplines: they celebrate the merits of the present and the supposed progress of these disciplines, or more pessimistically, they recall how perceptive the founding fathers were. They also sometimes constitute, as Bourdieu remarked, a strategic element in the construction of researchers' academic legitimacy by appropriating well-chosen predecessors. A full history can fulfill this type of function only occasionally. On the other hand, turned toward understanding the past, it constitutes an instrument better adapted than presentist history for the use of past analyses by current researchers.

Some Uses of the Standard History of Social Sciences

I will give an example of the fruitfulness of borrowing from the past by returning to the Chicago sociologists of Thomas and Park's generation. Studying the enterprise that Chicago sociology was, by replacing it in the academic and sociopolitical contexts where the work was carried out, lets us discover a universe profoundly different from that of any current researcher. For researchers who are not American, this experiment lets us measure the difference both temporally and culturally. We can thus discover the affinities, as well as the differences, between the abstract analyses of the Chicago sociologists and the viewpoint of the "dominant minority"—Protestant Anglo-Saxons—on ethnic relations. The focus of the analyses of Park and Thomas—the recent arrival and the coexistence of populations of varied cultural origin and physical appearance on the same territory—is no more than what the middle classes then saw as the source of the major public problems of the United States. The Chicago sociologists thus started off from what appeared to the middle classes as "facts": immigrants and the problems they brought with them. The sociologists, however, distanced themselves from the way social reformers, politicians, and journalists defined these problems in terms of ethnic attributes, by reasoning in terms of relations between groups. The sociologists also studied the entire process of contacts between these populations, as well as the significance of behavior, which the subjects themselves sometimes did not understand. Some dimensions of these contacts did not hold the sociologists' attention any more than that of the social reformers: they paid little attention to work relations or to class and gender differences.

At the time the Americans were carrying out their research, researchers on the other side of the Atlantic did not find their conceptual schemes very relevant: public controversies in France, as in England, were not revolving around problems of ethnicity and immigration but around the "social question," which is to say class antagonisms. In France, which had been a country of immigration since (at least) the middle of the nineteenth century, social scientists did not study this problem, due to the unanimous, and for a long time shared, conviction that immigrant populations were rapidly assimilated, in a republic whose founding act refused to recognize differences of religion and ethnic origin, and thus were not a "problem" that needed study.

Three-quarters of a century later, the social representations that gave birth to these analyses of American and French societies have been deeply shaken. The study of contacts between immigrant groups has belatedly become an area of research for French sociology, just as social classes—and genders—have become analytic domains dealt with, to a certain extent, by American social sciences.[7] This is what an earlier mutual understanding of the analyses carried out on both sides of the Atlantic might have produced.

Drawing a parallel between sociological analyses and the historical situations in which they were born also reminds us how much the research and conceptual schemes elaborated by the social sciences, often with difficulty and at great length, depend on social representations of the objects studied in the researchers' societies. It also suggests the benefits to be gained from borrowing analytic schemes developed in other historical situations. Comparison with other societies and other situations is in fact the main tool the social sciences have to free themselves from social representations that arise in public controversies in a given period. Such comparison presupposes in-depth knowledge of the history of the society and of the social sciences produced during the same period.

But a full history of social science offers not only the possibility of borrowing analytic schemes elaborated by past research. It also makes possible a conception of social science and its products disentangled from the conceptions of its practitioners and from their professional ideologies. Some research on the history of American social science—Richard Gillespie's (1991) work on the Hawthorne experiments, for example—has thus contributed to a critique of the "scientistic" ideology that prevailed in the social sciences after 1930, at times recalling criticisms made during the 1970s.[8] By bringing the diverse elements that influenced the finished research products out of obscurity—uncertainties in the collection of data and its interpretation, rivalries and alliances between researchers, subjective relations of researchers to their careers—these analyses help define a renewed and deepened conception of empirical research and its results. By leading us to pay attention to these elements so often left in the dark, historical analyses allow, as an indirect consequence, a control of their effects. The history of social science can thus make a major contribution to the rigor of research in these disciplines, as well as to reflection on their foundations. As Stefan Collini (1988), an English historian of social science, put it, "Part of the historian's function is to help us to escape from, or at least to loosen the hold of, those categories of thought we take so much for granted that we become almost unaware of their existence" (p. 387).

[Recent analyses of history of social science] try to understand products of research in the context of their time . . . they aim to objectify norms of judgment and do not apply today's criteria to works of the past.

The conception of social science to which these historical analyses lead converges with the one developed in the analyses of researchers—mainly sociologists and anthropologists who have been writing about their own research practices since the 1970s. Some study the techniques involved in writing reports;[9] others study the writing and selection of field notes in ethnographic studies;[10] still others, since the 1950s, study the consequences of different kinds of relations between researchers and their subjects and the uncertainties and the dynamics of these relations.[11] This process of explaining research practices itself is worth historical study; here, too, the experiences of past generations of field researchers can be passed down and not forgotten.

I have not yet answered the question with which I began. The answer I have outlined is more linked than I would have hoped to my own research path, but it contains elements that can be generalized. To get the distance necessary for social science analyses of the universes we are studying, we need a comparative approach, which helps us understand research that was carried out in a universe of which we were not part. A true history of social sciences—not a presentist history lacking rigor—is one of the best ways to achieve such mastery. Undoubtedly, this knowledge is especially fertile when its object is a going concern of empirical research on a certain scale, which has lasted enough to allow the progressive elaboration of its chief ideas. The Chicago tradition is such a case, as are the histories of *The Annals*, English social anthropology, and others.

                    Translation by Maureen Healey, revised by H. S. Becker

Notes

1. Edited by Ken Plummer (1997).

2. Of course, the development of urban ethnology also has other filiations, such as the multidisciplinary group that founded the *Human Organization* review in 1944. On urban sociology, see David A. Smith (1995).

3. Twenty years ago, this orientation was almost exclusive concerning the history of sociology (see Jerzy Szacki 1981). The explicit criticism of this orientation for the history of social sciences began in 1965 with an article by George W. Stocking (1965). This article contains a somewhat ambiguous criticism of presentism.

4. On the United States, see Kuklick (1999).

5. We can observe the same phenomenon in the domain of the history of the life sciences and of the natural sciences. The development of a nonpresentist history has simply been a little more precocious in this case.

6. To understand the Chicago sociology in the terms and the context of the time, I sought to specify a research program when writing my book on this subject. I did not discover until afterward that this had already been clearly formulated by a historian of life sciences, Jacques Roger, and partially by Lucien Febvre. The expression "histoire à part entière" was used as the title of a posthumous book of papers by Febvre (*Pour une histoire à part entière*, SEVPEN, Paris, 1962), which was translated in English under the title *New Kind of History* (1973).

7. I analyzed the progressive integration of an analysis in terms of class in the United States during the thirties in an article titled "L'Étrange Carrière de la Notion de Classe Sociale dans la Tradition de Chicago en Sociologie" (Chapoulie 2000).

8. See, among others, Julius A. Roth's (1965) suggestive article, Howard S. Becker (1967), John I. Kitsuse and Aaron V. Cicourel (1963), and Irwin Deutscher (1973).

9. See, in particular, Gusfield (1976) and Becker (1986).

10. See, in particular, Emerson, Fretz, and Shaw (1995).

11. Some of the first contributions to these reflections on ethnographic practices can be accessed in the collection of Adams and Press (1960). A second collection of contributions, now too often overlooked, can be found in the issues of the first years of the review *Urban Life and Culture*.

References

Abbott, Andrew. 1999. *Department and discipline: Chicago sociology at one hundred*. Chicago: University of Chicago Press.

Adams, Richard N., and Joseph J. Press, eds. 1960. *Human organization research*. Homewood, IL: Dorsey Press.

Becker, Howard S. 1967. Whose side are we on? *Social Problems* 14:239-47.

———. 1986. *Writing for social scientists*. Chicago: University of Chicago Press.

Briand, Jean-Pierre, and Jean-Michel Chapoulie. 1991. The use of observation in French sociology. *Symbolic Interaction* 14 (4): 449-69.

Bulmer, Martin. 1984. *The Chicago School of sociology: institutionalization, diversity, and the rise of sociological research*. Chicago: University of Chicago Press.

Carey, James T. 1975. *Sociology and public affairs: The Chicago School*. Beverly Hills, CA: Sage.

Chapoulie, Jean-Michel. 1973. Sur l'analyse sociologique des professions. *Revue française de sociologie* 14 (1): 86-114.

———. 1984. E. C. Hughes et le développement du travail de terrain en France. *Revue française de sociologie* 25 (4): 582-608. English translation in 1987. Everett C. Hughes and the development of fieldwork in sociology. *Urban Life* 15 (3-4): 259-98.

———. 2000. L'étrange carrière de la notion de classe sociale dans la tradition de Chicago en sociologie. *Archives Européennes de sociologie* 46 (1): 53-70.

———. 2001a. Comment écrire l'histoire de la sociologie: l'exemple d'un classique ignoré, *Le Paysan Polonais en Europe et en Amérique*, et l'histoire de la sociologie. *Revue d'Histoire des Sciences Humaines* 5:143-69.

———. 2001b. *La tradition sociologique de Chicago, 1892-1961*. Paris: Éditions du Seuil.

Collini, Stefan. 1988. Reflections on the historiography of the social sciences in Britain and France. *Revue de Synthèse* 3-4:387-99.

Deutscher, Irwin. 1973. *What we say/what we do: Sentiments and acts*. Glenview IL: Scott, Foresman.

Emerson, Robert M., Rachel I. Fretz, and Linda L. Shaw. 1995. *Writing ethnographic fieldnotes*. Chicago: University of Chicago Press.

Faris, Robert. 1967/1970. *Chicago sociology, 1920-1932*. Chicago: University of Chicago Press.

Febvre, Lucien. 1942/1968. *Le problème de l'incroyance au XVIe siècle: La religion de Rabelais*. Paris: Albin Michel. Translated in English in 1982. *The problem of unbelief in the 16th century: The religion of Rabelais*. Cambridge, MA: Harvard University Press.

Fine, Gary Alan, ed. 1955. *A Second Chicago School? The development of a postwar American sociology*. Chicago: University of Chicago Press.

Gans, Herbert. 1992. Sociological amnesia: The non-cumulation of normal science. *Sociological Forum* 7 (4): 701-10.

Gillespie, Richard. 1991. *Manufacturing knowledge: A history of the Hawthorne experiments*. New York: Cambridge University Press.

Gusfield, Joseph R. 1976. The literary rhetoric of science: Comedy and pathos in drinking driver research. *American Sociological Review* 41 (1): 16-34.

Kitsuse, John I., and Aaron V. Cicourel. 1963. A note on the use of official statistics. *Social Problems* 11 (2): 131-39.

Kuklick, Henrika. 1999. Assessing research in the history of sociology and anthropology. *Journal of the History of the Behavioral Sciences* 53 (3): 227-37.

Platt, Jennifer. 1996. *A history of sociological research methods in America, 1920-1960*. Cambridge, UK: Cambridge University Press.

Plummer, Ken, ed. 1997. *The Chicago School: Critical assessments*. London: Routledge.

Roger, Jacques. 1995. *Pour une histoire des sciences à part entière*. Paris: Albin Michel.

Roth, Julius A. 1965. Hired hand research. *The American Sociologist* 1 (1): 190-96.

Smith, David A. 1995. The new urban sociology meets the old. *Urban Affairs Review* 30 (3): 432-57.

Stocking, George W. 1965. On the limits of "presentism" and "historicism" in the historiography of the behavioral sciences. *Journal of the History of the Behavioral Sciences* 1:211-18. (Republished in Stocking, G. W. 1968. *Race, culture and evolution*. New York: Free Press.)

Szacki, Jerzy. 1981. Réflexions sur l'histoire de la sociologie. *Revue International des Sciences Sociales* 33 (2): 270-81.

The Making of Black Metropolis

HENRI PERETZ

Black Metropolis, an exemplary monograph about the South Side of Chicago, was written mainly by St. Clair Drake and Horace R. Cayton and was published in 1945. Both authors had former experience in research and field work. *Black Metropolis* was initially a Works Progress Administration project in collaboration with Lloyd Warner to use the money coming from federal funds. Drake and Cayton divided the work of studying different social components of the black community. Cayton was familiar with upper class and Drake with lower class and churches. A large team was set up to undertake the Cayton-Warner project from 1936 to 1941. There was no initial project for a book, and the expectations of the different members of the team were highly diverse. It was not until 1940 and 1941, once the study had been completed, that the three main researchers had the idea of publishing a book based on it.

Keywords: black community; Chicago; *Black Metropolis*; Horace R. Cayton; St. Clair Drake

B*lack Metropolis*, an exemplary monograph about the South Side of Chicago, was written mainly by St. Clair Drake and Horace Cayton and was published in 1945. I will discuss two aspects of this project: the book as the product of the collective work of a team and the way the research produced a book that had never been planned. The two main authors of the book had acquired skills, notably, those of doing field work, earlier in their lives as researchers. They could thus contribute to collecting some of the ethnographic material, in addition to training some of the team's investigators to do similar work. Indeed, the scale of the documentation gathered and analyses proposed is dumbfounding. The involvement of the main authors in the black community and the multiplicity of collaborators organized as a team help to explain the numerous situations described: historical scenes based on secondary accounts, as well as scenes

Henri Peretz is an associate professor of sociology at the University of Paris 8. He is the author of L'Observation *(1998). He is presently working on the ethnographic tradition of Chicago.*

DOI: 10.1177/0002716204267185

168

ANNALS, *AAPSS*, 595, September 2004

of contemporary action directly observed by the investigators or the authors. From this accumulation of statistical, ethnographic, and historical data emerged a book that had not been envisaged in the initial research project.

In this article, I will mainly rely on Horace Cayton's (1964) autobiography and on the archives deposited in the Schomburg Library.

A Federal Project

The project began with considerable federal financing. The initial project, from 1935 to 1937, was the work of two researchers of different status: Lloyd Warner (1898-1970), who was then a professor of anthropology and sociology at the University of Chicago, and Horace Cayton (1903-1970), a graduate student research assistant. At that time, Warner headed several different projects including *Deep South*, an investigation of the caste and race system of the American South. I will not describe Lloyd Warner's career here. But I will mention Cayton's previous training. He was the son of a journalist and the grandson of the first black senator; he had studied sociology and then had different research experiences, including his collaboration in research on the black political world of Chicago.

His first experience as a researcher was from 1932 to 1933, as research assistant in the department of political science of the University of Chicago, probably under the influence of Park, who was his teacher (Cayton 1964, 184). In this context, he worked with Harold Gosnell (1935), who was studying the "black political machine" in Chicago and the rivalries between Republicans and Democrats to secure jobs and win voters. Cayton (1964, 184) carried out fieldwork, doing interviews, particularly of policemen. Working with policemen was familiar to Cayton; he himself had been a member of the police force (a deputy sheriff) to pay for his studies. His contribution to Gosnell's work was not restricted to these interviews. Surviving documents show his observation of political meetings that took place in the 1930s in the South Side. He wrote, for instance, field notes, based on observation and typed out in two parts, devoted to a Republican meeting held on April 9, 1932, on the South Side (Cayton 1932). This text describes these meetings as having an atmosphere identical to that of certain South Side churches. Cayton continued going to these political meetings in the South Side. *Black Metropolis*, whose chapter on political expediency was greatly inspired by Gosnell, contains similar accounts of political meetings, without mentioning the investigator's identity.

After this first experience, Cayton became Louis Wirth's assistant in 1933 and 1934. It was in Louis Wirth's office, in 1933, that he met Richard Wright, who had come to collect a list of books to read (Rowley 2001, 81). During this period, Cayton also worked for the federal government, as an assistant to the secretary of interior, doing fieldwork in factories to discover the effects of the National Recovery Act (legislative measures designed to change working conditions): "There [in New York] I met Georges S. Mitchell, a professor of economics at Columbia University, who was to be my colleague on the study and for the next year I travelled all over the country interviewing, and observing the formation of the Congress of

Industrial Organization, the C.I.O., and the role of the Negro worker in the steel, meat packing, and railroad car shop industries" (Cayton 1964, 207). This study was the source of the book *Black Workers and the New Unions* (Cayton and Mitchell 1939).

The Cayton-Warner Project

After a period teaching at Fisk University, Cayton returned to Chicago in 1936 and 1937 as a research assistant and instructor in the anthropology department. It was then that the Works Progress Administration (WPA) project was born in collaboration with Lloyd Warner. Together, they set up a research project to use the money coming from the WPA, a federal agency for unemployment aid (Drake and Cayton 1945, xiii; Cayton 1964, 236) They focused on juvenile delinquency in the black community. They arranged the required institutional backing with the Institute of Juvenile Research (Chapoulie 2001, 262), which then played a central role in delinquency studies. This project was a pretext to study the entire structure of the black community (Cayton 1964, 237). This research was part of an Illinois WPA project, alongside an ensemble of projects turned more toward the arts and literature but in which black writers like Richard Wright had an important place.

Many people took part in the Cayton-Warner project, among them St. Clair Drake (1911-1990). Drake, who was then at Dillard University, went to Chicago in 1937 with a Rosenwald grant to continue his graduate studies in anthropology at the university (Drake 1985) and to contribute to the publication of *Deep South* by the Chicago Press. There, he found Lloyd Warner and met Cayton, joining the Cayton-Warner project for which he took some responsibility. Shortly after the beginning of the research, Drake took charge of the study of churches and voluntary associations. He then took up a position alongside Cayton and Warner in the management of the project. He also had a position in another organization, the Illinois State Commission, from which he drew other data.

He headed the research devoted to South Side churches and voluntary associations "in their relation to social stratification and to ethnic social action" (Drake 1985). Drake, the son of a minister, had received his training as a researcher, and particularly as an interviewer, by participating for two years in the study of white and black communities in the South. This research led to the publication of *Deep South*, under the management of Allison Davis and with the backing of Lloyd Warner (Davis, Gardner, and Gardner 1941). Drake previously had considerable experience of interracial relations and black institutions. During the *Deep South* period, he was trained as a participant observer and learned to reconstruct interviews from memory without taking notes. Thanks to his past experiences, he knew how to establish links with black institutions. He also contributed to analyzing data and to writing the book.

Drake and Cayton divided the work of studying different social components of the black community. Cayton was familiar with the elites of this community. He had observed the lifestyle of the two components of the black upper class: the

"Upper Respectables" and the "Upper Shadies," the rich racketeers. His selection in 1939 as head of Parkway Community House—a sort of cultural and social center established in the middle of the black area—gave him a position as activity leader, manager, and observer of the social, political, and intellectual life of the South Side. St. Clair Drake already had experience of the religious milieus and the working classes from his research in Mississippi. In Chicago, he rapidly became familiar with the milieu of the lower class and visited families who did not go to church. He also became a voluntary teacher at the Chicago Baptist Institution. Drake did participant observation with lower-class families. We see evidence of this in the note at the beginning of chapter 20 of *Black Metropolis*, which recounts his six-month observation of lower-class households. The account begins on Christmas Eve at the home of a doctor called in an emergency to an injured person. It is a detailed report of an extreme situation, followed by an account of the life of this household over a long period.

How the Team Was Organized

A large team was set up to undertake the Cayton-Warner project. The research assistants—there were about twenty of them—were recruited among graduate students. Most were white, for few blacks had reached this level at the time (Cayton 1964). More than 150 other people, 20 to 30 percent of whom were white, also worked on the project: office staff, documentation staff, typists, and statisticians (Cayton 1964, 237). Some accounts tell of two hundred contributors, including a large number of black and white investigators who carried out interviews; Drake helped train the investigators, interviewers, and observers. He taught them how to carry out and memorize an interview and to draft an account in the correct format.

The scale of the project entailed considerable personnel management, which Horace Cayton dealt with in part. In his autobiography, he evokes the pressure put on the organization of the research by unions, particularly that exerted by its communist members. Even though the team itself had few members with these sympathies, Cayton had to establish a balance between the different union and political factions. He said he never recruited researchers on the basis of their political affiliation (communists, anticommunists, Trotskyists, etc.) but on that of their competence, thus satisfying the diverse factions by favoring none of them (Cayton 1964, 239). Cayton also had to maintain a balance between white and black researchers. The collective and interracial organization of this work was supported by black liberals, the CIO unions, and the communists. It was also subjected to "the illegitimate pressure of gangsters, . . . the idiosyncrasies of academics and the close scrutiny of government auditors" (Drake 1970).

The project was supported by such institutions as the Julius Rosenwald Foundation and the Church of the Good Shepherd, which became the Parkway Community House under the management of Horace Cayton himself in 1939. This social assistance institution and black cultural center, located right in the middle of the

South Side, received some of the documentary material collected. Thus, a photograph taken in this institution in 1939 shows an exhibit of reports and documents collected by the research assistants (Anonymous 1939). We can see large volumes on a table, and on the walls are maps of Chicago on which we can make out the dark patches representing the black area. The caption of the photograph mentions twenty-three projects and underlines three of them. They were the most quoted in

---

During the Deep South *period, [Drake] was
trained as a participant observer and learned
to reconstruct interviews from memory
without taking notes.*

---

the book itself, especially St. Clair Drake's report on the churches and voluntary association (Drake 1940). This research is mentioned in the chapter devoted to black churches in Gunnar Myrdal's *American Dilemma* (1944). Drake's report, a large volume of 314 pages, includes a sort of review of the Chicago tradition, referring in particular to Park, Wirth, and Thomas. A veiled reference is made to Marx, concerning social stratification. This is followed by a long historical development based on diverse sources and presenting the evolution of churches and women's organizations like the Ida B. Wells Club. Then begins the purely empirical part, devoted to a numerical analysis and to case studies of churches and associations on the South Side. We find some of this documentation in the book (Drake and Cayton 1945, 614), notably, the implantation charts of churches and those of the participation in female clubs (Drake and Cayton 1945, 703).

This is how some of the research work of the Cayton-Warner project presented itself. Nothing indicated that it would be the source of a book.

Project for a Book

How was the book put together from extensive documentary material of such a diverse nature? There was no initial planning for a book project, and the expectations of the different members of the team were highly diverse. It was not until 1940 and 1941, once the study had been completed, that the three main researchers had the idea of publishing a book based on it. The first mention of the book dates back to 1940. Lloyd Warner wanted to integrate the extensive material into his concept of social stratification and to address a scientific and academic audience of sociologists and anthropologists. His first idea was to have the two works *Deep South* and *Black Metropolis* published by the University of Chicago Press. Cayton wanted a more commercial publisher—Harcourt—who would give the book wider distribution (Drake 1980). Going to war changed the publication climate: "The time seemed propitious for the publication of a book which would present the material in a more popular style and relate it to contemporary events" (Warner, Cayton, and Drake 1943). Indeed, the interracial climate became tense, particularly due to the discrimination problems created by the presence of blacks in the army. There were riots in Detroit and in Los Angeles. To give an account of the situation in Chicago, but also to put forward a general type of development of black cities, a plan for the book was outlined:

1. The arrival of blacks in Chicago since the end of the nineteenth century and more particularly around the World War I, which included the 1919 riot.
2. The relations between blacks and whites, mainly between 1935 and 1943, on the basis of direct observations.
3. The black community.
4. The future.

The first draft of the book was written by three people and took the form of a thousand-page manuscript, three hundred of which were in a definitive state. Two-thirds of the book was written by Drake. In 1942, the manuscript was read successively by Warner and Cayton and sent to Drake, who was then in the Navy in Brooklyn. To complete the manuscript, a work plan was drawn up to circulate the texts between the authors. Drake's wife, Dr. Johns, was hired as editor. The detailed plan for the manuscript confirms that Drake was the main writer and that critiques from the coauthors were numerous and severe. The publisher wanted the book to have a double audience, the lay reader and the professional reader, and thus to avoid the erudite apparatus of notes, bibliography, tables, and diagrams, as well as pedantic rhetoric. The many extracts from interviews and field notes in the final edition, and probably also the graphics with which the statistical and cartographical data are reconstructed, must have been a response to this type of demand.

It was not until 1944, however, that Cayton had a definitive agreement from Harcourt to publish the book. He explained the situation in a letter to Lloyd Warner dated October 1, 1944, and made a decision concerning the respective allocation of responsibilities: "Drake has written about two-thirds of the book without the assistance from either of us."

> As I am the only person that is completely familiar with all the material . . . and as Drake has already completed two-thirds of the book, I feel that just two signatures, his and mine, should appear on the book and your assistance in the whole project should be acknowledged much in the way as it was done in *Deep South*. (Cayton 1944)

But publication was not immediate. The publisher had two more requirements: that Richard Wright write a preface and that Lloyd Warner's methodological note be placed at the end of the work. Warner wrote the note mainly on the theme of class and caste and on the difference between the context of *Deep South* and of *Black Metropolis*. To ensure a wider circulation of the book, the publisher wanted Richard Wright's name attached. The novelist had become familiar with the South Side of Chicago after his emigration from the South. His first novels, notably, *Native Son*, evoked the social life of blacks in Chicago and their relations with whites.

Black Metropolis has endured as an exemplary monograph on the black community; it remains an extraordinary book because of the diversity of themes it covers.

The link between the two men made it possible for Cayton to ask Wright to write a preface to *Black Metropolis*. The preface begins with a commendation of the book and, more generally, of the Chicago tradition in sociology, which Wright undoubtedly knew through his reading and, above all, through the references the authors made to it. Wright established a parallel between the work and his novels, especially with respect to delinquency and to the hero of his novel *Native Son*. He then denounced the conditions that had been created for blacks to live in. Cayton expressed his gratitude to Wright for this preface. That was part of the general allocation of tasks in the production of the book, nothing of which could have been foreseen at the Cayton-Warner stage of the project.

Black Metropolis has endured as an exemplary monograph on the black community; it remains an extraordinary book because of the diversity of themes it covers. Only teamwork could allow such documentation to be gathered. If I had to choose one of the most pertinent traits of the work, the descriptions of the social life of Bronzeville would carry it off in my eyes. Undoubtedly, these multiple episodes will remain as a testimony of a past state of the black community. It is these scenes, written from notes gathered by the diverse investigators whom Drake and Cayton had hired, that give this research the character of an account and a testimony, which historians as much as sociologists still recognize in this book today. Everything the work owes to the social, political, and intellectual context of the time, and notably to the local context, remains to be shown.

References

Anonymous. 1939. Photograph of exhibit of WPA research materials. Horace Cayton Papers, The Vivian G. Harsh Research Collection, Chicago Public Library.

Cayton, Horace R. 1932. Republican mass meeting, April 9. Archives, Drake's Papers, Schomburg Center for Research in Black Culture, New York Public Library.

———. 1944. Letter to Lloyd Warner 10th January 1944. Archives, Drake's Papers, Schomburg Center for Research in Black Culture, New York Public Library.

———. 1964. *Long old road.* New York: Trident Press.

Cayton, Horace R., and George S. Mitchell. 1939. *Black workers and the new unions.* Chapel Hill: University of North Carolina Press.

Chapoulie, Jean-Michel. 2001. *La tradition sociologique de Chicago.* Paris: Le Seuil.

Davis, Allison, Burleigh B. Gardner, and Mary R. Gardner. 1941. *Deep South: A social anthropological study of caste and class.* Chicago: University of Chicago Press.

Drake, St. Clair. 1940. *Churches and voluntary associations in the Chicago negro community.* Mimeograph. Report of Official Project 465-54-3_386, Works Progress Administration.

———. 1970. To Horace Cayton from St. Clair Drake. Obituary. Archives, Drake's Papers, Schomburg Center for Research in Black Culture, New York Public Library.

———. 1980. Letter of 6th of January to the University of Chicago Press. Archives, Drake's Papers, Schomburg Center for Research in Black Culture, New York Public Library.

———. 1985. On the 40th anniversary of the first edition of *Black metropolis.* Archives, Drake's Papers, Schomburg Center for Research in Black Culture, New York Public Library.

Drake, St. Clair, and Horace R. Cayton. 1945. *Black metropolis: A study of negro life in a northern city.* New York: Harcourt Brace.

Gosnell, Harold F. 1935. *Negro politicians, the rise of negro politics in Chicago.* Chicago: University of Chicago Press.

Myrdal, Gunnar. 1944. *An American dilemma.* New York: Harper.

Rowley, Hazel. 2001. *Richard Wright: The life and times.* New York: Henry Holt.

Warner Lloyd, Horace R. Cayton, and St. Clair Drake. 1943. Scope and significance of the study. Archives, Drake's Papers, Schomburg Center for Research in Black Culture, New York Public Library.

Discovering Ink: A Mentor for an Historical Ethnography

By
WILLIAM KORNBLUM

Ethnographers often find that the discovery of a mentor, someone who generously unlocks doors and shares invaluable experience with a naive outsider, is a critical turning point in the research process. This article explores a mentor-investigator relationship in ethnographic research within the more specialized field of historical ethnography and through a case of historical ethnography: fieldwork in Chicago's jazz and blues music scenes from August through October 1924, where the discovery of a mentor has brought an unexpected and original perspective to the research.

Keywords: historical ethnography; fieldwork mentors; Chicago jazz

Finding Ink

This project is a form of sociological time travel, in an effort to fill in a gap or two and possibly to extend our knowledge of Chicago in the early 1920s, when the city was the center of perhaps the most important cultural movement in American history: the creation of jazz music as a multiracial art and entertainment institution. Using what I have learned about the fieldwork process, I am attempting to project myself, or someone rather like me, back to a time when sociology was a much newer field even than it is now. I want to try to recreate as accurately as possible an experience of Chicago field research in the heady days of early empirical urban sociology. Thematically, the work explores the joys and frustrations of interracial sociability and friendship in the jazz world and, ultimately, the heavy toll that racism takes on the American soul.

William Kornblum is a professor of sociology at The Graduate Center, City University of New York. His research focuses on contemporary urban issues such as public housing and public spaces.

DOI: 10.1177/0002716204267484

Historical ethnography to explore the known city

In his well-known tribute in *Black Metropolis* to the Chicago sociologists, Richard Wright called Chicago "the known city" and credited sociologists, white and black, for much of that knowledge (Drake and Cayton 1945). One hesitates to quibble with this rare tribute to American empirical sociology from a writer of enduring fiction. But it is also true that in the historic and entirely original work produced under Park and Burgess and their colleagues, there are outstanding gaps in the accomplishment. One wishes there had been more students and more resources to have allowed a greater number of firsthand accounts of that extraordinary time in American urban history. Among the classics are studies of the Gold Coast and slum, of gangs and hotels for workers newly arrived to the city, of the origins of racial tensions and violence, of the Madison Street Skid Row or "hobohemia," of the Taxi Dance Hall, and of the Jewish Ghetto. But what about the factory areas and stockyards, the political backrooms, the syndicate towns with their roadhouse speakeasies, and the vast outdoor markets in Jewtown? These were among the "natural areas" of the city that never quite made it into the literature, just as today so many worthy urban ethnographic research subjects never get under way due to changes in intellectual fashion or because there was no funding or sufficient faculty support (Bulmer 1984; Chapoulie 2001).

Eventually, Chicago sociologists, inspired by the models of the classic period and under the guidance of Blumer, Hughes, and Warner and later of Janowitz, Suttles, and Howard Becker, also filled in some of the blanks with rich ethnographic descriptions of the black-belt street corners, of the "Mother Wards," of the factories and neighborhoods in the industrial zones, and of the political clubs of the inner-city wards. Yet a great many subjects remain that might have been studied using the basic methods of the Chicago school but were not. This article, therefore, offers an example of how it is possible to reexplore specific scenes and places in Chicago during the classic period and to construct a sociologically plausible version of what might have occurred in a social milieu that with historical hindsight, clearly deserved far more sociological attention than it ever received. In recapturing what it would have been like to do a dissertation under Park and Burgess, we may gain a better understanding of culture and race relations when Chicago was the "shock city" of American urbanization and the crucible of interracial contact (Suttles 1990).

In the early 1920s, jazz music was emerging in Chicago as a powerful but still disreputable popular cultural form, just as an empirical sociology of urban life was developing at the University of Chicago. Unfortunately, no sociologist produced a dissertation about any aspect of jazz as a new urban phenomenon. Paul Cressey's *Taxi-Dance Hall*, a richly ethnographic study of wayward girls and the "dime a dance" phenomenon in Chicago during the late 1920s, may be as close as the classic Chicago School scholars came to an analysis of music's influence on urban youth and street life (Cressey 1932). Thrasher's seminal work on youth gangs in Chicago and the extensive work on the Illinois Youth Commission on juvenile delinquency have references to fads in leisure time among teenagers and young adults, but

Cressey's monograph deals most explicitly with one aspect of the dance craze that swept America in the Jazz Age. Jane Addams's *Youth and the Spirit of the City Streets*, W. I. Thomas's *The Wayward Girl*, and Ernest Burgess's classes on youth and play in the city clearly had a lot of influence on Cressey's and others' field research on urban youth and social change (Deegan 2002). In these authors' works or teachings, the emphasis is on how popular music and the temptations of the dance halls, night clubs, and small street theaters often led vulnerable young people astray. Although Park sought to avoid moralizing in his work and in that of his students and was particularly interested in fads and fashions himself, his tastes in entertainment, like those of most of his colleagues, tended to center on classical music and opera. There is no evidence that he had much interest in the then-controversial new music known as jazz. On the other hand, his enormous curiosity about changes in urban life would likely have led him to be sympathetic had an enterprising graduate student brought the subject of jazz music, and the multiracial community that was forming around its performance, to his attention (Shils 1997).

An accurate rendition of what it would have been like to conduct field research in the early Chicago jazz community requires a combination of historical research and retrospective ethnography. *Historical ethnography* is the term contemporary anthropologists often use to describe this eclectic set of methods, but it is not yet a common term of science or art in sociology. Anthropologist Ann Sutherland describes the central substantive issue in the method this way:

> Historical Ethnography still takes seriously the traditional anthropological method of intensive, personal fieldwork to find out how people think, what they do and what it means to them. But traditional ethnography has not usually asked the question: So how did this culture come to be this way? Today, ethnographers no longer take for granted that culture (or identity) is a given. Instead it is problematized, something that has to be explained. If culture persists, or identities of ethnicity and nation are key features of culture, then we must try to understand how they are constructed and reconstructed over time. (Sutherland 1999, 1)

This statement is not far from Michael Burawoy's perspective that it is impossible to understand current social conditions or cultures using ethnographic methods without developing a historical understanding of the phenomena under study (Burawoy 1991). In addition to bringing in the living influences of the past, many contemporary sociologists and anthropologists would agree with Ruth Behar who wishes to "recommend that fieldworkers lend their own experience to the process of enriching and dynamizing the fieldwork material itself" (Behar 1967). But these exhortations fall short of making it quite clear what historical ethnographies are or how they depart, if at all, from some of the classics of urban ethnography. In *Street Corner Society*, for example, William F. Whyte provides plenty of historical background and clearly sets himself in the fieldwork as an actor, without self-conscious assertions about "reflexivity" (Whyte 1943). Innumerable examples of ethnographies in sociology use historical material to show that the past continues to shape contemporary events and social processes. But that does not automatically qualify them as historical ethnographies.

None of the contemporary advocates of historical ethnography refers to it, but *The Delight Makers*, Adolph Bandelier's 1890 anthropological study of the ancient Anasazie Indians of the Southwest, created a model for what historical ethnography could achieve. Bandelier's extensive fieldwork with the Hopi and Navaho peoples, his years of linguistic research, his archeological investigation, and his wide travels throughout the U.S. and Mexican deserts prepared him to recreate what

---

Innumerable examples of ethnographies in sociology use historical material to show that the past continues to shape contemporary events and social processes.

---

daily life was like in the Frijoles Canyon on the Pajarito Plateau in what is now New Mexico. The work explores, in novel form, how conflict within and among the Indian clans and societies of the region led to dramatic social change. *The Delight Makers* has remained in print since it was published, and its author's work is commemorated at Bandelier National Monument in New Mexico, at what is no doubt the only national park named after a social scientist. This book is a model of historical ethnography because it is based on exhaustive social scientific research; it successfully reconstructs the time and cultural complexity of the Indian, clan-based villages, among people who lived in cliff dwellings or pueblos long before any contact with Europeans. Written as a novel, the book has reached readers outside the academic world. For my own research, as was true for Bandelier, the possibility of finding living informants is absent; the original musicians, club owners, promoters, record producers, gangsters, academics, and others who know the Chicago jazz scene are long gone, but their descendents can still be interviewed, and the places where they performed can, in some instances, offer fresh perspectives on the emergence of jazz (and the African American musical traditions on which it is often based) as the nation's premier contribution to world musical culture (Bande- lier 1890).

More specifically, this research is about race relations in the social world of jazz and blues in Chicago in the summer and fall of 1924. Chicago was briefly at the epicenter of jazz as a distinctly American cultural complex that spawned new styles in music, dance, entertainment, recording, and radio (Peretti 1992). For African

American and white jazz musicians alike, the music was a compelling way of life, as it was for many of the college kids and urban intellectuals who idolized the music and the musicians. But as Howard Becker and Irving Goffman have noted, jazz was also something of a deviant cultural movement, associated in "respectable society" with the taboos of race and race mixing and the life of the cabaret, prohibition alcohol, gangsters, loose women, and everything that was on the moral edge of the city (Becker 1963; Goffman 1963).

Getting to Know the Chicago Jazz Scene of the Early 1920s

The literature on jazz is rich to say the least; there is no end of accounts of different jazz scenes in Chicago and Indiana during the Jazz Age. Most of the prominent musicians wrote autobiographies—Louis Armstrong, to name the greatest example, wrote two of them and kept a tape recorder going for most of his life. These tapes were recently archived and are becoming available at the new Louis Armstrong home and museum in Corona, Queens, where he lived most of his life after leaving Chicago in 1924. There are autobiographies by Hoagie Charmichael (he also wrote two), Eddie Condon, Mezz Mezzrow, Benny Goodman, and many others, and an excellent firsthand account of the early Chicago days of Bix Beiderbecke by Ralph Berton, brother of the drummer Vic Berton, who frequently played with Bix and some of the other original Wolverines. The secondary literature is voluminous and still booming, although new discoveries are becoming infrequent. For the Chicago jazz scene of the early 1920s, there is a definitive history by William H. Kenney and firsthand accounts by Bricktop, Dempsey Travis, and others who witnessed or knew people who witnessed the legendary jazz sessions at the Royal Gardens and in the after-hours joints. One can rather easily find accounts of sessions with Ma Rainey and Bessie Smith and Louis Armstrong just before the migration of many of the greatest jazz originals, including Louis and Bix, to New York City (Peretti 1992; Kenney 1993).

As a jazz-struck teenager, I devoured the original musicians' autobiographies, although my passion was for the midcentury jazz of Bird, Monk, Coltrane, Bill Evans, and Gerry Mulligan. Years later, when doing reading and field research in South Chicago and the Indiana steel towns for my own Chicago dissertation, I read more of the Midwest jazz literature, out of personal interest and for the firsthand accounts they afforded of areas on the far South Side of Chicago where I was hanging out. Even in the sixties and seventies, the effects of prohibition and the mob lived on in the roadhouses, after-hours joints, and sleazy brothels that lined the otherwise insignificant commercial centers of towns like Calumet City, Chicago Heights, and Indiana Harbor. During the Jazz Age, some of these syndicate joints were also hot spots for music and dancing. Milton "Mezz" Mezzrow's fascinating autobiography (with Bernard Wolf) *Really the Blues* (1972) includes a number of detailed scenes of jam sessions with Bix, Davey Tough, and others among the white jazz originals. These sessions took place in and around Indiana Harbor, South Chicago, Gary, and over the prairies to the college fraternities of Indiana University in Bloomington, where Charmichael invited Bix and other white Chicago musicians to perform with him at fraternity parties.

About twenty years ago, I got the idea of using some of this material along with my own knowledge of the places and people of Chicago's South Side to write about what the early jazz era was like in and around the mill towns along the lower basin of Lake Michigan. Prohibition resulted in the dispersal of jazz venues to speakeasies and roadhouses, usually mob controlled and often located either in the entertainment zone of Chicago's Bronzeville or in the industrial zones between Chicago and the corrupt small towns on the Indiana-Illinois border, where the music and its followers were banished even further to the margins of the city.

After playing around with various approaches and forms, I simply began writing a set of field notes of some jazz experiences that were based on reading original sources and on my own field trips to the actual places where remnants of the twenties still existed. For example, taking a scene from a session Mezz Mezzrow fronted at the mobbed-up Martinique roadhouse in Indiana Harbor on the weekend of August 19, 1924, I wrote notes as if I were a beginning field researcher lucky enough to be on hand that evening when Bix Beiderbecke joined the session and lit up the room as only he could do. Fresh from the social science building on the Midway in Hyde Park, I somewhat timidly entered the Martinique at far too early an hour to hear the music. Doggedly, I pushed myself in the faces of the people who made the scene around that roadhouse bar. Some of these were people I actually knew years ago when my wife Susan and I lived in South Chicago, among them were steelworkers, gangsters, promoters, college kids, and various types of colonizing communists and socialists. Of course I never knew Mezzrow, Bix, and the other musicians, but I knew these communities where they briefly lived and performed during this culturally revolutionary moment.

My field notes brought a fresh perspective on the historical material. As a participant observer on the scene at the Martinique back in August 1924, I was very much in the moment. I could have no advantage of hindsight. Like any field researcher writing notes, I could not know what would become important in the future. So my notes also described other bars and scenes in Indiana Harbor, where tamburitza, polka, and Mexican guitars mingled with the sounds of the new musical form called jazz. I also described how the powerful sounds of the coke plants and furnaces of the giant steel complex that became Inland Steel melded with the jazz and other music of Indiana Harbor at the time. And I began to see how such retrospective field notes might work to create a historical ethnography of jazz in its local contexts.

But the stark racial segregation of the era created its own methodological problems. As a white guy, an outsider of about the same age and race as the white musicians, it was not hard to imagine getting to know Eddie Condon, Bix, Mezz, Davey Tough, and those around them. But under the informal rules about race mixing in a Jim Crow society, white musicians and ardent white jazz fans could visit and patronize many of the black clubs, but that did not mean someone like me, ethnographic ardor notwithstanding, could easily get close to Louis Armstrong, Lil Hardin, King Oliver, or the Dodd brothers. At the time, these musicians were easily approachable. They were not yet celebrities with huge coteries. But when they were not entertaining, they lived and circulated in Bronzeville, a world apart. To be introduced into the black jazz scene, to hang at the clubs where the most talent and experience was on show, I needed a mentor—a Doc, a Sea Cat, a Herman, a Boggs, a Hakim—who would become my Virgil of the Black Metropolis. To my great delight, I found such an ethnographic mentor in the person of Ink Williams, an A&R (Artists and Repertoire) man and "race-record" producer for the Paramount label of Chicago in the early twenties.

Getting to Know
Mayo "Ink" Williams (1894-1980):
Race-Record Pioneer

My first encounter with Mayo Williams came thanks to William Howland Kenney's indispensable book *Chicago Jazz* (1993). The historian devotes two pages to Williams as a producer of race records in Chicago of the early twenties. He informs us that Mayo Williams, as Kenney refers to him, signed artists and produced records for the race market, first for the Black Swan label, a short-lived, black-owned music company, and then for Paramount Records. Mayo Williams produced some extremely important jazz and blues recordings, featuring artists like Ida Cox, Louis Armstrong, Ma Rainey, Freddie Keppard, Thomas Dorsey, Ethel Waters, Alberta Hunter, and many other legendary creators of African American musical culture. But one paragraph in Kenney's brief account of Mayo Williams's career in the early recording business became etched in my memory:

> Mayo Williams personally regarded the separate retailing category printed in company catalogues as demeaning to blacks. Moreover the company refused to allow Williams "to be identified with white records or the white side of the situation at all." He was completely isolated from his employers, who never set foot in his South Side office, and when he was summoned to the yearly meeting with company of officers in the Palmer House, he took the service elevator to the appropriate floor. (Kenney 1993, 126-27)

Kenney further characterizes Mayo Williams as a rather shrewd intuitive sociologist who became an expert on the trends in musical taste in the black community of Chicago. But he also tells us that Williams had limited interest in the music. Apparently, he preferred opera. What does one make of this enticing but contradictory glimpse of a pioneer in early jazz and blues recording? He comes across as an accommodating pragmatist who was at the center of all the musical currents in the black community but seems not to have cared much about the music. Of course, I had to know more and went directly to Kenney's sources.

It turns out that almost anyone who has mentioned Mayo Williams since the late 1980s is quoting or paraphrasing from an interview with him reported on by

Stephan Calt, a music historian and collector of early 78 records. Calt used the interview, although with few direct quotes, in an invaluable two-part article on the history of Paramount Records and its race-record producer Mayo Williams. Almost all of Kenney's material about Williams is selected from the Calt article (Calt 1988, 1989). But few libraries subscribe to the 78 *Quarterly*. To find it in New York City, I would have to make a trip to the Lincoln Center music library. And after I found the Calt article, not a sure thing in this age of digital reproduction, there were few other promising leads. So I did what is normal in fieldwork nowadays, I put the name Mayo Williams into Google.

My notes also described other bars and scenes in Indiana Harbor, where tamburitza, polka, and Mexican guitars mingled with the sounds of the new musical form called jazz.

Google brought me to a Jay Mayo Williams who had graduated from Brown University in 1921. There was a photo of him from the Web page history of his fraternity, Alpha Gamma, Brown University Chapter. The page included this tribute to him from his college yearbook:

> Introducing "Ink," the star end. We have seldom seen him miss a tackle, and have never seen him emerge from scrimmage without a 5 inch grin. Not only does he excel in making his way thru interference, but also in executing end around plays. He has a warhoop that defies description. This dusky warrior is as fast as on the cinders as he is on the gridiron. In the dashes he shakes a fleet pair of heels. Au revior, "Ink." (From Brown University yearbook *Liber Brunensis*, 1921)

Could this dashing fellow known as "Ink" be the Mayo Williams of Chicago who liked opera better than jazz? I ran to the Lincoln Center music library and actually found the Calt articles. That handsome college graduate whose eyes peered into mine from the 1921 Brown yearbook photo was indeed the pioneering Chicago A&R man I hoped would lead me further into the world of jazz and blues on Chicago's South Side. Ink had returned to Chicago in 1921 after graduating from Brown. His primary motivation was to be closer to his mom, who had moved to Chicago, in turn, to be closer to a younger son who was in prison (why I do not yet know).

Ink played professional football for the Hammond Stars on the weekends and produced race records for the Paramount label during the week. The football team was owned by a liberal doctor in smoky Hammond, on Lake Michigan, just over the state line in Indiana. The Paramount record company was owned by a conservative and largely unmusical family of furniture makers up north on Lake Michigan, in Port Washington, Wisconsin. When Ink went to that all-white town to see his employers, he was an instant curiosity to the local children, who followed him through the streets. Of course, he could not dream of staying overnight in the white-only hotel. In Bronzeville, however, he was a man-about-town, very much one of the "talented tenth." At Brown, he had majored in philosophy and, through fraternity and sports connections, had become a very close friend of Paul Robeson. (It seems to have been Robeson who helped Ink appreciate the beauty of grand opera.) Yet Ink never became aloof from the people of the blues. His office, where the artists and would-be artists came to do business, was on Thirty-Sixth Street and State, in the heart of what the locals called "the stroll" and what the Chicago sociologists designated as "the bright light zone." The office was surrounded by theaters and cabarets where Ink and his assistant Althea Dickerson, the piano player and record-store owner, could find all the potential recording talent they might want.

Mayo "Ink" Williams was an extremely down-to-earth athlete, amateur bootlegger, and politically engaged black man who also enjoyed high-level conversation. He wrote critical articles about race and sports in the *Whip*, a slightly more militant competitor of the *Chicago Defender*. He even conducted some sociologically informed market research about musical taste among black Chicagoans. I am confident that he would have been receptive to informally mentoring an educated university fellow with many of his same interests. But what would it be like to speak with him? I wondered if it would be possible to find a recording of his voice and, from it, to learn how he expressed himself. Again on a Google search, I learned from the University of Chicago Jazz Archives Web site that Studs Terkel had apparently taped an interview with Ink Williams sometime before his death in 1980. My search for Ink in the primary sources led me back to contemporary Chicago.

Edward Sadlowski, the Chicago labor leader, is one of my closest friends and in every way a mentor for me in the world of blue-collar Chicago. He is extremely close to Terkel, and through him, I had met Studs a few times. I stayed with Sadlowski for a week in June 2003 on the East Side, between Hammond and South Chicago, and helped him and a group of steelworker friends rehearse a dramatization of the Memorial Day Massacre (at Republic Steel in 1937), which Studs was going to introduce when they were ready to perform. We arranged to have lunch with Studs to discuss how to find his Ink Williams tape.

At ninety-three, Studs Terkel was a living Chicago legend and remained extremely productive, having just published a new book at the time of our meetings in 2003. But he had lost much of his hearing and was still grieving the recent death of his wife. Studs did not remember Ink very well, nor did he remember doing an interview with Ink alone. He remembered that Ink had produced some of the early Bill Broonzy blues records, and for that alone, he was a hero. Studs also remembered that Ink had participated in a radio tribute to Paul Robeson years ago. He was fairly sure that tape could be located, and from it, I would get to listen to Ink's voice and manner of speaking. During most of the time we spent together, Studs talked about blues and jazz in Chicago during the era he remembered best, which was somewhat later than the time when Ink was recording jazz and blues in the early twenties.

I am still waiting for the tape and for my chance to hear Ink's voice. Studs's archives were in disarray because the friend who was sorting out hundreds of hours of his radio tapes died suddenly. Now the project is stalled. Terkel did not choose to devote his increasingly precious time to sorting out his own past; he was too busy keeping up with his work, the baseball scores, and politics. His modest home near the lake was strewn with piles of unsorted books and papers. The loss of past work haunts him, however, and with evident sorrow, he told the story of how all the tapes of his early Chicago television show *Studs' Place*, a show he lost during the McCarthy witch hunts, had been destroyed after he was fired. He did not have the Robeson tape in his home but promised that his recording engineer would know where it was and he would send it to me.

If Studs ever found the Robeson tribute, he forgot to send it. In time, there is no doubt I will secure the tape, but oral history interviews with Terkel and others help put detail on the exciting picture of Chicago during the Jazz Age. More important, they demonstrate that the memories of living experts are increasingly informed by work of contemporary filmmakers and historians who create the scripts for televised histories such as those of Ken Burns. Thus, in Chicago, most people with an interest in early jazz history remember that Clarence Williams was an important African American record producer who also accompanied Bessie Smith and others on the piano. Ink Williams, whose career was perhaps more fascinating because of his greater involvement in many different social worlds, was sinking further into obscurity. Yet Ink was not only a key player in early jazz recording, but his career also paved the way for the discovery after World War II by white musicians of the living legacy of the southern blues musicians. In Ink Williams, therefore, I had discovered an ideal mentor to bring me into the scenes and situations I needed to explore in this project. As the Terkel episode suggests, there are innumerable possibilities for learning more about Ink and the local characters who surrounded him. Oral history work, field research in the old jazz neighborhoods from Chicago's first ward out to Gary and Bloomington, Indiana, continues to breathe life into a career that needs to be rediscovered.

Although Ink Williams died a quarter of a century ago, people in Chicago, in addition to Studs Terkel, remember him and the famous and obscure musicians who pioneered the music, dance, and comedy of the period between the wars. One of Ink's discoveries, for example, was a country-blues singer and guitar player named Papa Charlie Jackson. Few living Chicagoans remember Jackson, but under Ink Williams's guidance, he became an extremely popular figure in the African American clubs in the late twenties and thirties. With Ink's help, Jackson recorded a number of successful race records throughout the mid- and late 1920s. Better-known African American blues musicians, like Muddy Waters, Lightnin' Hopkins, Bill Broonzy, and Howlin' Wolf, are credited with influencing the birth of rock and roll in the late fifties and sixties, but Charlie Jackson was representative of an earlier generation of blues musicians who were part of the Great Migration.

Long before the birth of rock, their music exerted a powerful influence on jazz and popular music. Ink knew and recorded these musicians, and my interest in his career has naturally led me to learn more about Jackson and other blues musicians whom he first recorded.

Ink apparently discovered Charlie Jackson one day in 1924 when he saw him playing on the famous blues street corner of Chicago's Maxwell Street market, also known at the time as Jewtown. As a graduate student in Chicago in the 1960s, I often listened to the musicians who sang and shouted the blues on the same street corners, near the shops of the Jewish clothiers that had originally given the area its name. This famous blues scene persisted until the last remnants of the market were razed in the late 1990s, so it is not difficult to recreate what it must have been like

---

From everything I have learned about Ink Williams, . . . I believe that an appeal to his intellect and his sense of adventure would make him extremely likely to be willing to mentor a white graduate student.

---

decades earlier to be in this cradle of the urban blues with a street-smart talent scout like Ink. Ink's account of his first encounter with Jackson revealed some fascinating aspects of the producer's talents. He was immediately taken by Jackson's country-blues style and his unusual instrument, a guitar with a banjo-like body, which created a unique sound. But Ink was also captivated by Jackson's music because it was the best tap-dancing accompaniment he had ever discovered. From this unexpected bit of information, I learned that my mentor, an accomplished professional athlete, philosophically minded and urbane intellectual, street-smart man-about-town, and successful record producer, was also a devoted tap dancer. How could a budding ethnographer of the urban music scene of the early twenties not be attracted to such an unusual and multifaceted character?

But how does one learn more about a largely forgotten country-blues player like Papa Charlie Jackson, whom Ink helped to become fleetingly famous? Again, the Internet is an essential research tool, for one learns that Charlie Jackson's music is available on discs produced by a group in Austria that is distributing many of the original blues artists of the Great Migration. Thanks to dedicated blues and jazz historians like Stephen Calt and Gayle Dean Wardlow (1990) in the United States and others in Europe, Internet Web pages offer some background on these original recordings. By listening carefully to the songs Ink's artists performed, the ethnographer can, in a sense, "hang out" with the musicians. Tracing their lyrics and melodies to other musicians who influenced them brings the network of musicians and the ideas about their social world that they expressed in their lyrics vividly to life.

Bluesman Charlie Jackson, to continue this example, mentioned that he took some of the lyrics and blues licks he played from his mentor and personal hero, an itinerant musician named Blind Blake. Ink Williams also recorded Blake, who played a ragtime, piano-style guitar, for Paramount in the midtwenties. Blake and Jackson and other blues and jazz musicians often played at raucous Chicago rent parties. Their lyrics are a sociological gold mine of reflections on the rewards and temptations the migrants found in the city's new and freewheeling urban lifestyles. The lyrics from the classic blues song "He's in the Jailhouse Now," for example, recorded by Blake and sung as well by Charlie Jackson, point the ethnographer to a significant aspect of the new freedoms and temptations the migrants found in cities like Chicago:

> Remember last election
> Everybody was in action
> Tryin' to find themselves a president?
> There was a man named Lawton
> From Chicago out to Boston
> Representin' the colored people we had sent.
> My brother was a voter, also a great promoter
> Goin' round town givin' advice
> Says "go down to the polls and vote"
> Stead of votin' once we voted twice
> He's in the jailhouse now,
> He's in the jailhouse now,
> Goin' downtown to jail
> No one to go his bail,
> He's in the jailhouse now.

If one excludes the subject of prohibition, references to politics in the lyrics of the jazz and blues musicians whom Ink Williams recorded during the twenties are far outnumbered by refrains about money troubles or lovers' quarrels. But Blake's verse about the business of electoral politics is a reminder that in the North, despite its own versions of Jim Crow, the world of politics had opened up to African Americans. Later in his life, Ink described himself as somewhat to the right of W. E. B. Du Bois, who was moving steadily to the left, but as an educated man-about-town, Ink would have remained the pragmatist and have made sure to know some of the significant political players of Chicago's First Ward, or "Mother Ward," where Negro urban politics became the compelling combination of community building and street theater it remains to this day. Ink's knowledge of local politics would have been essential in a world in which for every churchgoing musician like

Lil Hardin and Louis Armstrong, there were many more hard-drinking and carousing figures like Blind Blake and Charlie Jackson. To keep his musicians out of trouble, or to rescue them when they fell afoul of the law, Ink had to be at least modestly "connected."

Most graduate students feel the opposite of connected when they first enter a field-research situation. Feeling like the intruder or interloper, we seem to have little to offer and limited ways to reciprocate. Why should someone like Ink Williams want to take any time to bring a young stranger inside his community? In fact, when we first begin to frequent a new social milieu, the people who are busy leaders are unlikely to have much time for us. Individuals or groups we do meet at first are often marginal types themselves, who seek some small advantage by getting to know us. At times, the connection to a potential field mentor like Ink depends on a third-party introduction or recommendation. Or it may take only an opportunity to introduce oneself and to ask for a meeting to explain one's project. Gradually, the ethnographer learns that she or he has something very important to offer in return for a mentor's time and attention. Above all else, we are educated and sympathetic listeners who sincerely care about the social world the potential mentor is best equipped to explain.

From everything I have learned about Ink Williams and his role in the early days of jazz and blues recording, I believe that an appeal to his intellect and his sense of adventure would make him extremely likely to be willing to mentor a white graduate student. His interest in philosophy and social justice, and his very personal views about the music and musicians, never had adequate outlets, even later in his life when, now and then, he was asked by Chicagoans like Studs Terkel or by record historians like Calt and Wardlow about his career.

In most versions of the early period of blues and jazz, the stereotypical record producer is a bored, white (often Jewish) man who pays the performers a pittance for work that is to become immortal. In becoming a mentor for my historical ethnography, Ink has a chance to tell his side of what it was actually like, as one of the rare African American pioneers in the popular music field, to work with the musicians who were playing jazz and blues in Chicago at a time when "race music" was about to change the world.

References

Bandelier, Adolph. 1890. *The delight makers*. New York: Dodd, Mead. Full text available at http://www.sacred-texts.com/nam/sw/tdm/tdm00.htm.

Becker, Howard. 1963. *The outsiders: Studies in the sociology of deviance*. Glencoe, IL: Free Press.

Behar, Ruth. 1967. *The vulnerable observer: Anthropology that breaks your heart*. Boston: Beacon.

Bulmer, Martin. 1984. *The Chicago School of sociology: Institutionalization, diversity, and the rise of sociological research*. Chicago: University of Chicago Press.

Burawoy, Michael, ed. 1991. *Ethnography unbound: Power and resistance in the modern metropolis*. Berkeley: University of California Press.

Calt, Stephen. 1988. The anatomy of a race label. Part 1. *78 Quarterly* 1 (3): 9-23.

———. 1989. The anatomy of a race label. Part 2. *78 Quarterly* 1 (4): 9-30.

Calt, Stephen, and Gayle Dean Wardlow. 1990. The buying and selling of Paramounts. Part 3. *78 Quarterly* 1 (5): 7-24.

Chapoulie, Jean-Michel. 2001. *La tradition sociologique de Chicago, 1892-1961*. Paris: Éditions du Seuil.

Cressey, Paul G. 1932. *The taxi-dance hall: A sociological study in commercialized recreation and city life*. Chicago: University of Chicago Press.

Deegan, Mary Jo. 2002. *Race, hull-house, and the University of Chicago: A new conscience against ancient evils*. Westport, CT: Praeger.

Drake, Saint Claire, and Horace Cayton. 1945. *Black metropolis*. New York: Harcourt Brace.

Goffman, Irving. 1963. *Stigma: Notes on the management of spoiled identity*. Englewood Cliffs, NJ: Prentice Hall.

Kenney, William Howland. 1993. *Chicago jazz: A cultural history, 1904-1930*. New York: Oxford University Press.

Mezzrow, Mezz. 1972. *Really the blues*. With Bernard Wolfe. Garden City, NY: Anchor.

Peretti, Burton W. 1992. *The creation of jazz: Music, race, and culture in urban America*. Urbana: University of Illinois Press.

Shils, Edward. 1997. A gallery of academics, mainly in Chicago. In *Edward Shils, portraits*, edited by Joseph Epstein. Chicago: University of Chicago Press.

Sutherland, Anne. 1999. Review of *Myths of ethnicity and nation: Immigration, work and identity in the Belize banana industry*, by Mark Moberg. *Journal of Political Ecology: Case Studies in History and Society*, vol. 6.

Suttles, Gerald D. 1990. *The man-made city: The land-use confidence game in Chicago*. Chicago: University of Chicago Press.

Whyte, William F. 1943. *Street corner society: The social structure of an Italian slum*. Chicago: University of Chicago Press.

Beyond *Mysterium Tremendum*: Thoughts toward an Aesthetic Study of Religious Experience

By

OMAR M. MCROBERTS

Much sociological ethnography of religion values an objective distance between observer and subject to the point of reducing religion to a catalogue of doctrines and rituals, failing all the while to take seriously the subjective experiences of believers and the experiences of ethnographers themselves. The association of religious experience with transcendent feelings of awe or ecstasy, coupled with the methodological impossibility of perfect empathy, further drives the ethnography of religion away from the consideration of religious experience. I offer thoughts toward an aesthetics-oriented method of studying lived religiosity, whereby the ethnographer becomes sensitive to aspects of religious experience that are precognitive but not necessarily spiritual.

Keywords: ethnography; religion; aesthetics; congregational studies

Of all the commonly perceived strengths of ethnographic methodology, empathy stands out as the most mysterious and powerful. Whether or not we make explicit empathic claims, ethnographers often implicitly claim to understand the actual experiences and perspectives of the people they study, as well as the micro-interactive mechanics, cultural codes, and exogenous forces that define and reproduce social settings. Building perhaps on Max Weber's injunction that *verstehen*, or social understanding, be a central preoccupation of sociology, ethnographies commonly suggest what it might feel like to be a part of the social worlds we study, even when these empathic gestures are not built into a formal account of how those social worlds operate. Those who consume ethnographic accounts reserve special praise for those works offering gripping, gritty,

Omar M. McRoberts is an assistant professor of sociology at the University of Chicago. He is most recently the author of Streets of Glory: Church and Community in a Black Urban Neighborhood (*University of Chicago Press, 2003*).

NOTE: The author thanks Andrew Abbott for helpful feedback on a draft of this article.

DOI: 10.1177/0002716204267111

or otherwise moving tales. Such tales are prized because they seem to offer emotional access to the lives of ethnographic subjects. They give readers the sense that without leaving their armchairs, they have touched a system of experiences distant from their own but rendered uncannily familiar by the ethnographer's skillful transmission of the subjects' inner states.

Especially compelling are those accounts depicting the ethnographer's own measured conversion to the worldview in question. It is "conversion" because the ethnographer tries to enter some of the social categories he wants to study. Sometimes, the ethnographer existed inside one of these categories prior to beginning the period of official study. In either case, the claim of empathy with subjects issues in part from the ethnographer's attempt to inhabit the lifestyle in question. It is "measured" because, even as she moves toward immersion, the ethnographer leaves behind a gumdrop trail of analytical observations and questions, which she (perhaps) remembers to trace back home to the typewriter daily.

In studies of secular settings, this arching toward empathy through conversion tends to signal the ethnographer's special authority and dedication to the goal of deep sociological understanding. Michael Burawoy's (1982) classic analysis of the dynamics of worker "consent" on a shop floor surely would not have been as insightful had he himself not become a machinist, asking himself from this viewpoint whether the questions that dominated industrial sociology were the most incisive ones. As Burawoy confessed,

> In the beginning, largely out of fear and ineptitude, I shifted between contempt and awe for what I thought was an excessive expenditure of effort and ingenuity. Why should workers push themselves to advance the interest of the company? Why cooperate with and sometimes even exceed the expectations of those "people upstairs" who "will do anything to squeeze another piece out of you"? But it wasn't long before I too was breaking my back to make out, to make the quota, to discover a new angle, and to run two jobs at once—risking life and limb for that extra piece. What was driving me to increase Allied's profits? Why was I actively participating in the intensification of my own exploitation and even losing my temper when I couldn't? (p. xi)

Rather than generating doubt about his status as an objective observer, Burawoy's personal experience as a machinist adds a certain *intimate validity* to his claims about the everyday psychology of industrial labor.

Howard Becker (1997), in the pieces that appear in his *Outsiders*, is far less confessional than Burawoy; yet it is clear that he has gained access to regular marijuana users and jazz musicians in large part because he himself worked for years as a "professional dance musician." In other words, he had established himself in a "deviant" subculture about which he would later write. He viewed his immersion in this subculture and donning of the "deviant" viewpoint not as a breach of scientific distance but as a prerequisite for gaining access to the set and scene and for generating original sociological insight. "If we study the processes involved in deviance," Becker posits, "we must take the viewpoint of at least one of the groups involved, either those who are treated as deviant or of those who label others as deviant" (p. 172).

Perhaps the most intense ethnographic conversion in recent years, and the most explicit justification for conversion, is related in Loic Wacquant's (2003) work on boxing culture on Chicago's South Side. In his prefatory call for an authentically "carnal" sociology, Wacquant goes as far as invoking the very term, for

> there is nothing better than initiatory immersion and even *moral and sensual conversion* to the cosmos under investigation, construed as a technique of observation and analysis that, on the express condition that it be theoretically armed, makes it possible for the sociologist to appropriate in and through practice the cognitive, aesthetic, ethical, and conative schemata that those who inhabit that cosmos engage in their everyday deeds. (p. vii-viii; emphasis in original)

I need not mention that Wacquant became a boxer, reporting often from his own fleshly vantage point the sociological significance of this boxing lifeworld. While he will never, despite his conversion, be an African American male ringed into boxing by disparaging socioeconomic conditions, it is obvious that Wacquant has gone to great personal lengths to understand this culture of psycho-physiological discipline.

Religious Experience and the Empathic Dilemma

I mention these works not because I find anything acutely wrong with them nor because I find ethnographic conversion to be an inappropriate scholarly approach. Rather, I mention them with a sense of irony, even a touch of envy. For as an ethnographer of religion, I am aware that the goal of empathy in general and the path of ethnographic conversion in particular are understood quite differently when the researcher is in the pew or on the meditation cushion or prayer rug. Somehow, the idea of an ethnographer using his status as a minister to gain research access to a church, or joining a religion to understand *experientially* how the spiritual motivates human action, seems suspect from a sociological standpoint, at least compared to working as a machinist, gigging as a jazz musician, or joining an ascetic order of boxing adepts.

The very desirability of empathy with people's experiences comes into question when religion is the subject. What does it mean to relate to the experience of a person who has undergone a powerful conversion to Islam, been overtaken by the Holy Ghost, been overcome by the ineffable Truth of the Upanishads, or been lifted out of an existential crisis through participation in a shape-note singing choir? What does it mean to empathize with people who routinely experience religion from the position of thoroughgoing conviction? Such empathy could imply subjective *spiritual* conversion as well as a behavioral conversion to a way of life. This gesture toward empathy would not be different from any other ethnographic conversion, except that it would involve accepting the metaphysical system posited by the religion and, apparently (who knows, until tried?), experienced by believers.

When ethnographers operating in secular settings convert to the worldviews and worlds of experience they study, they need not claim to have experienced a spiritual order. It is enough to claim experiential understanding of a cultural system, an emotional order, a tactile alcove. One need not claim to understand the Holy to explain the paradox of agency on the shop floor. Wacquant uses the ethereal language of "mystery" and "cosmos" and "soul" to describe his boxing conversion, but he did not, say, give his soul to Christ to explain how giving one's soul to Christ alters one's status in a social order.

The experiential, empathy-seeking sociology achieved so skillfully by certain ethnographers of secular settings has been nearly absent in the sociology of religion. In the latter, the zone of experiential access to subject worldviews seems narrower than in the former, and the meaning of *objectivity* appears less flexible. In reportage at least, ethnographies of religion commonly take a more distant, agnostic, "realist-tale" stance (Van Maanen 1998). Few sociological ethnographers of religion claim any level of empathy with the people they study. When they do, their remarks on the matter resemble apology more than justification since the implication is that the ethnographer has experienced the spiritual truth of the religion under study. Compare the matter-of-fact, even celebratory confessions of the authors presented above with the words of Margaret Poloma (1982), a scholar of Christian charismatic movements, who prefaces one of her remarkably perceptive and disciplined analyses this way:

> In 1974, my newly found religious faith began to merge with my previous training as a social scientist. Since then, the latter has never ceased to challenge the experiences of the former, and the challenge grew as I proceeded to research unfamiliar aspects of the charismatic movement for this book. I have thus attempted to maintain the objectivity desired by all researchers. No doubt it has eluded me at times, just as it has escaped others who have conscientiously sought it. Both my particular orientation toward social science research and my own religious experiences have surely but unintentionally colored my study. (n.p.)

Later in the preface, Poloma describes her approach as an "existential sociology," which "seeks to understand human experience primarily, but not exclusively, through direct personal experience" (n.p.; on existential sociology, see Douglas and Johnson 1977). Is this so different from Becker's viewpoint adoption, Burawoy's occupational engagement, or Wacquant's initiatic immersion? It would seem so, not only to Poloma but to many others who produce and consume ethnographic accounts of religious life, because religious empathy, at least as it involves experiencing the truth of particular metaphysical claims the way believers do, is widely understood as a unique compromise of scholarly objectivity. The implication is that one cannot really be a participant and an observer in a religious setting. To seek empathic understanding of religious experience is to "go native" in a way that could preclude a return back up the gumdrop path to an ostensibly objective theoretical and analytical stance.

To avoid the slightest hint of such compromise, sociological studies of religion have too often thrown out the proverbial baby with the bathwater. Limited to the role of observer, the ethnographer of religion becomes a cataloger of doctrines and formal moral codes, a removed sketcher of organizational structures and networks of association, a play-by-play raconteur of ritual processes, or an interpreter of linguistic representations of worldviews. None of these roles is problematic in and of itself; on the contrary, all of them are critical to our understanding of religion. Meanwhile, though, the idea of religious experience as something at least partly accessible and even transmittable by the skilled ethnographer is all but lost. While sensibly avoiding intimate engagement with the metaphysical claims of believers, we miss many of the other aspects of religious experience, which we might try to "convert" to in the pursuit of sociological understanding. Subsequently, our theorizing about how religious commitments structure and motivate social action remains somewhat anemic.

The experiential, empathy-seeking sociology achieved so skillfully by certain ethnographers of secular settings has been nearly absent in the sociology of religion.

As a remedy, ethnographers must question deeply a key ontological assumption we make about religion. The assumption is that religion, at its core, is all about what Rudolph Otto (1958) famously referred to as the *mysterium tremendum*—the inexplicable and unutterable sense of a wholly transcendent Holy. The assumption is that the human taste for, and native capacity to experience, the Holy is indeed the main thing from which religion emerges. Religious experience is only numinous experience. Moreover, one cannot merely hear about another person's spiritual experience and claim to have understood it. To understand religious experience, one must experience the Holy. The ethnographer who implicitly turns away from Otto's emphasis on the Holy as something fundamentally unobservable too often implicitly accepts Immanuel Kant's understanding of religion (Kunin 2003, 62), or at least the parts Kant thought we could talk about, as something emerging from humanity's ethical capacity. From this standpoint, the researcher takes formal church teachings, organizational structures, cultures of social interaction, recurring ritual practices, and the entire religious standpoint as things that enshrine and propagate some idea of the Good. In other words, these observable, accessible things embody and act out a moral system and remind the community of its corporate relationship with that system.

Notice, however, how this particular flight from the Holy in the name of scholarly objectivity amounts to a flight from the consideration of religious experience. It is a reduction of religious life to a series of interpretable, translatable utterances, gestures, and written statements. It does not pursue the sociological significance of the believer's interiority, which, as a presumably numinous realm, is beyond ethnographic empathy and beyond direct observation and interpretation.

The Limits of Phenomenology

Even phenomenology, which is most famous for boldly declaring the primacy of internal experience and the secondary nature of interpretable social phenomena (e.g., Garfinkel 1967; Schutz and Luckmann 1973, 1989), does not adequately solve this problem when it turns to religion. In itself, the advent of phenomenological thought represents, among other things, a critical, if sometimes impractical, departure from symbolic interactionist thinking, and there are many lessons in this departure for the sociology of religion (see Young 1997; Neitz and Spickard 1990; Spickard 1993). Metaphorically, symbolic interactionism takes the social world as a "text" that can be read and interpreted after some period of study. The concern is what various signs mean. The ethnographer spends enough time in enough situations to feel confident that she has digested the deep grammar of the social milieu. She then produces an ethnographic account: a Rosetta Stone presenting fragments of raw data alongside remarks that translate the data for an outside audience, thus explicating the social system in question.

Phenomenology transcends this linguistic, translative imagery by taking the social world as, first and foremost, a world of mysterious, individual *internal states*, which are squeezed into the available categories of shared language to give rise to an endlessly complex set of symbolic interactions. The social, in other words, begins with and rests upon subjective landscapes, the morphology of which cannot be interpreted or translated any more than the color red, the fragrance of ripe melon in a glass of sauvignon blanc, or the actual *swing* of Thelonius Monk's piano stylings. Yet, somehow, people at least claim to "get" all of these things, and individuals are confident that what they get is the same substance as what the next person got. The experiential data in question are not languages to be interpreted or codes to be cracked. The ethnographer can only try to feel them for herself and then speculate about how they acquire individual meaning, shared meaning, and influence in social systems. Phenomenology is particularly useful as a humbling and sensitizing device for the ethnographer who is tempted to think that he really gets his subjects simply because he understands their social universe more than any other scholar. Ever aware that he cannot achieve full empathy with subjects, or with anyone for that matter, the researcher still becomes more alert to those things he can *re*late to as well as *trans*late. He submits to the experiential universe of the culture in question to see if he can taste what others claim to taste, and to see how a particular collection of sensory thuds came to be understood as a taste at all. Not satisfied with his mastery of the social text, he pursues the social *texture*, the intersubjective matrix out of which social things emerge.

Phenomenologists of religion, nonetheless, have still tended to theorize religious experience in terms of *mysterium tremendum*, thus rendering it beyond the methodological purview of the ethnographer. For example, in his writings on the matter, Peter Berger (1980) argues for a sociology of religion that begins with the appreciation of experience but takes the ecstatic "breakthrough" to "other realities" as the main substance of that experience. This returns us to the original problem of reducing religious experience to the innermost and loftiest subjective states

---

*For the ethnographer of religion,
aesthetic experience lies somewhere between
the entirely subjective realm of stereotypically
mind-blowing religious experiences and
the ostensibly objective social
scientific outlook.*

---

of exaltation, the understanding of which would require that the researcher convert to the believer's metaphysical infrastructure and then write about the inscrutable. This problem, I believe, explains why few even among the phenomenological fold have actually done *ethnographies* of religion. It is simply impossible for the student to understand and write about religious experience when that experience is defined at the outset as belonging to the realm of ineffable qualities. Rare sociological attempts to do so have justly been criticized for failing to prove the ethnographer's strong claim to see things through other people's eyes (e.g., see Yamane's [2000] critique of Spickard [1991]).

Other phenomenological works on religion avoid such claims of deep experiential empathy, aiming instead to depict the interpretive worldview in which religious experiences are made meaningful. An example is Arthur Paris's (1982) highly erudite and sensitive *Black Pentecostalism*. This pivotal analysis, resting as it does on the phenomenological understanding of social reality as linguistically constructed, is built mainly upon the verbal culture of believers. That is, Paris took people seriously when they *said* that religious experiences emerged and operated a certain way in their lives, and he reconstructed their viewpoints by following and explicating the inner logic of their discourse. Of course, this gesture alone is highly significant since, as Paris observes, many of the studies on black "sectarian" movements "have often allowed the distinctive practice of these groups to blind them to the underlying framework that informs their religion activity" (p. 87). Ignoring the complexity of religious people's own meaning systems and existential sense making, these early works interpreted the faiths mainly in functionalist, compensatory terms; that is, these religions can be explained as systems of emotional consolation for people situated at the bottom of the racial and economic order.

Still, in its reliance on verbal cues about inner spiritual experience, Paris's treatment does not communicate the experiential viewpoint of the believer much differently than Howard Becker's, a symbolic interactionist, who communicated the experiential worldview of marijuana users. It is true that when the ethnographer grapples with the believer's innermost experiences, she has little option other than to rely on the believer's own stated ideological positions on what they consist of and mean. After all, as Paris (1982) states, "a determination of the ontological status of the religious world is beyond the methodological capability of sociology. Given this position, however, one must regard the real existence of the supernal religious world as moot and therefore beyond the limits of social science determination" (p. 85). Indeed, the supernal world, including the numinous experience of that world, is beyond our methodological capability and is probably better off moot— but is this true for all of religious experience?

Beyond *Mysterium Tremendum*

I highlight Paris's work because I believe I understand (even empathize with) his predicament to no small degree. My most recently completed ethnographic work, like Paris's, examined religious life in a predominantly poor African American neighborhood in Boston (McRoberts 2003). I too tried to avoid reductionist explanations and aimed for an account that took seriously people's own intimations of why ecstatic experiences of the Holy mattered to them. Consider, for example, the following passage, which draws on the anthropological lexicon of Victor Turner (1995) but attempts also to explain the worldview of the believer:

> Ritual antistructure begins with the descent of the Holy Ghost, which is manifested in glossolalia, ecstatic shouting, and dancing. At such times it appears that the entire structure of the service, with all its assigned roles, has irreparably broken down. Men and women alike weep and "fall out" under the Holy Ghost. Church leaders become nearly indistinguishable from common congregants in the emotional outpouring. After this liminal period, while individuals are still drying tears and riding out the last shudders of the Spirit, congregations often sing in unison a slow hymn of thanks, as if to solidify the *communitas* generated during the liminal period. During these parts of religious services, the "cosmic power" referred to above reveals itself to believers as more than a feel-good rhetorical device; that power actually descends into the room and demonstrates its ability to level social distinctions. Migrant churches used this ritual leveling not to separate members from the world but to affirm their ability to operate, however cautiously and selectively, in the world. (McRoberts 2003, 104)

In this passage, I moved from technical description to a somewhat more expressive mode, but this was still a matter of interpreting religious experience according to the worldview articulated to me as I had not experienced their Holy Ghost myself. Rather, I had merely witnessed others experiencing their Divine. The following passage employs a similar device:

> Thus, at Remembrance [church], protecting religious authenticity in exile meant remaining true to intensely personal forms of worship that helped the believer to *metabolize* suffering and need—to burn them like mere calories in the fallen fire of the Holy Ghost. Here, the individual's confessed woes and wants were offered to God, who consumed them and faithfully returned the principal byproduct: peace of mind.

In both passages, I offer a condensed imagery to convey to the reader the deep meaning believers ascribed to religious experiences. But again, these attempts to explain a worldview do not communicate an *experience*. The actual inner experiences to which these excerpts refer were beyond description even for the people having them and were therefore not available to me to transmit to the reader. Believers did, however, return from these experiences with meaning-laden narratives (Yamane 2000) in the form of testimonies, the significances of which I harvested.

I felt, however, that aspects of religious experience were accessible to me as a participant. These aspects did not approach the spiritual, but they seemed highly salient nonetheless. Moreover, despite their relative ordinariness, these experiences did not lend themselves to definitive interpretation via the worldview-constructing languages of believers. What I am referring to are my appreciative experiences of styles of religiosity, which varied greatly from church to church, more so in fact than the formal religious ideological formulations I encountered. I could not explain, for example, a particular pastor's way of preaching or laying on of hands solely in terms of her church's Pentecostal worldview since these styles varied considerably even among churches with identical Pentecostal worldviews. Neither could I explain decorative configurations, manners of postworship interaction, nor modes of doctrinal talk and testimony solely in terms of systems of belief. Yet I felt I could see why these peculiarities were beautiful to members of those churches and how they contributed to the deep appeal of worship and fellowship in a particular church. In other words, while these stylistic elements could be interpreted according to the religious worldviews they served, they could not entirely be reduced to any articulated worldview. People certainly sang, preached, and arranged worship spaces within the parameters of their own meaning systems, but they also did so in a great many beautiful ways. Congregants and clergy could talk about the styles, but they could not rationalize the beauty of the styles. Neither could I, even though I felt that I had gotten it. Through my ethnographic encounters with people in many churches, I came to understand beauty as a key part of religious experience and religious communities partly as spaces where people generate and appreciate certain kinds of beauty.

In the meantime, I began to avoid limiting "religious experience" to the things that scholars of religion commonly identify as religious experiences (ecstasy, epiphany, breakthrough, etc.) at the expense of everything else people experience as they do religion. All experiences associated with religion, including communication about religious experiences, are religious experiences, whether or not they involve contact with supernal realities. And while it remains impossible to empathize completely with another being and to describe that experience with absolute fidelity, (even among coreligionists) the relatively mundane religious experiences I have in mind are not completely out of reach for the ontologically agnostic ethnographer. The feeling of a hard wooden pew, smoothed by decades of use, pressing uncompromisingly against the sitting bones and spine, and the very cadence of an order of service must be considered as much a part of religious experience as any sort of Divine intoxication. There is no reason to take these relatively accessible and mundane experiences as any less important to our sociological understanding of religious life than the more esoteric ones beyond our social scientific reach.

An Aesthetic Approach

The aesthetic approach to the study of religious experience, which I tentatively prescribe here (tentatively, because I have not specified and realized it fully in my own research), assumes that religious experience includes intuitive, precognitive elements that are not necessarily spiritual. It presumes that people who choose to practice religion find the more mundane aspects of that practice beautiful; it then sets out to understand experientially the stylistic aspects of religious experience. As such, it resonates with Friedrich Schleiermacher's view that religion is based not only on the human capacity to experience the Holy (Otto) and to discern the ethical (Kant) but also on our faculty of aesthetic appreciation (Kunin 2003, 62). It takes an additional cue from Clifford Geertz (1973), who described religious people's "ethos" (to be distinguished from religious "worldview") as "the tone, character, and quality of their life, its moral and aesthetic style and mood; it is the underlying attitude toward themselves and their world that life reflects" (p. 127). Moreover, for the ethnographer of religion, aesthetic experience lies somewhere between the entirely subjective realm of stereotypically mind-blowing religious experiences and the ostensibly objective social scientific outlook. To deploy an analogy, an open-minded student of early twentieth-century art can appreciate and discuss what the surrealists mean by "the marvelous," even if that student does not believe in the reality of subconscious realms. Likewise, an ethnographer of religion can reasonably, if humbly, try to relate to believers who find aspects of ritual or doctrine beautiful or sublime, even though that ethnographer is not directly concerned with the transcendent realms to which those religious expressions ultimately refer. We can try to appreciate or get "it," at least try to write about what "it" is, then speculate about the social significance of "its" appeal to believers.

The point, at least initially, is not for the ethnographer to mine the aesthetic for meaning the way we might mine the verbal content of a sermon or testimonial. First, the ethnographer seeks conversion: she takes a voluntary step into a universe of aesthetic appreciation. The religion as meaning system can then be described from this aesthetic standpoint, even as the aesthetic viewpoint is made significant in the context of the meaning system. The ethnographer who views the religious setting as an aesthetic universe thus struggles to understand the aesthetic experience of the believer, as well as to analyze and interpret the more formal aspects of religious practice. The result, it seems, would be a richer sociological account of, or a deeper speculation about, what makes religion compelling. Such an account would humbly make use of the ethnographer's own experiences (humbly, because the ethnographer's experiences are not presented as perfectly empathic) but nonetheless avoid evaluating adherents' metaphysical claims.

I present this approach in full agreement with David Yamane (2000, 173) that "more explicit attention must be paid to what we study when we study religious experience." Yamane's concern grows out of his conviction, which I also share, that we cannot directly study religious experience, or any experience for that matter, since a person cannot verbalize an experience without imposing upon it a layer of interpretation and since we can never know whether our empathic eavesdropping on another's experience is real (pp. 173-74). I therefore cannot directly perceive a worshipper's experience of beauty, nor can he describe the actual feeling of beauty to me, but we can talk about the things that make something beautiful for him. In addition, as a participant observant, I myself can experience something as beautiful and compare notes, as it were, with him about what made it beautiful; I can then use ethnographic writing to try to transmit not only the interpretive worldview but also my own grasp of that beauty to the reader. The process would be understood more as the translation of a poem than as the exegesis or interpretation of prose.

It is my belief in this last possibility that leads me to disagree with another of Yamane's assertions: that our inability to empathize perfectly means we may only study the language that people use to make sense of religious experience. This may be true for experiences of the Holy but not necessarily for other, comparatively mundane aspects of religious experience that the ethnographer himself might pick up on by being there. In other words, Yamane's language-based, narrative-focused solution to the problem of empathy is ideal for the in-depth interviewer but does not take sufficient advantage of the ethnographer's willful participation. As participant observers in religious settings, we experience many of the same stimuli as believers. The believer's linguistic sense making may explain the ideological significance of the stimulus, but the words, by themselves, cannot make the ethnographer perceive the stimulus as beautiful. When the ethnographer does perceive the stimulus as beautiful, it is not simply because she has understood the believer's articulated worldview. In fact, believers may have spoken little or nothing about the thing the ethnographer found so appealing. But the ethnographer's recognition of beauty might signal that something is compelling to others in the setting, thus inspiring a new angle of investigation into the believer's religious experiences. Recall that Burawoy honed in on the machinists' ironically self-sacrificing work ethic mainly because he experienced it as his own existential dilemma. Rather than calling this experience an instance of pure empathy with other machinists, on one hand, or a purely objective observation, on the other, he used his experience of the dilemma to question the social context more deeply than he had before. He used his experience as a machinist to discover the unique problematics of life on the shop floor. Likewise, the ethnographer of religion can use his experience of beauty to discover deeper questions about the believer's universe of experience. His subsequent ethnographic account, if it is to convey any of the beauty of the stimulus, will then build at least partly on his own experience of it. The point is, as a participant observer, the ethnographer of religion must necessarily study his own experiences as well as the words people use to describe theirs.

Aside from its practical disfavor of the experiences of the ethnographer, the language-only approach to religious experience eclipses the fact that religious talk itself can be a part of religious experiences of the beautiful. The narratives people use to "emplot" (Yamane 2000) dramatic experiences of religious conversion, for example, are a part of experienced religious life; they do not merely describe religious experience. For this reason, we should examine conversion narratives as much for their aesthetic impact as for the way they signal the neophyte's ideological "alignment" (Snow and Machalek 1984) with the religious group. The conversion narrative may then be seen not just as a meaningful story but as a style with aspects that are probably experienced as beautiful to the convert. Ideally, our ability to relate to this beauty and to emote it through ethnographic writing would transcend the important alignment analysis, allowing the reader to understand better the convert's attraction to the religion. We would say something about the appeal of this or that style of conversion story and show, perhaps, how people attempt to beatify their lives by viewing its details through the aesthetic of that narrative.

Conclusion

In the present format, there is barely room to raise, let alone to resolve, this truly vast issue. I can propose, nonetheless, a twofold agenda for the ethnographic study of religious experience. The first part of the agenda is to reconsider the seemingly antipodal ideals of empathy and objectivity. It is especially important that this take place in the study of religion, for while these ideals are potent in all of sociological ethnography (indeed, in all of ethnography), it is perhaps in the study of religion that their consideration is tetchiest. I assume that our response to the challenge of studying religious experience more carefully and cautiously should not be to purge from our methodological cache any mode of study that seeks experience or that involves an empathy-seeking act of conversion. These modes are not the problem in the study of religion any more than they are in the study of nonreligious settings. Rather, we should re-envision the gesture toward empathy as a highly provisional one in which the ethnographer uses her own experiences to speculate more deeply about the experiences of others. The ethnographer, in other words, takes seriously his own experiential point of view as data but makes this point of view a dynamic part of the inquiry rather than an end in itself. The empathic assertion then appears not in the form of "I experienced thus and so, and will now describe it as what others experience," but instead "I experienced thus and so, which prompted me to pursue a more incisive line of inquiry about the experiences of others."

Likewise, objective distance loses its status as a discrete methodological accomplishment that grants special validity to ethnographic inquiry. Only when held in tension with empathy—the impulse toward experiential understanding—does objective distancing become useful. Such tension "does not seek to remove the actor from the perceptual act, so that he can 'objectively' know its object. Nor does it require a 'subjective' commitment to the predefinitions and categories of the everyday world. . . . The participant side of participant-observation thus affords nearness, while the observer side lends farness" (Brown 1989, 49-55). Objectivity, then, is not merely about achieving and holding the proper analytical distance from the phenomenon one studies; rather, the objective stance accommodates intimate experience, even relishes ethnographic conversion, but perpetually disciplines the ethnographer's reactions to that experience with doses of critical dispassion. In this way, the inquiry makes use of the ethnographer's sense of being in a social world but avoids degeneration into narcissism and memoir, both of which tend to result when the ethnographer presumes the possibility of perfect empathy.

Thus, neither empathy nor objectivity appears on this agenda as an achievable goal in itself. Instead, the two appear in dialectical tension as a methodological heuristic: a "mental move" (Abbott 2004) that primes the pump, or perhaps clears a space, for fresh sociological insight. In particular, this understanding of empathy and objectivity opens up new possibilities for the appreciation of nonnuminous religious experience. The ethnographer, freed from the idea of religious experience as being almost exclusively spiritual and viewing objectivity and empathy not as static goals but as alternating mental dispositions possessing deep heuristic value, can turn her attention to the styles of being that get embodied in, perpetuated through, and enjoyed during religious practice.

The second part of the agenda, on that note, is to rethink and expand dominant notions of what religious experience encompasses. The most formidable barrier to our appreciation of religious experience is our a priori banishment of religious experience to the most inaccessible reaches of *mysterium tremendum*. While cautiously, and appropriately, interpreting such experience by using only the sense-making languages of informants, we become nearly blind to the more mundane religious experiences that we might appreciate more directly as participants. The aesthetic approach I briefly outline here is only one approach to the study of such experience. It is significant mainly because it highlights intuitive, precognitive aspects of religion that the ethnographer may nonetheless appreciate experientially and use to deepen inquiry and enhance reportage. But the point is not to reduce religion to or explain it by aesthetics, as religion previously has been reduced to emotionality, morally integrative functions, the numinous, and so on. Neither is the point to generate arguments for why particular religious practices or beliefs must be seen as beautiful from all standpoints. The point is to expand our understanding of religious experience, thereby deepening the sociological consideration of such experience while realizing more of the rich potential of our own ethnographic presence in religious settings. We should offer this richness with epistemological humility, for certain, but not apology.

References

Abbott, Andrew. 2004. *Methods of discovery: Heuristics for the social sciences*. New York: W. W. Norton.

Becker, Howard. 1997. *Outsiders: Studies in the sociology of deviance*. New York: Free Press.

Berger, Peter. 1980. *The heretical imperative*. Garden City, NY: Doubleday/Anchor Books.

Brown, Richard Harvey. 1989. *A poetic for sociology*. Chicago: University of Chicago Press.

Burawoy, Michael. 1982. *Manufacturing consent*. Chicago: University of Chicago Press.

Douglas, Jack D., and John M. Johnson. 1977. *Existential sociology*. New York: Cambridge University Press.

Garfinkel, Harold. 1967. *Studies in ethnomethodology*. Englewood Cliffs, NJ: Prentice-Hall.

Geertz, Clifford. 1973. *The interpretation of cultures*. New York: Basic Books.

Kunin, Seth D. 2003. *Religion: The modern theories*. Baltimore: Johns Hopkins University Press.

McRoberts, Omar. 2003. *Streets of glory: Church and community in a black urban neighborhood*. Chicago: University of Chicago Press.

Neitz, M. J., and J. Spickard. 1990. Steps toward a sociology of religious experience: The theories of Mihaly Csikszentmihalyi and Alfred Schutz. *Sociological Analysis* 51:15-33.

Otto, Rudolph. 1958. *The idea of the Holy*. New York: Oxford University Press.

Paris, Arthur. 1982. *Black Pentecostalism: Southern religion in an urban world*. Amherst: University of Massachusetts Press.

Poloma, Margaret. 1982. *The charismatic movement: Is there a new Pentecost?* Boston: Twayne.

Schutz, Alfred, and Thomas Luckmann. 1973. *The structures of the life-world*. Vol. 1. Evanston, IL: Northwestern University Press.

———. 1989. *The structures of the life-world*. Vol. 2. Evanston, IL: Northwestern University Press.

Snow, David, and Richard Machalek. 1984. The sociology of conversion. *Annual Review of Sociology* 10:167-90.

Spickard, James. 1991. Experiencing Navaho rituals: A Schutzian analysis of Navajo ceremonies. *Sociological Analysis* 52:191-204.

———. 1993. For a sociology of religious experience. In *A future for religion?* edited by William Swatos Jr. Newbury Park, CA: Sage.

Turner, Victor. 1995. *The ritual process*. New York: Aldine de Gruyter.

Van Maanen, John. 1998. *Tales of the field: On writing ethnography*. Chicago: University of Chicago Press.

Wacquant, Loic J. D. 2003. *Body and soul: Notebooks of an apprentice boxer*. New York: Oxford University Press.

Yamane, David. 2000. Narrative and religious experience. *Sociology of Religion* 61:171-89.

Young, Lawrence A. 1997. Phenomenological images of religion and rational choice theory. In *Rational choice theory and religion*, edited by Lawrence A. Young. New York: Routledge.

Experimental Ethnography: The Marriage of Qualitative and Quantitative Research

LAWRENCE W. SHERMAN
and
HEATHER STRANG

Experimental and ethnographic research methods are often described as mutually exclusive. This article suggests how they could be combined in the method of "experimental ethnography." Building ethnographic methods into the separate branches of randomized controlled trials could substantially increase the range of conclusions that can be produced by experimental research designs, as well as by ethnographic methods. Experimental designs offer greater internal validity for learning *what* the effects of a social program are, and ethnographic methods offer greater insight into *why* the effects were produced. The prospects for such integration depend on the capacity of two different communities within social science to work together for the common goal of discovering truth.

Keywords: randomized controlled trials; restorative justice; sampling; experimental research designs; quantitative; qualitative

Everyone loves a good story. Yet most of us are suspicious about "anecdotal evidence." We often say we prefer "solid data" for making big decisions, especially in spending trillions of dollars in taxes. But if the numbers do not make sense to us, we often reject them as flawed or biased.

Audiences may be even more likely to reject program evaluations when they come to surprising or counterintuitive conclusions. Many people are shocked and incredulous when they hear that an expensive mentoring and summer-camp program in the 1930s caused harmful effects on

Lawrence W. Sherman, president of the American Academy of Political and Social Science, is the Albert M. Greenfield Professor of Human Relations and chair of the Department of Criminology at the University of Pennsylvania.

Heather Strang is the director of the Centre for Restorative Justice at the Research School of Social Sciences, Australian National University.

NOTE: The authors would like to thank the Jerry Lee Foundation for the support it has provided for analyzing twelve randomized controlled trials on restorative justice in England and Australia.

DOI: 10.1177/0002716204267481

204

ANNALS, *AAPSS*, 595, September 2004

a large sample of teenagers for the rest of their lives (McCord 1978). They may find it hard to believe that arresting men for wife-beating can increase rather than reduce the frequency of violence by these men in the future (Sherman and Smith 1992; Pate and Hamilton 1992). They may be skeptical that young mothers visited in their homes by registered nurses will be much less likely to abuse their children and that those children will become much less likely to commit crimes when they grow older (Olds et al. 1998).

These conclusions are hard to accept when they are stated only in terms of numbers. Yet if the numbers are linked to stories about how these program effects actually happened with real human beings, an audience might be more likely to understand and accept the numerical conclusions. More important, social scientists themselves might be more likely to discover the truth about the program effects and to reach more understanding about why effects may vary across individuals exposed to a program.

In this article, we propose that social science unite the insights of stories and numbers. This merger should increase the contributions of social science to the reduction of human misery. The unification of stories and numbers can be achieved by introducing ethnographic methods into the best-known research design for producing unbiased conclusions about the average, numerical effects of almost anything on human beings, who vary widely in their reactions to almost everything (Cox 1958). Ethnography focused on finding—or falsifying—differences between randomly assigned treatment groups would not be "experimental" from the standpoint of ethnographic methods; standard methods of observation and interviews would suffice. From the standpoint of field experiments, however, the introduction of ethnography as a form of data collection would create an entirely new domain within work already dubbed "experimental," such as "experimental physics" or "experimental criminology." This work could quite properly be called "experimental ethnography."

Experimental ethnography is a tool for answering questions about *why* programmatic attempts to solve human problems produce *what* effects, on average, in the context of the strong internal validity of large-sample, randomized, controlled field experiments (Campbell and Stanley 1963). The hypothesis that the two methods are "a thousand steps removed" from one another (Maruna 2001) can be falsified by the joint efforts of ethnographers and experimentalists. This strategy can achieve experiments that create both a strong "black box" test of cause and effect and a rich distillation of how those effects happened inside that black box, person by person, case by case, and story by story.

The article begins with a brief historical context for the proposal for experimental ethnography. It then tells a story about one case in a controlled experiment testing a radical new approach to criminal justice. Using that story as the example for experimental ethnography, the article describes the sampling strategies and qualitative research methods that could be used to enrich any field experiment. The article then turns to the question of systematic reviews of experiments and the crucial role experimental ethnography can make in learning "what works." It concludes with a brief look at the likely or possible future of the invention of experimental ethnography.

The Rise and Fall of the Wall

For the past two centuries, the study of society has been divided by a visceral difference in taste among scholars. For several millennia, historians and biographers have recorded the *stories* of human society, emphasizing the unique facts of each event and its specific antecedents. Since the early nineteenth century, however, natural philosophers (later called "scientists") have computed the *averages* of human society: the central tendencies and distributions of the human condition that encompass millions of stories in a few numbers. Ever since then, students of society have gathered in two camps, separated by a thick wall: those who prefer stories (e.g., Mayhew 1861-1862; Anderson 1978) and those who prefer numbers (Quetelet 1835; Stouffer et al. 1949). Perhaps the high point of this wall was captured in W. H. Auden's 1946 poem "Under Which Lyre":

Thou shalt not answer questionnaires
or quizzes upon world affairs.
Thou shalt not sit with statisticians
nor commit a social science.

At the close of the twentieth century, the wall began to fall between the two camps. Scholars began to integrate qualitative and quantitative materials to generate and test hypotheses in history (e.g., Cannadine 1990), psychology (e.g., Sulloway 1996), sociology (e.g., Massey and Denton 1993), political science (e.g., Putnam 2000), economics (e.g., Reuter 1983), criminology (e.g., Sampson and Laub 1993), and psychiatry (e.g., Vaillant 2002). While by no means unprecedented, the integration of stories and numbers in these "natural history" analyses created a new climate in which the assumptions of two centuries of division could be reexamined.

Ironically, the branch of social science that had first advocated the integration of stories and numbers has yet to achieve it. Program evaluation, the applied social science that blossomed with the War on Poverty of the 1960s, created textbook doctrine about the integration of *process* evaluations and *impact* evaluations (Weiss 1972). Process evaluations were designed to tell the story about how a program was (or was not) implemented as planned, while impact evaluations were designed to analyze numbers measuring the effects that the program caused to occur on the people exposed to the program.

In theory, both methods were to be used in evaluations of every type of social program, from Head Start to welfare reform. In practice, so many programs broke down during implementation that there was only a story to tell and no numbers to analyze. This repeated experience led to a rising distaste for impact evaluations among the more story-centric process evaluators, who began to attack the wisdom of even attempting to generate numbers that could measure average effects of programs across large numbers of people (e.g., Schorr 1997). Rejecting homothetic views of program effects on the medical model, some evaluation researchers have cast the idiographic or contextually "situated" conclusion as the only kind of knowledge that is possible.

Medicine and individual differences

Nowhere has the wall between numbers and stories in treatment evaluations been more rigid than in medicine. When the bloodletting of patients was first subjected to a numerical impact evaluation (Louis 1835), the study was widely attacked by physicians who objected to the basic idea of generalizing about treatment effects. (Note that this was the same year, in the same city, in which Quetelet first published the idea of using social statistics to describe the "average man.") One critic of Dr. Louis's "numerical method" of evaluating medical treatments, Dr. Benigno Juan Isidoro Risueno D'Amador, said that the method could lead to a substitution of "a uniform, blind and mechanical routine for the action of the spirit and individual genius of the [physician] artist" (quoted in Millenson 1997, 98-99).

Almost two centuries later, many would say that D'Amador was right: that medicine has become far too blind to individual differences and that the quest for average effects has produced a uniform approach that ignores the variability of responses to medical treatments. Few modern critics of the method would want to give up the many benefits of the numerical method of medical impact evaluations: a vaccine for polio (Smith 1990), a cure for tuberculosis (Streptomycin Tuberculosis Trials Committee 1948), and a life-extending treatment for AIDS are but a few examples. But even a pharmaceutical company executive has declared that most drugs "don't work for most people"—in the sense that average effects may reflect successful treatment of only a minority of patients in a randomized clinical trial—and that individualized pharmacotherapy based on individual DNA differences will lead to much higher rates of successful treatment among all patients with the same disease (Connor 2003).

The era in which DNA differences might also be taken into account in evaluating the effects of social programs may not be far off, given the advances in the basic science of interactions between genes and social environments (e.g., Caspi et al. 2002). The precision contributed by such new measures, however, is likely to be more numerical than narrative. As long as people are highly influenced by situational-specific emotions in their reactions to attempts to influence their behavior, the need will be great for adding knowledge about a social individuation in program effects that may be equivalent to DNA differences in medical treatment effects. And as long as people generally feel more qualified to hold opinions about the causes and cures of human behavior than about the causes and cures of disease, it will be more important to address those opinions with individual-level stories as well as with numbers.

A Story from an Experiment

One story that illustrates this point comes from an experiment in a series of tests of a new program called "restorative justice" (RJ) (Braithwaite 2002; Strang 2002). The story describes the way the program works and sets the stage for proposing the structure of an experimental ethnography research design to examine key questions about RJ—or any other randomized trial that requires consent from one or more parties to create eligibility.

RJ offers new values and processes for society's response to crime. New values, endorsed by the United Nations and many religious organizations, stress healing over punishment, reconciliation over anger, and reintegration over rejection. New processes include participation by victims, offenders, and all persons affected by a crime in decisions about how offenders should repay their debts to society—and to their victims. The processes also provide a forum for expressing the emotions about a crime that are intentionally suppressed by the fact-finding procedures of conventional criminal justice.

The research question of ten separate tests involving more than 1,000 crime victims and offenders in England and Australia (Sherman and Strang 2004) is whether RJ can change people's lives for the better. Can it cure the post-traumatic stress and improve the health of crime victims? Can it help offenders to stop committing crimes? Can it motivate offenders to accept drug treatment, get jobs, and turn their lives around? And can such effects persist over the life course, lasting decades rather than a few months or years? All of these are questions that can be studied both quantitatively and qualitatively, although research funding tends to be limited to quantitative measures.

In its best-known form, RJ consists of a two- to three-hour conference led by a police officer or other trained facilitator. The agreements reached at these conferences may either take the place of formal court sentencing as a diversion from court, inform court sentencing prior to judges' deciding the sentence, or follow court sentencing as a supplement to prison or probation.

A conference in prison

One such conference took place in a London prison for women in late 2002. The conference was about the robbery of a sixty-something woman nurse at the doorstep of the emergency room where she worked. A young woman—a crack-cocaine user—approached the nurse to grab her purse. When the nurse resisted, the offender hit her over the head with a glass Coca-Cola bottle. The nurse staggered into the nearby emergency room, where she was given more than sixty stitches to heal the cut on her scalp. The nurse returned home, where she remained a recluse for over a year. During that time, she refused to buy another handbag or to leave a room without a member of her family escorting her.

When the robber was caught and pled guilty, a Scotland Yard police officer asked whether she would be willing to meet with the victim to discuss the crime before her sentencing date in Crown Court. When she agreed, the officer asked the nurse whether she would also consent to a meeting. In both cases, the officer explained that there would be only a 50 percent chance of a meeting, even if both parties agreed because of the experimental nature of the meetings. The officer also said that agreement to meet in principle was just as valuable for the research as an actual meeting and that both victim and offender would make an important contribution to improving justice by their agreement to participate in the study. With this fully informed consent, first the offender and then the victim agreed to participate in the randomized controlled trial (RCT). Immediately after the victim gave her consent, the London officer called a research office in Philadelphia, where a staff member consulted a computerized formula that selected the case for a RJ conference.

Ironically, the branch of social science that had first advocated the integration of stories and numbers [program evaluation] has yet to achieve it.

After a series of telephone calls to family and friends of the victim and offender, all the parties arrived at a small room in the prison, where the offender was in custody awaiting sentencing. The police officer who would be the facilitator of the conference sat everyone down in chairs arranged in a circle, introduced all the participants, and outlined the discussion that would take place. He then asked the offender to tell everyone present what she did; she responded with a brief, shame-faced account of the crime. He then asked the victim to describe the harm caused by the crime to her and to others. While the victim said very little, her family members and friends spoke at length. Similar statements were then offered by the offender's family.

Supporters of both the offender and the victim expressed a great deal of anger, including the offender's grandmother. "How could you do this to somebody's else's granny?" she demanded. "Would you ever want someone to do this to me?"

The offender repeatedly asked the victim to forgive her, but the victim remained silent. When the harmful effects of the crime had been fully aired, the facilitator asked the entire group what the offender might do to repair the harm that the crime has caused. At this stage in the conference, victims often ask for the offenders' commitment to turning their lives around. Offenders often suggest ways in which they might do something for the victim, such as donating money to a charity or performing a community service. Only rarely does the group agree on an actual restitution payment in cash to the victim. In this case, the group asked that the offender commit herself to getting off drugs and never going back to them.

Once the agreement was reached, the facilitator called a recess in the proceedings to write up the agreement. The participants stood up to get tea and biscuits from a sideboard. Supporters of the victim and the offender, as usual, talked informally over tea about common concerns, such as raising children. The normal release of tension was interrupted in this case, however, by the victim calling the offender over to her seat, where the victim had remained motionless throughout the two-hour conference. The offender complied.

The victim took the offender's hands, pressed them to her forehead, and began to pray—loudly and at length. She asked divine guidance for the offender and offered her own forgiveness as a means to help the young woman find the path to God's mercy and redemption.

The next day, the victim bought a handbag and later went back to work. The offender was sentenced to five years in prison.

Counterfactuals: The conferences that did not happen

So far, this story is consistent with the numerical evidence available. Robbery victims who volunteer for and participate in RJ conferences in this RCT are significantly less likely to suffer post-traumatic stress disorder and more likely to maintain (or resume) their normal employment patterns than are victims who volunteer for but are not randomly selected to participate in RJ conferences (Angel 2003; Strang 2004). It is only possible to draw that conclusion, however, by comparison of the stories of those victims who have the conferences and victims who do not.

Ethnographic studies of programs rarely make these comparisons, qualitatively or quantitatively. Ethnography naturally focuses on the people participating in a program and tells the story of how the program intersects with their lives. The logic of causation implicit in a chronological narrative is a before-and-after comparison. Interpreted through the language of a participant, the program observer can suggest plausible hypotheses about the causal links between program event X and human development Y. But these hypotheses cannot be tested rigorously within the cases participating in the program because there is no comparison to those who do not participate.

It is only by comparison to those with no program, or a different program, that we can reach valid conclusions about the effect of a program relative to some other option (Cox 1958; Campbell and Stanley 1963). Otherwise, causal analysis is vulnerable to the fallacy of *post hoc, ergo propter hoc*. Only a comparison to what happens in the absence of a program can rule out the possibility that a benefit would have occurred anyway. In this story, for example, the victim might have been just as likely to go back to work and buy a handbag even if she had not participated in an RJ conference. The only way to know if the effect of RJ is to increase the chances of victims' going back to work—on average—is to compare victims who had RJ to victims who would have, but did not, come to an RJ conference. While we can never know what would have happened in the individual case if the treatment had not been available, the great strength of an RCT design is that it allows us to estimate the average effect across the entire range of cases in treatment and control groups.

Nothing in this logic requires an RCT design, however, to measure results in numbers. In principle, it is possible to imagine an RCT in which all events after random assignment were studied in purely qualitative ways. Numbers merely simplify and summarize the comparisons of program cases to counterfactual cases. For someone steeped in factual narrative, such as a historian, it is quite manageable to interpret the effects of a program on a hundred cases, with fifty in the treatment group and fifty in the control. Without ever committing a single number to the page, a qualitative analyst comparing the RJ and control group would still "commit a social science." It is the logic of the RCT design, and not any particular method of data collection, that gives it internal validity—as long as most cases are treated as randomly assigned and as long as all cases are analyzed by intention to treat rather than by treatment actually received (Boruch 1997; Sherman and Strang 2004).

The use of qualitative materials in quantitative social science is often designed to "illustrate," or to bore deeper into, patterns that are evident from quantitative summaries. Thus, for example, in a study of five hundred juvenile delinquents through age seventy, Laub and Sampson (2003, 9) drew a sample of fifty-three men for interviews, stratified on the basis of the three lifelong patterns of criminal offending ("desisters," "persisters," and "intermittents"). But as these interviews revealed, hypotheses emerge from such qualitative material that would be very interesting to test. In the case of retrospective interviews after quantitative data have already been collected and analyzed, the feasibility of testing new hypotheses is limited.

In the case of prospective ethnography, however, it is possible to both develop and test grounded theory (Glaser and Straus 1967) as the research progresses. The hypotheses that are generated from interviews or observations of one case can immediately be tested against new data on the same hypotheses collected on other cases. Even if these hypotheses and their tests are later reduced to quantitative form, the fact that they would not have emerged without ethnographic work provides a strong justification for the added cost and effort of experimental ethnography. In our story, for example, the severity of the victim's reaction to the crime may suggest this hypothesis: the magnitude of potential benefit of RJ on the victim's mental health is directly proportionate to the magnitude of the harm the victim suffered from the crime. Because only limited quantitative data were being gathered on the severity of victim harm, the introduction of qualitative evidence offered both a way to "discover" this grounded theory and a way to test it—on average, in constant comparisons between treatment and control groups.

This kind of testing is best done when all the cases in an experiment can be included in an ethnography—an expensive but not unimaginable strategy for at least smaller samples of a hundred or so. Even the use of a much smaller sample, however, has the potential to generate hypotheses that could be tested against more comprehensive but less direct measures. If only ten cases—five treatment and five controls—could be studied ethnographically out of a sample of a hundred, for example, the selection of those cases (preferably at random from within each treatment stratum) for detailed "boring down" could yield hypotheses that could be tested in future questionnaire interviews sought from the entire sample of a hundred cases. Just as Laub and Sampson (2003) used a 10 percent sample to illustrate quantitative patterns retrospectively, experimental ethnography could use 10 percent—or even less—samples to generate hypotheses for testing prospectively.

To the extent that one ethnographer can compare cases from both treatment groups, it may be easier to detect hypotheses that emerge only from comparisons. With five program cases and five control-group cases, major differences in treatment effects may well emerge through qualitative work that might never appear in

---

In the case of restorative justice, the fact that both offenders and victims must give consent multiplies the possible comparisons.

---

preconceived quantitative measures. In some RJ conferences, for example, victims have said that they were moving away from the city because of the crime. Victims in the control group may have done the same. It may be only from the frequent contact with victims that ethnographic work entails that a comparison of rates of moving away because of the crime (at least according to victims' accounts) would become possible. This would be harder to estimate in a 10 percent sample than in a full sample, but if it were a very large effect, it would at least be noticed and be measurable against other kinds of data. With a good relationship to research subjects, ethnographers may also get a call from a victim who moves back into town after a brief period away. Constant comparisons by each ethnographer between treatment and control cases may lead to discovery of many such hypotheses.

Comparisons that did not happen

What RCTs usually fail to do is to make enough comparisons. Beyond the volunteers who are treated as assigned (control or treatment groups), there are many other people whose lives are affected by a RCT. This critique has several components. One is comparisons of people who volunteer to those who do not. This comparison is extremely important for external validity, in knowing how far to generalize the results of a program evaluation. That issue is especially important for programs likely to be imposed on the kinds of people who did not volunteer for the test phase. The results obtained from volunteers and nonvolunteers could be completely different. But neither medical nor social program evaluations invest much, if any, research effort in studying those who do not volunteer and in comparing them to those who do.

In the case of our story, there would be three possible comparisons. One is between all volunteers and all refusers, on average. A second would be between those volunteers who attended RJ conferences and those who did not volunteer. The third would be between volunteers assigned to the control group and refusers. All three comparisons would be biased by self-selection and would lack the internal validity of a randomized design. But both comparisons would yield insights from qualitative exploration that could be important in understanding the limits, or even the potential, of the program being tested.

Imagine, at the case level, the kind of data that could emerge from ethnographic comparisons of volunteers and refusers. What is the story of at least one refuser? How many days or years did that victim who refused participation suffer from the robbery—missing work, getting divorced, moving to another country to escape the associations of the crime? How was her child–raising affected? Her religious faith or respect for the law? Did she herself commit any crimes in the future? Or did the ones who volunteered get over the crime much more quickly and suffer less long-term effects than those who participated? And with similar stories from other refusers, how typical do any of the stories seem to be? If cardiac epidemiologists study the risk of death in men who differ in how angry they get (a self-selection or at least not a randomly assigned difference), then why not study the correlates and stories of self-selection out of a potentially beneficial program?

Similar comparisons can be made in asking questions about how volunteers assigned to the control group differed from refusers. Were the controls worse off than those who refused consent? Did they get their hopes up about what could happen in an RJ conference, only to have them dashed by their assignment to the control group? Or were they relieved that they did not actually have to go to prison to sit down with someone who hurt them? What happened in their life stories from the time they were assigned to the control group until some years later? Whether by numbers or narrative, this comparison is relevant to understanding the effect of general adoption of the program, especially if the program may not always be possible after a victim agrees.

Another comparison too often omitted in RCTs is between those who drop out and those who do not—except that such comparisons alone are sometimes used, in error, to estimate the true treatment effects, which can create disastrous selection bias and terribly mislead the research audience (Gorman 2002). Victims who consent and are assigned to the program but then change their minds may suffer the most. They may have more remorse about having refused a sure thing, never knowing why the criminal chose to rob them and never hearing the apology that they thought was their due (Strang 2002).

In the case of restorative justice, the fact that both offenders and victims must give consent multiplies the possible comparisons. All of these comparisons between people who attend conferences and those who do not are tripled, depending on the reason that they did not attend conferences. Offenders as well as victims who volunteer are placed by random assignment into the experimental and control groups. In addition, the "would-have-if-could-have" offenders who consented but whose victims did not join the victims who would have consented but their offenders did not. Since offenders are asked first, and victims are not approached unless offenders say they would consent, some victims never know that they lost the opportunity for a conference. Police tell the offenders who consented that they will not have a conference, although they do not say why. Placing the story in the full context of counterfactual stories would require examination of fourteen groups and 196 pairwise comparisons (14 squared) logically possible across the groups:

Offender Groups:

O-1. Offenders who do not consent and whose victims would have consented had they been asked.
O-2. Offenders who do not consent but whose victims would have refused had they been asked.
O-3. Offenders who did consent but whose victims refused when asked.
O-4. Offenders whose victims said yes but whose cases were assigned to the control group.
O-5. Offenders whose victims said yes and whose cases were assigned to have an RJ conference, which was held with a victim present.
O-6. Offenders whose victims said yes, whose cases were assigned to have an RJ conference, but who changed their minds and refused to meet with the victim.
O-7. Offenders whose victims said yes, whose cases were assigned to have an RJ conference, but whose victims changed their minds and refused to meet with the offender.

Victim Groups:

V-1. Victims who would have consented but were never asked because offenders refused.
V-2. Victims who were never asked but would not have consented even if they had they been asked.
V-3. Victims whose offenders consented but who refused their own consent.
V-4. Victims whose offenders consented and who gave their own consent but whose cases were randomly assigned to the control group.
V-5. Victims whose offenders consented, who gave their own consent, whose cases were randomly assigned to the RJ group, and who participated in an RJ conference.
V-6. Victims whose offenders consented, who gave their own consent, who were randomly assigned to an RJ conference, but whose offenders changed their minds and refused to meet with the victim for RJ.
V-7. Victims whose offenders consented, who gave their own consent, who were randomly assigned to an RJ conference, but who changed their minds and refused to meet with the offender for RJ.

These categories are depicted in Table 1.

Most of the 196 possible pairwise comparisons in the fourteen victim and offender groups would not be of much theoretical or policy interest. Comparisons between victims and offenders, for example, might not be of interest to an analysis focusing on victim effects or to one focusing on whether RJ reduces repeat offending. The main comparisons of interest would be between groups 4 and 5, for both victims and offenders, respectively, with the other groups compared with both 4 and 5. Smaller investments could also be made in studying the groups other than 4 and 5. Just how large or small an investment in ethnography would be appropriate,

TABLE 1

TREATMENT AND COMPARISON GROUPS IN A
CONTROLLED TRIAL OF RESTORATIVE JUSTICE

Victim and Offender Group No.	Offender Consent	Victim Consent	Random Assignment	Offender Change	Victim Change
1	No	Yes			
2	No	No			
3	Yes	No			
4	Yes	Yes	Control		
5	Yes	Yes	Program	No	No
6	Yes	Yes	Program	Yes	No
7	Yes	Yes	Program	No	Yes

or possible, in any of the groups merits a separate discussion of the sampling issues inherent in the logic of an RCT design.

Sampling for Experimental Ethnography

The question of "how many cases" bedevils qualitative social science. The direct tradeoff between depth and breadth is unavoidable, given a fixed amount of resources. Whether it is a choice of the lone scholar, with only so many hours to work on a research project, or of a research team with many members, the tradeoff is the same: very detailed insights on a small and perhaps atypical sample of people versus less detailed insight on a larger and perhaps more typical cross-section of people relevant to the research question.

In the case of experimental ethnography, the question of how many cases can become more sharply focused. Rather than seeking to represent the experience of a huge class of people, such as all poor black men in big cities or all women who work in suburban offices, experimental ethnography is challenged to say something only about the specific categories of people in the "pipeline" of the experiment's universe of eligible cases (Boruch 1997, 14). The sampling frame and the universe are identical for experimental ethnography, a truly rare opportunity for ethnography to be based on systematic sampling methods. The challenge of creating probability samples remains immense, of course, even for relatively small experiments with only fifty cases per treatment group. The ratio of potential cases to available resources may result in a sample that is too small to create a stable estimate of population parameters.

One solution to this problem is to focus entirely on the cases in the randomly assigned groups. With ten ethnographers and a one-year time frame following up an experiment in criminal sanctioning, for example, each ethnographer could be assigned ten offenders to interview or observe each week. By design, five of the offenders in each ethnographer's sample could be taken, by random selection, from the randomly assigned treatment group, while the other five in the sample could be taken from the control group. This would allow each ethnographer to be making "grounded theory" comparisons (Glaser and Strauss 1967) as they gathered their data, sharpening the things they look for in each treatment group by real-time comparisons to the other. While the cost of ten ethnographers for one year is not trivial, it is not inconceivable. The cost-benefit ratio would be especially high for evaluating a treatment, like RJ, in which the accumulation of findings shows highly diverse and unpredictable responses of different kinds of people (or offense types) to the same treatment (Bottoms, Gelsthorpe, and Rex 2001, 229).

The sampling frame and the universe are identical for experimental ethnography, a truly rare opportunity for ethnography to be based on systematic sampling methods.

Even a 10 percent sample of cases, or smaller, as discussed above, would serve the role of generating hypotheses and of illustrating the patterns of reaction. Sampling for ethnographic cases on the basis of initial reactions to random assignment would sharpen the differences to be explored and about which more grounded theory could be developed.

The main argument in favor of focusing only on the randomly assigned experimental sample is that it would increase the internal validity of the test. This is true at the exterior of the black box, in which the experimental design rules out alternative rival hypotheses at a quantitative level. It is also true within the black box, where the qualitative level could more precisely describe the causal mechanisms that allow the treatment to succeed or to fail in changing behavior. The combination of the two would be virtually unprecedented at the level of cases as randomly assigned.[1]

Another argument in favor of focusing on treatment and control groups is that it offers a clear basis for sampling on theoretical grounds based on early differences in experience. In RJ conferences, for example, most offenders and victims come away fairly well satisfied (Strang 2002), but a small minority come away unhappy. Similarly, among control-group cases some are angrier about the conventional process than others. If only ten victims and ten offenders can be included in an ethnography, the use of initial posttreatment interviews with the full sample could allow the selection of an ethnographic sample on the basis of treatment evaluation. In each group of ten, six "satisfied" (three treatment and three control) and four "unsatisfied" (two treatment and two controls) could be selected for ethnography. While these samples are so small that they could easily generate atypical results, there would still be more basis at the outset to expect differences that would affect the comparison of treatment and control groups.

The argument against focusing only on the experimental sample is that it would limit the external validity that could be gained from experimental ethnography. The unasked questions about the groups excluded from the sample (by self-selection or someone else's decision) could be best explored through qualitative methods. While a quantitative analysis could examine differences in demographic characteristics, health or crime outcomes, and other officially recorded variables, it would not be possible to use such records to tap into emotions and life experiences. Only ethnography—prospective and ongoing, by definition—would be likely to learn what questions should even be asked about why and with what consequences people do or do not consent, for example, to participate in an experimental test of a new idea. When the process of consent is conditional upon the consent of others, the various pipeline categories become even more difficult to understand without the open-ended scope of ethnography.

The external-validity argument is simultaneously strengthened and challenged in situations of high refusal rates. The argument is strengthened by the greater need to understand why people refuse to participate. The better the benefit that may result from an experimental test, the greater the need to understand why people may refuse to accept the benefit. This argument for experimental ethnography is challenged, however, by the problem of the large numbers to be sampled. Wherever the number of refusals exceeds the numbers of consents, the use of ongoing ethnography with refusal cases becomes more problematic.

In the 2002-2004 Thames Valley postsentencing RCTs of restorative justice, for example, the numbers of eligible cases outnumbered the randomly assigned cases by almost five to one. Of the 706 eligible offenders, 699 could be contacted to request their consent. Of the 699 contacted offenders, 443 (73 percent) consented. Of those 443, victims could be contacted in only 367 cases (83 percent) and consented in only 147 cases (33 percent of all 443 offender consents and 40 percent of victims contacted). With only some 100 offenders and victims lost to contact, almost 450 people refused to participate. Ethnography on all of them would be impossible (unless the authors won the lottery). Yet even sampling 10 people each from categories 1, 2, and 3, for offenders and victims (see Table 1) would require six ethnographers, a high price for such a small sample of each large group. One ethnographer, on the other hand, could handle two cases from each category.

One justification for ethnography in such a context would be the generative function of identifying research questions. Neither the ethnography nor the experimental design could identify causal relationships between the offenders' (or victims') decisions to refuse consent and some later developments in their lives. What the ethnography could do, however, is to explore how the kinds of people who refused, their circumstances, and the circumstances of their offenses differed from the kinds of people and circumstances where consent was forthcoming. This exploratory analysis could lead to future analyses drawing on quantifiable measures that could be gathered at low cost per case.

One option for adding qualitative information to the universe of cases in the experimental pipeline would be to ask each operational person seeking consent to prepare a short memoir of each case. This memoir could be required to follow a standard set of questions, such as how the offenders felt about the crimes, the victims, their lives, and their futures, and how the idea of participating in the experimental treatment looked to them in light of all those factors. The items could also cover the social context of the decision: who in their family or friendship network did they consult in making the decision? Who was in favor, who was against, and why? These are all questions that ethnographers could ask and interpret with greater objectivity. But for direct recall of the emotions and discussions at the time, in relation to cost of measurement, enlisting operating people after the fact may be a compromise approach to collection of qualitative materials at manageable cost from people who did observe the research participants prospectively and directly.

Experimental Ethnography and Systematic Reviews

A further justification for focusing ethnography on the experimental sample is the increasing use of systematic reviews of randomized trials (Chalmers 2003). With each experiment seen as merely one tree in a forest of evidence, the importance of knowing how each tree compares to all others becomes even greater (Sherman and Strang 2004). Rather than writing off the average effect of a series of RCTs as negligible or negative, it may be more useful to isolate the one or two most successful RCTs and determine how they differed from the majority. It is possible or even likely that the difference in question was merely due to chance. But there may also be substantive differences in the sample or the way the treatment was delivered that could help explain the difference in outcomes. Those substantive differences may even point to refinement of the treatment for future RCTs, treating the accumulated knowledge as a trial-and-error process of invention rather than as a verdict based on the average result.

At present, the methods of systematic reviews do not accommodate the kinds of data that ethnography could generate. Yet there is no reason such methods could not be developed. Sensitivity analyses can already be done by quantitative sorting of the RCTs on various criteria, such as the nature of the control group comparison (see Fonagy et al. 2002; Assendelft et al. 2003). Similar methods could be used for qualitative data.

RCTs that enjoy the benefit of experimental ethnography could be coded in very rich and surprising ways, such as a strong tendency of the control group to resent the fact that they were not randomly assigned to the treatment group. While such resentment is occasionally suggested (e.g., Killias, Aebi, and Ribeaud 2000), it seems unheard of to study it systematically. How this hypothesized resentment might play out in the lives of the control group, or disappear after an initial complaint or two, is exactly the kind of question that ethnography could raise. Comparisons to samples of similar offenders who were never eligible for the randomly assigned experimental treatment might also help inform such analysis. Since the issue of control-group reactivity is one of the most fundamental threats to the external validity of RCTs, this task should be reason alone for funding experimental ethnography.

The rising power of systematic reviews to dominate the policy conclusions about innovative ideas makes it all the more important to get them right.

The rising power of systematic reviews to dominate the policy conclusions about innovative ideas makes it all the more important to get them right. Black-box conclusions may be much more likely to mislead, especially if the contents of the black box actually vary. While some quantitative measures can examine the consistency of black-box causal mechanisms, few would doubt the increased insight that could be gained from ethnographic materials.

Some may argue about how large a sample would be needed to generate reliable insights about the causal processes operating with the randomly assigned groups. The possibility of placing an ethnographer with every research participant—victim or offender in our example—should cut short such an argument. Even with a 50 percent sample in RCTs of fifty cases per treatment group, many would place great credence in consistent conclusions found across a research team of five or ten ethnographers each studying both experimental and control cases.

The more detailed the descriptive material gathered and published about each RCT, the greater the possibility for systematic reviewers to comb the details looking for ground theory (Glaser and Strauss 1967) about why some RCTs produced better outcomes in the treatment group than other RCTs did. This "tertiary" analysis of the data from multiple RCTs would strengthen the use of RCTs to discover things that do work and not just to reject the treatments that do not work.

Given the greater likelihood that more rigorous methods (compared with less rigorous designs) will find that promising ideas are ineffective (Weisburd, Lum, and Petrosino 2001; Glazerman, Levy, and Myers 2003), the risk of prematurely rejecting promising treatments may rise along with evaluation rigor. One protection against that risk could be experimental ethnography. As former Attorney General Janet Reno often said about negative program evaluations, "Please don't just tell me that the crime prevention program doesn't work. Please tell me *why* it doesn't work, and how it *might* be made to work if it were improved in some way."

It is hard for quantitative analyses of RCTs to respond to such a request from a public official who seeks out the guidance of social science. No one could be better placed than an experimental ethnographer to answer the call. After we know that in one RCT, or in a series of them, a program does not work, there still may be substantial public pressure to continue a program. Generating ideas for revising the program is just what experimental ethnography could do, before handing a revised approach back to the general experimental evaluators (also known as inventors) for further RCTs.

The Prospects for Experimental Ethnography

This proposal requires two necessary and sufficient conditions to become a reality. One is that ethnographers and experimentalists be willing to work together. In our case, at least, we have invited several distinguished ethnographers to join us, and in principle, they have agreed to do so. Which brings us to the second necessary condition: funding.

The campaign to encourage evaluation funding to allow RCTs has been difficult wherever it has been mounted. Adding ethnography to the cost may just break the bank. Then again, it may just sweeten the package. In social science cultures that have strongly opposed RCT designs (e.g., Pawson and Tilley 1997), the addition of experimental ethnography may be just the compromise needed to bring greater value to the high costs of nonexperimental evaluations. Those who attack RCTs say that while they may tell what worked in one sample, they cannot tell why, and therefore, the RCTs' value for developing externally valid policy conclusions is limited. Those who attack nonexperimental evaluations say that because they cannot tell what worked, their insights as to why a program functions the way it does will have little value. Rather than choosing between more "whys" than "whats" or more "whats" than "whys," experimental ethnography could provide the win-win answer that works. What a story that could make!

Note

1. Multisite randomized trials, with many cases randomized at each site, sometimes include qualitative observations about the site. But conclusions from such analyses do not directly address variability across individual cases within randomly assigned treatment groups.

References

Anderson, Elijah. 1978. *A place on the corner*. Chicago: University of Chicago Press.

Angel, Caroline M. 2003. Effects of restorative justice on post-traumatic stress symptoms of burglary and robbery victims in London: A preliminary report. Jerry Lee Center of Criminology, University of Pennsylvania.

Assendelft, Willem J. J., Sally C. Morton, Emily I. Yu, Marika J. Suttorp, and Paul G. Shekelle. 2003. Spinal manipulative therapy for low back pain: A meta-analysis of effectiveness relative to other therapies. *Annals of Internal Medicine* 138:871-81.

Boruch, Robert. 1997. *Randomized experiments for planning and evaluation.* Thousand Oaks, CA: Sage.

Bottoms, Anthony, Loraine Gelsthorpe, and Sue Rex. 2001. *Community penalties: Change and challenges.* Devon, UK: Willan.

Braithwaite, John 2002. *Restorative justice and responsive regulation.* Cambridge, UK: Cambridge University Press.

Campbell, Donald T., and Julian C. Stanley. 1963. *Experimental and quasi-experimental designs for research.* Chicago: Rand-McNally.

Cannadine, David. 1990. *Decline and fall of the British aristocracy.* New Haven, CT: Yale University Press.

Caspi, Avshalom, Joseph McClay, Terrie E. Moffitt, Jonathan Mill, Judy Martin, Ian W. Craig, Alan Taylor, and Richie Poulton. 2002. Role of genotype in the cycle of violence in maltreated children. *Science* 297 (5582): 851-54.

Chalmers, Iain. 2003. Trying to do more good than harm in policy and practice: The role of rigorous, transparent, up-to-date evaluations. *Annals of the American Academy of Political and Social Science* 589: 22-40.

Connor, Steve. 2003. Glaxo chief: Our drugs do not work on most patients. *The Independent*, December 8, p. 1.

Cox, D. R. 1958. *The planning of experiments.* London: Wiley.

Fonagy, P., M. Target, D. Cottrell, J. Phillips, and Z. Kurtz, eds. 2002. *What works for whom? A critical review of treatments for children and adolescents.* New York: Guilford.

Glaser, Barney, and Anselm Strauss. 1967. *The discovery of grounded theory: Strategies for qualitative research.* Chicago: Aldine.

Glazerman, S., D. M. Levy, and D. Myers. 2003. Nonexperimental versus experimental estimates of earnings impacts. *Annals of the American Academy of Political and Social Science* 589:63-93.

Gorman, D. M. 2002. The "science" of drug and alcohol prevention: The case of the randomized trial of the life skills training program. *International Journal of Drug Policy* 13:21-26.

Killias, Martin, Marcelo F. Aebi, and Dennis Ribeaud. 2000. Learning through controlled experiments: Community service and heroin prescription in Switzerland. *Crime & Delinquency* 46:233-51.

Laub, John and Robert Sampson. 2003. *Shared beginnings, divergent lives: Delinquent boys to age 70.* Cambridge, MA: Harvard University Press.

Louis, Pierre Charles Alexandre. 1835. *Recherche sur les effets de la saignee* [Research on the effects of bloodletting]. Paris: De Mignaret.

Maruna, Shadd. 2001. *Making good: How ex-convicts reform and rebuild their lives.* Washington, DC: American Psychological Association.

Massey, Douglas, and Patricia Denton. 1993. *American apartheid: Segregation and the making of the underclass.* Cambridge, MA: Harvard University Press.

Mayhew, Henry. 1861-1862. *London labour and the London poor: A cyclopaedia of the condition and earnings of those that will work, those that cannot work, and those that will not work.* London: Griffin, Bohn.

McCord, Joan. 1978. A thirty-year follow-up of treatment effects. *American Psychologist* 33 (3): 284-89.

Millenson, Michael. 1997. *Demanding medical excellence.* Chicago: University of Chicago Press.

Olds, D. L., C. R. Henderson, R. Cole, J. Eckenrode, H. Kitzman, D. Luckey, L. Pettitt, K. Sidora, P. Morris, and J. Powers. 1998. Long-term effects of nurse home visitation on children's criminal and anti-social behavior: 15-year followup of a randomized controlled trial. *Journal of the American Medical Association* 280:1238-44.

Pate, A. M., and E. H. Hamilton. 1992. Formal and informal deterrents to domestic violence: The Dade County Spouse Assault Experiment. *American Sociological Review* 57:691-97.

Pawson, Ray and Nick Tilley. 1997. *Realistic Evaluation.* Thousand Oaks, CA: Sage.

Putnam, Robert. 2000. *Bowling alone.* New York: Simon and Schuster.

Quetelet, Adolphe. 1835. A treatise on man, and the development of his faculties. Paris: Bachelier

Reuter, Peter. 1983. *Disorganized Crime*, Cambridge, MA: MIT Press.

Sampson, Robert, and John Laub. 1993. *Crime in the making*. Cambridge, MA: Harvard University Press.

Schorr, Lisbeth. 1997. *Common purpose: Strengthening families and neighborhoods to rebuild America*. New York: Anchor.

Sherman, L. W., and D. A. Smith. 1992. Crime, punishment and stake in conformity: Legal and informal control of domestic violence. *American Sociological Review* 57:680-90.

Sherman, L. W., and H. Strang. 2004. Verdicts or inventions? Interpreting results from randomized controlled experiments in criminology. *American Behavioral Scientist* 47:575-607.

Smith, Jane S. 1990. *Patenting the sun: Polio and the Salk vaccine*. New York: William Morrow.

Strang, Heather. 2002. *Repair or revenge: Victims and restorative justice*. Oxford: Oxford University Press.

———. 2004. Victims and restorative justice. Presentation to Second Winchester International Restorative Justice Conference, *Restorative Justice Approaches: From Inspiration to Results*.

Stouffer, Samuel A., Edward A. Suchman, Leland C. DeVinney, Shirley A. Star, and Robin M. Williams Jr. 1949. *The American soldier: Adjustment during army life*. Vol. 1. Princeton, NJ: Princeton University Press.

Streptomycin Tuberculosis Trials Committee. 1948. Streptomycin treatment of pulmonary tuberculosis: A Medical Research Council investigation. *British Medical Journal* 20:769-82.

Sulloway, Frank J. 1996. *Born to rebel: Birth order, family dynamics and creative lives*. New York: Pantheon.

Valliant, George. 2002. *Aging well*. Boston: Little, Brown.

Weisburd, D., C. Lum, and A. Petrosino. 2001. Does research design affect study outcomes in criminal justice? *Annals of the American Academy of Social and Political Science* 578:50-70.

Weiss, Carol H. 1972. *Evaluation research: Methods of assessing program effectiveness*. Englewood Cliffs, NJ: Prentice Hall.

The Liberty Bell: A Meditation on Labor, Liberty, and the Cultural Mediations That Connect or Disconnect Them

By
PAUL WILLIS

A visit to the Liberty Bell has an unexpectedly penetrating effect on the author. He recasts a planned talk on the crisis of British working-class culture into a wider meditation, shaped by the metaphor of the bell, on the role of culture in popular struggles from below. The bell calls up the centrality of human labor in popular struggle and experience, from that embedded in the physical making of the bell to all the symbolic and communicative labors entailed in the grassroots *cultural production* of the historical meanings now condensed into it. In the past, these labors have helped to produce trade unions, abolitionist political forces and organizations, and the civil and women's rights movements. But devastating economic and social changes seem to have fractured the everyday cultural forms of today, made them invisible, and unwound their links with political organization: the bell is cracked anew. But human labors, physical and cultural, continue even in "new times." Ethnographic social science must recognize, record, and dignify their many forms, seeking, where possible, to make *visibility* a means to self-direction and repair.

Keywords: culture; cultural production; working-class culture; cultural commodity; logic of practice; ethnography and cultural therapy

Philadelphia! An Englishman new to a foreign city, an ethnographer to boot, and a day to spare before the conference. What to do? Of course, the Liberty Bell!

Buried fuses on a time-killing tourist visit suddenly detonate my ethnographic imagination. After a lengthy queue and boring, never-ending security checks, honestly expecting to be bored further, I turn the first corner into the Liberty Bell Pavilion to find the famous embla-

Paul Willis's work has focused on the ethnographic study of lived cultural forms in a wide variety of contexts, from highly structured to weakly structured ones, examining how practices of "informal cultural production" help to produce and construct cultural worlds "from below." Currently, he is working on conceptual and methodological ways of connecting or reconnecting a concern with identity/culture to economic structure, with particular reference to "shop floor culture." In 2000, he cofounded the Sage journal Ethnography.

DOI: 10.1177/0002716204267529

zoned quote, the inscription from the rim of the bell: "Proclaim Liberty through-out All the Land unto All the Inhabitants Thereof" (*Leviticus* XXV, V10). This is vaguely familiar. I follow the crowds around, turn the second corner, and cast my eyes up. Boom! A quote you never hear, "Let the Bell Be Cast by the Best Work-men," gets equal prominence. *Labor* made the bell; they wanted the *best* labor to make the bell! The quote is from the letter written on October 17, 1751, by Isaac Norris, the Speaker of the Pennsylvania Assembly, ordering the 2,000 pound bell for the steeple of Pennsylvania's State House. Boom! The letter is addressed to Robert Charles, the assembly's London agent, who, as directed, ordered the bell from Thomas Lester's Whitechapel foundry. The bell was made in England! Labor, England . . . Boom! This famous transglobal floating signifier/symbol is actually a material object produced by human labor, concrete human labor, specific in time and place. English labor made the bell in 1751![1] Everyone remembers the symbol, but no one remembers the labor, nor its time or place. Labor, hidden in history, made the bell! The bell resonates through my head.

Reaching the end of the pavilion hall where the famous bell hangs, standing before the heavy, mysterious object, I fall into a strange reverie. This solid bell and all that it signifies, made so long ago by English labor, reminding me that taken over a long historical period, the experiences and struggles of labor, even if from a sub-ordinate position, have profoundly modified the social and economic systems that have sought to dominate workers, limiting the predatory powers of free-reign capi-talism and ensuring basic rights and freedoms for the majority.[2] Labor, embodied in the materiality of this bell "made by the best workmen," has conditioned and limited the arrogance of power and its ability to do with and dispose of the social body of labor as it wishes for private profit.

The ringing of the bell in my imagination, however, reminds me of a different though connected kind of hidden labor: communicative or cultural labor. The Lib-erty Bell is material and is the product of physical labor, but it is also a powerful instrument of human communication and culture making—that is, of *cultural pro-duction*.[3] The bell calls; the bell is heard. Although they may not be conscious of it, all hear the bell knowing that all others hear it too. The bell is a product of physical labor and also, and immediately, a source and means of symbolic connection draw-ing in a community of previously atomized individuals now sharing a common communication.[4] Add in the famous inscription, and the bell calls for specific pur-pose, for freedom. The bell is calling me now in this and in another way, presenting a task of intellectual labor. The bell *is* physical labor; the bell *is* cultural production. For me, the bell condenses material, social, and semiotic themes long strung out in different social science traditions but which now cry out for reconciliation.

In the British case, the brute materialities and bodily pains of manual labor had to be spoken, sung and written about, and organized and projected through sym-bolic labor for them to become the cultural force of labor, a working-class culture[5] from which political power could grow. There had to be a cultural formation of a historical persona before "the people" could enter on the stage of power. In Amer-ica, this labor, this cultural production of meaning in different forms, stands behind the many different histories of the bell as the labor of multitudes of activists has

How the Bell Was Made

Workmen dug a hole deep enough that ground level would be six inches higher than the top of the finished bell and wide enough to provide working room around the completed bell. They then built a hollow brick oven in the shape of, but slightly smaller than, the inside of the bell, and open at the top. Next, a profile of the inside of the bell was cut from a board and this template was mounted on a pole standing in the center of the oven, resulting in sort of an over-sized draftsman's compass. Then, layers of clay or loam mixed with horse manure, horse hair and hemp to increase cohesion were added to the brick oven, shaped with the template and dried until this inner mould, or core, was complete. Drying was speeded by putting burning coals in the oven. The core was then lubricated with ashes or pig fat, a template of the inside of the bell cut, and a model of the bell built from the same material and by the same process used to form the core. The clay "bell" was then lubricated, and an inside mold, or cope, built up. When the cope was sufficiently thick, it was very carefully lifted clear of the core, and the clay bell was broken up and removed. . . . The cope was carefully lowered over the core. A separate mold of the cannon (the loops used to attach the bell to its yoke) was lowered into place, the pit was filled with sand to keep the cope from shifting, and the molten bell metal poured into the space between core and cope.

From *The Story of the Liberty Bell*, by David Kimball
(pp. 22-23), on sale at the Liberty Bell Pavilion.

relocated its materiality within different discourses and movements. It is cultural production that has placed the bell, like a jewel in the crown, in pride of place at the pavilion exhibition. First associated with American Independence, in the late 1830s and 1840s, it became known as the Liberty Bell to symbolize and focus the struggle for freedom of four million slaves: "Ring loud that Hallowed Bell! Ring it till the Slave be free" (HRH Moore, "The Liberty Bell," 1844). In 1915, in fine demonstration of the condensations of labor, physical and symbolic, the Penn Women's Suffrage Association commissioned a copy of the bell, dubbing it the Women's Liberty Bell. In 1965, the bell was the scene of civil rights demonstrations. The annual "Let Freedom Ring" ceremony celebrating the life of Martin Luther King Jr. begins at the Liberty Bell.

These examples are rather grand, but the cultural production echoing through my reverie, though including these formative and defining institutional moments, is generally really rather a modest thing, a quotidian nitty-gritty affair. The bell is ringing in my mind to recognize and dignify the countless small struggles running through daily life, the sea of meanings that only occasionally gather into historical storm-force waves. This view of cultural production is distinct from views that see culture as a passive transmission of traditions from the past, from views that see it only as a field for the operations of ideology, from views that see it as a passive reflex of structures and structural location, and from views that see it as structured only from the internalities of symbolic and discursive structures. Cultural production highlights the activity and creativity of social agents, the essential element of which is transformative labor: the active work of producing something new from given materials, producing something not in the same way there before. I am thinking of the labor of the English workmen making the bell and also of workers struggling to form early combinations and trade unions, the grassroots struggles to form the antislavery, civil rights, and women's rights movements. I am thinking that in various forms and guises, practices of the labor of cultural production are the essential and defining feature of our humanness, our self-making of humanness. I am undertaking cultural production now in my reverie: trying to make sense of this heavy material object as an intersection of physical, social, and semiotic labor.

Of course, cultural production cannot simply invent its own materials to work upon. The English workmen needed iron ore, copper, tools, materials (including horse manure), a furnace, and time (see sidebar). So, too, informal cultural producers work over time with materials that are given or inherited. The raw materials and tools for processes of cultural production come in a wide variety of forms—plastic, oral, textual, musical—and from a wide variety of sources—historical and contemporary, local and mediated, commoditized and noncommoditized. The textual "treasure troves" of history should not be underestimated, nor the "horse shit" from contemporary culture, nor the funds of oral history and advice passed on from elders. Ideological accounts and texts also play a variable part, sometimes in negative formation against them. The traditions, continuities, and social inheritances of sex, gender, race, and ethnicity provide their own grist to the mill of every new generation. Many of the symbolic resources used in cultural production have not been named yet by social science classification but are the interstitial stuff of ethnographic accounts of real lives in progress. Because they are subject to the work of cultural production, all of these resources can be made into new shapes and put into new articulations producing new hybrid forms.

Part of the active, unprefigureable, and creative nature of cultural production in situ is that its labors produce insights or penetrations of the locating conditions of existence of those who undertake it and of its own practices and forms—cultures of the manual working class focused, for instance, on the conditions and experiences of wage labor—so contributing to lived judgments of how identities and actions can be best developed in their light, limiting the force of constraint and exploiting unexpected flashes of freedom in the structural and discursive locations of living cultural forms. Cultural forms are of intense interest for the ethnographer not because they show readouts of meanings made somewhere else or because they preserve a set of quaint customs and hypostasized self-maintaining values to be recorded for the ethological record but because they contain a certain elegant cruciality in context, embedded and lived insights with respect to their own conditions of existence.

The Liberty Bell is material and is the product of physical labor, but it is also a powerful instrument of human communication and culture making—that is, of cultural production.

In my reverie, I am thinking that there really is something in left-leaning romantic conceits that informal modes of cultural production might link culture and structure in privileged and creative ways for dominated and subordinate groups and in a manner that yields critical or new knowledge, consciousness, and possibility differentially for them.[6] The bell, the product of so many different labors that present it here for me today, sits there quietly ringing out a whole different way of hearing, seeing, and being in the world than what is central in the boardrooms and cabinet offices. For dominated groups, the experience not just of oppression but of their own cultural productions in relation to it provides a counterposing resource to put against official and ideological explanations of their position, exposing the latter as meant mainly to reconcile them to subordination. Cultural practices provide the resources to make it possible to act and feel differently, to just say "no," upon occasion to feel superior: practically, critically, sensuously, and creatively to engage with the conditions of labor, with the conditions of gender, and with the conditions of segregation. Though associated with particular verbal registers, cultural practices often work against the flow of language, which, especially in more formal contexts, may reflect dominant, especially individualistic ideological paradigms, bending meanings their way. "Alternative knowledges," or better perhaps, states of "knowingness," exist separately from dominant and legitimate forms of meaning, verbal, textual, and institutional. The conditions of advanced capitalism enforce a kind of schizophrenia of *self* and *selves* on the subordinate classes; on one hand, inhabiting the unitary official public stories of *self* policed by language and institution; on the other, inhabiting bodily, cultural, and sensuous *selves* registering the multiplicities of social suffering of want and exclusion as workers, women, minorities, and so on. Meaning comes about, at least in the first instance, neither as an abstract expression nor as an asserted human universal but as an experienced and creative form of exploring the possibilities of the concrete with the resources and potentialities of a given culture. Sensuous powers indicate possibilities within the self for creative autonomy and independence. Outside and ideological definitions of the self are exposed as one-sided, partial, and tending to limit or close wider potentials. The bell rings for me the possibilities of different embedded worldviews arising from the concrete labors, physical and symbolic, of those stuck on the wrong end of the many tendrils of power, control, and authority.

New Times

I stir uneasily in front of the bell, shifting my weight from foot to foot, oblivious to the stares around me. I reproach myself that my reveries have been backward looking so far, too abstract, and unduly romantic. Get a grip! What of new times? How does the bell fit in today? As I stand in front of the massive weight, I pretend that its dark history skin is bright and burnished—like a mirror empirically reflecting what is around it now rather than its past of agglomerated labors. What do we see reflected of the conditions in Philadelphia and other major industrial metropolitan centers across the Western world?

Well, things have certainly changed. Whatever victories took place in the past, the position of subordinate and dominated groups now seems to be changing in most ways for the worse. They seem to have become dislocated from social process. We were all Marxists once and used Marxist metaphors to address the imponderables of the connections between levels of the social totality. The capitalist system of production produced a ruling ideology as well as a ruling class. But this ideology and power were challenged by the cultures and eventually the institutions of the dominated, building up from below, registering their concerns and interests finally on state forms of power (all that is held in the material symbol of the bell). But it is certainly very noticeable now that as the structural conditions of the working class in the United Kingdom, for instance, have markedly deteriorated, particularly for its lower half, there has been no resurgence in working-class culture and no apparent increase in outrage or clear cultural or political articulation of the interests of the new poor and dispossessed on a wider stage.[7] Now, we seem to be in a world of apparently severed or severely damaged relationships between, on one hand, the historical conditions of labor and of social subordination and, on the other, working-class or subordinate cultural forms; between grassroots cultural forms and community formation; between community and organizations expressing their interests; between organization from below and political representation; between political representation and state power. Once, we could assume that all thinking people shared some broadly Marxist view of the likely relations between levels of the social formation, even if we could not spell out exactly how determinations, up or down, operated in this big picture. The big picture would show clear organizational and political expression of one kind or another rising from below. Now, we are stuck with ruined pictures, broken grand narratives, and with marauding commodity culture. Does the bell chime only for the past, I ask myself? What are some of the changes that seem to have put the bell out of tune with modern times?

Perhaps the most dramatic change has been in the material conditions of the working classes. Residents of the so-called core countries have experienced a deep and profound worsening of their economic position. In the late 1970s and early 1980s, the United Kingdom was the first industrialized country to experience massive losses of the manual industrial work that had previously been available to the working classes. This trend is now firmly established across the old industrialized world. In the United Kingdom, more than half of the manufacturing jobs that existed in the 1970s have been destroyed with a slightly larger reduction in related trade-union membership. At the same time, industry has instituted a virtually epochal restructuring of the kind of work available. Taken together, the new customer-service call centers and the hotel and catering industries now employ more than double the number of workers as the old "smoke-stack" industries—cars, ship building, steel, engineering, coal mining.[8] The whole working class has been badly affected by the diminution in both the quality and the quantity of jobs available, especially young people, older workers, and ethnic minorities. From the point of view of the working class, work opportunities have shifted away from relatively abundant and reasonably-paid skilled or semiskilled industrial work to much lower-paid service and out-of-reach white-collar work. The new high-tech jobs and the higher-level training and educational programs designed to fill them are irrelevant to most of the displaced and to-be-displaced manual industrial workers.

A new and developing feature is that the state has also intervened much more massively in the operations of the labor market and a reregulation of collapsing traditional transitions from school to work. For many working-class youth, the choice is now compulsory training programs, workfare, being forced into low-wage labor, or risking the freedoms of the street whose ultimate terminus is often jail or a revolving door between jail and the street.[9] This is a state-mandated attempt to regulate and reform the labor power of the working class wholesale, attempting to drive the price of labor down and effectively impose a new category of the working poor on large sections of the population. It is also to be noted that the state and local state forms are attempting an ever-long reach into local cultural and social affairs—court orders against "antisocial behavior," on-the-spot fines for public drinking and littering, eviction for "antisocial" tenants in state housing, "acceptable behavior contracts"—which have long been the province of local actors to regulate within local cultural norms. Instead of the state, its powers, and its agencies being formed partly at least by the upward influence of working-class culture, the state is reversing the flow in renewed attempts to form and dominate working-class culture.

At any rate, the objective probabilities of a reliable and decent wage through manual work have been radically decreased for substantial parts of the working class, and the threat of its removal has become a permanent condition for all workers. The old expectations often continue in some form but have been thrown into permanent crisis. Plenty of male working-class kids are still or perhaps more willing than ever to take on exploited manual work in traditional masculine and antimentalist ways, but there is not enough work to go around, and many are left in suspended animation on varieties of state schemes and dead-end training programs. Many simply disappear from the radar screens. These dramatic changes have destroyed or substantially weakened working-class paths from school to work and have shaken the material foundations of traditional working-class cultural forms, sidelined the centrality of labor and of cultures of labor within the whole social formation.[10]

Young people are becoming less defined by neighborhood and class and more defined by their new relations of commodity and electronic culture.

With staring eye and widening space around me, in my reverie, I imagine that in so many ways, we are now plunging into an epochal and possibly catastrophic social void. We are seeing in the current postindustrial revolution a shakeout of especially male industrial labor on a scale similar to that of the shakeout of agricultural labor in the first industrial revolution. Nor is this one simple transition but an accelerating vortex of change as the new service industries, call and business data-processing centers, for example, that replaced the old industrial ones themselves disappear or are outsourced overseas almost as they arise.[11] During the first industrial revolution in England, the world's first, the shakeout of agricultural labor was accompanied by mass internal migration from the country to the city. Though lived through suffering, massive dislocation, and countless personal tragedies, this constituted, ultimately, a way out of the void as it faced displaced peoples then. Displaced landless laborers moved to the new cities, forming there new urban relations; through struggle and their own cultural production finding and making new psychic, cultural, institutional, and material homes. But when you are displaced from the city, where do you go? What cities are the new mostly male work-less workers bound for? If you have just arrived with diasporic bags unpacked, where do you go? Cities of the sky? Derelict cities of alienated souls hovering over the decaying city centers where once they were welcome? Falling into its cracks and crannies, making new cities of the sidewalk? Cities of vastly expanded penal institutions?[12] Signed Training Centers, cities of state warehouses for the unemployed? Schooling as we know it was developed for the expanding Victorian cities of the first industrial revolution; what of schooling now for the new ghostly cities of the postindustrial revolution?

Apace with these profound material changes affecting the world of work has been a profound social recomposition of working-class communities and of labor supply for the vastly different (or disappearing) kinds of jobs available. Against the overall gloom, social diversity and some aspects of equal opportunity have progressed but at a cost of cultural fragmentation and potential discord, which heightens atomization and leaves subjects open to individualizing state and educational ideologies. In some ways inversely reflecting the decline in demand for male manual labor power, women across all classes are achieving higher education levels and rates of labor-force participation, though for the unskilled at rock-bottom wages in "feminized," highly insecure, often caring professions. Continued waves of migration, now driven politically as well as economically, flow into the metropolitan centers cumulatively changing their race/ethnic compositions forever and expanding labor supply even as the "proper jobs" dry up. Furthermore, Britain now has a substantial third generation of predominantly Asian British and African Caribbean British youth who do not willingly accept the conditions their grandparents suffered in silence. They conduct their struggles on the edge of an abyss their parents never knew: vertiginous decent into the new cities of the street, mind, and institution.

For white, working-class youth, just as their economic maps are being forcibly redrawn, they have to redraw their ethnic and cultural maps. They are having to recognize themselves, often unwillingly or with resentments, as a newly marked ethnic group, apparently no more privileged than any other, as they lose or can no longer automatically take for granted the central advantages conferred by the (white) proletarian inheritances of a decent industrial wage. Here lie potentials both for new forms of white antiracism, for racial solidarity, for racial cultural borrowing in diverse forms of white ethnicity, and for possible pits of resentment to fuel more conscious and virulent forms of racism replacing the old unconscious and taken-for-granted forms of superiority. The multiplying groups constituting the working class and their multiplying representational forms, schisms, and instabilities have helped to further fracture the possibility of single unifying cultures emerging from below.

Alongside these material and social changes, further complicating their own internal dynamics, has been an accelerating epochal change at the specifically cultural level whereby symbolic resources, from wherever derived and of all kinds, have been subject to commoditization and turbo-charged electronification. Communicative potentials that may have been used for community building are sublimated into the shiny fetishism and imaginary relations of the cultural market. Of course, commercialized cultural forms have been of great importance for at least the last century, but the sheer weight of commercial provision, the massive increase in broadcast TV channels, and the faltering of public service, or at least of its ethic, accumulate to render quantitative into qualitative change. Commoditization of objects, artifacts, and cultural services has become the norm. New global electronic forms of communication are sidelining old sensuous communities—face-to-face interactions with known others—with now literally hundreds of TV channels available through digitalization. This is furthered by the huge

growth of commercial leisure forms. The postmodern cultural epoch is characterized by this qualitative expansion of commodity relations from the meeting of physical needs—food, warmth, and shelter—to the meeting and inflaming of mental,
emotional, expressive, and spiritual needs and aspirations. You could say that the
predatory productive forces of capitalism are now unleashed globally not only on
nature but also on human nature, further eroding and dislocating the possibilities
of solidaristic cultural and community development from below.

Young people are becoming less defined by neighborhood and class and more
defined by their new relations of commodity and electronic culture. Even as their
economic conditions of existence falter, most young working-class people in the
United Kingdom would not thank you now for describing them as working class.
They find more passion and acceptable self-identity through music on MTV, wearing baseball caps and designer sneakers, and socializing in fast-food joints than they
do through traditional class-based cultural forms.

You could say that the commoditization and electrification of culture have
helped to produce a double articulated crisis of the void; not only are the material
conditions of the working and subordinated classes profoundly changed, but the
cultural resources and forms through which that crisis may have been understood
and responded to have also eroded and been devalued. Though exaggerated and
sometimes mythologized now, too easily forgiven for their racism and sexism, the
traditional forms of, for instance, white working-class culture did at least give a cor-
poreal and embedded sense of the self in relation to a larger group and a logic for
understanding the relations of that larger group to other groups, not least dominating ones. Just as this domination deepens dramatically and as material conditions
change profoundly for the worse, the means for placing the self and understanding
are plunged into crisis as well. It is certainly conceivable that if the old cultural
forms and their institutional extensions and expressions had held, people would
have resisted more soundly or made much better collective settlements within the
multiple crises now engulfing working class and subordinate groups. As it is, mar-
ket-led processes of individuation have helped to render structural change and
deepened subjugation apparently into matters merely of personal misfortune.

Cultural Production in New Times

So, in my reverie, the bell rings in some bleak new times for popular struggles
from below. We are plunging into a kind of void. But my thoughts suddenly take on
a more positive hue and my expression lightens, much to the relief of a park ranger
at the bell, who, for some reason, has started keeping rather a close eye on me. I am
thinking that in addition to indicating the unknown, a void is a vacuum; a vacuum
sucks new things in. What is being sucked into the void? Only extended state forms,
welfare-to-work, and tougher penal policy? What from below; what are the sucking
sounds there?

I am returning to the central theme of my reverie: human labor as a central
defining category, especially as it is engaged in cultural production. Cultural pro-

ductions will fill the vacuum! Even in new times, they will not disappear, only perhaps disappear from view as their successive articulations to power and politics have broken down or been broken down. In fact, diverse forms of informal cultural production will take on more importance as manual industrial labor, the manual cultural repertoire, and the traditional forms of organization based on homogeneous social groupings no longer stand at the apex of economic and social process. As never before in recent times, the poor are submerged under an enormous weight of negative stereotyping, assumptions of passivity, and increasingly, suspicions of various kinds of social pathology and dysfunction. Against this, we need an openness to new fields, forms, and retuned sensitivities with which to understand the importance of the creative labors of the popular classes, more specifically now as symbolic labor, labor on and among new symbolic materials. Here is an urgent need for a renewed and retheorized ethnography capable of picking up new forms of life in the bottom of social space as they engage creatively with and make sense of the new conditions.

I return again and again in the cyclical nature of my reverie to the transformative role of labor. Culture is not a passive reflection or homology of structure but, through cultural production, includes a creative element with respect to not only its own practices but also larger societal or structural change. Now more than ever, we must allow an independent social and aesthetic energy to subordinate groups, so often assigned the worst hands and put in category boxes of appropriate behavior, culture, and meaning arising mechanistically (although the mechanism is never explained) from structural constraint. Of course, the latter evidently sets certain limits beyond which variation cannot venture (the poor in England cannot fly to Jamaica to develop their homegrown reggae), but equally, we must have a theoretical way of allowing humans to be seen as living not only through but also beyond the historical norms and limits associated with their structural conditions of existence as they engage in the collective and cultural explorations of the possibilities of social becoming. Thereby, they may more fully reveal the contours of changing conditions, not only the brute economic facts of change but also the orders of how symbolic forms intersect with and embody them, helping to form the parameters of how modern subjects are formed.[13]

What are the possible new forms, materials, and practices of cultural production? What might make up the fabric of the bell in the future? In my reverie, I grapple with the fact that subordinate cultural production simply cannot avoid the commodity and the engulfing world of electronic communication. It is certainly commodity culture that has helped to erode the solidarities of traditional organic communities and their ability to represent themselves at successive levels of the social whole. But perhaps these old laments that have so recently depressed me are still too backward looking. There is always another side to contradiction. Shifting on my feet again, it occurs to me now, lowering old social ambitions, that actually, commodity culture might be quite an interesting thing. Perhaps we must sift the rubbish of the present rather than the rubble of the past. Strangely, I am thinking that there might be intrinsic connections between the cultural commodity form and use, which informal cultural labor can take advantage of, where legitimate and official culture back off. There is an intrinsic double naturing of the cultural com-modity. It is fetishized (breaking itself off from communities, labors, and histories of meaning) simply because it is a commodity, but as a commodity, it must also offer use value to sell, and because it is a *communicative* good, this value must offer forms of shared human meaning.[14] The communicative bit, so to speak, has to bat-tle with the fetishized bit of the commodity, distilling usefulness and shedding overloads of social or cultural value assumed or read into form for its own sake. Fetishistic acid burns away history so revealing the communicative possibilities that survive the fire, making it easier for new informal users to adapt them to the users' own forms of cultural production. Compare this, I am thinking, to the subsi-dized galleries and museums (bulging attics, storerooms, and cellars too) of high material culture preserving holy "auras" (actually another kind of fetishism) around objects and artifacts in a way almost designed to prevent plain or everyday use. So I am ruminating that whatever we may think of them individually, commodified forms may offer up something socially new: profane use value to be taken up by informal cultural production. Shunned by the powerful, meanings, often subversive, promiscuously get through to nonelite receivers/viewers/users without being framed through forms of social dependency or, for that matter, geo-graphic belonging. If objects and artifacts seem to belong to someone else, then they cannot be yours. If they are orphaned, they can be adopted. If the poor in Eng-land cannot get to Jamaica, Jamaican music can get to them—rap and hip hop too. Fetishism cuts the nonrandom past; antifetishism opens the random future. Inher-ited cultural genes are broken, opening up new possibilities for variation. The half-formings and semidecodings of cultural commodities and the recodings they incite may play an increasingly important part in making meaning from below, creating sensuous, social identities and possibilities as *lived difference*.

Here may be clues to understanding lived dimensions of and possible futures for new forms of gender, ethnic, and even class identities. Of course, class-based, antiracist and feminist struggles of the past have opened the doors and laid the ground for new kinds of emancipated identity, but it is through commodity forms that majorities now experiment with actual styles of difference. Women have taken on a new assertiveness at least partly through the mediations of popular culture, clothes, popular cultural images, and more dominant roles in film and TV. With newfound confidence, ethnic minorities are exploiting electronically freed-up symbolic resources of diasporic networks and commodity-borne postcolonial hybrid and syncretic cultural forms to subvert insulting stereotypes and explore possibilities for new identities to set against traditional assumptions of racial homogeneity.

Commodity cultures move with their own flows and their own specific states of consciousness including sometimes an explicit aim to find escape and transcen-dence. Part of postcommodity and mediatized lived culture, especially for the young, seems to be about celebrating transitional states for their own sakes because there is no prospect of actual transitions to final destinations. Both ends of the tran-sition are detached from material reality or purely symbolic referents are found for them. Richard Hoggart (1956) wrote in the 1950s about the brief period in which young working-class women in prewar traditional working communities in northern England enjoyed a brief period of "butterfly" existence of going out with friends after leaving school and before settling down to a humdrum existence in their new marital homes. It is almost as if this butterfly stage has been extended now into a permanent social aspiration. It may well be that it was always the case that the fun associated with the very short period of the transition to independent living, getting a job, and settling down was always more fun than what came before

---

Part of postcommodity and mediatized lived culture, especially for the young, seems to be about celebrating transitional states for their own sakes because there is no prospect of actual transitions to final destinations.

---

or after. But if insecurity is everywhere, then why not undertake the symbolic labors and investments to try to turn the froth of life into the meaning of life?[15] It may be, I am thinking, that something of the *puer eternis* exists in all of our commodity-related lives, adults too, where we are all becoming, if you like, permanently adolescent where the rituals and fun that were associated with a short period of moving onto another life stage have been exploded into new possibilities and new sets of, so to speak, horizontal relations to be enjoyed for themselves in new and very extended forms of living for today. Though with important imaginary components, this also has real collateral effects through the labor involved, including possible formations of new identities displacing previous identities because they have no fixedness in expected destinations. In the world of commodity culture and the market imaginary, nobody knows whether you are working class, which part of town you come from, or what your political views are likely to be. Apparently, you can leave your old skin behind.

So, in my reverie, I am trying to locate the crucial areas where theoretically retooled ethnographic antennae might be raised to register new forms of cultural production. Important areas, I am thinking, are simply the textures and differences (from dominant, overground patterns) in consumption practices of working-class and subordinate groups. What new ways are being crafted for occupying concrete sexed/raced/classed bodies; what new sensuousness embodiments of a working-class manualism are forming, not in production but in consumption? But, I pause,

glancing sideways and catching the eye unexpectedly of a park ranger already looking at me. I know that this cannot be the whole story. These are possible cultural
productions in the realm of choice. What of the realms that are still determined by
necessity, especially, for instance, school, work, training, and state schemes? How
does the necessary connect with the voluntary under new conditions? Of course,
even if attenuated, patterns of traditional compliance and resistance will continue,
but what real effects will flow when the puer eternis, the geriatric butterfly, and a
broadly retread live-for-today attitude meet the also death-defying figures of
capitalist exploitation and state mandating in concrete sites?

Talking to myself now, the ethnographer inside reminds me that real social
agents live simultaneously and in the same life space—the dislocations of the void
together with the recompositions of the social together with the commoditization
of communicative social relations. Ethnographic work must encompass the
interpenetrations of these too-often separated worlds as they constitute the practical field on which agents live and act. How will accelerating deindustrialization be
understood through and in relation to new social representations and identities,
through a world of commodity communication whose materials are out of reach for
the new workless, barely in reach for the new armies of the working poor keeping
their heads just above water in seas of symbolic plenty. The new assertiveness and
confidence of previously invisible or representationally fixed groups produce complex changes for all representations of social difference and multiple opportunities
for ethnic, gender, and class cross-dressing[16] as ordinary possibilities for social
agents to intervene in the symbolic orders of their own social universes. But how
are the new orders of symbolic experience related to structural features of contemporary experience and to the positions and relations of a deepening oppression that
seem oddly to be have been made invisible by the new diversity of social and cultural forms? How will the necessities of new times, economic and institutional, be
lived and understood through these resources? How will the new relations of
exploitation and/or subordination be actually embodied and/or opposed in living,
breathing, cultured, clothed bodies? If culture must now be understood at least in
part as the creative uses of the resources of the imaginary world of commodity culture—changing gender relations and identities, diasporic cultural networks,
postcolonial cultural topographies, syncretic and hybrid combinations of all
these—then what will happen culturally in the welfare offices? What will happen
culturally in work-placement and training schemes? What will happen culturally in
McDonalds? What will happen culturally in the still-existing but sped-up Fordist
factories? What revelations and new knowledges will be generated?

The Crack

Tracking across the bell in my excited state, my eyes fall upon the crack, slowing
my thoughts right down again. Oh dear! The bell rings much clearer in my imagination than ever it did during most of its long life. Just as the bell is both physical labor
and cultural labor, so its crack denotes faults in both physical labor and cultural

labor. Cultural labor suffers from its own self-limiting faults. How can I ask for new public and critical knowledges to ring out without facing some of the faults I know prevent just that. There is the crack in front of me now, stopping the bell's ringing. I reach out but the newly watchful ranger restrains me from putting my finger into it.

I fell into this reverie in surprise at seeing the workmen called forth, seeing usually hidden physical labor made public. But cultural labor is much more hidden— invisible even—especially when it is emergent or when its traditional manual-related forms are disconnected, which is increasingly the case now as we spin into the void, from institution and organization, which at least give some vocabulary for belonging, interest, and intention. At least in part, cultural labor is invisible precisely because we have no means of talking about what it is we do. Five minutes in another class, ethnic, regional, or foreign culture tells us that the mode of informal life and the use of often the same cultural commodities and artifacts are quite different, but still, we do not have a public language to name what is different as the specificities of informal cultural production. The possibilities of recognizing and naming informal practices are further obliterated by the dominance of the languages for talking about the symbolic forms that are highly valued and that attract finance and recognition, which are mobilized for controlling or attempting to control the common understandings of art. These understandings and related practices control the fields of subsidy, access, and influence. The hidden cultural productions of the masses, though vibrant in experience and sensuous knowingness, are never seen, recognized, analyzed, or taught. Perhaps the biggest fault in informal production is precisely its invisibility to itself.

Invisibility curtails social and revelatory possibilities. In commodity culture, for instance, the self-misrecognition or invisibility of cultural production can render its social or socially derived meanings apparently into intrinsic properties of the self (being stylish, cool, hip, or whatever in school for young people; crucially, being popular), which in turn, rather than being understood as an ordinary feature of located, informal practice are seen as magically deriving from the cultural commodity that has bestowed this blessing on the individual from its own fetishized and internal resources.[17] The hidden work of cultural labor that has actually transformed market commodities into meaningful human possessions becomes a steady state for *conscious experience* of the always already singular nature of the category of cultural commodity even after it has been de-fetishized in personal possession and use. Fetishism lives in new clothes. Ever-more devious and cunning marketing practices try to insert commodities as potential possessions ever-more accurately into the interstices of informal production (retail theatre, interactive media, product placing, fluid logos, experiential products). Commercial practices also learn from and expropriate the street and their possessions to redesign commodities, moderating and calibrating them ever-more cynically for insertion into new rounds of informal production. The semiotics of the commercial designers and marketers are no better nor more creative than those of the street, home, or dance floor, but they are conscious of their own practices, which can therefore be directed. There is economic power behind this direction. Meanwhile, consumers are atomized from each other, pursuing their cool essences instead of combining to recognize and strengthen their own cultural productions, the revelations they might produce, and the common interests and demands that might flow from that.

That commodity-related informal production grows more important but is not dignified or recognized leads onto other circles of confusion. For the young especially, low wages and unacceptable working conditions in paid work may be accepted or tolerated, out of not only grim economic necessity but also desperation to get hold of commodities as a means of access to informal cultural production. This is motivated by a profound psychic energy, generated not by a guilt-inducing thing called consumerism (falling prey to fetishism) but by an unconscious or semiconscious recognition that enabling cultural production—getting hold of its tools and materials (actually for processes of de-fetishization)—is becoming increasingly a matter of cultural life or death and of individual viability. Meanwhile, many of the old categories and measures—a fair day's pay, union membership, decent conditions of work—simply fall by the wayside as far as paid work is concerned, so devalued are they now compared with the hidden but profound measures of worth supplied by informal cultural production and meaning.[18]

My troubled thoughts turn to other, related aspects of the crack in subordinate cultural production, the unintended consequences and self-entrapments that can arise from its more traditional forms in more pernicious ways when organic, grassroots institutions become atrophied or disconnected. Take masculinity as style and presence; this is a permanent theme of cultural response. Now hypermasculinities[19] are developing that may be effective in strategies for short-term street survival, for opposing school, for training schemes, or for work regimes but that also produce wider schisms and oppressions for women and other men who are not recognized as neighbors in suffering. Furthermore, their likely intersections with antimentalism[20] defeat hopes of economic mobility and forms of wider social understanding. Similar processes can be traced for feminine and ethnic forms of resistance or oppositional sense making in local sites, which finally wind up producing identities fitting only too well with the exclusions and hierarchies of wider society.[21] Cultural practices make sense of structural location, but these same practices, all the more believed because of their creativities, can be complicit with the maintenance through time of those very power structures and interests that seem to be opposed, giving form for their livings-out in concrete practice. Informal cultural production is blind to the temporal dynamics and ironic sequential relations of how reproduction works where resistance in one site at one time can lead to accommodation or subordination within other sites at other times.

Furthermore, as cultural productions come to define particular factions, mistaken as intrinsic properties of individuals and groups (overlooking that in different time and place, altogether different outcomes would be produced), then widening circles of negative representation and destructive stereotyping can take root, not only in the dominating classes but also among subordinate groups themselves. In popular common sense, different cultural geographies can develop with hierarchies of negative markings of "out" or more "other" groups with attendant struggles to escape from the most marked categories as they are perceived in different regions of social space. A red (neck), blue (collar), black (skin), pink (feminine)

game of jockeying for relative advantage can emerge with groups at pains to differ-
entiate themselves from other groups: "respectable" from "rough," "street" from
"decent," "lads" from "the bosses' men," "white" from "black," "black" from
"blacker black,"[22] and so on. All of these have gender permutations with feminine
cultural capital, for instance, used to put space between an aspirant working-class
femininity and negative and increasingly masculinized class and/or racial markings.[23] In fact, the permutations are endless for flights between (as well as sometimes purposive "code switching" in the opposite direction to gain street advantage
or aid resistant tactics in particular contexts)[24] least and most marked categories or

---

*Just as the bell is both physical labor and
cultural labor, so its crack denotes faults in both
physical labor and cultural labor.*

---

the optimal combination of categories with respect to any set of material, social,
or economic conditions that are faced. Often, categories might be nested within
each other, changing the specific meanings of the enclosed categories.[25] We always
use the categories of the social immersed in the social, so that in conventional contexts, resistant or deviant forms might be used in tactical ways, for instance, without
any intended or at least full subscription to that wider social meaning, though it
might then be taken as such by others. The problem is that competition between
groups over positions in overlapping hierarchies tends to underwrite and reproduce that order (class) hegemony that holds them all together. It need hardly be
added that stereotyping and stigmatizing processes are exacerbated by widening
economic disparities and that all divisions are seized upon with alacrity from above
by dominating groups. Talk about divide and rule!

To be clear, in my reverie, I am not discounting the importance of the bell as
solid cultural production from below; it still hangs there in all its materiality defying
all idealisms. I am not entertaining thoughts of false consciousness or of seeing the
oppressed and subordinated as simply the dummies of structural processes—hapless marionettes jerked about by strings the analyst sees but they cannot. That is
entirely counter to the stream of my thoughts concerning all that is creative in all
the labors that have produced the bell as it hangs before me. It is more a question of
recognizing that nothing straight can be molded in the metal of human intention.

There are dilemmas for us all in seeking to drive back the murkiness that clouds
the cultures through which we think and act. I remember Achilles in Shakespeare's
Troilus and Cressida: "My mind is troubled like a fountain stirred / And I myself see
not the bottom of it." The opacity here is the warrant for social science. If subordi-

nate insights or penetrations offered full transparency to cultural forms or practices, neither ethnography nor its frames of theory would be needed. But if this
opacity is the founding condition for social science, its progress depends on prospects for transcending it within the scope of local knowledge rather than freezing it
within new institutional and academic orders of the mental/manual divide.

I ruminate in front of the bell that seeking after clarity in social thought requires
a double and to some extent contradictory focus: (1) respect for and sympathetic
understanding of the processes of lived cultural forms and (2) an awareness of the
power of the structural conditions under which those cultures form, not simply as
supplying a context or frame but mediating what they are. This puts an onus on the
privileged analyst to take a position, through a separate politics if necessary, on
those structures and the measures that might alleviate their weight. A burden of
inescapable bad faith also exists, I am thinking, in reaching over a class divide you
have not made: on one hand are the dangers of romantic individualism in returning
as hero from the underworld clutching accounts of the netherworld; on the other,
the recognition that what the poor really need is not a cultural vote of confidence, a
"culture fix." What they really need is a "poverty fix" you cannot hope to provide.
Also enforced is a critical perspective on subordinate cultures, not just as a free-
standing moral exercise but the latter as conditioned by a recognition of the complexity of the distorting weight of history bearing down on subordinate cultures.
History structures, conditions, disorganizes, and confuses—not only from the outside but also from within. The very forms that oppose or deal with oppression are
complicit with the way it operates and sometimes thereby are also pushed into a
pathological register. Structure always knocks twice: once at the front door of fate
and once ingratiatingly at the open back door of how we make our human homes.

It is the instabilities and difficulties of maintaining this double and contradictory
focus that cause much heat in the social sciences.[26] The autonomies and agencies
and the creativities and surprises of lived culture have to be granted, and
ethnographic texts of all kinds play a crucial role in that. But, equally, a
nonreductive grounds must be found and shown for their surprising, final complic-
ity and sometime collusion with structure. The same points could be made about
any practice, including our own. Respecting the lived, however, (no marionette
strings) requires the possibility for a means of sharing and laying bare the forms of
this complexity within the lived. To the dismay of the casual bystanders, I am staring even more intently at the crack now, as if to delve into its inner recesses. With
growing exasperation, a ranger stops me from trying to put my finger in the hole
again. The $64,000 questions: Is there a repair for the crack? Are there therapies
for the injuries of life in subaltern culture? In some important sense, cultural forms
achieve, through their own resources, the work of structural determination. Can
they be used, in reverse, to undo their own work? What are the prospects for a cultural reverse engineering? The problem is to find cultural levers, level-specific
means of change (politics), or ways of converting cultural meaning into explicit
meaning thereby limiting the scope of new fetishisms, unintended consequence,
and self-entrapment and lifting the prospects for awareness of collective interest

for collective organization and action to effectively pursue glimpses of freedom flashing from those same cultural resources.

Of course, the obstacles are immense. One could say that a good part of social science is precisely about seeking to go beyond the folk categories of common sense and beyond the norms and limits of everyday intuition in a way that is irrecoverable to them. Perhaps the principal contribution of the most eminent sociologist of modern times, Pierre Bourdieu, is to distinguish between what he terms the "logic of practice" and the "logic of logic." It is not possible to conduct both simultaneously.[27] You might say that it is impossible to be aware of a practice at the same time as conducting it. If you recognize the logic of a practice, you cannot conduct it. Culture cannot work on culture. The rangers watching me suspiciously will never understand what I am thinking about. That would be a sociological tautology.

But trying not to attract further attention to myself, I mutter under my breath that I just cannot accept that only those beyond the crack can see the crack or that it is not possible to work from the outside to aid inside repairs within the grain of already existing cultural production. Important countertendencies can be put against the arguments for the necessary lack of self-consciousness in the logic of practice. Part of the problem here may well be an unconscious assumption by elite theorists of a symmetry in how subordinate cultures work that mimics actually the wholeness and hermetic sealing of how their own *dominant* (white, bourgeois, male) cultures operate in their own more complete mastery of culture and conditions, immune from blunt intrusions of want or naked domination. Historically, cultures of subordination have been riven with brutal disjunction and contradiction, in part making sense of them in personal projects, never complete, and in part through joining the larger social movements for which the bell stands. In our current situation, the fractures, ragged edges, tips of suffering icebergs, and almighty tears in the fabrics of personal projects are all potential grip points for unmasking folk categories, making them more self-conscious while preserving their good sense and laying bare their propensities for entrapment.

Movements in the wider culture also provide possibly propitious conditions for an increase of critical self-awareness. The contemporary mediated and mediatized society provides countless images and representations of different cultures and ways of life from reality TV to documentaries to crime drama, often reflecting deviant or criminal behaviors and alternatives. The latter are sensationalized and supplied cynically for profit by uncaring corporations, but they are decoded in different and sometimes oppositional ways on the ground. The internal development of cultures now, as never before, includes a crucial moment of externality—images, commodities, styles, music styles supplied by the market—and so, an external dimension can be detached and studied. Countering what I was arguing to myself before, the very operations of the capitalist commodity circuits bring restless change, even self-invalidation, in the form of those materials so, for those with eyes to see, continuously subverting unconscious assumptions of unchanging essence and universalism in the materials and cultural forms of commodity culture.

What can be termed the therapy society has grown, where it is okay to let it all hang out, confess to personal problems and weaknesses, and seek solutions whether on *Oprah* or with friends. Sociological gurus have added legitimacy to the quest for personal narratives and self-reflexivity and for seeking clarity in the foun- tains of the self. But the superfocus on the self gorges its membranes to bursting point. Looking inward will never resolve problems and feelings that originate in cultures and their relations to structures that lie outside of the self. So the therapy society uncovers problems it can never solve. It seeks ambitions for which there is no destination in the circles of the self. Impossibilities fuel desires for meaning that may just flash across to the overburdenings of meaning in invisible cultural produc- tion, giving momentary insight into self as historical work in progress rather than given essence. All this cries out for sociological direction. These tensions, thirsts, and fears are openings for critical cultural perspectives and for making visible the cultural continents that lie behind experienced personal problems.

Nothing straight can be molded in the metal of human intention.

There is a huge expansion in another interesting arena: higher education. It is expected that up to 50 percent of eighteen-year-olds in the United Kingdom will participate in higher education. Educational institutions themselves have become primary sites for and of cultural production, formal and informal. For all the prob- lems and contradictions arising between the public and the private, in some impor- tant sense, the official focus on self-consciousness and on the focusing and direc- tion of human powers must have some knock-on effect with respect to the same vectors in informal cultural production. New students, many from working-class and minority backgrounds, are opting in large numbers for noninstrumental sub- jects such as sociology, anthropology, cultural studies, and media studies, which supplies some indication of a thirst for self-understanding in rapidly changing soci- eties and cultures that may cross over or blur public and private realms of knowl- edge. These subjects, allied topics, and themes are also gaining grounds in schools not least in an attempt to interest students reluctant to be in school at all. Training and expanded educational programs for the unemployed also often build in some social studies component. All these provide opportunities both for interrupting or challenging unconscious and received "logics of practice" and for aiding students to look at their own cultural experiences more reflexively. While individual con- sciousness may be taken up, at least in part, with the chances of individual mobility, locating cultures are more likely to address the implications of living in and through subordination.

Capitalist production sites are increasingly embedded in global systems, surveyed, and subject to the threat of export overseas if labor indiscipline, wrong attitudes, or anything else threatens their smooth and profitable operations. But state and educational sites cannot be exported and may increasingly come to bear the weight of contradictions and cultural stresses displaced from production. Cultural insights and analyses can play a role in countering new forms of moral panic about rebellious or disaffected student cultures as well as making more visible their inner social logics.

I am becoming exhausted thinking about the long front of cultural change. I come to the end of my ruminations in front of the bell with my fist at my lips, wondering about a modest proposal. What are the chances for a specifically ethnographically based "therapy" for the injuries of subordinate culture, especially in light of the vastly expanded scope of educational and quasi-educational programs? Using ethnographic texts, or fragments, or enactments, or role plays, or media forms drawn from them, might give a critical distance and a focus on nonpresent cultural forms that are nevertheless similar to those experienced invisibly in daily life, making them visible and offering the prospect of embedding analytic concepts in life worlds. Rather than attempting a circular logic of the cultural interpretation of culture, though, I am trying to narrow down to name a handful of catalytic concepts that might act as bridges between submerged or preverbal experience and a language for grasping its social meanings analytically. What can we add to the symbolic resources already streaming into cultural production? What fuses, buried and other, would I throw into ethnographic classes: discuss X ethnographic text in relation to . . . um . . . here goes, in relation to cultural labor, penetration, invisibility, sign shifts, possessions, new fetishisms, ironic social reproduction, red/blue/black/pink games of pass the social parcel.

Is this "culture working on culture"? No! It has a separate though related logic. Catalytic resources can be thought of as groupings of a social semiotics to be united with the praxis of how cultural production undertakes its labors. The latter are effaced in part by a lack of understanding of contingency and the almost rhetorical relations of parts in social life so that the results of actions can seem to be their causes or essences. Social forms are concrete yet continuous and malleable, but the most recent configuration might seem to contain the whole history of their meaning. Crucial sign shifts can take place between categories so that class meanings arising in relation to conditions and sites of capitalist control and exploitation, for instance, may be registered in male or ethnic terms as intrinsic parts, apparently, of being male or black. There, they are judged positively or negatively as may be but either way stop revolving in the limits of these essentialist orbits. So can class meanings enfold within race or gender insurgency but find there only class stasis or defeat? The social outruns its various incarnations. The point is to disaggregate and to supply a technology for thinking[28] for straightening out social aspects of cultural production even if large parts of cultures and their internal histories and operations remain mysterious, arcane, or impenetrable. Cultures are acted on and also make themselves at least in part as lived, if mediated, struggles to understand their own location in baffling historical formations. The aim is not to bring something new in from the outside but to strengthen and make true, in connecting purpose and outcome, this internal impetus. This is to strengthen something that is already there, consistently and properly naming the social and its meanings thus redirecting their force to ring—instead of silence—freedom's bell.

I cry out aloud, too loud, gesticulating at the bell, "Freedom sleeps: let the 'best workers' repair the bell for today!" I am finally led away by protesting rangers. But there will be another day. In Philadelphia.

Notes

1. Actually, subsequent research revealed that that this was merely the first bell, which was cracked almost immediately by a stroke of the clapper as it was hung up to try the sound (Kimball 1989, 21). The metal was recast locally by Pass & Stow with a higher proportion of copper, though this bell, too, cracked some time between 1817 and 1846 (Kimball 1989, 43). The specific labor that made the bell was even more hidden in history than I at first supposed, as well as revealing only too early and too well the crack that I go on to discuss later.

2. A history of more than a 250 years of successive waves of industrialization and urbanization labor and the institutions of labor have played a profoundly formative role in the history of politics, state formation, and public policy in Britain and America. Outside the offices of the Trades Union Congress (TUC) in London stands a proud statue of a manual laborer. The entrance to the AFL-CIO, the U.S. equivalent of the TUC, boasts two huge murals of scenes of working life with captions "Labor is Life" and "Labor Omnia Vincit." The British Labour Party, itself, was formed by the institutions of the labor movement in the early part of the last century to take a direct hand in parliamentary affairs and to help fashion the state to encompass, or at least to take account of, the interests of workers and to enshrine certain basic citizenship rights, not least universal suffrage, freedom, and equality under the law. For all the current revisionism, it is also worth noting that it was a Labour government that after the World War II, introduced the world's first comprehensive and inclusive welfare state offering universal rights to free health and education and entitlements to social security payments during illness or unemployment: still a model for introducing basic civic, citizenship, and economic rights for workers across the world.

3. See the foreword and chapter 5 of *The Ethnographic Imagination* (Willis 2000) for a full account.

4. Lest my romanticism runs too far ahead of the narrative and anticipating my own later arguments, let a discordant note ring: in 1772, people living near the state house petitioned the assembly "that they are much incommoded and distressed by the too frequent Ringing of the great Bell in the Steeple" (Kimball 1989, 32).

5. For historical accounts of the "self-making" of working-class culture and its institutional forms and influence on the wider society in Britain, see Thompson (1963) and Williams (1956, 1958).

6. This is not to reduce creativity to a social meaning or function or to see *cultural production* as driven by social meaning. Creativity and expressive cultural development are their own things, striving within and for their own potentials, but I would argue that their sustenance and reproduction, in turn, rest upon how well they illuminate their conditions of existence. A metaphor drawn from gas-heating technology helps me to think this through. When you light a gas fire, a safety mechanism called a thermo-coupler transfers heat along a tube back to the gas supply to keep the supply valve open, maintaining the burning of the gas. The flame is its own combustion, a unique and singular reaction of oxygen and carbon, but the heat it produces, through none of its own intended purpose, maintains the conditions of its own functioning. If for any reason the flame goes out, the thermo-coupler goes cold, contracts, and switches the gas valve off, thereby cutting the supply and preventing the free escape of unburned gas—so with the informal creativities of expressive development. The flame of creativity is its "own thing" but survives only so long as it really burns, producing heat and light, which are useful for other purposes in context. As soon as an apparent systemic usefulness is lost, the flame dies. The flame is not lit by social usefulness, but it will not burn in isolation; its autonomous functioning is a conditional. "The lads'" counter–school culture, for instance, described in *Learning to Labour* (Willis 1981), occupies all of the school landscape for them; it gives them meaning, fun, and diversion, as they see it, in more

fully developed ways than does the life of the conformists. But although the mediations of the lads' culture individualism and meritocracy is penetrated with a group logic that shows that certification and testing will never lift the whole working class but will only inflate the currency of qualifications and legitimize middle-class privilege. They frame the giving of their labor power in wearing circumstances without career illusions, judging the minimum which is necessary, thereby avoiding the double indignity of living their practical subordination twice, once really and once in ideology. This guarantees the longevity of such cultures.

7. I do not underestimate the importance of new national and global movements for peace and antiglobalism protest, but as yet, they have not, I would argue, meshed with cultures and/or movements arising from below articulated around worsening social and economic conditions for the popular classes. Of course, this might change depending on future organizational and cultural developments from below and above. Despite its difficulties in organizing the armies of the unemployed, under-employed, part-time, and low paid, there is also continuing resilience in the trade union movement. It remains the best, last bastion of traditional working class interests.

8. For a roundup of changes in employment patterns in the United Kingdom, see Roberts (2001).

9. See Teresa McGowan (2002) for an ethnographic account of the circuit between homelessness, street life, and jail in San Francisco and St. Louis.

10. See Savage (2000, 34-39) for a comprehensive account of the decline in importance of what he calls "manual cultures of independence" in the United Kingdom.

11. See a report by Rebecca Harding (2003), chief economist of the Work Foundation, London, who argues that around ten million posts in the United Kingdom could be "performed anywhere in the world." From an internationalist and developmental perspective, some of this might be welcomed, and just as jobs, capital, and factories are exported to developing countries, so will the conditions be created for new or renewed struggles from below. Be it noted, though, that the same globalizing processes will transform newly industrialized countries perhaps at an even faster pace than the old core countries. They may be industrialized and de-industrialized within a generation rather than the two hundred years it took in the United Kingdom.

12. For the British case, see *London Times* (2003, 17).

13. Especially as ethnographers, we must, in an important sense, continue to believe in culture as the most important level in our considerations of how new totalities may be unfolding: not only, what all ethnographers share, in the sense of immersion in the flow of the engulfing human river, that which connects past and present sustaining tradition and continuity, but also in the sense of the vital clues it delivers for how things external may shape the water's course. Unable to elevate ourselves above the river, its complex flows and eddies are an important guide to the shape of the unseen riverbanks, guides to how and within what limits its courses may be changed. Culture can also be seen in some sense as a preeminent category because it has a prior existence or continuity with respect to any given set of conditions. Actually, then, some of its forms and logic exist (the materials coming into cultural production) before what might seem to cause it. This poses difficulties for all cause-effect schemas in human affairs, for orthodox views of determinacy, and for all linear thinking. Determinant relations may not be of a one-way flow type from cause to effect, a billiard ball knocking another billiard bill, or the billiard table setting the frame for the possibilities and type of play: possibilities usually posed in general, abstract (frequently mystified) ways with specific pathways never specified. Determinant relations between structure and culture may be ones of subjective disclosure—revelations of the nature and scope of the cause from resources preexisting it.

14. See chapter 4 of *The Ethnographic Imagination* (Willis 2000).

15. For an interesting account of the central importance of night-life culture to young people in the north of England, which deals with some of these issues, see Chatterton and Hollands (2001).

16. See comments on "ethnic cross dressing" in McCarthy (2002).

17. In a somewhat different context, in her book *Consuming Passions*, Judith Williamson (1986, 13-14) makes a similar point rather elegantly: "Consuming products does give a thrill, a sense of both belonging and being different.... Our emotions are wound into these forms, only to spring back at us with an apparent life of their own. Movies seem to *contain* feelings, two-dimensional photographs seem to *contain* truths. The world itself seems filled with obviousness, full of natural meanings that these media merely reflect. But *we* invest the world with its significance. It doesn't have to be the way it is, or to mean what it does."

18. For a fuller account and further developments of these arguments see chapter 6 of *The Ethnographic Imagination* (Willis 2000).

19. For an account of masculinities in school cultures in England and for an exploration of this term, see Mac an Ghaill (1994).

20. See *Learning to Labour* (Willis 1981) for an analysis of how masculinity in counter–school culture combines with some categories and shuns others, especially mental work, which is associated with (disapproved of) feminine ways of being in the world.

21. Working-class girls perform more "silent" forms of resistance and disaffection, with similarly ironic processes of reproduction to be observed with respect to their destiny in unpaid domestic work and within low-paid "feminized" occupations (e.g., Anyon 1983; Llewellyn 1980; Payne 1980). Other variants of informal and resistant cultures of school borrow from, recycle, and adapt elements of various race and ethnic cultures, sometimes with marked effects for social reproduction (e.g., Fordham 1996; Mac an Ghaill 1994; Portes 1995; Raissiguier 1995; Sewell 1997, 2002).

22. Dillard (2001, 182) argues that rightist multiculturalism is often based on "to restate the matter bluntly, not to be like blacks."

23. For an ethnographic account and analysis of how a group of working-class women in England utilize what the author terms "feminine capital" in pursuit of respectability, see Skeggs (1997).

24. See Anderson's (1999, 98-106) detailed presentation and analysis of the dilemmas of maintaining both decency and security in the street-oriented environment of Philadelphia's inner city.

25. Salzinger (2004, 17) writes fascinatingly about recodings of a (softer) masculinity on the shop floor within the feminized maquila sector, Mexico's border export-processing industry. She notes that gender categories are "fractal" depending for specific local meaning on specific context and how, and how far, they are concretely nested in wider frameworks, such as the maquila sector in her example.

26. See the heated exchange in the review symposium in the *American Journal of Sociology* (May 2002) where, in critiquing three recent books on urban sociology (Anderson 1999; Duneier 1999; Newman 1999), Loïc Wacquant emphases structural conditions with culture seen as an homology of structural position, and in their replies, Mitch Duneier, Eli Anderson, and Kathy Newman in different ways emphasize the importance of a humanistic assessment of lived cultural forms.

27. Commenting on Bourdieu's *Pascalian Meditations*, Wacquant (1999, 277) describes how "Bourdieu refines and draws out the full implications of what is arguably his greatest 'discovery' and contribution to social theory to date: the specific logic of practice and everything that separates it from the 'logic of logic.' . . . The ordinary knowledge that makes us competent social agents is an embodied, situated, 'knowing-how-to' that is blind to itself and operates beneath the controls of discursive consciousness and ratiocination." Bourdieu is by no means alone in positing impassable differences between folk and scientific knowledges. In a well-received book on class analysis, Savage (2000, xii) outlines the "paradox of class" in the United Kingdom whereby the "structural importance of class to people's lives appears not to be recognized by people themselves." In a concluding chapter titled "The Epistemological Fallacy of Late Modernity," Furlong and Cartmel (1997, 109) argue, in their magisterial review of youth research in the United Kingdom, that "although the collective foundations of social life have become more obscure, they continue to provide powerful frameworks which constrain young people's experiences and life chances. Over the last two decades a number of changes have occurred which have helped to obscure these continuities, promoting individual responsibilities and weakening collective traditions . . . [young people's] subjective understanding of the world can be seen to misrepresent these underlying structures."

28. From the different tradition of philosophical logical behaviorism, much more decontextualized and universalistic but sharing the same in his case more behaviorist antidualism, Gilbert Ryle (2003) makes some rather similar points to Bourdieu's, which may help us to come at the issues involved from another direction. In his famous passage on digging (from *The Concept of Mind*), he claims that "to say that a person has been enjoying digging is not to say that he has been both digging and doing or experiencing something else as a concomitant or effect of the digging; it is to say that he dug with his whole heart in his task, i.e. that he dug, wanting to dig and not wanting to do anything else (or nothing) instead. His digging was a propensity-fulfilment. His digging was his pleasure, and not a vehicle of his pleasure." Again, we see the claimed impossibility of performing everyday spontaneous activities at the same time as appreciating their meaning or import. To focus on "enjoyment" destroys or is something else from "digging." The conduct and understanding/appreciation of practice are held to be incompatible. But after the digging is over, surely, it is possible to look at some of its elements, preconditions, and outcomes. Hard or soft soil, with what kind of spade, for planting or fallow? Was the experience more pleasurable than going to the pub? If not, it should be the pub next time. Was there a

productive outcome, was there backache, or was there a good night's sleep? Crucially and comparatively, was the digging undertaken in free time or wage-labor time (not in the slightest an issue for Ryle)? How might the digging experience be differentially analyzed in its elements, thereby revealing them: boredom, toil, harmony with nature, alienation, speed of earth turnover, appearance to others (like your employer) of speed of earth turnover? Surely, there are starting points here for making practices and experiences of digging more self-recognized in thought and for directing not destroying digging practices in the future.

References

Anderson, Elijah. 1999. *Code of the street: Decency, violence and the moral life of the inner city*. New York: W. W. Norton.

Anyon, J. 1983. Intersections of gender and class: Accommodation and resistance by working-class and affluent females to contradictory sex-role ideologies. In *Gender, class and education*, edited by S. Walker and L. Barton, 19-37. Lewes, UK: Falmer.

Chatterton, P., and R. Hollands. 2001. *Changing our Toon: Youth, nightlife and urban change in Newcastle*. Newcastle, UK: University of Newcastle.

Dillard, A. D. 2001. *Guess who's coming to dinner now: Multicultural conservatism in America*. New York: New York University Press.

Duneier, Mitch. 1999. *Sidewalk*. New York: Farrar, Strauss and Giroux.

Fordham, S. 1996. *Blacked out: Dilemmas of race, identity, and success in Capital High*. Chicago: University of Chicago Press.

Furlong, Andy, and Fred Cartmel. 1997. *Young people and social change*. Buckingham, UK: Open University Press.

Harding, Rebecca. 2003. Millions of British posts seem ripe for export as companies look to cut costs. *Financial Times*, October 18.

Hoggart, Richard. 1956. *The uses of literacy*. Harmondsworth, UK: Penguin.

Kimball, David. 1989. *The story of the Liberty Bell*. New York: National Park Service.

Llewellyn, M. 1980. Studying girls at school: The implications of confusion. In *Schooling for women's work*, edited by R. Deem, 42-51. Boston: Routledge.

London Times. 2003. Twice as many blacks in jail as at university. December 14.

Mac an Ghaill, M. 1994. *The making of men: Masculinities, sexualities and schooling*. Buckingham, UK: Open University Press.

McCarthy, C. 2002. Understanding the work of aesthetics in modern life: Thinking about the cultural studies of education in a time of recession. Paper presented at the annual meeting of the American Educational Research Association, New Orleans, April 2002.

McGowan, Teresa. 2002. The nexus: Homelessness and incarceration in two American cities. *Ethnography* 4 (4): 500-534.

Newman, Kathy. 1999. *No shame in my game: The working poor in the inner city*. New York: Russell Sage.

Payne, I. 1980. A working-class girl in a grammar school. In *Learning to lose: Sexism and education*, edited by D. Spender and E. Sarah, 12-19. London: Women's Press.

Portes, A., ed. 1995. *The economic sociology of immigration: Essays on networks, ethnicity and entrepreneurship*. New York: Russell Sage.

Raissiguier, C. 1995. The construction of marginal identities: Working-class girls of Algerian descent in a French school. In *Feminism/postmodernism/development*, edited by M. H. Marchand and J. L. Parpart, 79-93. London: Routledge.

Roberts, K. 2001. *Class in modern Britain*. Basingstoke, UK: Palgrave.

Ryle, Gilbert. 2003. *The concept of mind*. Chicago: University of Chicago Press.

Salzinger, L. 2004. Revealing the unmarked: Finding masculinity in a global factory. *Ethnography* 5 (1): 6-27.

Savage, Mike. 2000. *Class analysis and social transformation*. Buckingham, UK: Open University Press.

Sewell, T. 1997. *Black masculinities and schooling: How black boys survive modern schooling*. London: Trentham.

———. 2002. I know why black boys fail at school—And racism isn't to blame. *Mail on Sunday*, December 15, p. 59.

Skeggs, B. 1997. *Formations of class and gender: Becoming respectable*. London: Sage.

Thompson, Edward. 1963. *The making of the English working class*. London: Gollancz.

Wacquant, Loïc. 1999. The double-edged sword of reason: The scholar's predicament and the sociologist's mission. *European Journal of Social Theory* 2 (3): 275-81.

Williams, Raymond. 1956. *Culture and society*. Harmondsworth, UK: Penguin.

———. 1958. *The long revolution*. Harmondsworth, UK: Penguin.

Williamson, Judith. 1986. *Consuming passions*. London: Marion Boyars.

Willis, P. 1981. *Learning to labour*. New York: Columbia University Press.

———. 2000. *The ethnographic imagination*. Cambridge, UK: Polity.

Bureaucracies of Mass Deception: Institutional Review Boards and the Ethics of Ethnographic Research

By

CHARLES L. BOSK
and
RAYMOND G. DE VRIES

Ethnographers have long been unhappy with the review of their research proposals by institutional review boards (IRBs). In this article, we offer a sociological view of the problems associated with prospective IRB review of ethnographic research. Compared with researchers in other fields, social scientists have been less willing to accommodate themselves to IRB oversight; we identify the reasons for this reluctance, and in an effort to promote such accommodation, we suggest several steps to reduce the frustration associated with IRB review of ethnographic research. We conclude by encouraging ethnographers to be alert to the ways the procedural and bureaucratic demands of IRBs can displace their efforts to solve the serious ethical dilemmas posed by ethnography.

Keywords: research ethics; institutional review boards; ethnography; research methods

One score and seven years ago, the National Commission for the Protection of Human Subjects of Biomedical and Behavioral Research met in February to identify the ethical principles that would serve as guidelines for the protection of human subjects of biomedical and behavioral research. The discussions from those meetings culminated in *The Belmont Report.* In

Charles L. Bosk is a professor and graduate chair of sociology, a senior fellow of The Leonard Davis Institute for Health Services Research, and a professor in the Department of Medical Sociology at the University of Pennsylvania. In 2003 and 2004, Bosk was a member of the School of Social Science at the Institute for Advanced Study, Princeton, New Jersey. He is also an elected fellow of the Hastings Center. He is author of Forgive and Remember: Managing Medical Failure *(University of Chicago Press, 1979/2003) and* All God's Mistakes: Genetic Counseling in a Pediatric Hospital *(University of Chicago Press, 1992). His* What Would You Do? The Collision of Ethics and Ethnography *will be published by Chicago in 2005. His research interests include medical mistakes, misconduct, and the culture of patient safety; genetics; medical education; and research ethics. He was a recipient of the John McGovern Award from the Association of Academic Health Centers.*

Raymond G. De Vries is a professor of sociology at St. Olaf College in Northfield, Minnesota, and a visiting

DOI: 10.1177/0002716204266913

ANNALS, *AAPSS*, 595, September 2004

249

the summer of 2003, The Social and Behavioral Sciences Working Group on Human Research Protections convened a conference at, fittingly enough, the Belmont Conference Center. The title of the conference was *IRB [Institutional Review Board] Best Practices in the Review of Social and Behavioral Research*; the working group invited a collection of persons—with "considerable expertise in human research protections and the review of social and behavioral science protocols"—to join them at the Belmont Center. Topics for the various sessions of the conference included "IRBs that Work"; "Back to the Basics for Social and Behavioral Research," that is, what is and what is not research, the meaning of generalizable knowledge to subjects, the concept of the human subject; "Challenging Protocols—Methods of Inquiry"; "Challenging Protocols—Contexts and Populations"; "Barriers in Reviewing Protocols"; "Best Practices in the Consideration of Consent, Disclosure, and Deception"; and "Research Risk and Best Practices in the Determination of Exempt and Expedited Review." The Office of Behavioral and Social Science Research of the National Institutes of Health provided support for the conference.

It is difficult to fully assess how successful the participants were in identifying "best practices."[1] Since the conference itself was held a mere six months before we began writing this article, it is too soon to say how effectively the results of the conference will be disseminated or, for that matter, to whom. If the goals of the conference were to identify a set of best practices, to operationalize those practices in a set of procedures, and to distribute those procedures as a set of guidelines to those in academic or commercial organizations with responsibility for administration and compliance with federal regulations, then there is no reason to expect anything less than a successful outcome. Working groups experienced in the production of such documents can produce guidelines on most anything. Administrators charged with translating vague principles into coherent procedures often find such documents a great comfort. At the very least, guidelines stored in a binder and filed on a shelf provide grounds for arguing later about whether institutions discharged responsibilities properly.[2] However, if the working group hoped that conference participants would help produce a document that quells the considerable resentment that the bureaucratic regulation of research has created among social scien-

professor at the Center for Bioethics, University of Minnesota, Minneapolis. He is the author of numerous articles on the sociology of medicine and the sociology of bioethics and the editor of Bioethics and Society *(Prentice Hall, 1998). He is the recipient of a "Mentored Scientist Development Award in Research Ethics" from the National Institutes of Health (NIH), and he is currently a coinvestigator in two other studies, both funded by the NIH: "Work Strain, Career Course, and Research Integrity"—a study of the norms of conduct in science—and (in conjunction with the Minnesota Center for Health Care Ethics) "Ethical and Policy Problems of Deep Brain Stimulation (DBS)"—a look at the unique ethical problems that surround the development and dissemination of new medical technologies. He is now busy creating a team of researchers to examine the international "market" in research protections and how this market is negotiated by companies that make and market medical devices and pharmaceuticals.*

NOTE: Work on this article was supported in part by a grant from the National Institutes of Health (K01 AT00054).

tists, then they are likely to be severely disappointed, no matter how sensible, adequate, and nonintrusive the recommendations are. In fact, for those whose behavior the guidelines seek to regulate, the mere existence of one more document trying to get right the vexing question of how to assure the proper ethical conduct of qualitative researchers through organizational oversight is a symbol and symptom of a deep misunderstanding of the realities of ethnographic research and an even deeper misapprehension about how conduct is effectively regulated. In the current environment, one more working group's recommendations are more likely to fuel rather than to extinguish the flames of discontent. The burden of this article is to illustrate why this is so.

---

*Social and behavioral research encompasses
a vast amount of ground to cover with
a single set of regulations.*

Some of the reasons for this are structural. First, social and behavioral research encompasses a vast amount of ground to cover with a single set of regulations. Just how vast this ground is becomes clear when we look at the membership of the Social and Behavioral Sciences Working Group on Human Research Protections, the well-intended conveners of the second Belmont Conference on the ethical conduct of research. The working group had representatives from demography, education, family and community medicine, sociology, and psychology.[3] The working group also includes representatives from numerous federal agencies who fund or conduct social and behavioral science research: the National Institutes of Health, the Federal Bureau of Prisons, the Department of Education, the National Science Foundation, and the Agency for International Development. The executive officers of the American Sociological Association and the American Education Research Association are also members of the working group. Those charged with applying regulations are also represented in the working group composition—there is an associate dean for research, a director of ethics education, and a director of a Native American research and training center.

Even with this extensive disciplinary and organizational coverage, qualitative research is underrepresented in the membership of the working group. One member of the working group, who attended the conference, mentions in his or her biographical sketch participating in projects using a wide range of methodologies from clinical trials to ethnographic research but then claims a special expertise in "the distribution and use of public-use data files," an important topic to be sure but not one that is reassuring to those who desire to see the special problems that research regulations present to ethnographers fully understood, adequately described, and realistically addressed. In all fairness, the list of attendees at the conference supplemented the expertise of the working group—qualitative researchers from sociology, anthropology, and political science participated in the conference. But the influence of these participants in the documents prepared by the working group remains to be seen. This structural flaw in representation is a generic one for tasks where a consensus that satisfies a vast array of interest groups needs to be reached, but to promote effective deliberation, the size of the working group must be limited. Still, to assemble a working group without a symbolic representative of those practitioners within the social sciences—ethnographers, who have grumbled and groused the loudest about the hindrances that the current regulatory structure imposes—seems to be a grave tactical error. After all, conversion and co-optation are, as ethnographers of deviance and social control have demonstrated, two very effective strategies for neutralizing problem populations.[4] The voices of social scientists who have complaints about IRBs and their operation deserve a fuller hearing.

If the problem of representation is a generic structural problem, the title of the conference reflects a second structural problem, quite specific to social and behavioral science research of the qualitative kind.[5] To title the conference *IRB Best Practices* is to link the regulation of social science research with the current regulatory regimes of clinical medicine, supported by rationales drawn from evidence-based medicine. Conferences or research aimed at identifying best practices have become a staple of the modern world of medical practice, especially in those domains that attempt to link clinical practice to findings supported by "outcomes research." The language of best practices is part of the Quality Improvement (QI) or Total Quality Improvement (TQI) movement in medicine. The aspirational goals of this movement are entirely laudable; it seeks to adapt some of the management practices from other industries into medicine to create a more efficient, effective, and safer system for health care delivery. The title of the conference, then, reinforces the link between the rules that regulate biomedical research and the rules that regulate social and behavioral science research. For many social scientists, this linkage is precisely the problem.

IRBs can develop best practices for routine review and approval of qualitative research proposals; however, many in the social science community feel that those best practices will never be good practices so long as research is modeled on the standard clinical trial. Even if the conference conveners intended to move away from the clinical model, the banner under which the conference was convened belies their intention. In the standard research proposal, a hypothesis or set of hypotheses about the effect of intervention x on condition y is being tested. The researcher generally has a clearly bounded relationship with the research subject. The procedures involved, their risks and benefits, and the alternatives can usually be described in some detail.[6] Roles, rules, and procedures are clear and time limited. Subjects can be fully informed, a goal that is realized more in the breach than in the fact.[7] For some types of social science research—the laboratory experiment, the fixed-item survey, the longitudinal panel study—the relationship of researcher and subject closely tracks the biomedical model that informs IRB procedures: a highly structured, objective relationship.[8]

But ethnographic research fits this model poorly. For ethnographers, the primary data-gathering tool consists of the relationships that we forge with those whose lifeworld we are trying to understand. Few of us start with specific hypotheses that we will later test in any systematic way. Furthermore, to the degree that we can restate our disciplinary curiosity as a set of testable propositions, these hypotheses are likely to be trivial. We cannot state our procedures any more formally than we will hang around here in this particular neighborhood and try to figure out what is going on among these people. We want to know how they make sense of their world, how they navigate in it, and how understanding their world helps us better understand our own. Neighborhoods vary: this store that serves as front for the crack dealers (Bourgois 1995); these clubs where the blues musicians congregate (Grazian 2003); this neonatal intensive-care unit (Anspach 1993; Heimer and Stauffen 1998); these neighborhoods where people sell their kidneys (Cohen 1999); these laboratories where biologists seek to unravel the mystery of peptides (Latour and Woolgar 1986). Neighborhoods change but methods are remarkably constant—really, they have not changed much for sociologists since Whyte (1942) or for anthropologists since Malinowski (1922).[9] We observe, we may tape-record, we may videotape, we all take notes, and we code those notes according to our own various schemas—some of us use computers to sort data, and some of us still cut and paste and shuffle file cards.[10] We do not know in advance what questions we will ask or, for that matter, where we will draw a curtain and choose not to inquire— or decide not to report.

We cannot inform our subjects of the risks and benefits of cooperating with us for a number of reasons. First, the risks and benefits for subjects are not so different from those of normal interaction with a stranger who will become a close acquaintance, an everyday feature of a lifeworld, and then disappear, after observing intimate moments, exploring deep feelings, and asking embarrassing questions. There is the risk inherent in any fleeting human relationship—the risk of bruised feelings that come from being used, the loss when a fixture in a social world disappears, or the hurt of realizing that however differently it felt in the moment, one was used as a means to an end.[11] This risk is magnified by a certain unavoidable deception in every ethnographic investigation, a certain pretense that comes from trying to have both researcher and informant forget that what is going on is not a normal, natural exchange but research—not just everyday life as it naturally occurs but work, a job, a project—"No really, I'm interested in what you have to say, think, feel, and believe for more than my own narrow instrumental academic purposes." To some degree, we cannot specify risks because we do not know what we will find, what interpretive frameworks we will develop for reporting what we do observe, and how the world around us will change to make those findings seem more or less significant.[12] Finally, we cannot define risk because few of us believe that being an ethnographic informant is a risky business. We believe this despite considerable anthropological and sociological evidence to the contrary.

IRBs also review proposals to make sure that the confidentiality and anonymity of study subjects is adequately safeguarded. In general, this last element is relatively easy to promise. However, some situations are highly problematic. For those of us who work with highly literate populations, confidentiality and anonymity are much easier to promise than to assure. We can do nothing to prohibit a sufficiently determined reader from trying to decode the text, to stop a figure in an ethnographic narrative from identifying himself or herself, or to prevent an institution from coming forward and saying, "We are 'made-up-ville'" (Bosk 2000).[13] Typically, such decodings are harmless but not necessarily. If read as romans à clef, ethnographic works among hospital workers can make tense and fractious workplaces even tenser and more fractious for the workers within them, who now know what they previously only suspected, who see on the printed page what was once said only behind closed doors.

In anthropology, regimes already in place have used a rich lore of ethnographic works to root out troublesome populations. This has happened despite the best efforts of anthropologists to foresee risks to subjects and to veil identities. Political climates change. What seemed a harmless remark yesterday may appear to be an insurrectionary one tomorrow. A group that no one seemed to care about can grow central when regimes shift. In addition, the requirement of subject confidentiality and anonymity, if stretched too far, does not permit ethnographic work in public domains. The workings of government, for instance, at the local, state, or federal level, would be hamstrung by an overly rigid insistence on confidentiality and anonymity. Certain forms of public controversy could not be explored as well. Because of the risks posed when confidentiality and anonymity are breached, IRBs, at least in the minds of researchers, have imposed consent requirements that themselves are out of character with the type of research being proposed. Bruner (2004) provides two different examples: (1) being asked to get written consent from illiterate peoples and (2) having colleagues refuse to answer questions about difficulties with IRBs until they were assured that the inquiry itself had been sanctioned by an IRB.[14]

So to restate the obvious, social scientists and behavioral scientists, in general, and ethnographers, in particular, are not thrilled with current federal regulations that require prospective review of research projects; they are skeptical that such review improves the ethical quality of research; and they believe that such review does nothing more than hinder the pace of research. Truth be told, medical researchers have never been much thrilled with the regulations either. They have done their public grousing and grumbling, and generally, they have figured out what it is that IRBs want to hear and figured out ways to say exactly that. Since IRB review is almost entirely prospective, there exists very little check on whether researchers in clinical domains do exactly what they say they are going to do.[15] Why have social and behavioral science researchers not done the same? Why have they not adopted a policy of weary, self-resigned compliance coupled with minor or major evasion? Or even, if they have used passive-aggressive strategies of compliance and evasion, why are there also so many public complaints and so many public calls for resistance?

Both the complaints and the calls for resistance seem peculiar on any number of counts. First, there is an inaccurate stridency to some of the complaints. Some of those who are opposed to the current regime of IRB research have complained that the regulations violate a First Amendment right to unfettered speech. This absolute interpretation of the First Amendment neglects the considerable jurisprudence that indicates that reasonable restrictions might be placed on the time, place, and manner of speech. Others have complained that journalists, especially those journalists who do investigative reporting, are not hemmed by requirements for informed consent or the need to respect confidentiality. Why should sociological researchers, they ask, be held to a higher standard? One deceptively simple

---

We cannot specify risks because we do not know what we will find, what interpretive frameworks we will develop for reporting what we do observe, and how the world around us will change to make those findings seem more or less significant.

---

answer is that perhaps we should aspire to a higher standard than the average journalist. Journalism is, after all, a commercial enterprise, many of the workers in which lack what are often thought of as the prerequisites of a professional occupation—long adult socialization in a specialized body of theoretic knowledge.[16] Journalism is not supported by public funds. Because we are not journalists, however many similarities one can identify between ethnographic research and investigative journalism, we have no reason to expect the same rules to apply.

Next, something is vaguely uncollegial and distasteful to the social scientist's objections to IRBs on two counts. First, much of the social science critique of both the research and the clinical practices of physicians centers on how poorly patients or subjects are informed of what is being done to them, why it is being done, and what alternatives exist. Freidson (1970), for one, has argued that physicians have used their technical authority as scientific experts to make normative decisions, choices that patients or research subjects ought to make for themselves in a democratic society. The early sociological writing on death and dying (Glaser and Strauss 1968) stressed how much information control by physicians robbed patients of autonomy and dignity. Emerson (1969) characterized the desperate measures that patients used to try to gain accurate information on their conditions. Davis (1960) described how physicians manipulated and feigned uncertainty to control and limit patient choices. Sociologists decried these practices of information control. To a degree, when coupled with the revelations of past ethical abuses such as those Beecher (1966) catalogued or those that revealed the suffering of vulnerable, minority populations at Tuskegee (Jones 1981), these critiques led to the recommendations of the first Belmont report (Rothman 1991) that stressed informing patients so that they could reasonably exercise decision-making capacity.[17] There is more than a whiff of hypocrisy in imposing obligations on others—in this case, physicians and medical researchers who cannot be trusted because their self-interest makes unreliable their judgments of others' best interests—while resisting those very same obligations for oneself because our work is harmless, our intentions good, and our hearts pure.

A second dimension of the uncollegial spirit of the social and behavioral reaction to IRB review is its uncharitable nature. If we were honest, we would recognize that IRBs and the regulatory and administrative regimes for research now have a fair amount of bureaucratic momentum behind them. How much good IRBs accomplish and how much harm they prevent remain open questions. How procedures might evolve so that they better meet the realities and contingencies of social and behavioral research as it is actually done in a real world of real people is certainly open. What is not open is whether a prospective review of research will exist.[18] So at the very least, we social scientists ought to recognize that the committee work involved by our colleagues on IRBs is like a lot of other committee work. It is thankless; it is done in pursuit of some communally shared objectives, even if these are poorly articulated; it is underfunded; and if it were not done by these colleagues, we might have to do it ourselves, which would mean that we would have less time to do our own research. We should all, then, be a bit more forgiving of the imperfections of the whole structure even as we remember them—all the better to correct them. If all this were not reason enough to be a bit more constructive and cooperative in our critique of IRBs, we can add one more: none of us truly objects to the goals of IRB research—we all wish subjects to be treated with respect, protected from harm, and saved from embarrassing exposure.

Therefore, we need some constructive suggestions for making the system work better, we need to educate IRB members about the nature of qualitative social science research, and we need to do a better job of educating ourselves about the regulations—if only because such education will make clear to us that the system is less onerous than we fear. We need to explore the different ways that the system can be streamlined and made more efficient. It is in this spirit that we offer the following suggestions, all of which have been floated in the vast literature on IRBs.

Encourage more and better studies of how IRBs work. Given the continued and high level of displeasure with IRBs, we would expect ethnographers to be studying the way IRBs work. When it comes to IRBs, social scientists are cobbler's children. Like the hapless waifs whose feet remain unshod while their parent makes shoes for others, social scientists complain about the many shortcomings of IRBs while using their skills to describe and analyze nearly every other sphere of human activity. Reports on the shortcomings of IRBs are rarely supported by data. A recent American Association of University Professors (2001) report is based on anecdote, a nonscientific survey of social science researchers, and testimony given to government committees; the report of the National Research Council lists only eight studies in an appendix, "Selected Studies of IRB Operations: Summary Descriptions." One might assume this small number is the result of careful selection, but as the authors of the study note, "There is little regularly available systematic information about the functioning of the U.S. human research participant protection system" (Citro, Ilgen, and Marrett 2003). We need to better understand what IRBs look like and how they work (De Vries and Forsberg 2002).

Increase social scientist participation on IRBs. In institutions with multiple subcommittees of IRBs, create a specialized IRB for vetting social science research. IRB composition has specific requirements: multiple disciplines must be represented, there must be a community representative, and there must be at least five members. There is no reason why one subcommittee cannot specialize in social science research. This will assure that research is reviewed by colleagues who have some understanding of social science methodologies.

Increase social scientists' knowledge of IRB rules. We all need greater understanding of what the rules require of us. A good deal of ethnographic research falls under the category of expedited or exempt research. We need to familiarize ourselves with these categories of research. We need to make clear to IRBs why we believe that our research falls into one category or the other. We need to be familiar with those situations where the regulations allow something other than written consent; generally, in situations of minimal risk, alternatives to written consent are permissible. We also need to know which populations are defined as vulnerable and the set of special protections afforded such populations.

From experiences as a member of study sections for the Ethical, Legal and Social Implications part of the Human Genome Project, one of us often found that researchers submitting proposals using qualitative research methods are defensive when specifying what they will do and are incomplete when discussing consent procedures. As a consequence, methods are left vaguer than they need to be, and the requirements for consent appear to be evaded rather than embraced. We understand why this happens: it is a pain (really, there is no other word for it) to try to shape a proposal for a qualitative research effort into the format required by a National Institutes of Health RO1 Grant application. But if we wish funding for our projects, it is a pain we must endure. Specifying to an IRB how we will meet the requirements of informed consent is likewise a pain, but it is one that can be borne with a bit more grace than we have managed so far. We can begin to engage the process creatively if we know the rules. The more familiar we become with those rules, the more we can work around them, find the loopholes, and yes, even amend them so that they make sense given the kinds of inquiry in which we engage.

Educate IRB members. Social scientists have complained about the "mission creep" that occurred when IRB jurisdiction expanded from biomedical research to all research involving human subjects. Whether this truly was mission creep or just a natural extension of a mandate is for others to debate and decide; however, the fact that IRBs began to review proposals with biomedical research in mind has had a number of implications for social scientists using qualitative methods. First, the personnel who serve on IRBs are, as a consequence, overwhelmingly drawn from the ranks of biomedical researchers.[19] Research protocols themselves are then reviewed in narrow terms: What was the risk/benefit ratio? How adequate was the consent form? When faced with qualitative research proposals, whatever normal operating procedures and rules for deliberation committees had evolved break down. In addition, the template of the research being proposed makes little scientific sense to committee members who have a trained incompetence when it comes to the inductive methods of qualitative research. Under these conditions, too many IRBs have members who decide that qualitative research has no scientific validity; hence, it can offer no benefit; and as a consequence, there is no risk worth contemplating for human subjects. Qualitative researchers then have reasonable proposals turned back with what seems like a set of unreasonable objections and appears to be a willful obtuseness about the nature, conduct, and purpose of the proposed research. To avoid this situation, two types of education for IRB members are required. First, IRB members need to learn to extend beyond their own disciplinary boundaries. They need not like, approve, or be advocates for qualitative research. They do need, however, to have enough education in its methods and the theories of social life that undergird them to appreciate that this is a legitimate form of inquiry. With this understanding comes the knowledge that there are better and worse ways to proceed with qualitative projects, that there are criteria of judgment that can be applied, and that reasoned decisions can be made rather than positivistic prejudices enacted. Second, IRB members, like their social science counterparts, need to be familiar with their own rules of operation. They need to know which research qualifies as minimal risk, which projects are exempt from review and which can receive expedited review, and which research projects are allowed alternatives to written consent. If IRB members are not well versed in the rules that they are charged with applying, then they will have difficulty applying those rules correctly.

Have in place a speedy appeals process. One thing that frustrates researchers, whatever methods they employ, is delays encountered when IRB approval stalls the start of projects. For qualitative researchers, this frustration is multiplied when it seems that a failure to win approval grows out of a misreading in what was involved in the research process. Resubmissions that require answering nonsensical objections are not an adequate remedy. For the requirements imposed to make a research proposal pass muster may also make that same project impossible to do. Beyond that, the delay between original submission, response to objection, and resubmission may erode whatever access to a field setting that has been negotiated. Finally, there is little confidence that the same folks who made such a seemingly arbitrary decision so recently will now act with the requisite wisdom. Institutions need to have in place appeals mechanisms that allow researchers a speedy hearing before a body of colleagues who will not be made defensive or be constrained by their prior rulings, who understand what qualitative methods entail, and who are familiar with the rules governing research with human subjects. IRBs need to

---

There is more than a whiff of hypocrisy in imposing obligations on others . . . while resisting those very same obligations for oneself.

---

remember that few researchers design projects with the intent of harming people. Researchers need to remember that IRBs have a specific job to do. An appeals process that puts the ball in a different court reminds each of them that neither of them is infallible.

Explore other ways of organizing review of social science research. The United States was a pioneer in the creation of ethics review boards, but we have much to learn from the ways other countries have responded to the need to protect the subjects of research. There are other ways to organize ethics reviews and other ways to approach review of social science research. In the Netherlands, for example, social science research is exempt from review unless it places a demonstrable physical or psychological burden on its subjects. Paying attention to the way our colleagues in other countries have approached this problem will create solutions to our dilemmas.[20]

So that is the gist of the argument. IRBs are here to stay. The review process may impose more harm than benefit, but it is hard to imagine turning back now. Social scientists are not bureaucratic incompetents or mutes. They can find ways to work within the system at the same time that they work to change it. When the requirements for approving research with minimal risk are looked at, the entire review process seems to impose fewer burdens than what we actually complain about. The system is highly imperfect. We can make it better. The system is underfunded and understaffed. Given this, a spirit of cooperation rather than belligerence seems the appropriate way to respond to our colleagues who have either volunteered or had their arms twisted to perform this onerous task.

All that said, we cannot help but feel that one more thing is worth saying. We do not think that the system of prospective review that we have adopted does much to protect subjects from harm or guarantee ethical conduct from researchers. The ethical problems that we meet in the field are so complex and the situations are so fraught with the moral and existential dilemmas of leading a life that consent does little to assure our subjects or ourselves, for that matter, that we will do the right thing when the situation presents itself. What should the sociologist studying faith healing in suburban New Jersey do when parents refuse to take a sick child to the physician? What does the sociologist studying an intensive-care unit say when a doctor, nurse, or family member contemplating treatment withdrawal asks what he or she should do? What does the anthropologist studying the drug-addicted home-less do when an informant, copping some heroin, is a few dollars short and asks for a loan? In his book *The Secret Army: The IRA, 1916-1974*, J. Bowyer Bell (1970) includes a series of photographs depicting a bomb attack.[21] Four plates detail the loading of the bomb into the car, the moments before the explosion, the explosion itself, and the damage done. It turns out that these photographs were not taken by Bowyer Bell, but one can easily imagine that the qualitative researcher studying a group like the IRA, or a teen gang, or professional gamblers, or sex workers would come upon such scenes. In scenes when the last item in the sequence is "the dam-age done," it is certainly reasonable to ask what are the obligations of the researcher to his or her informants, as well as to third parties. Resolving this sort of ethical dilemma is not the sort of thing that is amenable to prospective review, to an abstract calculation of risks and benefits, and to consent. The problem with IRBs and qualitative research is that they are such a distraction from the real difficulties that we face and from the real ethical dilemmas that confront us that we may not recognize and discuss the serious and elemental because we are so busy with the procedural and bureaucratic.

Notes

1. One of us (De Vries) was present at the conference. Attendees generated useful and long lists of (1) the problems of reviewing the research proposals of social and behavioral scientists and (2) the solutions to those problems; staff members of the working group are in the process of refining these lists.

2. A wise law school faculty member once told one of us (Bosk) that contracts do not regulate working relationships among parties. When there is an adequate working relationship, there is no need for a con-tract—the parties can work out differences on the hoof as it were. In fact, that ability to make adjustments and move on is as good an operational definition of a working relationship as one might ever hope to find. Con-tracts set the ground rules for the dispute when working relationships fall apart. Guidelines are a bit the same; it is only when disaster fails to be averted that one needs to check if guidelines were followed. One conse-quence of this is, as Snook (2000) points out, that there is a great deal of organizational drift in everyday prac-tice as the need for practical contingencies gets dislodged from formal organizational rules.

3. Anthropology, political science, social work, and nursing are nowhere to be found in the individual dis-ciplines of the working-group members or among the professional associations with representatives on the working group. A note from the editors in the January 2004 issue of *Anthropology News* informs readers that "work on a position paper defining ethnographic practice with reference to IRB [institutional review board] guidelines has been begun by the AAA [American Anthropological Association]" (p. 10).

4. There are two other groups that went unrepresented. Here, the lack of representation is likely to go unnoticed, but it is not unimportant on that account. First, there were no representatives from the increasing number of organizations that provide institutional review board (IRB) review of protocols for a fee. Second, there were no representatives of commercial research organizations, a fast-growing organizational segment

within the research marketplace that is responsible for a good deal of social and behavioral research in the clinical/medical domain (e.g., research on compliance with medication regimes; Petryna, forthcoming).

5. Identifying this problem, as one that is specific to "social and behavioral research of a qualitative kind," points to another larger, definitional problem, hiding behind the problem of representation. There are multiple kinds of qualitative techniques. Calling interview studies ethnographies, or identifying focus groups as a technique for providing a "thick description," does little to solve the confusions induced when trying to write rules that assure that firsthand observational research conducted in settings where behavior naturally occurs—research that cannot be done effectively without rapport, trust, assent, and consent of subjects—is "ethical."

6. Here, one might need to exercise caution. Even with the medical model, the identification of risk to both research subjects and IRB members often depends on the thoroughness of the investigator, the completeness of the literature review, and the willingness of the researcher to provide what Weber called, in a far different context, "inconvenient facts." A healthy subject died in an asthma trial at Johns Hopkins when researchers failed to discover for themselves or failed to inform the IRB and, surely, as a consequence, failed to inform a volunteer in a clinical trial that a pulmonary antagonist intended to induce asthma so that the efficacy of a new therapeutic agent could be tested had caused death in animal trials. Even in the most straightforward and mechanical of research designs, the adequacy of regulations rests on what Parsons (1951) called the "institutionalized integrity" of the profession—its willingness to face inconvenient facts. To state the same point a slightly different way, Freidson (1970, 1975) long recognized that the monitoring, surveillance, and social control of those who possess highly specialized, abstract, esoteric, theoretic knowledge depends on the cooperation of those with that knowledge. To Plato's old question, "Quis custos custodes?" (Who governs the governors?), the answer appears to be the *custodes* themselves.

7. Since the implementation of IRBs, there has been a body of evaluative research that documents the gap between the goals of the regulatory schema and their fulfillment. This research documents that consent forms are difficult to parse (the standard aimed for is that of the average eighth-grade reader), that subjects fail to understand the nature of research (double-blind nature of clinical trials is particularly problematic), and that subjects conflate the roles of researcher and clinician, as well as the nature of research and therapy. So when we say that ethnography poses special problems for IRBs that clinical research does not, we are not comparing a system that works perfectly in one domain but fails to fit another.

8. Even here, the relationship is not perfect. For example, forced-compliance studies like the Asch or Milgram experiments—and here we are leaving aside all the other ethical questions that surround these experiments, as well as the enormous lore that mis-describes them—could hardly have been practiced without deception. This, we suppose, means they are great fodder for the conference session on "Best Practices: Consent, Deception, and Disclosure." For a hilarious send-up of what it must have been like to be a subject in the Asch experiments, see the description in the novel *Kinflicks* (Alther 1976). In fact, the general requirement of informed consent—disclosure of the purpose of the study—poses problems at many levels for social scientists of all stripes. A great deal hinges on how complete the disclosure needs to be to satisfy the requirements of informed consent.

9. We could have invoked Park and Boas. Origins are tricky things. We cannot speak at all authoritatively about anthropology. We are not historians of social science. But as sociological researchers using qualitative methods, self-consciousness about what is happening here seems to us to begin with Whyte's second edition of *Street Corner Society*, published in 1955.

10. Our methods have not changed, but in both sociology and anthropology, there is a considerable amount of self-reflexiveness that has developed relatively recently about those methods. There is rather more of this in anthropology than in sociology, but in both fields, there is a rather thorough chewing over of such questions as what does it mean to represent "the other," whose voice does the ethnographer authentically represent, and whose interests do ethnographic representations represent.

11. This is phrased to deliberately echo the violation of Kant's categorical imperative. Careful readers will notice that the word *solely* has been omitted; this surely makes an ethical difference.

12. Two examples serve to illustrate this point. One is drawn from reality; one is hypothetical. Jeffrey Goldfarb's (1982) work on art and theater in Poland obtained a salience when the Solidarity movement became politically active and visible that the work did not have when he designed his study. Second, imagine the ethnographer studying the integration of the Arab American community in the United States and its continuing ties to countries of origin before 9/11 and after 9/11.

13. All of these forms of decoding have consequences. A reader who decodes a text, incorrectly or correctly, may cause others to give pause before consenting to observational studies. An individual who, or an institution that, comes forward vitiates the promises that the researcher made to all the others in the study who have not chosen to come forward (Bosk, forthcoming).

14. This second example highlights the difficulty of what is research and what is not. We wish to know if a group of colleagues share a problem with us because we wish to know if we are dealing with a "private trouble" or "a public issue." At what point does my inquiry shift from purely personal curiosity to a formally organized search for generalized knowledge? Or, to put it another way, are we, as Bruner fears, reaching a point where "we will not be able to have conversations about research with our colleagues without IRB approval"?

15. A new bureaucratic level of scrutiny, the data safety monitoring board (DSMB), has been created to make sure that research is as safe as promised; how well these boards will work in practice remains to be seen. Once again, like all such reporting schemes, the efficacy of DSMBs depends on the institutionalized integrity of researchers both recognizing and reporting adverse events.

16. Compare the importance of graduate training to on-the-job training in sociology or journalism. It is hard to imagine sociologists without Ph.D.s holding down positions at major research universities. On the other hand, journalists need not have attended journalism school or have advanced degrees to obtain positions of respectability. Of course, lines that are drawn sharply can be just as easily blurred. Robert Park, one of sociology's first advocates for the primary observation of social life in natural settings, came to sociology from journalism. But he did attend and receive a doctorate from a German university.

17. In a recent online article in *Spiked*, Richard Shweder has argued that the historical evidence does not support the accepted narrative of Tuskegee as racist, deceptive, and unethical research. Shweder offers a counternarrative that attempts to argue that Tuskegee was not so bad as to justify the regulatory regimes justified in its name. Whatever the merits of Shweder's argument, it is hard not to feel that the point of the article is not to correct the historical record but rather to undermine the justifications for the federal oversight of research with human subjects (available at http://www.spiked-online.com/articles/0000000CA34A.htm/).

18. We put up with quite a bit of bureaucratic nonsense as academics. We sit on strategic planning committees whose documents are often ignored or risible—we will strive for intellectual excellence and equip our students with the skills they need to excel in the world of the twenty-first century and with the skills necessary for lifelong learning. We participate in external and internal departmental reviews. We sit and try to figure out what the general requirement in liberal arts education means and how it can best be accomplished. We go to faculty meetings and discuss the same inanities in the same inane way month after month, year after year. We may feel the occasional moment of self-pity about all this; we may joke about it. But, at some level, we all recognize that these sorts of meetings only seem pointless; we recognize that they are a way of discussing what kind of community we have been, we are, and we hope to be. The discussion of research ethics in IRBs is the same kind of community-making discussion, but curiously, we social scientists have some trouble recognizing this even as we debate among ourselves how much and which Durkheim our students ought to read.

19. So much was this the case that when Bosk came to Penn and became a member of the IRB there, he was designated an outside community member. This seemed strange not only to Bosk but to a federal regulator, although it took two years for Bosk to be redefined as a token for disciplinary breadth. In their recent survey of IRBs, De Vries and Forsberg (2002) found that IRBs are dominated by those working in medical occupations.

20. De Vries (forthcoming) contrasts the requirements for membership on IRBs in the Netherlands and in the United States, observing how the regulations in the United States are based on *identity*, while those in the Netherlands are based on *expertise*.

21. We would like to thank Michael Walzer for pointing us to this volume.

References

Alther, Lisa. 1976. *Kinflicks*. New York: Knopf.

American Association of University Professors. 2001. Protecting human beings: Institutional review boards and social science research. *Academe* 87 (3): 55-67. Also available at http://www.aaup.org/statements/Redbook/repirb.htm.

Anspach, Renee. 1993. *Deciding who lives: Fateful choices in the intensive-care nursery*. Berkeley: University of California Press.

Beecher, Henry K. 1966. Ethics and clinical research. *New England Journal of Medicine* 74:1354-60.

Bell, J. Bowyer. 1970. *The secret army: The IRA, 1916-1970*. London: Blond.

Bosk, Charles L. 2000. Irony, ethnography, and informed consent. In *Bioethics in social context*, edited by Barry C. Hoffmaster, 199-220. Philadelphia: Temple University Press.

———. Forthcoming. *What would you do: The collision of ethics and ethnography*. Chicago: University of Chicago Press.

Bourgois, Phillippe. 1995. *In search of respect: Selling crack in El Barrio*. New York: Cambridge University Press.

Bruner, Edward. 2004. Ethnographic practice and human subjects review. *Anthropology Newsletter*, January.

Citro, C. F., D. R. Ilgen, and C. B. Marrett, eds. 2003. *Protecting participants and facilitating social and behavioral sciences research*. Washington, DC: National Academies Press.

Cohen, Lawrence. 1999. Where it hurts: Indian material for an ethics of organ transplantation. *Daedalus* 128 (4): 135-66.

Davis, Fred. 1960. Uncertainty in medical diagnosis: Clinical and functional. *American Journal of Sociology* 66:41-47.

De Vries, Raymond. Forthcoming. How can we help? From "sociology in" to "sociology of" bioethics. *Journal of Law, Medicine and Ethics*.

De Vries, Raymond, and Carl Forsberg. 2002. What do IRBs look like? What kind of support do they receive? *Accountability in Research* 9:199-216.

Emerson, Joan. 1969. Negotiating the serious import of humor. *Sociometry* 32:169-81.

Freidson, Eliot. 1970. *The profession of medicine: A study in the sociology of applied knowledge*. New York: Harper and Row.

———. 1975. *Doctoring together*. New York: Elsevier.

Glaser, Barney, and Anselm Strauss. 1968. *Time for dying*. Chicago: Aldine.

Goldfarb, Jeffrey. 1982. *On cultural freedom: An exploration of public life in Poland and America*. Chicago: University of Chicago Press.

Grazian, David. 2003. *Blue Chicago: The search for authenticity in Chicago blues clubs*. Chicago: University of Chicago Press.

Heimer, Carole, and Lisa Stauffen. 1998. *For the sake of the children: The social organization of responsibility in the hospital and the home*. Chicago: University of Chicago Press.

Jones, James. 1981. *Bad blood: The Tuskegee syphilis experiment*. New York: Free Press

Latour, Bruno, and Steve Woolgar. 1986. *Laboratory life: The construction of scientific facts*. Princeton, NJ: Princeton University Press.

Malinowski, Bruno. 1922. *Argonauts of the Western Pacific*. London: Routledge.

Parsons, Talcott. 1951. *The social system*. New York: Free Press.

Petryna, Adriana. Forthcoming. The human subjects research industry. In *Global pharmaceuticals: Ethics Markets, practices*, edited by Adriana Petryna, Andrew Lakoff, and Arthur Kleinman.

Rothman, David. 1991. *Strangers at the bedside: A history of how law and bioethics transformed medical decision-making*. New York: Basic Books.

Snook, Scott. 2000. *Friendly fire: The accidental shootdown of U.S. Blackhawks over Northern Iraq*. Princeton, NJ: Princeton University Press.

Whyte, William F. 1942. *Street corner society*. Chicago: University of Chicago Press.

Reproduced below is a conversation and question/answer session about the relationship of ethnography to public policy. The conversation took place in Philadelphia on November 7, 2003. Comments by Jean-Michel Chapoulie follow the dialogue (p. 277).

Keywords: ethnography; public policy; sociological concepts; knowledge utilization; NASA; politicians; underdogs

On the Value of Ethnography: Sociology and Public Policy

A Dialogue

By
HOWARD S. BECKER,
HERBERT J. GANS,
KATHERINE S. NEWMAN,
and
DIANE VAUGHAN

Becker [B]: This session began because Herb Gans and I got into a discussion about Erving Goffman. I had written a piece about Goffman's language, suggesting that his very neutral language (in Asylums [Goffman 1961], for example) was a productive way for social science to proceed. I thought that that neutral language was central to his enterprise—or was, at least, to one of the crucial things he did, which was to get away from conventional language and conventional categories of thought. Those are especially foisted on us by contemporary definitions of problems, contemporary ideas about what's important, what's hot, what needs to be taken care of, what needs to be dealt with. I think we're often better off to take a somewhat larger and

Howard S. Becker is the author of Outsiders, Art Worlds, Writing for Social Scientists, and Tricks of the Trade. He lives and works in San Francisco.

Herbert J. Gans is the Robert S. Lynd Professor of Sociology at Columbia University. His most recent book is Democracy and the News (Oxford University Press 2003, 2004), and his Deciding What's News will be republished in a twenty-fifth-anniversary edition by the Northwestern University Press later in 2004.

Katherine S. Newman is the Dean of Social Science at the Radcliffe Institute for Advanced Study and the Malcolm Wiener Professor of Urban Studies at Harvard University. Her research areas include urban poverty, downward mobility, and lethal violence in American schools.

Diane Vaughan teaches sociology at Boston College. She is the author of Controlling Unlawful Organizational Behavior, Uncoupling, and The Challenger Launch Decision, and is working on Dead Reckoning: Technology, Culture, and Cognition in Air Traffic Control.

DOI: 10.1177/0002716204266599

ANNALS, AAPSS, 595, September 2004

more general comparative view, never mind about the contemporary relevance of our research. That will find its own way to the surface. Herb took issue with that. I'm going to suggest that Herb respond right now to that and then we turn to Kathy Newman and Diane Vaughan, both of whom have been far more than me, and perhaps more than Herb, involved in things that are of contemporary interest, things that are problems now, to which sociology and ethnographic research might make some kind of contribution. Do you want to respond, Herb?

Gans [G]: Howie and I and Erving all went to school together, so we were brainwashed pretty much by the same people. Erving was always unfathomable, so this justified our discussion. I certainly didn't know what was in his mind. But I disagreed, first of all, because I thought *Asylums* was a plea for a mental health policy that rehumanized the patient. Whether Erving had that in mind or not is hard to tell. But I feel very much that sociology and anthropology, in order to survive—and I think this goes way beyond our e-mail—but in order to survive we have to be useful. But even if it wasn't a question of survival, we ought to be useful. Because to be general runs the danger of being irrelevant. Erving was certainly opposed to being irrelevant—fairly strenuously. That much I know. But also because sociology and anthropology ought to help in the making of social policy. You should not be in social policy unless you have expertise in it because it's a discipline unto itself and very different from the behavioral sciences, but we certainly ought to be relevant to it. And I think ethnography is particularly useful here because we come closest to the people who are being studied. We can tell policy experts what the implications are of their policy on other people. We can tell policy people what the people that we have studied need in the way of policy. Ethnography has always studied the underdog and the victim, partly because of how sociologists think and partly because that is funded by government and the foundations. The underdog that is troubled or makes trouble is one subject that keeps social science research money coming, after all. But we can communicate for the underdogs, for the victims to— and in opposition to—the perpetrators, as I think of them. We should also communicate with the decision makers, social hierarchies, institutions, etc., that enable perpetrators to victimize underdogs.

There's also another topic here. When you talk about the general, then you're coming close to the positivist analysis, the search for laws, for timeless laws. And the notion of having timeless laws for society boggles anybody's mind who's been on Earth for fifteen seconds. I think in that sense too, if Erving said that, I would be disagreeing very sharply.

B: I'll call your attention, Herb, to the last paragraph in Goffman's essay on total institutions, a category which includes mental hospitals but not only mental hospitals. It says something like this: that perhaps when we get the more general view that we get from the comparative study of institutions of this kind, when we look not only at prisons and mental hospitals but also army barracks, submarines, ships at sea, monasteries and convents, all of which come under his definition of a "total institution"—when we look at these kinds of places, perhaps we will see that we can't blame the people who run them, that it's a mistake to think there are evil people who are running these places. I'm adding a lot to what he said, but this is the idea behind it.[1] And he leaves you with the sense that I think a lot of people who have done field research have, which is that when you get through studying some situation, some organization, you sure as hell know that something bad is happening, but you're damned if you know who did it. It's very hard to pin it down because everybody is operating under some constraints that make what they're doing seem to them reasonable, make it seem difficult to do anything else, etc. And the only way we can feel secure in pinning down the evildoers is to not talk to them and so not find out anything about their situation. That's often read as a kind of counsel of despair, as saying in effect, "The hell with it. There's nothing that can be done." Which is not the case because every link in a chain like that is a link that's potentially weak and can be broken. But it is to say that it's very hard to pin down fault and to see where the moral responsibility lies. And that seems to me one of the things you have to do when you decide on a political solution to anything.

G: Obviously, in the last paragraph, Erving got very structural, and he said that there are no evil people. He is mostly right, but there are many good or morally neutral people whose actions have evil consequences, although perpetrators or victimizers may be the wrong words for them. Most people are agents, and there are constraints on them. As Howie said very nicely, there are weak links and our job is to help the policy analysts find the weak links and then to do something about them. How to get them done and how to mobilize and organize power to get them done is the big question, but as ethnographers, we cannot and do not have to answer it (although I wish we could, as sociologists or citizens). But I think there's a fine dividing line between the agent under constraint and the evildoer, and I think this is where you played the role you did [Diane Vaughan], because if it weren't for you, every nth shuttle in the future would certainly blow up. Because of what you did, at least only every second nth will blow up because you did point to the agents and the weak links and said things had to be fixed. And I think here's a natural place for you to take over.

Vaughan [V]: What he is alluding to is a book I published in 1996 titled *The Challenger Launch Decision*. The book itself is a historical ethnography, which means that I was using mainly archival documents to reconstruct structure and culture and explain why NASA blew up the space shuttle and why they made a decision to launch it when they were warned that there were problems. The explanation itself is one that is multilevel in that it takes into account history, macrolevel structural factors, NASA's political environment, the organization itself, and then connects those to individual decisions and actions and how they interpreted signals of danger. At the end of that book, because I saw that the accident was a result of systemic macro-, meso-, and microlevel factors, I actually was surprised when I was rereading it recently to see what I had done there that in the last paragraph of the book I had predicted an accident. I was finishing the book in May 1995, and I wrote that at the time the political context of NASA was changing back to what it was prior to Challenger. At that point, I had predicted another accident, but I had never really thought about the consequences for *me*. When Columbia blew up, my phone started ringing an hour and a half afterwards, and it virtually only recently has stopped. From February the 1st through the middle of September [2003], there were twelve-hour days that were very involved with what had happened. Initially, all the calls were from the press. I took this as professional responsibility in the sense that I had written something that was about history and the press didn't really have another source. But I also took it as a teaching opportunity. One of the things that was clear in the beginning was that a lot of journalists who had never done anything about space had been assigned to the space beat to cover this accident, and they didn't have a clue about NASA, NASA culture, what had happened with Challenger—nothing. So I spent a lot of time on the phone that was just teaching them. But soon I discovered that the sociological concepts that had driven the analysis in the book, like organization culture, the normalization of deviance, institutional failure—those words began appearing in the press whether I was being quoted or not.

The story that was going on at the same time was that a congressionally appointed investigation board had been called together, headed by Admiral Gayman. Two weeks after the accident, I learned, because of my association with the board, Admiral Gayman read my book. And what he saw was that the explanation of Challenger was analogical to what they were finding about Columbia. The press things continued. By mid-April, I was called to testify before the board investigating the Columbia accident and was there for two days, one day in which I was briefing the board. And then the second day was my testimony. I saw this as very adversarial. I'd never done anything like this. It was going to be live on NASA TV and videostreamed in all major press centers around the country and into home computers. I was also teaching, as you can imagine, so there was a scramble about how to prepare for this. But when I got there, I found a board that was already prepared and interested in and endorsing the sociological analysis. Everyone on the board—and they had 117 staff members—and they all had my book. Plus a short piece that I had written to translate the causal ideas and how you could connect strategies for change with the causes of organizational mistakes. And I put that in a management journal, so they had found that. And that had also led them to other social science literatures. After my testimony, they invited me to come and work with them.

So I spent the summer [of 2003], starting in June, in Washington, D.C., working with the accident investigation board and the staff—there were about forty of us— on the production of the report. And they had succeeding outlines of the board's report. When I got there for the testimony, the first working outline they had had a section on social causes that mirrored the chapters in my book that were on the social causes—the decision making, the macrolevel political history, and the organizational factors. So when I got there, I was truly in a teaching position that people were coming to me and asking me about these concepts and how they fit and showing me their data, so that I could begin to work with their data. And the concepts shaped their analysis in the book.

It was interesting. In one of my conversations with the admiral, who defies any military stereotype—the fact that (a) I was there and (b) he listened to me, as he did to everyone else—was one of the really amazing parts of these group experiences that I was fortunate enough to have. In the beginning, I saw that the outline in the "Social Cause, Part 2" of the accident was trying to distinguish between layers of cause. So one of the chapters was the proximate cause of the accident, contributing cause of the accident, and factors relevant to the accident. So, encouraged by the fact that he was obviously ecumenical, I went into his office and I said, "I can see what you're trying to do here, but no one is going to understand these different causes." So he was persuaded—and the degree to which he endorsed sociology shows up in the final report to the extent that this is the first accident report that has given equal weight to the social causes as to the technical causes. Being successful there, I thought I would try something else and so suggested that they move the history chapter away from the beginning of the social cause part to the end of it, and he wouldn't buy that. And I said, "Why?" He said, "History is a scene setter." And I said, "No, history is cause." And I explained to him how NASA historic political and economic environment had shaped that accident. He was still unconvinced, so I proposed that I write a chapter that drew paryllels between Columbia and Chamlenger and was called "History Is Cause." I proposed it as an experiment—you don't have to publish this or use this in the report in any way, but I would like to try to do this. He turned out to be delighted. He did not move his history chapter, but he was delighted with the chapter, and it's sort of a wrap-up to this part 2 of the book.

He was very much in touch with the press, and he began using sociological concepts early on. Just prior to the report's publication, he had a press conference. And there was an article that appeared in the *New York Times* that really outed me as the genie behind what he had in his magic bottle; that was the report and the author of chapter 8. So this volume of press continued. My name and the concepts of the book, especially "The Normalization of Deviance," became so commonplace in the place, it was almost generic. And the day after the report was issued, Sean O'Keefe, who was a NASA administrator, had a press conference. He said a few words and just opened it up to the press, and the first question by the press was, "Have you read Diane Vaughan's book yet?" Which got me an invitation the next Monday night to NASA headquarters for dinner, in which I tried to address something that's not so clear in the report, which is: if culture is a problem, how do you change culture? So I saw that again as a teaching opportunity. And since then, I've been working more closely with NASA. One of the things that I'm recommending is that you don't wait until you make a huge mistake in order to investigate your culture and think about how you thought it was and how it actually turned out to be, that you should have anthropologists and sociologists who are ethnographers in the agency at all times so that you would be getting feedback on your culture. And I suggested a fellowship program whereby they were enabled to do that. And people have been very enthusiastic about that. I don't know how it's going to work out.

There are a lot of things to say in the discussion in relation to Kathy's work as well. But I think that the reason I was able to have success—I don't know how you define success here, but if you define success as change, that's still up in the air. But

I think the reason I was able to teach effectively the connection between the two accidents is because the first book was ethnographic. The description in addition to the concepts really told the story. So when the Columbia accident investigation board and reporters are seeing that NASA had a problem flying with known flaws over the years since the beginning of the shuttle program with the foam, that naturally connected with the idea of normalization of deviance that was in my book in relation to the O-ring problem, that proceeded much in the same way, where they accepted some and then more and then more and then more. So it wasn't like they made two bad decisions; the bad decision was the first decision to accept anything that was a technical deviation and proceed with it. So it was both the ethnographic description, but it was also that the concepts made sense to them because the concepts also fit the data on the second case. And that is what I think gives ethnography particularly a role, not necessarily in public policy, but at least in shaping the public discourse so that people understand the sociological roots of the problem and have a way of analyzing it as you were describing what Erving Goffman did at the end of his book—so that you get it that there aren't really evil people, that there are evil systems and you have to change the systems.

Newman [N]: I want to pick up on that last point about the role of ethnographic work in defining problems in ways that people completely outside of social science can understand. That is one of the vital things that ethnographic work can do that other forms of social science have more problems with. In fact, I would say that what the ethnographic tradition does is to define social problems that have either not been recognized or have fallen off the radar screen, either because the presence of this problem contradicts cultural expectations about what kind of society we live in, what sort of organization we're working in, or because the problem plagues people who have been written off. We don't see them because we don't care about them or because we somehow think their problems are endemic to the kind of people they are. Those are the kinds of circumstances in which I think ethnographic work has the greatest promise.

I was asked by Howie to reflect on how this general perspective has influenced my own work. I've written two books on downward mobility, which, to pick up on Mitch [Duneier]'s point about social amnesia, was actually a topic of great importance to sociologists in the 1930s. Then it dropped completely off the radar screen, I would argue, because downward mobility flies in the face of what American culture defines as the normative experience. Yet even in huge technical tomes like Featherman and Hauser, we find evidence that there have always been a significant number of people falling down the class ladder. We just don't focus on them or write about them because their experience doesn't accord with the culture we live in. An ethnographer can turn that expectation on its head and look at a problem that is standing right before us and ask how it is constituted.

Another problem that I've worked on in collaboration with four of my graduate students, one of whom is here today, bears a resemblance to this. We have a book coming out in February [2004] on rampage shootings in American high schools. These are horrible tragedies that take place in the "wrong place." They are occurring in places that have very low background violence, that are known to be a great place to raise a family, and suddenly, they turn into murderous violence. It jars our sense of predictable social order and makes a perfect occasion for an ethnographic exploration. *Rampage* owes a great deal both to Diane's work and to Charles Perrow's work on normal accidents. Rampage shootings happen after an enormous amount of warning behavior, after a great deal of "evidence" piles up that in retrospect suggests that something horrible is going to happen. Yet nobody can see it beforehand. These concepts of structural secrecy, of organizational failure, turn out to be powerful explanations of why rampage shootings get as far as they do.

I've also written two books that fall into this latter category of issues, those that don't get attention in general, because their victims are on the wrong side of inequality. One book, *No Shame in My Game* [Newman 1999b], was about the working poor, and the other, *A Different Shade of Gray*, was about elderly minorities in the inner city who are aging in poor communities. Those books look at the lived experience of people who don't confirm the accepted paradigm of American culture. We think poor people are poor somehow because they don't want to work. Well, what about all those people who are working in low-wage jobs?

Another important service ethnography provides—and this may be a more anthropological take than a sociological one—is to expose or explore the subjective experience of victims or of perpetrators: What does it mean to ordinary people to be working poor or to be downwardly mobile, and why do they think this experience has befallen them? What is the folk sociology of this issue, and how does it differ from the way a sociologist or a more distanced analyst would explain the structural problem of downward mobility? Americans have a weak grasp on structural forces. They tend to pull their problems inward toward the self, to make them expressions of failures that are under personal control. Explorations of the subjective perspective are always embedded in a particularly critical approach to the understanding of American culture.

A third point that I think is crucial about ethnography in the public realm is its capacity, which I think Diane's work shows and Howie's and Herb's as well, to communicate beyond the academy through powerful narrative. Ethnography has the capacity to connect with the public, with students, and even with politicians—even with people who run NASA—because they can actually understand it, and they have a great difficulty often with structural equation models. It also then tends to attract media exposure. I've been on *Oprah* and the *Lehrer News Hour*, and at either end of that media spectrum, you find yourself with a teaching opportunity, a chance to convey to an enormous public the power of social science to capture a reality that matters, that helps to explain things that people find puzzling. Quantitative forms of sociology rarely have that opportunity, which is too bad because they offer insights into many important public problems as well.

Many ethnographers are tempted to move from the diagnosis to the remedy. You can't embed yourself for three or four years in a problem and then say, "Gosh, I have no idea how we could improve this situation, no opinion about how we could make the lives of the working poor better, no thoughts on improving the lives of the inner city elderly." But I do think there is a difference between diagnosis and remedy. We shouldn't confuse public sociology, or the exposure of social problems, with policy evaluation. I've never thought of myself as a policy wonk. I wasn't trained as a policy analyst. At Harvard, I work alongside people who've done it for a living for many years, and they bring tools to policy analysis that I genuinely don't have. Nonetheless, I would never back away from the challenge I pose to myself of offering whatever I can in the way of informed speculations, ideas, thoughts, possibilities, about how to make the problems I study go away or be less harsh in their consequences. But I guess in the end that's not a special brief of ethnography. It is something we can do. Some people do it, some people don't. It's not necessarily unique to our trade.

The special mission of ethnography, in my opinion, lies in its capacity to redefine the social landscape, to explode received categories, to cause students, ordinary readers, we hope politicians and people who have power to understand the social realities of our society. Ethnography has the capacity to develop different ways of thinking about a social universe that they often take for granted, to explore and make real the experience of people who have gone through hardship, through loss, through confusion, and possibly even a triumph against all expectations. That is a special mission that I feel makes it legitimate for me to take that paycheck that I get for doing this work I'm privileged to do.

G: Let me say two things. I e-mailed Diane Vaughan after I learned about all this and told her she was the heroine of sociology because she was in the right place at the right time when she could do something. I've been in some situations like this and made proposals. However, my proposals were generally ignored or rejected, but you were there with the right remedy and at the right time.

But I got up mostly to respond a little bit to Kathy because I think ethnographers can do more than she says they can do. If you've studied and worked among the working poor, you know even just by listening to them what kinds of changes could be made to give them access to an opportunity for upward mobility. And you can tell the policy people that. You can draw from the implications of your research; you can draw from the consequences of your research. The implications will provide clues to policy. The consequences will help you evaluate the policy or take a policy evaluator aside and give him or her helpful advice. So I think we can do something. Whether we ought to do something is up to each individual, but I certainly think that ethnography, by the virtue of being close to people, by seeing how they live and seeing their problems, enables us to take a bit more of an active role than she suggested.

N: You misunderstood, Herb. I didn't say that you can't or you shouldn't evaluate policy. I'm saying that it's something some people would like to do and other people don't find to be consonant with their mission. But I don't think it's something that is necessarily the sole province of ethnography.

G: Of course not. But it's one of the capabilities that ethnography gives us. That's what I was trying to say.

B: I'm a mischievous kid and I can't resist making a little trouble if I can. Seriously, I think it depends so much on the situation around the case. You're exactly right—Diane was in the right place at the right time. Hardly any of us ever are. What made me a complete cynic about the value of sociology for influencing anything were two experiences I had. One is: I did research on marijuana fifty years ago [Becker 1963, pp. 41-78]. It was part of a wave of research of various kinds—biochemical, pharmacological, psychological, legal, etc.—all of which showed that governmental policies with respect to marijuana were foolish and counterproductive. Those arguments are well known and widespread. Everybody has heard them and knows all about them. And the result of all that research is that the laws are even more punitive today than they ever were. This is enough to make a boy unhappy, I'll tell you.

The other experience is on a much smaller scale. It had to do with the research my colleagues and I did in a medical school. When we finished our research, we wrote a manuscript, we gave it to the faculty to read, and we had a meeting with some of the faculty, who said, "Well, where are your recommendations?" We said, "We don't have any recommendations. This is what it looks like." They said, "No, you've been here three years. You must have some idea of what could be made better." I said, "Look, I'm not a medical educator. I don't know what you people are trying to achieve. But you tell me what you don't like, and I'll tell you how to fix it." They said, "Well, for instance, we don't like the way students cram for examinations. They study very hard to pass these exams. And then they immediately forget everything they've learned. It's just for passing exams." I said, "What would you like them to know how to do? What is the exam is supposed to measure?" "We'd like them to know how to examine a patient—do a physical examination, take a medical history, order the appropriate laboratory tests, arrive at a diagnosis, and suggest a plan of treatment." I said, "Nothing easier. Give each student two patients. Let them do that. Then you examine the patient and you see how well they did." There was a dead silence. I said, "What's wrong?" "Well," they said, "that's not very practical." I said, "What do you mean?" They said, "It would take a lot of time." I said, "You'd better believe it. But if you're serious, this is what you would do." They said, "We can't do that." "Why not?" "Well, we have our research to do. We have our administrative work on various faculty committees. We have our own patients to take care of. We don't have time for that."

From this I developed the concept of a *panacea*. A panacea, in the technical definition I gave it, is a solution that takes care of exactly what you want to get rid of and doesn't cost a penny or a minute or anything that's of any importance to you. The problem I've always found with offering solutions based on ethnographic knowledge is that they cost too much and that we are never in a position to get the people who might be able to make the change we suggest to agree to bear the expense of doing it. I think, Diane, you may be in a position where what NASA is experiencing now is so heavy and so expensive that they're willing to pay the price to make some changes. But that's not a very common situation for a social scientist to be in.

G: Diane, you said before that you think the next blow up will be on the same schedule, so obviously you didn't think you achieved what you hoped to.

V: Well, I went to a conference of NASA's forty top leaders, and they are absolutely determined to make change and excited and having lots of ideas. I never saw a group of such smart people. They understand the social principles behind this. But a lot of it is outside their ability to make change. Their top leaders have responsibility to Congress and the White House, and as long as they are shortchanged in terms of funds, they are always going to have deadlines and schedule pressures, and their ability to make internal change is seriously challenged by that. As well as the fact that historically the roots of the agency are in the military. It's huge, so they have an exceedingly large system in terms of rules and protocol, which make hierarchy and change of command essential for them. It's a minisociety. It's just like changing society: there are inequalities throughout. You can't listen to engineers because engineers can only speak up under certain conditions. So systems are hard to change.

Audience Questions/Comments [Q]: With respect, there is another tradition of ethnography that might enlighten the discussion, and that is the ethnography of policy making itself. I would take issue a little bit with Herbert Gans's contention that we only look at the underdog. It's perfectly possible to look at the activities of politicians and policy makers, look at the way they proceed, and look at the way in which they have knowledge, and it becomes quite clear that we all as social scientists are still operating within a blue-book socialist or Fabian tradition, which believes, as it were, the facts will speak for themselves and they'll be effortlessly absorbed in the political process. That is not the way it works. It works very differently. What you're talking about is a world which is largely self-contained. You're talking about a world which has its own strong political priorities and its own discourses. Not least amongst the characteristics of those discourses is the anonymization of influences. Ministers, at least in the countries I've studied, are not interested in sources. They're not interested in the authors of particular documents. They're interested in what they conceive in a very immediate sense to be the political good sense of what is said. And the political good sense is not our sense at all. It's framed by constituencies. It's framed by political crisis. It's framed by long-term problems. It's framed by manifesto commitments. It's framed by obligations to parties and all the rest. That's one issue. The second issue is the timing is critically wrong. We often produce our results out of synchronization with the policy process. And the policy process has its own momentum. So there is not, as it were, a receptive audience. And it goes on.

In the field I know something about, which is justice, John Braithwaite has been the most distinguished and influential social scientist, but you will look very hard to see his name amongst any of the papers that talk about changes in justice systems. The whole way in which social science is treated is to bleach out authorship. And I don't think we know very much about the way in which social science does impinge. It's much more oblique. It's much more tangential. It's much more a matter of trickle down. It's much more a matter of casual conversation. And if we persist in the idea that somehow we will represent the sufferings of the poor and then the politicians will respond, I suspect we're not going to work very effectively.

N: Let me take a crack at that. I don't measure the success of what I'm doing by whether or not politicians find it attractive and act on it. I'd love it if they did, but I still think it's a worthy enterprise because the mission is something larger than simply trying to affect public policy or to study how public policy is made—though all of those things are available for ethnographic study, I don't deny it. The study of the political process and the extent to which it *ever* pays any attention to evidence as opposed to interest groups, I think, is very worthy as well. But I think we would make a big mistake if we evaluated the success or the intrinsic value of what we do by whether or not we can show the kind of change that Diane is able to show. I think it's wonderful, but I think it's rare. I don't think I was able to massively affect the course of mobility in the United States by writing *Falling from Grace* [Newman 1999a], but I changed a few people's way of thinking about the problem, and that modest goal is actually sufficient for me.

Q: Let me just respond very quickly. I said that we studied the underdogs and the victims in part because we were paid to do so. However, I do not think that is all we should do. In the sixties, Lee Rainwater and I argued that we should stop studying the poor and start studying the people who make other people poor. We got nowhere, of course, and things haven't changed very much. But I agree thoroughly that we ought to be studying the policy people and see if we can get to them that way.

V: If I could say one quick thing in relation to Kathy's comment. I think that we cannot really measure our effect, that you don't know when you put something into print who's reading it. Kathy and I are both outliers in a sense in that we do deal with the public a lot in terms of our research, but if you think not of policy change but of social change, and you think of the sociologists who are really public sociologists but are not teaching in universities because they can't do their work and simultaneously stay on a faculty and live up to those requirements but are doing grassroots organizing and trying to empower other groups of people, that those teachings are based on sociological principles. And it may be that in terms of their work and in terms of my work, the people I may have most influenced are the people who are on this accident investigation committee. We have to think of social change in terms of our outreach to our students, in terms of other kinds of examples of public sociology than just the kind that Kathy and I have had the opportunity to do. That's the kind that shows. What we don't see are the invisible work of all the sociologists in their classrooms. When a student leaves your classroom, you may have changed their life, and you may not, but often you don't hear. So I think changing organizations and changing lead structures is always going to be hard for us. But I think, as Kathy says, if we give people a different vision of how the system works, then we've done a lot right there.

Q: I think that skepticism is the enemy of sociology, and because of this skepticism, I ask, is that the reason that the Chicago slums are still there and that they are more miserable now than when this work was started in the Chicago School? And then I think sociologists sometimes are snobs. They are snobbish about their writing. They make their writing so complicated and incomprehensible for the policy maker, for the politician who is not always very smart maybe, but who needs to read simple texts. So don't we really have time to produce those, to help people? This is my question.

Q: I think that a lot of the graduate students in this room are probably thinking about a lot of what you've all been saying. And I think Diane and Kathy are beginning to answer the question that I have. A lot of us, especially those of us who study urban poverty, we want to do policy-relevant work, and we think about that, and we realize that there is a reality of the context that we work in. Eli [Anderson] and Mitch [Duneier] have both told me, and Kathy Edin has told me this as well, that our first goal should be to be good sociologists. We want to explain, we want to understand. And if we go into it motivated primarily by a policy agenda, we'll always be disappointed because policy makers will misappropriate and reinterpret our findings to say what they want to say. That's how people can read Kathy Edin and Laura Lane's *Making Ends Meet*, and liberals can say, "See, welfare moms can't make ends meet on welfare alone. Low-wage working moms can't make ends meet on a minimum-wage job." And conservatives can read the same book and say, "Look, here there is proof: welfare moms cheat on welfare. That's why we need welfare reform." So I guess the question that I have for all of you, for those of us who want to do that kind of policy-relevant work, what's the answer? Can we just hope we're in the right place in the right time, as Diane was? Or can we hope to influence just a few people, as Kathy Newman was saying? Or is there a way that we can try to gear our work to speak to policy makers and not have it misappropriated?

Note

1. The actual wording of Goffman's remark is as follows: "I have defined total institutions denotatively by listing them and then have tried to suggest some of their common characteristics. . . . the similarities obtrude so glaringly and persistently that we have a right to suspect that there are good functional reasons for these features being present and that it will be possible to fit these features together and grasp them by means of a functional explanation. When we have done this, I feel we will give less praise and blame to particular superintendents, commandants, wardens, and abbots, and tend more to understand the social problems and issues in total institutions by appealing to the underlying structural design common to them all" (Goffman 1961, 123-24).

References

Becker, H. S. 1963. *Outsiders: Studies in the sociology of deviance.* New York: Free Press.

Goffman, E. 1961. *Asylums.* Garden City, NY: Doubleday.

Newman, K. 1999a. *Falling from grace: Downward mobility in the age of affluence.* Berkeley: University of California Press.

———. 1999b. *No shame in my game: The working poor in the inner city.* New York: Knopf/Russell Sage.

Vaughan, Diane. 1996. *The Challenger launch decision: Risky technology, culture, and deviance at NASA.* Chicago: University of Chicago Press.

Comments by Jean-Michel Chapoulie on the "Value of Ethnography" Dialogue

Gans's position assumes the prior existence of accepted social policies that favor those at the bottom of the social scale. This is certainly not a social fact that one finds in all times and places. (Paul Veyne presents somewhere a conception of the Roman elites whose principal concern was to exploit the Roman plebeians and not to improve their morality and notes that the Roman elites differed considerably in this from the bourgeois elites of the nineteenth century.) Gans's position also supposes that the backers of research have this kind of goodwill toward those at the bottom of the social scale. What I know about American foundations of the 1930s does not completely support this view.

1. Gans claims that "sociology and anthropology, in order to survive, . . . have to be useful." The question is useful to whom? This point of view, the most common one on this question among sociologists, I think, ignores the conflicts of interest and perspectives omnipresent in all societies. I think we can go back to Becker's (1967) discussion in "Whose Side Are We On?" with respect to this question.

2. Diane Vaughn's experience with NASA seems completely different from that of people who do research on the categories of people who are thought to "make problems" and whose "problems" justify the research: it is a question of using the expertise of social science after an acute problem has been identified, not before. In experiences like Vaughan's, the contribution of the social sciences is taken up almost immediately by those who have and use the power of decision. But this use of social science occurs in a world of political decisions completely different from the world of social science. The world of politics has its own constraints, notably (as one questioner remarked), its own timeline whose rhythm, in the democracies of the West, is influenced by the timing of elections, the constraints of political careers, the ways of legitimating "interesting" problems, and so on. In general, the time frame of political decision making is much shorter than that of the slow changes the analyses of social scientists are often interested in. There is very little chance that any politician could make a career by making an issue of the problem of individual downward mobility. But a politician could reasonably hope to reform NASA, and one must not forget the case of the politician who could make a large

Jean-Michel Chapoulie has done field research on secondary school professors (Les professeurs de l'enseignement secondaire. Un métier de classe moyenne, Presses de la Maison des Sciences de l'Homme, 1987), historical research on the development of schooling in France since 1800 (Les collèges du people, with J.-P. Briand, Editions du CNRS, 1992), and a historical book about Chicago sociology (La tradition sociologique de Chicago, 1892-1961, Paris, Éditions du Seuil, 2001). He is currently a professor of sociology, Université de Paris 1 (Panthéon Sorbonne).

DOI: 10.1177/0002716204266964

public believe that he has reformed NASA, even though he knows that the problem he pretends to have eradicated will show up again: reforms of social policy in Europe provide numerous examples of this type.

Because social science analyses have very different modes of functioning, legitimation, and communication than do discussions of general social policy or policy in specialized areas (e.g., medical education), the transition from one to the other is very uncertain, depending on many unpredictable, conjunctural events. It is likely that the reinterpretations of social science made in the political world will often be radically different from the original interpretations made by social scientists.

Ethnographic work undoubtedly has a greater chance to influence public discussion and to reformulate the definitions of social problems than do other types of social analyses since they are a kind of translation of the world studied into the world of the cultivated middle classes—those who participate in public discussions. But that does not imply that this influence works in the direction desired by those who have produced the ethnographic analyses.

3. Social science analyses are almost always quite narrow and are often unaware of the specific and limited conditions under which their conclusions are valid, which can only lead to dead ends. School reform in France is a good example. The studies by the demographer Alfred Sauvy and the sociologist/economist Jean Fourastié, and their discussions with highly placed officials, played an important role in the adoption of the reforms that led to the creation of today's *collège*. This reform, intended to reduce educational inequality among children of different social origins, had been discussed for close to sixty years.

Prior to the reform of the 1960s, some children who had finished primary school at age eleven went to a *lycée*, where they took a "classic" or "modern" course for seven years, either of which prepared them to take the baccalauréat (the examination that had to be passed to be eligible for further education). Other students went to a different school (called *cours complémentaire*), in which they studied subjects similar to those studied in the modern courses of the lycée, for four years. Some students in the cours complémentaire (30 to 40 percent in my generation) could, after finishing the four-year program, enter the modern section of the lycée and prepare for the baccalauréat as well.

The reform created new establishments that brought together the first four years of the former lycées and the four years of the cours complémentaires in one unified collège, which all students were required to attend until the age of sixteen. After completing the collège, some students could go to lycée for another three years. This change was supposed to lessen the social inequalities created by different kinds of schooling.

The plan for the new unified collège was finally imposed, against the wishes of a large number of educational bureaucrats, the prime minister, and many other politicians, by the then president of the Republic. The research sponsored by Sauvy was an essential element in overcoming the resistance of some administrators, unions, and others to this change. But no one—neither social scientists, administrators, nor politicians—had thought about how school personnel, students, and families would react when they found themselves in the new situation thus created. The teachers had to deal with restless students, who were sometimes not very interested in scholarly work. Middle-class families had to find ways of avoiding the early elimination of some of their children due to bad grades, since there was not at this time any alternative for further study. A large number of working- and lower-middle-class families had decided that their children could not benefit from schooling and that the school and its personnel were hostile to them, and so on. And the official objective—the equalization of the chances for further education—was not achieved, at least with respect to access to elite schools. In the end, Sauvy and Fournastié contributed to the lengthening of schooling in France and, in this sense, to the "modernization" of France but not to the reduction of educational inequality nor to the recruitment of elites from the working and lower-middle classes (one of Sauvy's explicit objectives). In addition, one can wonder if years of schooling would not have been prolonged anyway, as elsewhere in Europe.

I do not believe the present generation of "experts" in education has shown itself any more efficient than that of Sauvy and for the same reason: it takes up one part of the problem—the fact that a large number of working- and lower-middle-class students do not like school and are undisciplined—and concludes that the school must adapt to this public. This ignores the present structure of the labor market, which is, of course, completely outside the mandate given to school reformers.

The role of consultants in the social sciences seems to me directly linked to the importance of "social problems" in societies where there is public discussion. The social sciences contribute to the public definition of these problems, but their contribution seems to me fundamentally the same as that of politicians, journalists, or spokespersons for different causes. The point of view of sociologists acting as experts is, in the vast majority of cases, only a variant of the common, middle-class point of view on the problem concerned. Some people can find gratifying careers there, however, and can benefit from the halo of the label of "science," as weak as that is in the case of sociology.

Reference

Becker, H. S. 1967. Whose side are we on? *Social Problems* 14 (3): 234–47.

On the Rhetoric and Politics of Ethnographic Methodology

By
JACK KATZ

In a variety of ways, all ethnographies are politically cast and policy relevant. Each of three recurrent political rhetorics is related to a unique set of fieldwork practices. Ethnographies that report holistically on journeys to "the other side" build policy/political significance by contesting popular stereotypes. Theoretical ethnographies draw on political imagination to fill in for a lack of variation in participant observation data and to model an area of social life without attempting to rule out alternative explanations. Comparative analytic studies build political relevance by revealing social forces that are hidden by local cultures. Each of these three genres of ethnographic methodology faces unique challenges in relating fieldwork data to politically significant explanations. By shaping the ethnographer's relations to subjects and readers, each methodology also structures a distinctive class identity for the researchers—as worker, as aristocrat, or as bourgeois professional.

Keywords: analytic induction; policy research; politics of science; research practices

Speaking of the ubiquitous relevance of legality, Vilhelm Aubert once remarked that even to assert authoritatively that "there is no law on that" is to make a significant legal statement (cf. Aubert 1983, 77-78).[1] Acting in an area not governed by law means you have a certain freedom to proceed and a certain vulnerability to be attacked. As with law, the hermeneutics of politics stop at no limits. (It is revealing to note that the same holds for religion and psychoanalysis [Ricoeur 1970].) To characterize a piece of ethnographic research as apolitical is a political statement.

Jack Katz is a professor of sociology at University of California, Los Angeles. His current research is on the intersections of work, household formation, and local area use in six neighborhoods that represent the range of social and ethnic stratification in Hollywood. His Web site is http://www.sscnet.ucla.edu/soc/faculty/katz/.

NOTE: I would like to thank Eli Anderson, Howie Becker, Angela Jamison, Rob Jansen, Diane Vaughan, and Maurice Zeitlin for very useful attacks on prior versions.

DOI: 10.1177/0002716204267475

A debate over whether research should be "policy relevant" has a false tone, in part because policy relevance is just one form of politics. It is hard for students of the collaborative construction of social facts to resist asking the following: relevant to which policy makers, in what ways, and the most difficult question of all, when? "Policy relevance" is an indirect way of demanding that political priority be given here and now to those with at least a foothold in institutions of power.

A debate over whether research can expect to find timeless laws can also be misleading, at least when the subject is ethnography. Railings against "positivism" tend to forget the pragmatic logic of methods. People who search for timeless laws do not necessarily believe they will ever find them. This appears absurd only if we forget that in the quest for perfect, certain, or universal knowledge (Turner 1953), one does different things than when ambitions are more limited. The quest for timelessly applicable forms of theory, like the quests for love, peace, equality, or god, leads one to do different things, and while arriving at a settled end may be fantasy, the challenges structured and overcome on the way are not necessarily quixotic.

Consider the romantic logic that organizes the work lives of our practical-minded colleagues, the survey researchers. It is always absurd to conduct a random sample to generalize to a sampled population since even if generalizations are qualified with probabilities stated in the timeless standards of quantitative logic, the population is never the same, in composition or at least in biographical reality, as the population to which the study's results will be extrapolated. Between any study and the application of its results, there is always the wild bet, always made against a better wisdom, that things do not change. But on the way to the survey researcher's absurd quest for generalizable certainties, some very real dragons of competing explanation can be slain, or at least seriously injured.

Several critical issues easily can be masked in a debate between advocates of neutral and comparative analytic language and advocates of research cast in language that will be perceived as relevant for assessing the impacts of power. By critical issues, I mean something empirical: whether self-consciously or sentimentally, every ethnographer will define his or her position on each of these issues in each research project; the stance taken will have major consequences for the demands of the research project. A central choice is one of genre. This article is essentially a discussion of the three dominant genres in sociological ethnography, each of which builds political significance for a text in distinctive ways. Within each, there are politically significant choices, but the challenges differ.

First, ethnographies can be made policy/politically meaningful by presenting a picture of social life that is juxtaposed to common stereotypes. I refer to this first genre as "worker" ethnography. To develop a politically powerful juxtaposition, the ethnographer operates in the field as a novice jack-of-all-trades, laboriously detailing varied regions of subjects' lives through relatively unspecialized description. Humbling his or her authorial posture, the worker ethnographer maintains a transcending respect for the subjects, who are rendered as fully human beings. Even through self-reflexive passages, the subjects remain at center stage in the text. This is the tradition started by William F. Whyte's *Street Corner Society* (1955) and continued by Gans, Anderson, and Duneier.

I label a second genre "aristocratic": the researcher either does not spend much time with subjects, avoids the drudgery of repeatedly describing everyday events, or at least fails to present in the text empirical materials showing variations in the lives of subjects that are directly relevant to the theory offered. While this kind of ethnography can make a significant contribution at certain points in the history of research on given types of social phenomena, the rhetorical strategy is usually to provide a flat, unvaried, morally sympathetic but relatively superficial picture of subjects in order to cast them into illustrations of theory. Begun by Radcliffe-Brown, whose structural-functionalist ethnographies came to be seen as politically conservative, the leading current examples of this tradition include the anticapitalist ethnographies of Burawoy (1979; Burawoy and Lukács 1985; Burawoy et al. 2000) and, in its most powerfully rhetorical aspect, the enormously popular, feminist/anticapitalist ethnography of emotional labor by Hochschild (1979, 1983).

The third genre, which I call "bourgeois professional," is the least formally political. The ethnographer works as a specialist studying a kind of social process, constructing and analyzing series of cases that show fine variations between similar events, biographies, and types of social action. Like a dentist, each "case" has a set of X-rays taken at more or less analogous times; because the dentist cannot control if and when patients will come in, some files are more or less complete than others; and a craftlike expertise is required to make sense of what will often be invisible to lay viewers without professional instruction. The resulting text becomes political only through conveying the indirect and subtle message that local culture obscures how universal social processes shape local life. For the bourgeois professional ethnographer, the key issues for defining the political significance of a study are which spatial and temporal dimensions of a social phenomenon to include in the composition of the set of gathered or constructed cases. Research projects in this genre are distinguished by the creation of sets of closely related data. The researcher amasses situationally specific observations of behavioral interaction and diachronically described cases, such as the biographies of collective phenomena (e.g., riots), natural histories of work careers (e.g., the public school teacher), the stages through which a given type of conduct is built up (e.g., opiate addiction), and status passages in personal life (see Vaughan on uncoupling, following). The first flourishing of this style of ethnography came in the 1940s and 1950s, in Second Chicago School studies (see Fine 1995).

Prologue: The Social Construction of a Text's Political Status

Ethnography is a relatively mushy field on which to hold a fight that pits advocates of neutral language against those favoring policy, political, or morally marked analysis. In the conduct of fieldwork, methods and theory interests are so closely mixed with each other and with historically and socially contextualized relevancies that neutrality is relatively hard to come by. The argument can be held more clearly in fields in which methods are more fixed relative to substantive focus and where theory is prima facie neutral (exchange theory, status expectations theory, network theory, conversation analysis, etc.).

Consider a study of conversation-analytic practices as demonstrated in transcribed recordings of interrogations of complaining victims in rape trials (Drew 1992). The author uses this corpus to analyze how prosecutor and witness contest each other's descriptions of legally significant events, but he draws no implications about the justice or injustice in which violence against women is either initially performed or subsequently administered legally. The issues addressed are technical; the themes are about court versions of universal conversation-interaction processes. That the substantive material is about rape trials is of no noted relevance.

I mean not to judge such work but to highlight the moral/political challenge it presents to the researcher. As an ethnographic parallel, one might imagine a study of the table manners of SS guards at extermination camps that made no analytic relevance of the context of their dining. At some level, that is what Norbert Elias (1994) indirectly did in his historical ethnography of "the civilizing process."

The bitterness of the irony in Elias's work, published in exile in 1939, his parents dead at Auschwitz and Breslau soon after, is transformed if not eradicated by the publication some sixty years later of an analysis of the de-civilizing processes that lead up to the Nazis (Elias, 1996, esp. 299-402). The earlier, morally neutral text is qualified and recast as a foundation for a comprehensive moral appreciation of the relationship between everyday modern culture and the structure of national political power.

All of this poses a question that is too often ignored in facile rejections of technical, policy silent, universally cast analyses: who determines the context in which a work should be read? Becker's (1953) marijuana-user paper has a bit of a protest against psychological explanations, but it reads primarily as a learner's manual, consistently dry and matter of fact, without tones that either hector or proselytize. But that is not how it ever has been read. Does a study of the interaction tactics at rape trials, which never mentions that cross-examination techniques incidentally compound the assault on a victim's subjectivity by attempting to thrust undesired meanings into her mouth, show a commitment to positivist science carried to amoral madness? What about a study showing table manners being honored a mere matter of feet beyond a view onto grotesque horrors? Seen in the right context, the latter becomes a study of how people collaborate to sustain identities as good people while doing dirty work (Hughes 1962).

In an important, neglected sense, the critic who would damn these studies as amoral covers up his or her failure to import the context that would bring out the political significance. Reading Elias on table manners on its own carries one line of political implications; reading it as a precursor to *The Germans* (1996) gives another spin. And before Elias published *Studien über die Deutschen*, what was the political status of his earlier work? That depends on whether the reader is willing to bring the substance of Elias's later work into the discussion before Elias does. The same is true with Drew (1992) and cross-examination practices at rape trials.

The study can be a resource for damning Drew's moral indifference or for using Drew to damn the way legal process compounds victimization.

To return to the initial discussion (by Becker et al., in this volume) of Erving Goffman's *Asylums* (1961), which is conceded by all sides to be both theoretically and policy/politically significant, we should note what an odd type of ethnographer he was. None of his writings have ethnography's usual monograph-like focus on people in a single organization, time, or place. All of his writings show the workings of a fundamentally simple, if extraordinarily agile, humanist mind: he takes the culture of a given institution (prison, con man's world, gambling, theater) and, with undaunted chutzpah, applies it to a range of institutions with mutually segregated cultures and distinctive languages for understanding themselves. What is locally grounded culture in one institutional setting becomes metaphor when applied to another. Something similar was the key to Georg Simmel's great fertility and was evocatively transmitted from Simmel through Park to Goffman's teacher Everett Hughes, who, as Hughes's students have reminded us, would make deliberately provocative comparisons, for example, of doctors and prostitutes as sharing intimate craft knowledge in body work.

Goffman provides an especially instructive example of the complex relations between ethnography's policy/political relevance and its use of theoretical language that transcends substantive relevancies as recognized in local institutions. In most of his writings, Goffman was not demonstrably concerned with policy or practical consequentiality. And yet *Asylums* has been directly relevant to policy formation. It has been cited prominently in judicial considerations arguing for the limitation of government powers over confined populations (see Justice Brennan's dissent in *O'Lone v. Estate of Shabazz*, 107 S.Ct. 2400, 1987). As a radicalizing perspective on the institutionalization of subordination, it also preceded, if it was a not a precedent for, the critique of modern power that became associated with Michel Foucault (1979). Before Foucault, Goffman used the prison as a metaphor for understanding the workings of power in a variety of institutions, some of them work institutions, some religious, some military. This line of critical perspective, which more or less directly challenges the distinctive cultures of each substantive institution as a misleading cover for the workings of oppression, continues in the more ambivalent political stance taken by Bruno Latour in his sometimes ethnographic, sometimes highly abstracted texts (Latour and Woolgar 1986; Latour 1993, 1999).

The example of Goffman's work points to three distinctions useful for this discussion. There is the distinction drawn by Becker et al. (in this volume), in which Gans advocates research that expresses policy/political relevance as defined by the culture currently maintained by a given substantive institution. This includes those within its central organizations and the constituencies regularly or irregularly interacting with it. Becker appreciates policy/political relevance as it appears from a perspective that transcends any one institution's culture, a perspective that uses neutral language to find commonalities across social settings segregated by distinguishing cultures.

There is a second distinction, between potential and realized policy/political relevance. Goffman gave a new political relevance to a series of ethnographies (and novels, diaries, and biographies) that, for their creators, were limited in focus to a given substantive institution. And much of Goffman's own work remains apolitical and irrelevant to policy concerns today, but only because the necessary further steps have not been taken. For example, consider his extensive studies of behavior in places that are "public," not in the sense of ownership but in access. Once this field of study matures to the point of analyzing comparatively the structure of social

In the conduct of fieldwork, methods and theory interests are so closely mixed with each other and with historically and socially contextualized relevancies that neutrality is relatively hard to come by.

process in the uses of public spaces managed by government (parks, beaches, museums) and public spaces managed by capitalists (restaurants, malls, museums), it is likely to lead to critiques of current public policies, which subsidize some spaces and not others. What the government does in subsidizing some spaces and not others is not only allocating public goods to the use of some populations and not others; it is also shaping patterns of segregation and integration in the histories of users' lives. If we compare interaction on site with users' patterns of social interaction in their off-site social lives, we are likely to find that some public spaces separate people who reside and work in proximity, while others throw types of individuals whose lives otherwise have no points of contact into common interaction arenas. It is not obvious that publicly managed public space integrates while privately managed public space segregates. (For some scraps of research in this direction, see http://www.sscnet.ucla.edu/nsfreu.) Research might tell, and when it does, Goffman will have taken another great stride toward becoming a policy researcher.

And third is the important distinction between the self-conscious purpose of research and its social significance. Goffman was above all intellectually playful. In a way familiar to much childhood play, he would make believe that social life in one area was governed by the forms and processes of social life in another. If brought off with the appropriate élan, such play can generate a veneer of charm that covers its fundamental disrespect for the authoritative boundaries of institutional culture.

The resulting text does not necessarily look political, much less radical, even though in the resources it provides for critique, in its potential, it is. Motive is important but not the political motives we are used to discussing. The key motive behind the distinctively sociological comparative analysis that characterizes a line of research running from Simmel through Hughes to Goffman, Becker, and now, Latour, among others (I would add de Certeau, but that is another line), is a celebration of the intellectual freedom involved in the distinctively sociological game of taking one institution's serious version of itself and insouciantly using it as a metaphor for undermining the self-proclaimed uniqueness of another.

Goffman's work shows the distinctive policy significance of using a uniquely sociological perspective that overrides what is currently considered relevant to policy formation. It also shows something that should surprise no ethnographer: that the making of policy or political relevance is the product of collaborative action. Work done in an emphatically bourgeois spirit celebrating the freedom to pursue intellectual fun can become powerfully political, depending on what others, in other research projects and in positions of power, do with it. Conversely, work done in a serious spirit of political relevance and with marked policy language will often be relevant only to the collectively related careers of other politically self-defined academics. After all, if we have reason to mistrust the cultures in which institutions proclaim their values and concerns, should we not also mistrust the culture of self-proclaimed policy and political relevance?

The Three Classes of Ethnographic Work in Sociology

At least three rhetorical strategies for claiming general significance for an ethnographic case study compete for researchers' affiliations. Each rhetoric draws in a different way on theory and political sentiments. Virtually all ethnographies can be located within these three types, although texts occasionally combine genres. Each genre can be used well or poorly. The three-class system used below is not intended as a simple rating device but as a way of focusing on the distinctive choices within each genre.

1. Worker ethnographies of the "other side"

First is work that documents social life in a given time and place, and within local terms, as its central contribution. (For leading examples from the current generation of ethnographers, see Duneier [1999] and Anderson [2003].) Displays of what life is like on the "other side" of mythological projections are a mainstay in ethnography's warrants (Katz 1997). In this genre of ethnographic work, policy relevance is built into the juxtaposition; what power misperceives, it is unlikely to govern well. Generalizability is essentially of the sampling not theoretical variety. That is, the people described at a given time and place are offered as representatives of a type of person, as addressed by public commentators, politicians, administrators, and academics: the homeless, crack users, gang members, men who hang out on ghetto street corners. Theoretical significance is often tacked on as protective bookends for the text, but the claim of significance for the study rests most firmly on the juxtaposition between the social realities documented by the ethnographer and those held to be true by people in power.

To provide a compelling juxtaposition to common stereotypes, it is essential for the researcher to operate as a relatively humble jack-of-all-trades, going along with subjects where they may travel, entering novel situation after novel situation with the anxiety of the novice, and displaying an unusual intimacy with the darker corners of subjects' lives. The text strives to present a picture of subjects that differs substantively from what some large segment of social thought and popular culture imagines to be the case; for rhetorical effectiveness, the text must also display a picture of subjects that is more rounded than stereotyped and less obviously touched up or "spun" than political commentary. The result is a diverse and relatively unspecialized set of data. The data are then sorted into chapters to depict sectors of a lifeworld in a way that always keeps the subjects whole as opposed to exploiting them as bearers of politicized categories.

Commonly, no effort is made to document or to analyze existing data to see whether the phenomena studied took the same or different forms in different social conditions. While this has long worked well to sustain a market for ethnographic research, there are dangers on this essentially theory-weak path to claiming significance. Here is an example from contemporary gang criminology.

Gang researchers create a model for the gang they study, without reconciling contradictions apparent if one reads other gang studies. For example, midwestern gangs are attributed to "rustbelt" realities of "deindustrialization," while even more populous, contemporaneous Latino gangs in the economically expanding Southwest are attributed by another researcher to their presumably unique "multiple marginalities" (for a detailed discussion, see Katz and Jackson-Jacobs 2003). Policy relevance depends on a commitment not to research comparatively.

Given the costs of immersion for ethnographers, a single geographic site is most common. A local focus also works well in the United States in part because state and local jurisdictions are pressed politically to find antigang policies, and they can independently fund social intervention solutions that make sense within local culture. Research monographs are offered in support of favorable stereotypes that are used to justify ameliorative policies. Stereotypes about causes of social pathology are locally shaped to fit local cultural realities. The Midwest knows it is a rustbelt; the Southwest knows that gangs are endemic to Latino culture. In each area, a different stereotype is used to fund antigang social programs. The contradiction remains inchoate. News, entertainment, and academic institutions ensure that every area has an unshakeable investment in a unique local culture, within which such mutually incompatible explanations resonate well and thrive (on contradictory news portraits of similar metropolitan crime realities by New York and Los Angeles media, see Katz 2003). Milwaukee residents do not vote in Los Angeles;

Los Angeles residents do not vote in Milwaukee. Local advocates virtually never contest these inconsistent parochialisms.

2. The aristocratic posture:
Singing theory versus documenting variation

A second strategy for claiming significance for ethnography puts extraordinary weight on theoretical discussions that resonate with moral and political sentiments compelling to academic sociologists. Michael Burawoy's (1998) is the most notable brief for this position. What Burawoy terms the "extended case method" should be understood as a rationalization for declining to do the work of extensive, in situ description or, if that work is done, to decline to present in texts descriptions of empirically documented variations of the explanatory ideas and/or of the matters to be explained. Instead, one predefines a problem to be researched from within academic debates and interprets the meaning of fieldwork encounters within that framework. The case is "extended" not by documenting the biography of the empirical cases studied, which was the original meaning of the concept (see Gluckman 1961, 1967), but by interpretively linking theoretical characterizations of field encounters to "macro" themes, which are referenced not through original data gathering but, at best, through readings.

I label this posture aristocratic because, besides demeaning the work of writing field notes that reflect members' meanings and incorporating them intact into the text, it proceeds from and constructs a position of privilege and power for the author relative to both the research subjects and the reader. One of the hallmarks of this posture is that it opposes the emphasis in "grounded theory," and more broadly, in the interactionist tradition of social research, by warranting a disregard for documenting social realities as experienced in situ by the people studied. Often this takes the form of a researcher's finding "problems" through a debate within the academy, through "theoretical considerations," and thus justifying overriding evidence that the people studied do not define their situation as problematic or that they define their situation as problematic in ways the researcher ignores. While the worker and bourgeois professional ethnographer humbles himself or herself to shape explanatory categories to fit what the people studied experience, the theory-informed ethnographer knows better. This posture inevitably leads to an assertion of false consciousness made from a position of presumptive superiority: what the people studied define as their reality itself is a product of powers they fail to appreciate.

Now, nothing is inherently wrong with forming initial definitions of problems from within academic debates, nor even with concepts of false consciousness. In the final analysis, few sociologists get by without resorting to notions of false consciousness or its rhetorical alternatives, such as subconscious meaning or latent function. And as members of society, we have all had the common experience of turning on our lives to realize that previously undiscovered forces were shaping us in ways we failed to appreciate. The problem is not with theory; the methodological problem of false consciousness arises when the researcher uses it as a basis for not describing and textually presenting descriptions of how the people studied in fact live and understand variations in the situations of their everyday lives. Whether or not the case is "extended" through theoretical discussion, the key issue is pragmatic, whether the reader is disempowered by presumptive interpretation or is enfranchised to participate in the discussion by being given access, to the extent the researcher can provide it through quotations and in situ field notes, to the subjects' realities as they experience it.

I label this posture aristocratic because . . . it proceeds from and constructs a position of privilege and power for the author relative to both the research subjects and the reader.

Feminist studies of beauty and appearance cultures, for example, can be handled in more or less aristocratic/democratic fashion, depending on the extent to which the researcher honors the concerns of subjects at least enough to present to the reader extensive data on the situations in their social worlds in which appearance makes a difference in the subjects' own experience and behavior. But the choice is real. I venture to suggest that virtually every U.S. graduate sociology research department has had multiple experiences of personal crises as M.A. and Ph.D. students, who typically seek to identify morally and emotionally with the people they study, discover an importance of cosmetic culture to black and Latina working-class women, which they describe in empathetic detail only at the risk of making their academy-based theoretical presumptions about the oppressive weight of appearance culture appear privileged and denigrating.

When texts fail to present data describing situated conduct as experienced by the people studied, another aristocratic feature is built into the ethnographer's posture: key explanatory categories become ambiguous, leading to an impairment of the reader's ability to understand, much less define, evidence that would directly counter the proffered explanation. In Michael Burawoy's studies of worker "consent," a label he derives from Marxian theory, it is never clear what this key phenomenon is. While he consistently takes consent as the matter to be explained, consent is not translated into indicators of strike activity, union militancy, tenure on the job, or even worker output.

In the 1970s, Burawoy entered a machine shop to collect field data for his dissertation. He came to realize that he had landed in the same machine shop that

Donald Roy had studied thirty years earlier. Roy sought to understand a variety of enigmas he found in his and his coworkers' behavior. Roy phrased the issues in commonsense terms about an observably varying explanandum. Why did they work hard at some times and hardly at all at others (Roy 1952)? They did not seem to be seeking to maximize their incomes, so what were their motives (Roy 1953)? Why were they intimately friendly to each other at one time and then in bitter conflict at another, and then friendly again (Roy 1959-1960)? Roy focused on situational variations in work effort and in the dynamics of workers' small group cultures. He created extensive, detailed data sets on the work output of different workers at different times and then took those differences as matters to be explained. Burawoy phrased his problem in a more singular, theory-derived, and academic fashion, taking workers' consent to labor, but no particular variation in their conduct, as the matter to be explained.[2]

It turned out that the level of worker output that Burawoy found in the 1970s was the same, he reports, as Donald Roy found his study in the 1940s. In both periods, workers sought to "make out" through a gamelike strategizing. Burawoy does assert changes in how workers were supervised, in how their pay was linked to their output, and in the direction of their conflicts, which he says turned from management toward each other. But in the sole description of output he provides as a comparison with Roy's extensive descriptions, he states,

> Their average "measured performances" for the entire year [referring to sixteen radial-drill operators] . . . were as follows [giving figures]. The average was 120 percent, which turns out to be precisely Roy's average in his second period. . . . The data do not suggest significant differences between the rates on radial drills in Geer's Jack Shop [Roy's site name] and on radial drills in Allied's [Burawoy's site name] small-parts department. (Burawoy 1979, 227, note 17).

Moreover, just as Roy found workers gaming around production quotas, Burawoy, searching to explain the mystery of workers' consent to work, found that "game-playing generates consent to the social relations in production that define the rules of the game" (Burawoy 1979, 82). In process and result, consent to labor remained essentially constant. Where is the variation that Burawoy would explain?

Burawoy claims that between the 1940s and 1970s, changes in the structure and managerial style of capitalism had an impact on consent, but the reader will struggle in vain to find descriptions of variation in the matter explained that correspond to differences in the explanatory categories.[3] Further ambiguities turned up when after working for a short stint in what he characterizes as an analogous machine shop in socialist Hungary, Burawoy reported that the output was much the same as he and Roy had independently found in Chicago (Burawoy and Lukács 1985). What, then, do changes in twentieth-century capitalism or in the contrast between capitalism and state socialism explain? Perhaps they explain the managerial style of relating to workers. But if managerial styles differ by political economy without affecting worker productivity, then capitalism does not exploit workers, at least not in the sense of extracting a greater value or output from them. (Notably, there is no serious argument that the Hungarian workers were better compensated than the

U.S. workers.) This minimizes Marxian theory to a brief for human relations at the workplace.

This would be fine, at least as a matter of logic, if managerial style were what Burawoy wanted to explain. But the theoretical excitement of his research comes from the promise to explain why workers go along with oppressive conditions. One way of reading Burawoy's 1974 study is that it was unnecessary: Roy had already documented variation in worker activity and attitude and had provided an explanation fit to the empirical variations he describes. Imagining this objection,[4] Burawoy provides a rhetorical rather than empirical answer. While Roy tried to explain "why people don't work harder," Burawoy tried to explain "why people work so hard" (Burawoy 2003, 654, note 9). The distinction is an esoteric version of half empty versus half full.

> I take as a point of departure the possibility and desirability of a fundamentally different form of society—call it communism, if you will—in which men and women, freed from the pressures of scarcity and from the insecurity of everyday existence under capitalism, shape their lives. . . . It is in terms of this possibility . . . that Marxists interpret the present and the past. (Burawoy 1979, xiii).

This imaginary invocation of differences in the thing to be explained, and in the explanatory conditions, might be termed *theory singing*. The ethnographer acknowledges that explanatory logic requires arguing a relationship between variations in explanandum and explanans, but that variation is supplied by "theory" not by any data describing variations in the explanandum or explanans. The power of theory, and of a theory club in sociology, is essential for this rhetoric to work. The result is reminiscent of the emperor's new clothes: readers who are haunted by their inability to perceive what it is that is being explained simply show their lack of initiation into the power club. They lack the right sensibility or, to echo Bourdieu, theoretical taste.

Another way ethnographies take on an aristocratic posture is by failing to offer materials that readers may use to develop and test ideas that were irrelevant to the author. When worker ethnographies are well done and when dossiers on individual biographies or types of social action are carefully assembled, an ethnography's readers can exploit the text's data without concern for, much less a show of obeisance to, the author's original purpose. (As noted above, Goffman's writing was full of such creative reuses of others' ethnographies.) These are relatively humble styles of work, the worker ethnography being the most malleable in the hands of subsequent users, in that they do not insist that the reader seek admission into the author's intellectual world to find value in the text. A common feature of the aristocratic style of ethnography is that the reader cannot see the subjects except as already dressed in the author's theoretical categories. There are few or no indented paragraphs or extensive quotations that show the reader what the researcher heard and saw in the field. Colloquialisms and situationally nuanced detail are absent. The reader must, in effect, accept the disciplinary guidance of the author to obtain any glimpse of the subjects. (For an extreme example, see Jankowski [1991], who

THE ANNALS OF THE AMERICAN ACADEMY

gives an extensive tour of reputedly dangerous worlds in which subjects can never be seen up close, heard in their own words, or otherwise appreciated outside the analytical lenses that the tour guide insists readers wear.)

Finally, the aristocratic style in ethnography can be identified by an exclusive focus on a preferred explanation. Alternative explanations are simply not considered or not considered seriously. The choice not to consider alternative explanations is rhetorically effective only if the text does not show variation in the phenomena to be explained. Put conversely, the author's failure to present variation in the explanandum is rhetorically obscured by the elaboration of a single explanation, for which the description of invariant phenomena provide illustrations.

The worth of a study should not be assessed outside of a triangular appreciation of the empirical relationship between author, subjects, and readers.

An example is Arlie Hochschild's (1983) book on the production of emotional displays by workers, especially female workers, as scripted and supervised by capitalist-controlled service firms. (Many of the following points have been made before [Smith-Lovin 1998].) Hochschild's book is a complex, and for that reason, a more informative, example of the aristocratic style in ethnography because it shares features with what I term the professional bourgeois style. Drawing on a wide range of interviews that she conducted and on a wide range of descriptive writings by others, Hochschild gathers a large, richly varied set of descriptions of situationally specific instances in which people interpret their emotions either as compelled by others or as authentic. Some of the situations are from personal life (e.g., romantic relations); some are from a variety of work settings; some cover the training of actors. On the basis of this varied data set, Hochschild develops concepts about "feeling rules" and "emotional labor" that are extensively grounded in her data. In an appendix, she relates the understanding of emotional experience and interaction that she develops through her data to the history of the study of emotions, from Darwin through Freud to Goffman.

Left to these conceptual contributions, the book would have been a valuable offering to the sociology of emotions, on the order of Candace Clark's (1997) study of expressions of sympathy in everyday life situations. Analytical tools are offered to subsequent emotions researchers in a form that is accessible and that promises to "cut at the joints of experience," to use William James's phrase, or that offers other researchers "sensitizing concepts," to use Herbert Blumer's phrase. But Hochschild raises the book's claims to a significantly grander status by developing a political/morally righteous theory that disdains capitalist-enforced demands for emotional labor by middle-class workers such as Delta Airlines flight attendants. The key to the great success of this project is the author's construction of a righteous sensibility that condemns corporate-enforced emotional labor in a withering regard.

What makes the study aristocratic in its posture is the refusal to be disciplined by the data. Again, the key failure is in documenting variations in the phenomenon to be explained. Hochschild claims that capitalist-institutionalized demands for emotional labor are broadly damaging to the middle-class workforce because they undermine the "signal" function of emotions: over time, the worker loses the capacity to interpret her or his emotions as self-indicating because the worker's emotions are in effect owned by management, which insists on a positive emotional expressiveness toward service clients. Hochschild massively documents the explanans: corporate demands that flight attendants display positive emotions. But the evidence for the existence of the damage claimed is meager and weak. Here and there, flight attendants are quoted in brief references to the negative effects of their emotion work (e.g., Hochschild 1983, 4), but as many or more data strips show positive effects, and many other strips show negative effects, or self-alienation from emotion, at nonwork sites (e.g., weddings).

It is telling that the most powerful data passage that indicates psychological damage to flight attendants from their emotional labor comes in the classic style of aristocratic ethnography, through the commentary of a headman, or in this case, headwoman. A sex therapist said to have fifty flight attendants as patients reports a pattern of "loss of sexual interest" and "preorgasmic problems," stating, "They hold onto their orgasmic potential as one of the few parts of themselves that someone else doesn't possess" (Hothschild 1983, 183). Scattered throughout the book, there are several passages in which passengers are described as abusing flight attendants, for example, spitting on them. But in this book of some 300 pages, a single sensational quotation from a sex therapist is virtually the only data indicating that emotional labor has negative aspects that endure situational ugliness.

We can see here the rhetorical relationship between the failure to present data describing variations in the explanandum and the failure to discuss alternative explanations of the data illustrating the explanandum. We learn at one point in the text that Delta management recruits for certain flight-attendant personalities. Whatever sexual problems these employees may have, there is no evidence they emerged after their employment began. There is no discussion of the possibility that whatever emotional problems flight attendants may have, they may have preceded working for the airlines, much less that they might even have been greater in scale. There is no discussion of the possibility that women who are similarly situated to the flight attendants but do not take emotional labor jobs may suffer greater emotional self-alienation. With respect to the startling figure of a caseload of fifty sex-therapy patients from one airline, there is no consideration that the therapist may build her practice through a referral network specific to flight attendants and that even more disturbed women, located in more isolated settings, suffer without treatment. There is no effort to provide evidence, or even discuss the possibility, that young women may seek therapeutic help at rates relatively high to males of the same age, regardless of employment status.

The political/moral thrust of the book rests on a series of empirical claims that remain more implicit than explicit. These include that service work increases the pressures on workers to manifest emotional expressions as opposed to the demands in off-work social life or nonservice work (were women better off when they were seamstresses in sweatshops?); that women face this pressure more than do men (what about Willy and Biff Loman?); that large-scale capitalism, especially the impersonal, multisited corporation, creates this pressure more than do alternative political-economic systems; and that management perverts, distorts, undermines, pollutes, alienates, or otherwise negatively affects workers' emotional makeup by demanding and disciplining emotional expression. We hear virtually nothing of the emotional lives of women, or men, at working-class jobs that lack a personal service component, or who are primarily homemakers, with the exception of a few passages that indicate that emotional self-alienation is also part of some nonwork, intimate relations. What we do not see includes descriptions of the psychological makeup of flight attendants when they start Delta jobs; descriptions of similar women who work for pay as lonely writers at home; materials on mothers who feel injunctions to maintain enthusiastic, positive interactions with their young children; descriptions of social interaction among men in machine shops, where emotional display to colleagues may be intensely scrutinized and frequently tense (Roy 1959-1960); and descriptions of professional and managerial men at home and at work. On the latter, I note that for eighty years, *The New Yorker* has run cartoons depicting executive-type males, and now, occasionally females, absurdly using domestic emotions at work and treating spouse, child, or pet like a subordinate employee at home.

Note the relationship between the lack of documentation of emotional problems increasing as women become flight attendants and the most subtle resonances of the book's theory singing. The failure to document biographical change for the worse among emotional laborers is a relatively minor problem. The greater problem is the unstated but constant inference that nonservice work, or nonemotional labor, or not working at all, is less emotionally self-alienating. Like Burawoy's imagination of a communist utopia but more in the style of a Chekhovian dreamer idealist than militant Marxist, Hochschild implies but never asserts the possibility of an alternative world of plentiful, wondrous orgasms.

In the style of aristocratic sensibility, Hochschild's argument sets up its own feeling rules. A powerful message conveyed to the huge masses of undergraduates who have been taught this book is that going along with corporate injunctions to smile is to betray one's colleagues. Flight-attendant unions, we are told, sometimes bargain with smiles, which they withhold until pay and working conditions improve (Hochschild 1983, 129). To smile on command, or even to come to experience emotional labor as natural and pleasant, is to sustain the management system that wrecks the psychological makeup of masses of other employees. This elegantly written book professes a superior moral perspective that instructs its young adult readers on the feeling rule that they should question their feelings, even when they seem otherwise unproblematic, if they find themselves in employer-demanded forms of emotional labor. I wonder if emotional labor reaches into tender souls more powerfully than does academic teaching by model mentors.

Hochschild does not limit her analysis or theory to the data she actually has accumulated. She will not be disciplined or humbled by her empirical materials; the successful aspirations of this ethnography are to a much higher and intellectually free position, one from which data are attended to primarily to discipline them into the outline of a transcending moral power. Instead of showing before-and-after or synchronic comparative descriptions of people in and outside of emotionally scripted service jobs, Hochschild sings theory by invoking a category, "deep acting," which conveys the idea that after enacting superficial emotion scripts long enough, their artificiality must reach deep into the soul.

As I stressed in the prologue, the worth of a study should not be assessed outside of a triangular appreciation of the empirical relationship between author, subjects, and readers. My point is to bring out the rhetorical relationship between monolithic theory singing and the presentation of data showing only constant rather than varying forms of key explanatory categories. Reading *The Managed Heart* in its historical context, my evaluation is uneasy but, on the whole, favorable. When first published, the book, and the journal article that preceded it, gave much-needed direction to countless researchers who wanted to study the intersection of gendered identities, the discipline of the workplace in a changing economy, and multinational capitalism. Emotional labor, feeling rules, and emotion scripts became indispensable descriptive tools. But to continue to sing the book's theory some twenty years later—that is, to use theory to elide the challenge of describing relevant patterns of experience over biographical time, home, and workplace and gender identity and occupational status—is increasingly to rely on the power of moral/political righteousness and its academic club to blunt criticism and to block research progress.

3. Analytic induction and bourgeois professional ethnography

Studies in the genre of journeys to the other side rely on political sentiments in stereotypes and powerful myths to give juxtapositional significance to the cases they detail. Theory singing leans on politically charged characterizations to evoke the variations necessary for a sense of explanation and to invite sympathy for side-stepping challenges to document and present data that would rule out plausible rival explanations. A third general ethnographic strategy for relating policy or politics and theoretical language puts data variation and emergent analysis at the center of the project.

Comparisons most vigorously test explanation when they are developed in data describing given cases as they change over time in multiple social contexts. The rhetoric of methods may be "constant comparative," "grounded theory," or simply, the familiar language of causal explanation's necessary and sufficient conditions (for a straightforward example of the last, see Newman 2004). As a matter of convenience, I will refer to this genre in terms of its most explicit explanatory form, as "analytic induction" (Katz 2001).

While any ethnography is likely to refer to its database by noting the raw amounts of field notes collected, the number of interviews conducted, and the time spent in the field, professional ethnography is the only style that can be said to work with the more or less self-conscious concept of the data set. A data set is an analytically formed collection of descriptive materials, typically organized around a given type of social situation or a given type of social process. Perhaps the first data set constructed in this style consisted of observations of medical-student perspectives (Becker et al. 1961); each observation is given equal or weighted value in relation to each other. There is a separable, explicit effort to create quality in the data set, independent of the substantive explanation. Contextualized, situated descriptions, for example, are treated as more probative than are descriptions of opinion or attitude that do not describe the context in which the opinion emerged.

I use the term *bourgeois professional* because the constitution of the data set is a task not unlike what dentists, lawyers, accountants, and others do in occupations focused on "cases," each of which has certain common features. For ethnographers, the common features are likely to be incidents of behavior that are situationally contextualized, in the sense of being described as occurring within an immediate context that is relevant to the actor's organization of conduct; descriptions of the stage in a larger process within which any described scene or act occurs; and descriptions of the social interaction within which the act or action emerges, meaning a description of how, in shaping his or her conduct, each person is taking into account the likely responses of others present and anticipated.

We can distinguish bourgeois professional ethnographies by the complexity of the variation they create for data sets. The greater the variation in the data examined, the stronger the resulting explanation. By greater variation, I refer not to the quantity of data but to its qualitative form. In particular, ethnographies may use three progressively challenging forms of data variation.

A first test comes when the researcher tries to fit her initial explanatory ideas to the variations she documents. A second test of the explanation occurs when the analyst draws on cases documented by others for further evidence. A third test is the one that the current discussion highlights. This occurs when the explanation is tested across a range of social areas that are segregated in culture and that may never have been considered in the same breath by anyone before the researcher, using distinctively sociological thinking, saw the analogy.

Consider Diane Vaughan's (1986) study of "uncouplings," or how people make transitions out of intimate relationships. Vaughan tests her theory primarily on information she collected on 103 people whom she interviewed at some point in their process of uncoupling. Second, she refines her explanation by examining others' descriptions of divorces and transformations out of nonmarital intimacies. Third, she develops her explanation by examining the process of ending other types of relationships and terminating other kinds of interaction: she compares what she has found about the phases of uncoupling with what she and others have learned about movements out of jobs, terminations of religious affiliation, and even experiences of "small girls" terminating a game of Monopoly.

While these comparative analytical data are less numerous than the other two types, they are especially critical to her analysis. This is the kind of "neutral" and seemingly policy-irrelevant thinking that Becker (2003) has advocated in his discussion of the language of Goffman's essay on "total institutions." At the time Vaughan conducted her study, uncoupling was a major emotional and therapeutic concern but not much of a political issue. And her reflection on what happens when small girls end Monopoly games is clearly entertaining but hardly seems meat for political debate.

A key challenge routinely ducked by ethnographers is confronting biases specific to the time and place of their work.

But her recollection of the cruelties involved when children stop playing with each other, along with other instances of "interaction termination" drawn from innocuous, everyday life situations, helped specify a key qualification of the phenomenon to be explained. Early on, Vaughan realized that *marriage* and *divorce* would not provide definitions of variation that could be explained. The formalities of marriage do not, she saw, make for uniform differences in the dissolution of relations among nonmarried intimates, whether they are homosexual or heterosexual. In the style of analytic induction, she redefined what others might have treated as a study of divorce into a study of *uncoupling*, a term she developed. While not a neologism, the term was somewhat independent of any precedent in popular culture.[5]

The example of girls' ending games of Monopoly was evidence for a further qualification of the explanation. Vaughan was seeking to specify necessary conditions or phases of uncoupling, not "why couples break up" but uniformities in the stages they go through. One of her most important findings was that despite the great pain and hostility common in uncouplings, there was also a great deal of mutual caring; she found evidence of caring in all cases, even the most bitterly contested (Vaughan 1986, 193). This was not what she recalled about how small girls stop playing monopoly. She recalled that frequently one would lose interest, but instead of confronting the other with the desire to end the game, the bored or distracted player would take advantage of a break in the action not to come back, break the rules so as to precipitate a fight, withdraw by attending to the TV, and so on. Caring among the uncouplers sometimes took the form of direct confrontation; that may seem harsh, but, Vaughan noted, it clarifies the situation for the other, giving the other an opportunity to define a new stage in their lives.

This third type of test of her theory, in which she examined events in substantively foreign types of social situations, provided a crucial specification of the importance of the public nature of the couple's commitment to caring in the process of breaking up. Although she does not formulate the analysis in quite this way, we may theorize that the public nature of a commitment, which can be constituted by marriage but also by an ongoing intimacy that has become an open fact within a couple's personal public, makes dissolution more kind by making it more difficult. The dissolution of a previously public relationship is more likely to be reviewed by others and thus more carefully handled by oneself.[6] This Simmelian irony had no particular policy relevance at the time Vaughan's book was published. What could be more lacking in relevance than observations of how girls end games, how bus passengers disengage from annoying seat companions, or how bored partygoers manage their exits?

Today, the gay-marriage debate suddenly makes this preeminently sociological comparative thinking directly policy/politically relevant, albeit ambivalent in its implications. If making public commitments are valuable, not necessarily in keeping people united but in humanizing their separation, then gay marriage, as an explicit form of public commitment, has much to recommend it. On the other hand, gays were already in her sample, and the knowledge of their friends that they had been a couple provided enough public commitment such that their dissolutions demonstrated phases similar to those of formally married heterosexual couples.

Note that we can clearly mark the point at which Vaughan's analysis goes beyond obvious relevance for understanding intimate dissolutions: when she starts drawing analogies that only sociologists would bring into the discussion of uncoupling. This seems a commitment to the kind of neutral analysis that Becker (2003) has recommended. And yet, years later, it has become a key move in shaping the relevance of the study for a hot policy issue. The possible uses of her study in the current gay-marriage debate are ambivalent, but they greatly contribute to the debate by helping transform what is a highly emotional and symbolic discussion into a consideration of potentially decisive empirical consequences. If, for example, marriage enhances gay couples' public commitments in a way that diminishes cruelties in breaking up, then that bolsters the legal case that limiting marriage to heterosexuals violates constitutional guarantees of equal protection.

Being Here and Being There: Current Biases toward the Parochial and the Present

Each class of ethnographic work, then, has political significance depending on the place it takes within a larger collective act that is shaped by readers and historical processes that the author cannot control. A key challenge routinely ducked by ethnographers is confronting biases specific to the time and place of their work. The field of ethnographic research as a whole is woefully indifferent to biases that push fieldworkers to limit their studies to the parochial and the present. Too often, when concerns arise that ethnographic research is too "micro" and not sufficiently contextualized historically, the response is to abandon fieldwork for reading and theorizing.

"Being here and being there" captures a constant dilemma for ethnographers. *Ethnography*, in this usage, means a coherent narrative picture of social life. Ethnography's subject may be social life as lived at a particular geographic or organizational site, a set of people whose way of life shares a common theme, or a theme that characterizes a social movement or episode of collective behavior. As sociological texts, ethnographies contrast with texts that show relationships between variables or the features of ideas without conveying the social context in which those who display the variables or embody the ideas live out their lives. It is the commitment to a contextualized narrative that sets up ethnography's central strategic challenges in defining the sets of data that will underlie and discipline analysis.

On one hand, a variety of intellectual traditions point ethnographers to appreciate that whatever site they study is an artificially bounded fragment of a larger social reality. Whatever the "here and now" that the participant-observation fieldworker can study up close, the events observed and the ways of the people encountered have always already been shaped by social experiences in some other "there and then." On the other hand, the social-psychological realities of ethnographic fieldwork as an occupational practice constantly tempt the researcher to limit data gathering and analytic perspective to the here and now. In addition to the fieldworkers' occupational egocentrism, there will always be an egocentric, current reality bias in local culture that obscures the artificiality of local boundaries. The people encountered by the fieldworker care principally about realities here and now because that is principally what they can affect and because others they regularly encounter insist that they attend to local exigencies, and soon. The first step in making a new advance in methodological quality is recognizing that the quality of ethnographic work is in this sense of the phrase formed at the crossroads of being here and being there.

Here are some of the challenges to move beyond parochial and (to borrow a term from historiography) presentist biases that contemporary ethnographers have yet fully to acknowledge. Large-scale immigration into the working class, for example, poses unrealized challenges for Arlie Hochschild's emotion theory. In 1979, I started buying garden supplies from an "OSH" store in Hollywood. As a newcomer to Los Angeles, I was struck by the bizarrely exaggerated greetings and farewells that I would receive from cashiers, who then were almost all black and white. Today, the cashier who greets me at OSH is likely to be a Ukrainian, Thai, or Guatemalan immigrant, and she is likely to utter an enthusiastic phrase that may sound to me like "Chuvahnashdee!" It is striking how much has changed demographically at this site, but sociologically, what is even more interesting is how little has changed. Despite the difference in accent and acculturation, I have no problem in hearing the merry mandate to "have a nice day!"

Now, if it is no problem for me to make out what the cashier is saying, it is also, in that situated work task, no problem for her that her accent is "heavy." The reason it is no problem for me is not because I am good with accents but because hers is a strictly regulated performance of emotion labor. I know what I am likely to hear at that place and at that phase of the shopping process. And the cashier knows I know. We both use the script of emotion work to obliterate the possibility that her "foreignness" will make her a less-than-effective worker.

The question of why some people stay in conditions of disadvantage and oppression while others leave is routinely neglected in urban ethnography.

For my imaginary immigrant service worker (and yes, here I am theory singing), it is a boon that she is doing closely managed, situationally specific, precisely scripted emotion work. Were I to encounter her elsewhere in the store and ask where to find fertilizer, the confusion that might result could be embarrassing. At the cash register, the routinized script of emotional expression provides the immigrant cashier with cultural clothing that she can wear perfectly well, even though it was not made for the body of ethnic culture she brings to the job.

Is emotion work dehumanizing, alienating, or otherwise harmful in this context? In areas like Hollywood, where emotion work has mushroomed as part of the exploding service economy, routinized scripts for expressing emotions fit remarkably smoothly with the predominately immigrant labor force now doing it. Perhaps after months or years of uttering these superficial niceties with an automaticity that rivals her cash register, the Ukranian immigrant cashier will become a "deep actor" of superficial California culture, profoundly alienated from her originally passionate folk soul.

What emotional labor might seem to mean to researchers from families that have been native-born for generations is not necessarily what it means to immigrants. The social distance between the biographies of university researchers and the current American workforce means that no amount of "reflexivity" will solve this problem: no single researcher is likely to be as diverse as the subjects he or she studies. If ethnographers are not to turn these questions over to survey researchers, they now need to strategize their research designs. The relatively comfortable fieldwork design of situating oneself at a work site, learning how to work there, and observing how others do the work needs to be supplemented by more dicey data gathering that will reveal how workers manifest emotions and deal with accent and cultural misunderstandings in other areas of their lives.

We need a new wave of ethnographic research strategically designed to reveal both the "there and then" and the "here and now" that together create the lived biographical and situated meaning of emotion labor. This new wave is likely not only to point in surprising policy/political directions but also to require a fundamental rethinking of basic theoretical preconceptions. For example, researchers will probably have to struggle with the dizzying complexities of the relationships between home and work, as revealed by Christena Nippert-Eng's (1996) creative study. How do we know which behaviors and sentiments to attribute to "home" and which to "work," given that formally defined work is increasingly done at home and as we increasingly appreciate how personal life is shaped and sustained at work sites? How can we hold onto these categories, which at once render their meaning in dialectical relation to each other and richly provoke people to undermine their opposition in practice?

The spatial metaphor in phrasing the ethnographer's struggle as one of simultaneously being "here" and "there" obscures an even more difficult challenge of documenting the extralocal temporal reaches of local social realities. I will use community research as an example. The tradition goes back at least to Jahoda et al. [1930/1971]). In community research, ethnographers are massively pressed to limit their focus to the meanings of events for current local residents. There is a revealing irony in the facts that ethnographies of neighborhoods threatened by displacement reveal the sacrifice of valuable social cohesion and community values (see Gans [1962] and Suttles [1968]. Was there ever a neighborhood studied by a sociologist that was not deemed worth saving? But studies of residential life formed after urban renewal and urban planning reveal a positive meaningfulness of local area that is scorned by critics of the plastic character of housing plans, who see only sterility rising in the wake of destruction. (See Gans [1967] and a study of how residents actually live in perhaps the most ridiculed planned community in Milton Keynes, United Kingdom [Finnegan 1998].)

A reliance on the boundaries of social realities as defined in the here and now usually fails the ethnography of community research in at least two fundamental ways. The social reality of any place exists not only as a present for those currently in occupancy but also as a past in the lives of those who have left and as a future denied to others who took courses of action that led them elsewhere. In the genre of community studies, we do not learn much about the lives of those who have left the town or city; we learn even less about the meaning of the local area to those who settled elsewhere. By studying only those present at the time and place of the study, the ethnographer biases the policy/political message and sidesteps the novel challenges for theory.

By studying those who leave, one may find otherwise hidden meanings of attachment among those who stay and, even more, that policies of preserving people in place may be shortsighted. As millions of low-income migrants have crossed vast geographic and social barriers to enter and move across the United States, ethnographers have continued to explain the pathologies suffered by low-income, urban populations by reference to local conditions. The question of why some people stay in conditions of disadvantage and oppression while others leave is routinely neglected in urban ethnography. Political sentimentalities may be at work here; it is a hard sell to convince local leaders to subsidize the costs of moving their constituents away. But political pressures aside, answering the question of persistence in place would seem to require carrying research beyond what can be learned in the current neighborhood. It is debatable whether policy/political conviction or methodological convenience is the stronger influence on research design.

Current populations are also shaped by processes in the lives of those who never arrived. What this means for the policy and theory limitations of urban ethnography can be quickly indicated by the challenge faced by ethnographers of California's coastal cities. (By coastal city, I mean not just where there is salt in the air but anything within ten miles of the coast.) Battles over land use and neighborhood preservation in coastal cities are constantly fought between those in place and agents who would bring in populations that do not yet have a local face. Most visible to the ethnographer are the local "growth entrepreneurs." Given their superior wealth, self-serving economic interest, corrupting contributions to the politically powerful, and relatively small numbers, developers routinely lose the narrative battle in the ethnography to the more numerous and usually less affluent residents allied against development, who seek no obvious material gain and are always at risk of becoming victims of politically corrupted capitalist schemes.

The joy with which ethnographers rail against capitalist developers is increasingly tempered by discomfort in defending what, in the most extreme cases, are becoming superrich communities. But the elephant in this collective act is not the capitalist developer; it is the mass movement of millions of workers who are deflected in their residential settlement further and further into desert communities toward the east. Dangers to historic preservation and to the precious coastal ecology are stressed by residents as they oppose development proposals. Meanwhile, workers' commutes mount to four-hour daily routines requiring countless tanks of gas to sustain lifestyles that must try to take root in new, air-conditioned desert homes.

A decisive theoretical commitment is necessary to break out of the increasingly unsatisfying political sentimentalities shaped by community ethnographies that give a priority in narrative voice to those living on site during the period of the research project. We must first be able to imagine a perspective that will include not only current residents, and not only those who commute in and out, but also the masses who never contemplated arriving because local conditions have indirectly but powerfully conveyed signals of blocked entry. At present, only the economists, through the concept of opportunity cost, know how to incorporate lost futures in their theoretical models. Unless we are to turn the field over to them or become servants of the privileged, what we need is a way to model the present that includes negative realities, the futures conditional that never materialized but that may even more powerfully shape the ethnographic scene than what is positively in evidence in the fieldworkers' encounters.

Any social place consists of positive constructions and of powerful negations. Our community studies must begin to enable us to describe how current residents live side by side with the ghosts of those who have left. We must also find a way to document how some live with their own unrealized possibilities of exit. And we need to bring the spirits of the banished into contact with the precious tranquility of California's Santa Barbaras. The ethnographic demographics of a local community exist not only in the lives of those who reside and work there but also in the unrealized fantasies of those who have never been and will never be present. The ability not just theoretically to evoke the locally absent but to bring them into the description of what the fieldworker confronts at his site is not well developed in American sociology, but in other traditions, there are strong leads as to what might work.[7]

Ethnography as a Search for Community

All research is essentially a search for community, at least in the sense of an effort to be embraced by an audience to which the study's results will be pitched. In its original meaning (Geertz 1988), "being here and being there" refers to a tension between communities. Genres of ethnographic research differ perhaps most fundamentally in how they handle this tension.

The locals we seek to know at field sites typically have their own sense of community, one independent of the researcher's academic home. After leaving the university for the field, one way for the researcher to reestablish community is to do relevant research—research that speaks to policies that are of local concern. The dilemma of being here and being there can be substantially resolved when research speaks in terms that locals see as advancing their causes.

But there are other ways of finding community, and I would submit that as forms of sociological practice, it is the strategy adopted to search for community that most fundamentally distinguishes fieldwork methodologies. Because community is always political, each search for community has its distinctive political aspirations or pretensions. Researchers who are suspicious of local cultures have two alternative escape routes. One is horizontal; the other vertical.

The horizontal route to escape is not back to the academy or to some vacation land outside of social research but into another immersion and then another. The trajectory is not unlike serial monogamy, with the passionate involvements and risk of treachery at every transition along the way. Analysis grows as one questions the claims of unique local culture that are made at each site, which one does by using as a critique not some overarching sociopolitical theory but the professions of unique culture at other sites.

The series of involvements across substantively segregated research projects encourages an appreciation that each site contains all the others. Play is discovered at work, and work, in the ethnomethodological sense of careful doings geared to a responsive payoff, is revealed in play. Education ethnographies do not turn up much evidence about learning in school; in ethnographic data, school looks more like a struggle between the classes. But education is highly visible in participant-observation evidence of life on the job. Art thrives in every corner of everyday life, from morning makeup routines to evening episodes of loving. Meanwhile, what people do in art museums has more in common with rituals of shame avoidance. Museum visitors train their attentions in anticipation of demands to identify artist, style, and epoch.

Community is sought not at any one site but in a sensitivity to the universalities of social process. Political significance comes from debunking the claims of authentic boundary made by local culture and by offering the liberating perspective of commonalities found across formally segregated sites.

An alternative escape from immersion in a field site is through a vertical movement. Whether because of personal precommitments (the fieldwork training course is over; it is time to get a job; another research opportunity beckons) or from the discovery that one cannot manage to make the self sufficiently malleable to become locally accepted, community is sought in some more powerful and elevated region. Escape may come through the always open doors of academic discourse, in the form of endless theorizing, teaching, and methodological reflection. Or escape from the field may be justified as an act of opposition to the powerful, who rule from distant, inaccessible sites: if the forces shaping social life in the lower regions that one can enter are really in higher locations, staying in the lower regions too long risks accepting the false consciousness that people there can really rule their lives.

Indeed, what does the growing global reach and consolidation of multinational corporate and political powers tell us about the source of the social patterns that occur in the small-scale settings that we may enter as participant observers? That our site is "here" seductively denies that the real causes are located "there," in socially distant, higher regions. Is it not increasingly foolish to immerse oneself in a search for explanation in *any* local site? And even if one could enter the halls of the powerful, theory tells us that the action really is not much there anyway but in the long course of history and in the structuring of large-scale social formations in which we can only aspire to be fleeting, tightly circumscribed, insignificant participant observers. In the increasingly common songs of theorized globalism, the only justification for participant-observation ethnography is to give a first-person witnessing of the sufferings and horrors that distant powers cause and then ignore (Bourdieu et al. 1999).

I have suggested that the following are three class strategies: the worker's, the bourgeois professional's, and the aristocrat's. Class in this application is a matter of the researcher's way of relating to the practice of fieldwork. In the working-class version of ethnography, the researcher operates like a jack-of-all-trades, hanging out with the guys and using relatively unspecialized skills to portray wide-ranging sectors of their lives. Because fieldwork is the closest thing we have to a sine qua non of the ethnographer's identity, in this social arena, if in no other, the usual stratification of class status often is turned on its head. Hence the extraordinary immediate recognition given to Duneier's (1999) *Sidewalk* and the extraordinarily enduring appeal of Anderson's (2003) corner study.

As bourgeois professional, the ethnographic fieldworker develops files that describe the evolution of cases over time. A set of case files is created by developing a specialized expertise that is substantively narrow. Over time and multiple studies in diverse substantive contexts, the researcher's self becomes shaped as a tool that facilitates subtle appreciations of how the fate of each case, regardless of substantive context, is shaped by what happens at given points in its trajectory (see, e.g., Emerson 1981, 1983). A common intellectual result is an ongoing suspicion of any local culture as artificially claiming distinctive social realities and causal forces.

That our site is "here" seductively denies that the real causes are located "there," in socially distant, higher regions.

The aristocrat may write at great length about his or her own theoretical preoccupations and in-the-field subjectivity. Spending relatively little time in the embarrassing business of shaping a self that strangers in the field will embrace, or at least tolerate, the aristocrat quickly develops the confidence to model the world from a removed study. Unlike the working-class or bourgeois professional, the aristocrat happily dispenses with the grunt work of ethnography, the laborious recording and meticulous examination of others' detailed doings. Or, having done some grunt work as a kind of rite of passage, the ethnographer may find life at that level unsatisfactory. Without any showing of relevant variations in the matters to be explained, the ethnographer may then elegantly select illustrations and invoke theoretical imagination to construct a narrative posture that operates as a tasteful sensibility, condemning what he or she cannot in fact explain.

It might be said, "You choose your class and you get your methodology," but as sociologists, we know that class identities are not freely chosen. If there is anything universally distinctive about participant-observation fieldwork as a research method, it is that it is a socially structured, existential crucible. What you will be able to do, as a matter of personality, you cannot know in advance. What you can do at one life stage is not necessarily what you can do at the next. Ethnographers always have a class status but, we may hope, not one that is fixed at birth.

Notes

1. In his ethnographic study of life aboard ships, Aubert (1982), a Norwegian sociologist insufficiently appreciated in the United States, provided some of the evidence that Goffman drew on in writing *Asylums*.

2. Roy's studies were exemplary of what I call the "bourgeois professional" style of ethnographic work of the Second Chicago School. He created similarly structured dossiers on the work activities of multiple workers at multiple times, then disciplined his explanation to fit with those differences. For an exemplary "worker" ethnography of related matters conducted at about the same time as Burawoy's study, see Kornblum (1974), who, in a text that is at once extraordinarily detailed and holistic in the understanding it conveys, studies social life on and off the job at several steel factories in South Chicago, relating differences in worker perspective to differences in ethnicity, immigration history, unionization, strikes, and local political history as well as to differences in the structure of the production process across factories. Stepan-Norris and Zeitlin (2003, 183) have recently noted that Burawoy ignored readily available evidence that would have shown variation in worker militancy. "While Roy was working in his shop, Orvis Collins was also working as a milling machine operator, in a shop employing 90 to 110 machine operators, in another factory. (Roy's shop employed only some 50 men). Collins worked in his shop for about six months and he also spent many months afterwards interviewing the men he had worked with there (Collins, Dalton, and Roy 1945). This ethnography is not cited by Burawoy." In Collins's shop, were substantial "radical" sympathies, as manifested in part in discussions about the Soviet Union, and greater militancy in union activities. In other words, Burawoy's failure to specify the meaning of consent by describing differences in worker perspective was not the result of a lack of available evidence that could do just that.

3. Significantly, Burawoy's own evidence on the timing of changes in the structure of capitalism and the introduction of a new, more humane managerial philosophy after World War II does not line up with his macroexplanation. The internal labor market, a relaxation in management constraints that increased workers' freedom to move around jobs, was created *before* Allied bought Geer. The managerial change was instituted *before* the change in the structure of capitalism. It appears that Milton Friedman, not Karl Marx, is sustained by his data: an increase in the demand for labor following the expansion of the economy after World War II led to an improvement in the bargaining position of employees, which received expression in a variety of ways: higher wages, more union strength, better working conditions.

4. Burawoy attributes this objection to a passage in Howard Becker's writing. If one reads the passage that Burawoy cites, one finds that Becker (1998, 89) actually treats Burawoy's work as an inspiring model for research. Apparently aware that his work is vulnerable to the critique of no difference, Burawoy creates a context to defend himself by imagining an attack.

5. This move from a popular cultural definition of a problem to a phenomenologically grounded definition of the problem from the standpoint of the people whose behavior is at issue is typical in the procedures of analytic induction. See Katz (2001).

6. While Vaughan says that she is aiming for "how" not "why" explanations, I would put it a bit differently. She is not aiming to explain why people break up, but she is trying to explain why breaking up has certain processual features, in this case, caring. Analytic induction inevitably presses toward causal, "why," sufficient condition explanations and makes great contributions in advancing knowledge, even if it usually gets only to "distinctive" as opposed to "necessary and sufficient" conditions.

7. I think of de Certeau, Derrida, and Latour. See, for a tantalizing example, Octave Debary's article in this volume.

References

Anderson, Elijah. 2003. *A place on the corner.* 2nd ed. Chicago: University of Chicago Press.

Aubert, Vilhelm. 1982. *The hidden society.* New Brunswick, NJ: Transaction.

———. 1983. *In search of law: Sociological approaches to law.* Oxford, UK: Martin Robertson.

Becker, Howard S. 1953. Becoming a marihuana user. *American Journal of Sociology* 59:235-42.

———. 1998. *Tricks of the trade: How to think about your research while you're doing it.* Chicago: University of Chicago Press.

———. 2003. The politics of presentation: Goffman and total institutions. *Symbolic Interaction* 26:659-69.

Becker, Howard S., B. Geer, E. C. Hughes, and A. L. Strauss. 1961. *Boys in white: Student culture in medical school*. Chicago: University of Chicago Press.

Bourdieu, P., P. P. Ferguson, et al. 1999. *The weight of the world: Social suffering in contemporary society*. Cambridge, UK: Polity.

Burawoy, Michael. 1979. *Manufacturing consent: Changes in the labor process under monopoly capitalism*. Chicago: University of Chicago Press.

———. 1998. The extended case method. *Sociological Theory* 16:4-33.

———. 2003. Revisits: An outline of a theory of reflexive ethnography. *American Sociological Review* 68:645-79.

Burawoy, M., and J. Lukács. 1985. Mythologies of work: A comparison of firms in state socialism and advanced capitalism. *American Sociological Review* 50 (6): 723-37.

Burawoy, Michael, Joseph A. Blum, Sheba George, Zsuzsa Gille, Teresa Gowan, Lynne Haney, Maren Klawiter, Steven H. Lopez, Seán Ó. Riain, and Millie Thayer. 2000. *Global ethnography: Forces, connections, and imaginations in a postmodern world*. Berkeley: University of California Press.

Collins, Orvis, Melville Dalton, and Donald Roy. 1945. Restriction of output and social cleavage in industry, *Applied Anthropology* 5:1–14.

Clark, C. 1997. *Misery and company: Sympathy in everyday life*. Chicago: University of Chicago.

Drew, Paul. 1992. Contested evidence in courtroom cross-examination: The case of a trial for rape. In *Talk at work*, edited by P. Drew and J. Heritage, 471-520. Cambridge, UK: Cambridge University Press.

Duneier, Mitchell. 1999. *Sidewalk*. New York: Farrar, Straus and Giroux.

Elias, Norbert. 1994. *The civilizing process*. Oxford, UK: Blackwell.

———. 1996. *The Germans: Power struggles and the development of habitus in the nineteenth and twentieth centuries*. New York: Columbia University Press.

Emerson, R. M. 1981. On last resorts. *American Journal of Sociology* 87:1-22.

———. 1983. Holistic effects in social control decision-making. *Law & Society Review* 17:425-55.

Fine, G. A., ed. 1995. *A Second Chicago School? The development of a postwar American sociology*. Chicago: University of Chicago Press.

Finnegan, Ruth H. 1998. *Tales of the city: A study of narrative and urban life*. Cambridge, UK: Cambridge University Press.

Foucault, Michel. 1979. *Discipline and punish: The birth of the prison*. New York: Vintage.

Gans, Herbert J. 1962. *The urban villagers: Group and class in the life of Italian-Americans*. New York: Free Press.

———. 1967. *The Levittowners: Ways of life and politics in a new suburban community*. New York: Pantheon.

Geertz, C. 1988. *Works and lives: The anthropologist as author*. Palo Alto, CA: Stanford University Press.

Gluckman, Max. 1961. Ethnographic data in British social anthropology. *The Sociological Review* 9:5-17.

———. 1967. *The judicial process among the Barotse of Northern Rhodesia*. Manchester, UK: Manchester University Press.

Goffman, E. 1961. *Asylums: Essays on the social situation of mental patients and other inmates*. Garden City, NY: Anchor.

Hochschild, Arlie R. 1979. Emotion work, feeling rules, and social structure. *American Journal of Sociology* 83:551-75.

———. 1983. *The managed heart: Commercialization of human feeling*. Berkeley: University of California Press.

Hughes, Everett C. 1962. Good people and dirty work. *Social Problems* 10:3-10.

Jahoda, M., P. F. Lazarsfeld, and Hans Zeisel. 1930/1971. *Marienthal: The sociography of an unemployed community*. Chicago: Aldine-Atherton.

Jankowski, M. S. 1991. *Islands in the street: Gangs and American urban society*. Berkeley: University of California Press.

Katz, Jack. 1997. Ethnography's warrants. *Sociological Methods & Research* 25:391-423.

———. 2001. Analytic induction. In vol. 1 of *International encyclopedia of the social and behavioral sciences*, edited by N. J. Smelser and P. B. Baltes, 400-484. Oxford, UK: Elsevier.

———. 2003. Metropolitan crime myths. In *New York and Los Angeles: Politics, society and culture*, edited by D. Halle, 195-224. Chicago: University of Chicago Press.

Katz, Jack, and Curtis Jackson-Jacobs. 2003. The criminologists' gang. In *Companion to criminology*, edited by C. Sumner, 1-34. Oxford, UK: Blackwell.

Kornblum, W. 1974. *Blue collar community*. Chicago: University of Chicago Press.

Latour, Bruno. 1993. *We have never been modern*. Cambridge, MA: Harvard University Press.

———. 1999. *Pandora's hope: Essays on the reality of science studies*. Cambridge, MA: Harvard University Press.

Latour, Bruno, and Steve Woolgar. 1986. *Laboratory life: The construction of scientific facts*. Princeton, NJ: Princeton University Press.

Newman, Katherine S. 2004. *Rampage: The social roots of school shootings*. New York: Basic Books.

Nippert-Eng, Christena. E. 1996. *Home and work: Negotiating boundaries through everyday life*. Chicago: University of Chicago Press.

Ricoeur, Paul. 1970. *Freud and philosophy: An essay on interpretation*. New Haven, CT: Yale University Press.

Roy, Donald. 1952. Quota restriction and goldbricking in a machine shop. *American Journal of Sociology* 57:427-42.

———. 1953. Work satisfaction and social reward in quota achievement. *American Sociological Review* 18:507-14.

———. 1959-1960. "Banana time": Job satisfaction and informal interaction. *Human Organization* 18:158-68.

Smith-Lovin, L. 1998. On Arlie Hochschild, *The managed heart*. In *Required reading: Sociology's most influential books*, edited by D. Clawson, 113-19. Amherst: University of Massachusetts Press.

Stepan-Norris, J., and M. Zeitlin. 2003. *Left out: Reds and America's industrial unions*. Cambridge, UK: Cambridge University Press.

Suttles, Gerald D. 1968. *The social order of the slum: Ethnicity and territory in the inner city*. Chicago: University of Chicago Press.

Turner, Ralph. 1953. The quest for universals in sociological research. *American Sociological Review* 18:604-11.

Vaughan, Diane. 1986. *Uncoupling: Turning points in intimate relationships*. New York: Oxford University Press.

Whyte, W. F. 1955. *Street corner society*. Chicago: University of Chicago.

Observations and Reflections of a Perpetual Fieldworker

This article is based on the author's five decades of experience as a "perpetual fieldworker, engaged ethnographer," and teacher of field methods of social research. After dealing with what she perceives as a false dichotomy between qualitative and quantitative methods of research, she considers some of the cognitive characteristics of ethnographic research and distinctive properties of field data. She pays special attention to the complex role of participant observer within which an ethnographer conducts field research, focusing on the delicate balance between involvement and detachment that it entails and between listening and questioning. The article ends with an acknowledgement of the pivotal part that informants play in this kind of inquiry and with a tribute to the enduring meaning of a researcher's relationship to these "companions in the field" and her indebtedness to them.

Keywords: fieldwork/fieldworkers; informants; listening; participant observation; qualitative research; questioning

By
RENÉE C. FOX

I am a perpetual fieldworker and an engaged ethnographer. Throughout the course of my more than fifty-year-long career as a sociologist, my primary methods of research have been participant observation, in situ interviewing, oral history-taking, and content analysis of primary and secondary documents. Most of the articles and books I have authored are written in the kind of ethnographic literary genre that anthropologist Clifford Geertz has characterized as "thickly descriptive," interpretive, and evocative of "being there" (Geertz 1973, 3-30; 1988, 1-24). And I have taught field methods of social research to generations of students—to nurses, physicians, social workers, occupational and

Renée C. Fox, Ph.D., a sociologist, principally of medicine, is the Annenberg Professor Emerita of the Social Sciences, a senior fellow at the Center for Bioethics, and a member of the affiliated faculty of the Solomon Asch Center for the Study of Ethnopolitical Conflict at the University of Pennsylvania. She is also a research associate at the Refugee Studies Centre, Queen Elizabeth House, University of Oxford, United Kingdom.

DOI: 10.1177/0002716204266635

physical therapists, historians, folklorists, and writers, as well as to developing social scientists.

As I have written, ethnographic research has been "more than a method" for me. It has entailed "vertical as well as horizontal journeying" that has carried me, "geographically, intellectually, and emotionally, to nearby and faraway places," and transported me into "deep layers of the real lives of real people, into real situations, and into the innermost recesses of my own life and psyche." It has also "enabled me to move beyond the boundaries of myself and my native land, [to] become acquainted with societies and cultures other than my own" (Fox 2003a, 266). Wherever my research has been situated—whether in the United States, Europe, Africa, or Asia—what I have been privileged to study through this medium, as a sociologist principally of medicine, has brought me face-to-face, in a flesh-and-blood way, with some of the most wrenching and exalting, tragic and comic, illuminating and enigmatic aspects of the human condition.

My sustained involvement in the field as a researcher and teacher has not only entailed "doing" ethnography but also observing and pondering what it entails. In that sense, I have been a participant observer of participant observation—the core modality of ethnographic inquiry. It is from this gamut of firsthand experiences and continual reflection on them that the insights about ethnography presented in this article have emerged.

The Relationship between Qualitative and Quantitative Methods

The interactive and documentary methods of investigation that ethnographic field research employs have been dubbed "qualitative"—usually to distinguish them from the so-called quantitative methods that are also part of the social scientist's repertoire.

Sociologists are overly inclined to think dichotomously and, in certain respects, invidiously about these sets of methods rather than to see them as a spectrum of ways of inquiring into social reality, each of which has its own assets and limitations. On one hand, there is a positivist tendency in the discipline to characterize quantitative methods as more authentically and rigorously scientific than qualitative methods. On the other hand, proponents of qualitative methods, especially those for whom, as physician and anthropologist Arthur Kleinman once put it, fieldwork is "a way of being-in-the-world," have a tendency to extol what they claim are the uniquely "humanistic" attributes of these methods and, by innuendo, of the social scientists who use them—particularly their "empathy," "sensitivity," and "perceptiveness." In my view, such partisanship about which methods are best, supported by ideologically driven ideas about the comparative virtues of science and humanism, is neither rational nor constructive. For competence and skill in social research require not only trained knowledge of which method to use, when, and how but also the "ecumenical" employment of several methods of research whenever possible, so as to maximize their individual strengths and offset their restrictions.

Some Cognitive Characteristics of Ethnographic Research

This admonitory statement notwithstanding, qualitative methods of research in general, and ethnography in particular, do have distinctive cognitive attributes. (I reserve the term *ethnography* for qualitative research involving prolonged immersion in the field and continuous, face-to-face interaction with informants and respondents that results in the generation of massive amounts of "thickly descriptive" data, in a potentially narrative form, that provide an intimate view of what is being studied. I distinguish it from *nonethnographic* qualitative research that employs observation and interviewing methods in more circumscribed, short-term, distant, and "thin" ways.)

Although ethnographic fieldwork does not usually call for the generation and testing of hypotheses, it does require both theoretical and empirical foreknowledge. Aspiring to enter the field devoid of any preconceived ideas of what one may be looking for, or might expect to find, in order to fulfill a purist conception of scientific objectivity and impartiality is neither warranted nor realistic. If it were possible to go into the field as a *tabula rasa*, with the aim of "letting the field speak," it is likely that when the data collection was finished, one would exit from the field in the same state, as a consequence of being overwhelmed by the voluminous, unfocused material amassed and by the difficulty of making patterned sociological sense of it. A complex, two-way process is called for, which is both inductive and deductive and through which pertinent sociological concepts, ideas, and information are carried into the field and are activated both by the observational, interview, and documentary data being gathered and by the process of sociological reasoning in which one is trained. Not only are the excellence and meaningfulness of the field research and its results contingent on the quality of the social science that goes into it, but it could be argued that a deeper internalization of sociological thinking than usual is a requisite for doing the kind of "on the hoof," running analysis and interpretation of continuously inflowing data that fieldwork demands.

A set of trained skills are also necessary for conducting field research. Foremost among these are skills in observation and interviewing and in remembering and recording; high pattern recognition; the capacity to use one's self as an instrument in a self-reflexive but nonnarcissistic way, and to empathically recognize the connection between "self" and "other"; the ability not only to listen to what people say but to hear what they say and mean; the attunement to the language of gesture and silence, as well as to verbal language; the appreciative awareness of the nonbanality of "everyday" aspects of social life, their eloquence and import; an unwavering capacity to do the around-the-clock, hard work that the faithful writing of field notes requires; and perhaps above all, the interpersonal skill to manage, understand, and constantly analyze the socially complex and emotionally evocative role of participant observer that lies at the heart of fieldwork.

Properties of Field Data

The data that the fieldworker gathers are microscopic in nature. The orbit of a field study is usually restricted to the physical and social terrain that can be covered and managed by a solo-researcher, engaged in collecting what Geertz has called "small . . . particular facts" (Geertz 1973, 23), through participant observation and interviewing. On its ground level, an ethnographic research project is a highly specific case study, made up of numerous, even smaller case studies and of the fastidiously detailed qualitative materials from which they evolve. Nevertheless, the significance of these data is not confined to "micro" matters. Through the at-once inductive and deductive processes of analysis and interpretation already described, the data's import is enlarged by "macro" sociological concepts (that they also illuminate) and by their bearing on larger issues. As Geertz has aphoristically stated, "small facts speak to large issues" in these respects (Geertz 1973, 23).

Ethnographic data are also intrinsically comparative and intercultural in outlook, even when the research is conducted in one's "native" society. Whether "at home" or "abroad," through participant observation and in situ interviewing, field researchers acquire firsthand knowledge of groups, communities, and subcultures within a society to which the researchers might not have had access otherwise. They thereby expand their capacity to see both the differences that exist between themselves and their subjects and the similarities that link them, socially and culturally. And fieldwork carried out in "other" societies usually enlarges and alters researchers' perspectives on their "own" society, while advancing their knowledge and understanding of the society that they have come to study.

In addition, field notes are historical records in the making. With the passage of time, the sort of contemporaneous chronicle by a trained observer and probing interviewer who was a witness "on the scene," which the collection of notes describes, can become documented past history of high veracity and value.

In my own experience, it is my relationship to Belgium from 1959 to 1993, that most fully illustrates these attributes of field research and data. What began as a rather specialized inquiry into how social, cultural, and historical factors affected clinical medical research and research careers in Belgium progressively evolved into a study of Belgium through the windows of its medical laboratories: "the gamut of social institutions and groups" that this small, continental European society "encompasses, its characteristic social processes, and the values and beliefs, symbols and images out of which its . . . culture, atmosphere, and worldview are fashioned" (Fox 1994, 5). The particularism of Belgium and its "centrality as an organizing principle throughout the society" proved to be one of its most striking characteristics. To an extraordinary degree, "Belgians' family, community, region, the social class into which they were born, the ethnic-linguistic group to which they belonged, the religious-philosophical tradition out of which they came, and the political party with which they were affiliated enclosed them in enclaves that were not only insulated from one another but also rivalrous" (Fox 1994, 6). Consequently, my research entailed both physical and mental "commuting" between particularistic enclaves to which I was given privileged entrée—paradoxically, because unlike Belgians, I belonged to none of them. One of the findings that emerged from the comparative opportunity that this afforded me was the discovery of how much these particularistic groups had in common culturally, despite all that they believed differentiated them from one another. This turned out to be one of my most disputed findings, not only because these groups were so insulated from one another but also because of Belgians' peculiar insistence that they have

---

Although ethnographic fieldwork does not usually call for the generation and testing of hypotheses, it does require both theoretical and empirical foreknowledge.

---

neither a distinctive nor a common culture and that their country is perpetually on the brink of "disappearing." Because this outlook is part of the shared culture that Belgians deny possessing and contains within it an inversely expressed pride in their country, my rather tautological-sounding conclusion that despite "its collective self-doubts about its historical authenticity, national reality, and cultural coherence, . . . Belgium does indeed exist" was received with covert appreciation as well as overt skepticism (Fox 1994, 7, 31).

As my research unfolded, I became increasingly convinced that to truly and deeply know Belgium, it was vital to have direct contact with its former colony, Congo-Zaïre, the immense African land over which this tiny European country had reigned for seventy-five years (1885-1960). More than political, economic, and social domination had been involved in this colonial relationship. "The vast African territory that stretched beyond the restricting [inner and outer] boundaries of Belgium, and yet 'belonged' to it, [had] provided Belgians with an horizon, . . . an existential as well as a geographical frontier," and a dreaming space (Fox 1994, 225). It was this realization that transported me to Zaïre—the former Belgian Congo, now the Democratic Republic of Congo—where, from 1962 to 1970, I did extensive field research.

The trajectory of this research involved moving back and forth between micro and macro foci and levels of analysis within Belgium and beyond it, while the overall scope of my study became more enveloping to include the imprint both of the

Congo on Belgium and of Belgium on the Congo. In a sense, Belgium became my second country—a bridge for me between the United States, Europe, and Central Africa. Over the course of the three decades that the research spanned, the socio-logical data that I collected acquired some historical significance as a chronicle of an important postcolonial era in Belgium and in the Congo and of a period marked by social ferment and concerted attempts to modify traditional structures within Belgium and throughout most of continental Europe. Africa opened up to me through this research and, along with Belgium, entered and altered my inner land-scape. It seems to me more than coincidental that both Belgium and Africa are so prominent in the major research project in which I am presently engaged: a study of *Médecins Sans Frontières* (MSF)—"Doctors Without Borders"—that is focused on the practical and moral dilemmas this organization encounters on the front lines of its medical humanitarian and human rights advocacy action. One of the five Operational Sections of the organization is MSF-Belgium, and a large proportion of MSF's resources, including 50 percent of its project expenses, are committed to missions on the continent of Africa. Program expenses for work in the Democratic Republic of Congo during 2002 and 2003 figured at the top of the list, surpassed only by the money that MSF spent for its missions in Angola.

As the foregoing suggests, there is a biographical dimension to ethnographic research, to the journeys into the field that the investigator makes, and to the role that he or she assumes to carry out that research.

The Role of Participant Observer

It is the role within which an ethnographer conducts field research that distin-guishes it from all other forms of social and cultural inquiry. This is a role that can and should be continually observed and analyzed in a self-reflexive way by the investigator throughout all the phase movements of a study. At its core is a dynamic equilibrium between participation and observation—a continuous balancing and rebalancing of involvement and detachment.

It is through ongoing interaction and a developing relationship with the individ-uals and groups who belong to the milieu being explored that the researcher enters ever-more deeply—psychologically and interpersonally, as well as intellectually—into its social structure and culture and the experiences, personae, and lives of those who people it. Maintaining equipoise as this increasing engrossment takes place, without becoming overly identified with certain individuals and groups, while piercing and progressively reducing the "otherness" that separates the research worker from "those among whom he [or she] seeks new knowledge" (Mead 1970, 152) must be recurrently achieved and re-achieved. Toward the end of the three years that I spent as a participant observer in a male, metabolic research ward in a university hospital—studying the patients and physicians of Ward F-Second, the ways of coming to terms that they fashioned to deal with the chronic and terminal illnesses, and the high levels of medical uncertainty, limita-tion, risk, and failure along with the conflicts between research and therapy that they mutually faced—I was introduced by a long-term patient to a new arrival on the ward in the following way: "This is Miss Fox. She is not a doctor exactly. She is not a patient exactly. But she falls somewhere in between" (Fox 1959/1997, 234). Such a stance, at once equidistant from and equally close to the individuals and groups being studied (in this case, doctors and patients), and yet marginal to both, is neither ready-made nor static. It requires a considerable amount of self-examination and self-monitoring by the participant observer throughout the trajectory of the research, which is likely to be punctuated by episodes of overrapport and of underrapport at certain junctures. On Ward F-Second, for example, many of the patients who were in advanced stages of renal or cardiovascular disease suffered from severe, sometimes life-threatening edema. During a particular period of my

---

No account of fieldwork would be complete without acknowledgement of the pivotal role that informants play in the conduct of ethnographic research.

---

research on the ward, my anxiety- and angst-ridden identification with their predicament resulted in my developing "angioneurotic edema" in my face and my legs—a somaticized manifestation of my inability at that point to maintain sufficient emotional "space" between myself and the patients with whom I was establishing increasingly close relations. And when twenty-seven-year-old Paul O'Brian (a pseudonym), one of my chief informants, with whom I had an especially strong bond, died of Hodgkin's disease, along with the grief that I felt, I experienced something akin to a vocational crisis about the meaning and justification of the fieldwork in which I was engaged. "It seemed to me all that I was doing was looking, listening, and taking notes, with the vague hope that someday, a Ph.D. dissertation still to be written might become a book . . . that would feelingly portray the [suffering] predicament of F-Seconders" (Fox 1959/1997, 221).

On the other hand, interludes are likely to occur in the course of prolonged ethnographic research when the participant observer feels strongly alienated from certain individuals or particular groups encountered in the field and from aspects of the culture that they seem to incarnate. An incident from my field experience in the Congo anecdotally illustrates this kind of disaffection. The sociological research that colleagues and I had been conducting in Kinshasa and in the many communities in the interior of the country to which we traveled included in-depth interviews with numerous African women who had shared disturbing accounts with us of the hardships they suffered as a consequence of the infidelity and neglect of their husbands, their willful withholding of money to feed and clothe their wives and children as a way of exerting control over them, and the greater group solidarity that the men appeared to have with their male age-mates than with their spouses. On the way home from work one afternoon, two of my colleagues and I stopped at an outdoor café for a cup of coffee. Seated at a table next to us were several young Congolese men absorbed in animated, laughter-punctuated conversation, as they each quaffed a cool glass of beer. I was startled by what negative, accusatory feelings their innocuous public behavior evoked in me. I had become so affected by the stories of mistreatment that women had confided in us that without any knowledge of who these men were or what their family lives were like, I was indignantly supposing that they were enjoying themselves and each other's company at the monetary and emotional expense of their wives!

When the participant observer notices her overinvolvement, she must recognize it, record it in her field notes, analyze it, and work to rectify it. Disentangling oneself sufficiently from strong feelings of antipathy and disapproval to proceed with the fieldwork in as receptive, open-minded, and inclusive a fashion as possible is not easy to accomplish, especially when the researcher's own social values and moral convictions are being challenged by what she is observing, learning, and experiencing in a firsthand, participatory way. It may become necessary to temporarily withdraw from the field for a while to regain a more composed, equilibrated perspective.

Managing this kind of emotion is rendered all the more difficult if it coincides with what I have come to think of as the "therapeutic temptation" to which fieldworkers are susceptible—that is, their desire to intervene in some of the situations they are observing to help to improve, remedy, or rectify them. One of the most vividly portrayed instances of this propensity and of the feelings that may accompany it can be found in Laura Bohanan's "anthropological novel" *Return to Laughter* (published under the nom de plume of Elenore Smith Bowen). As she writes in the author's note, although the characters in this book, except herself, are fictitious, its "ethnographic background" is based on the "incidents . . . of the genre [she] experienced" doing fieldwork in West Africa, in a tribe that "does exist," among people "of the type" she describes (Bowen 1954/1964):

> I stood over Amara. She tried to smile at me. She was very ill. I was convinced these women could not help her. She would die. She was my friend, but my epitaph for her would be impersonal observations scribbled in my notebook: . . . "Death in childbirth/ Cause: witchcraft/Case of Amara." A lecture from the past reproached me. "The anthropologist cannot, like the chemist or biologist, arrange controlled experiments. Like the astronomer, he can only observe. But unlike the astronomer, his mere presence produces changes in the data he is trying to observe. He himself is a disturbing influence which he must endeavor to keep to the minimum. His claim to science must therefore rest on a meticulous accuracy of observation and on a cool, objective approach to his data."
>
> A cool, objective approach to Amara's death?
>
> One can, perhaps, be cool when dealing with questionnaires or when interviewing strangers. But what is one to do when one can collect data only by forming personal friendships? . . . Was I to stand aloof observing the course of events?

I marched over to Yabo. "Do you wish Amara to live? . . . There are doctors who can save both her life and the life of her child. They have stronger medicines than yours to bring forth the child. If those fail, they know how to reach up into the womb. They even know how to cut open the living body, bring forth the child, and then heal the mother. I will send a messenger on a bicycle to the hospital and another for a truck. I will pay carriers to carry Amara up to the road and on it, until the truck meets them. I will write a paper to the hospital, asking them to give her the best medicine and telling them that I will pay. (Bowen 1954/1964, 184-85)

Although Amara's husband, uncles, and father, who were the gatekeepers in the situation, acknowledged that "the heart" of the anthropologist "wished [Amara] well" and expressed their gratitude for what Bowen/Bohanan had offered to do on Amara's behalf, "with unmoveable determination," they insisted that the doctors to whom she wished to entrust Amara did not have the capacity to "remove the magic" and deal with the witches that had brought Amara to the brink of death. They continued to enlist the aid of magico-religious practitioners and to perform certain ceremonies to ward off the magic and the evil it had produced. They would "not allow" Bowen/Bohanan to help. "Defeated," she was "forced to watch [Amara] in pain and steadily growing weaker. . . . In silence and bitterness, at nightfall, [she] left" (Bowen 1954/1964, 185-86).

After Amara's death, it took a long time for Bowen/Bohanan to "return to laughter" (the title of her book)—to recover not only from her grief and chagrin over what she was certain was a preventable death and from her powerlessness to do anything about it, but also from the sense of estrangement from the tribe she was studying with which the death left her—of "the gulf between their world and mine," as she put it. What became for her "symbolic" of this chasm was what she now felt was the "savage" way that these people "laughed at suffering" and "at the sight of human misery" (Bowen 1954/1964, 231). It was not until she had reached a later stage in her research, close to the time of her departure from the field, that she recognized the "courage," the humanity, and the resiliency that this ostensibly cruel laughter contained:

Such laughter has little concern with what is funny. It is often bitter and sometimes a little mad, for it is the laughter under the mask of tragedy, and also the laughter that masks tears. . . . It is the laughter of people who value love and friendship and plenty, who have lived with terror and death and hate. . . . They knew how to live at close quarters with tragedy, how to live with their own failure . . . [and] the terror of a broken society . . . and yet laugh. . . . [And] they knew how to come back . . . and create life anew. (Bowen 1954/1964, 297)

The introspective, odyssey-like story that Bowen/Bohanan tells of what it was like for her to be an anthropologist in the field contains within it allusions to other evocative aspects of the role of participant observer that it is important to handle perceptively, with skill, and whenever possible, with foresight. As she notes, social scientists are more likely to be trained to be aware of the observer effects that they have on the persons, places, and phenomena they are studying and to try to minimize those effects than to be prepared for the ways in which they themselves may be altered by their field experiences and relationships. I have referred to the vertical journeying that participant observation involves—the enlightening, frequently painful, and often transmuting encounters with the researcher's own psychological and social, moral and spiritual self that participant observation entails. The personal changes that the fieldworker undergoes may also result from her socialization into and by the community to which she is progressively given entrée. On Ward F-Second, a long-term patient, who was observing me at least as keenly as I was observing him, described my initiation and socialization into the "hospital life" of

---

When the participant observer notices her overinvolvement, she must recognize it, record it in her field notes, analyze it, and work to rectify it.

---

the ward to me in the following way. I can remember how "serious" you were at first, he said. "Once or twice there I was even afraid you'd bust out cryin'. After a while, though, you began to understand and take things, so you were able to laugh and make jokes like the rest of the fellows" (Fox 1959/1997, 218). In effect, what he told me was that under the watchful eyes of the patients of F-Second and their tutelage, I gradually learned to deal with witnessing the stresses of grave illness, medical uncertainty and limitation, human experimentation, and closeness to death that they faced by adopting some of the coping mechanisms that they used. Paramount among these was the impious, defiant, and macabre humor through which the patient community counterphobically expressed some of their deepest, most powerful, and threatening feelings (a form of humor kindred to the tragicomic laughter of the tribe that Bowen/Bohanan studied). Their teaching and my learning were implicit processes of which I was not aware until I startled myself by making a grim, F-Second-like joke in an extrahospital setting, wondered what accounted for this uncharacteristic behavior on my part, and in a state of raised consciousness, observed when I arrived at the ward the next day that I was an active participant in this kind of joking that constantly took place between F-Seconders. The patients who taught and permitted me to do this were not only pleased with the virtuosity that I had developed in wielding this humor; they also recognized that I was en route to understanding its coded meaning. And they knew long before I did that it would have an enduring influence on my emotional life.

The socializing effects of participant observation on the researcher are not always so felicitous. They may contribute to the sort of crisis of identity that it is not uncommon for fieldworkers to undergo. In the methodological appendix to *Street Corner Society*—his renowned study of the social worlds of street gangs and corner boys in an Italian American slum of Boston's North End that he called "Cornerville"—sociologist William Foote Whyte has recorded a memorable, personal account of such a crisis. It occurred in the context of his attempt to "gain an insider view" of the political life of the community. With this in mind, Whyte "enlisted as the unpaid secretary of the unpaid secretary" of George Ravello, the state senator who was a candidate in the mayoralty contest taking place at the time; when that was over, he reenlisted to be active in Ravello's subsequent campaign for election to a vacant seat in the Congress. "Fortunately for my study," Whyte wrote, "all the other Cornerville politicians were at least officially for Ravello. I therefore felt that I could be active in his campaign without creating barriers for myself anywhere else in the district." On election day, Whyte voted when the polls opened and then "reported for duty at the candidate's headquarters." But later in the day, after he got home, he "began hearing alarming reports from the home ward of the Irish politician who was Ravello's chief rival. He was said to have a fleet of taxicabs cruising around his ward so that each of his "repeaters" would be able to vote in every precinct of the ward. It was clear that if we did not steal the election ourselves, this low character would steal it from us." Responding to the commands of one of the senator's chief lieutenants, before the polls closed that night, Whyte voted three more times for Ravello in different parts of the ward. At one polling place, his vote was challenged, and he came within a hair's breadth of being arrested. Looking back on his "performance on election day," Whyte realized that his "first-hand personal experience" of being a "repeater" had very little research value because he "had been observing these activities at quite close range before, and [he] could have had all the data without taking [the] risk" of getting arrested or jeopardizing his entire study. But the most serious and enduring problem that this experience retrospectively posed for him "transcended expediency":

> I had been brought up as a respectable, law-abiding, middle-class citizen. When I discovered that I was a repeater, I found my conscience giving me serious trouble. . . . I could not laugh it off simply as a necessary part of the field work. . . . I . . . had to learn that the field worker cannot afford to think only of learning to live with others in the field. He has to continue living with himself. If the participant observer finds himself engaging in behavior that he has learned to think of as immoral, then he is likely to begin to wonder what sort of a person he is after all. (Whyte 1993, 309-17)

"What am I doing? Why am I doing it? Who am I? Who and what am I becoming?" These questions, which usually occur in response to a critical field event, touch the core of the researcher's sense of self, personal integrity, and fundamental values. They are triggered by his or her startled realization of having been changed by the field and a *prise de conscience* about the moral and psychological implications of this change. And they are related to an array of structural strains inherent to the role of participant observer and their cumulative impact on the person cast in this role.

I use the phrase "cast in this role" advisedly because although the well-prepared, scrupulous fieldworker carefully thinks through how she will present herself to the people being studied—without deceit or falsification, in a manner that is "acceptable to the people among whom [she] works and is congruent with the activities that they will see [her] carry out" (Mead 1970, 155)—in the end, that role is not self-determined. Like any other social role, it is shaped in part by the persons with whom one interacts. For example, six years prior to the time that I undertook my research on Ward F-Second, I had contracted a severe case of poliomyelitis that kept me in the hospital for months and, after a long convalescence, left me with a moderate degree of residual, right-sided muscle weakness and paralysis. "Though my ex-patient status was an important and relevant fact, I did not intend to include it in my self-presentation. . . . Because I hoped to understand the ward . . . from the point of view of physicians as well as patients, I did not wish to be overly identified with either. Discretion about my former illness, I felt, would be a precaution against too closely aligning myself with patients." But I had not accounted for the perceptiveness, medical expertise, and outspokenness of Leo Angelico (pseudonym), a veteran patient on the ward, whose legs and left arm were paralyzed from what was thought to be a spinal tumor. In the course of the first day that I appeared on F-Second, he asked me if I had been "a polio"; I answered affirmatively. By the day's end, as the "news" of my patienthood traveled the length of the ward, I was viewed not only as a sociologist engaged in a doctoral dissertation study of the patients and physicians of F-Second but also as a former patient, who "understands, because she was a patient herself" (Fox 1959/1997, 214). In this instance, the way that the patient community reformulated my role accelerated the community's acceptance of me and helped to validate my research in its eyes. However, being perceived and defined by the community one enters in a manner that fits its system of statuses and roles can be problematic. Such was the case, for example, in connection with the research that I conducted in the People's Republic of China (Fox and Swazey 1982, 1984). Whereas the fact that I was seen as a senior in age and in professional standing, who was a teacher and a scholar, was regarded as an asset and facilitated my research, my statuses as an unmarried woman, with no children, who was marginally handicapped were anomalous in the Chinese social system. They were regarded as deviating from the normal, as well as from the common order. Although these aspects of my status-role set were handled by respondents with politesse, they were impediments that also had the deeply inward, psychological effect of making me feel like a disvalued nonperson.

As fascinating and fruitful as it may be to do fieldwork in the complex role of participant observer, the process of obtaining information in this fashion, as anthropologist Margaret Mead wrote, is "a very curious and exacting adventure"—physically, socially, and emotionally. The prolonged, continuous, and absorbing "experience of immersing oneself in the field" that it demands; the months, sometimes years, of "trying to step as fully as one can" into the ongoing life of other people and "the reality" of their social world and culture that this involves; the "suspen[sion] for the time [of] both one's beliefs and disbeliefs, and of simultaneously attempting to understand . . . this other version of reality"; the intensifying "inclusion of the observer within the observed," yet "the delicate balance between empathic participation and self-awareness" on which the research depends; and the changes that fieldworkers undergo "with each step of the journey" (Mead 1976, 1, 6, 7, 15)—all these are features of the participant observer's role that not only require attention, care, and skill but may entail considerable stress. Over time, they can even result in the emergence of the kind of "participant-observer burnout" that medical historian Judith Swazey and I detected in ourselves after some twenty-five

---

[T]he role within which an ethnographer conducts field research . . . distinguishes it from all other forms of social and cultural inquiry.

---

years of collaborative research on the development of organ transplantation, the artificial kidney, and the artificial heart. Eventually, this led to our decision to call a permanent moratorium on our fieldwork in this sphere. Our exit from the field, we stated in *Spare Parts*, our final book on organ replacement, was impelled by the "need and desire" that we had developed to "distance ourselves . . . emotionally" and to make "a value statement." "By our leave-taking," we declared, "we are intentionally separating ourselves from what we believe has become an overly zealous medical and societal commitment to the endless perpetuation of life and to repairing and rebuilding people through organ replacement—and from the human suffering and the social, cultural, and spiritual harm we believe such unexamined excess can, and already has, brought in its wake" (Fox and Swazey 1992, 199, 209-10).

Participation, Listening, and Asking Questions

The chief mode of participation in which the fieldworker engages is talking with people, individually and in groups. This in situ talking can take several forms. The most "natural" and least interventionist of these involves being present and listening when people in the field are conversing with one another, silently registering what is being said, and recording ex post facto in one's field notes—ideally, in as close to verbatim speech as possible—the sociological crux of the exchanges that occurred. Being an interested listener may also provide opportunities to ask specific questions about the discussion that is taking place, without unduly disrupting it or overly influencing its content. In addition to these going-with-the-flow ways of listening and questioning, being a participant observer on the scene facilitates access to individuals with whom more formal interview arrangements can be made to obtain needed information or explanations or to probe for below-the-surface attitudes, feelings, values, and beliefs. Because they are grounded in the lived situation of which the fieldworker is a part, these interviews are likely to contain questions of focal importance that might not have occurred to outside researchers whose interview schedules are conceived and constructed from a distance. In addition, the participant observer has the built-in advantage of the rapport that her sustained relationship to interviewees has established. Not only does this rapport ease and enrich communication; it often leads to relevant data being brought to the investigator by contacts in the field, without her having to ask for it.

"One has to learn when to question and when not to question, as well as what questions to ask," William Foote Whyte advised. "Go easy on that 'who,' 'what,' 'why,' 'when,' 'where' stuff," Doc, his primary informant, once cautioned him. "You ask those questions, and people will clam up on you" (Whyte 1993, 303). Discerning what not to ask is crucial. In the context of my own field research, there have been at least two major instances where I decided that the wisest course of action was to refrain from posing questions about what I was observing or from taking the initiative of probing into more inward phenomena. The first of these concerned what I came to think of as the "game of chance" behavior of the Metabolic Group, the team of physicians who cared for the patients of Ward F-Second and also conducted research upon them. Recurrently, at their evening rounds, behind the closed doors of the conference room where they met, these physicians made wagers on such serious medical matters as the diagnosis of a patient's illness, the impact of therapy upon it, its prognosis, the laboratory and clinical outcomes of particularly important and hazardous experiments for which their patients were subjects, and even on whether a particular patient would live or die. Although I was the only outsider who was allowed to sit in on their evening meetings, and they displayed this behavior in my presence, I felt that irrespective of how adroitly I phrased the question, there was no way that I could ask them why they took bets on such grave matters, without embarrassing, offending, and alienating them. No matter how neutral or tactful my phraseology and tone of voice might be, I thought, they might assume that I was shocked as well as surprised by such brazenly unscientific and seemingly inhumane antics. So I made the decision to confine myself to observing the game of chance—noting when it occurred and when it did not, what the surrounding circumstances were, and what other behaviors accompanied it. I was particularly struck by the facts that the team was most likely to take bets when the levels of uncertainty and of risk surrounding their clinical and research interventions were especially high, that the giving and taking of bets was usually carried out in a rather ceremonious fashion that centered on recording the bets on the same kind of paper they used for laboratory findings, and that it was accompanied by the "blasphemous hilarity" of counterphobic medical humor (Fox 1959/1997, 82-85). Without recourse to discussing their game of chance with the physicians, based solely on the patterns that emerged from my microdynamic observations over time, I gradually reached the following understanding of their ritualized, laughter-accompanied wagering:

> On one level, it is a collective way of "acting out" the chance elements that are inherent to medical science and practice. It is also a way of "acting on" them, for it involves a group of health professionals in a game-like contest, in which they pit their knowledge, experience, skill, and powers of reasoning and prediction against the unknown, adventitious, hard-to-control . . . aspects of medical work. "Winning" the bet, by "guessing" right, represents a symbolic mastery of these chancy forces, and a schematic victory over them. This wagering is fundamentally ironic in nature. It mimics probability reasoning-based medical scientific thinking, and it is playfully structured around the premise that what physicians . . . know and do not know, what they can and cannot do, and how their interventions affect patients—all have much in common with a game of chance. At the same time, the betting behavior is self-depreciatory and self-mocking, depicting supposedly professional medical expertise and action as highly speculative, full of guesswork and gambles, and fraught with luck –both good and bad. Finally, the game of chance is both a protest and a petition. It is a ritualized way of declaring that what health professionals know and can do for patients, and whether or not their patients get better or worse, live or die, should have more order and meaning than the throw of the dice or the turn of a roulette wheel. (Fox 1988, 582-83)

In the end, when they read my doctoral dissertation and my subsequent book *Experiment Perilous* (Fox 1959/1997), based on my three years of field research in their midst, the members of the Metabolic Group thought not only that my interpretation of their game of chance was correct but that it was also one of the most insightful conclusions I had reached. I am convinced that if I had asked them questions about their wagering while I was still in the field, they would not have been forthcoming in answering them, and that showing overt curiosity about this behavior might have made them less willing to admit me to the inner sanctum of their conference room.

A second major instance where I have exercised deliberate restraint about asking questions is of another order. It concerns phenomena that are neither visible nor audible and thus cannot be directly observed—namely, the reactions of donors and recipients of organ transplants and their families to this extraordinary act of giving and receiving. Over the decades of our firsthand research on transplantation, Judith Swazey and I were made aware of the buried, often animistic sentiments that people have about their vital organs and the integrity of their body that this "exchange" is likely to evoke. Many recipients of cadaveric organ transplants, for example, grapple with the haunting sense that along with the organ they have received, psychic, social, and physical qualities of their unknown donor have been transferred into their bodies, personhoods, and lives. Some recipients dream recurrently of an individual who they suppose was their organ donor. Others notice changes in the activities and foods they enjoy, in their daily habits, and in their personality traits that they attribute to characteristics of the donor that have somehow been infused into their beings. Their feeling that the spirit of the donor lives on in a personified and transforming way within them is augmented both by the magnitude of the "gift of life" they have received, which is of such surpassing significance that it is inherently unreciprocal, and, in the case of cadaver transplants, by the recipient's realization that an unknown, unseen human benefactor had to die for them to live and flourish (Fox and Swazey 1992, 36-37; Fox 2003b, 237-38). Judith Swazey and I never took the initiative of questioning organ recipients about these experiences. In our judgment, we had neither the professional competence nor the right to try to enter and probe the regions of their psyches from which such anthropomorphic reactions emanated. We were concerned about how disturbing it might be for recipients if we attempted to explore these feelings with them, and on

---

[An ethnographer] must find ways to observe, participate in, and come to understand the social world she is studying from the vantage points of as many persons who belong to it as possible.

---

a strictly pragmatic level, we thought it would be counterproductive. Through the spontaneous testimonies of donors, recipients, their families, and transplant surgeons and nurses to which we were privy, however, we learned a great deal about these subterranean aspects of organ transplantation. Somehow, seemingly because they felt we were acquainted with these phenomena and did not regard them as strange or irrational, many recipients were willing, and in some cases eager, to talk to us about the phenomena without our asking. An anthropological adage comes to mind in this connection: "The tribe will tell you its secrets if you already know them."

Participant Observers and Informants

No account of fieldwork would be complete without acknowledgement of the pivotal role that informants play in the conduct of ethnographic research. It is not an exaggeration to say that their collaborative participation in this sort of inquiry, of which they are also subjects, is indispensable. There is a sense in which virtually all the members of a group, an organization, a community, or a population being studied in this way take part in the research. But there are certain individuals among them with whom the fieldworker develops a particularly close and continuous collegial relationship. In effect, this special kind of informant becomes the participant observer's observing participant, adviser, and counselor and, in many instances, more than a friend.

One of my chief informants inside the social world of F-Second was Jennie P., a young woman of my own age and head nurse of the ward at the time I did my field research. I never saw her again after my study was finished, but we have exchanged annual Christmas/New Year's cards and messages ever since. "Is it 45 or 46 years since we shared the hope and sorrow of those very special patients on F-Second?" she wrote in December 2000. "I've always felt fortunate to be able to share with you my love and frustration of my special 'fellas.'" And among those "very special" men who were part of the "experiment perilous" that united us and with whom we have been linked in "hope and sorrow . . . love and frustration," over time and space, are Paul O'Brian and Leo Angelico, my most important patient informants on the ward.

I dedicated *In the Belgian Château*, the book that is based on my research in Belgium and Congo/Zaïre, to "Moeder Clara" and "Sabine" (pseudonyms), two other informants who "welcomed me into their 'houses' . . . opened their lives and their lands to me . . . played cardinal roles" in my field work and the writing of the book and who "occupy special places in my life" (Fox 1994).

Relationships like these may raise questions about the Olympian objectivity of the ethnographer. Both through the association that she develops with the informants who are her closest companions in the field and through means that extend beyond it, she must find ways to observe, participate in, and come to understand the social world she is studying from the vantage points of as many persons who belong to it as possible. But as the corpus of ethnographically based works attests— whether the names attributed to the informants are "Amara" or "Doc", "Jennie," "Paul," or "Leo", "Clara" or "Sabine"—these persons to whom field researchers are deeply tied and profoundly indebted "live on in [their] memory," in images and words, "transfixed in time" (Mead 1976, 16).

References

Bowen, Elenore Smith. 1954/1964. *Return to laughter: An anthropological novel*. Garden City, New York: Doubleday, Anchor Books, Natural History Library Edition.

Fox, Renée C. 1959/1997. *Experiment perilous: Physicians and patients facing the unknown*. Republished with a new epilogue by the author. New Brunswick, NJ: Transaction.

———. 1988. The human condition of medical professionals. In *Essays in medical sociology: Journeys into the field*, 2nd ed., 572-87. New Brunswick, NJ: Transaction.

———. 1994. *In the Belgian château: The spirit and culture of a European society in an age of change*. Chicago: Ivan R. Dee.

———. 2003a. Exploring the moral and spiritual dimensions of society and medicine. In *Society and medicine: Essays in honor of Renée C. Fox*, edited by Carla M. Messikomer, Judith P. Swazey, and Allen Glicksman, 257-71. New Brunswick, NJ: Transaction.

———. 2003b. Through the lenses of biology and sociology: Organ replacement. In *Debating biology: Sociological reflections on health, medicine, and society*, edited by William J. Simon, Lynda Birke, and Gillian A. Bendelow, 235-44. London: Routledge.

Fox, Renée C., and Judith P. Swazey. 1982. Critical care at Tianjin First Central Hospital and the Fourth Modernization. *Science* 217:700-705.

326

THE ANNALS OF THE AMERICAN ACADEMY

———. 1984. Medical morality is not bioethics: Medical ethics in China and the United States. *Perspectives in Biology and Medicine* 27:336-60.

———. 1992. *Spare parts: Organ replacement in American society.* New York: Oxford University Press.

Geertz, Clifford. 1973. Thick description: Towards an interpretive theory of culture. In *The interpretation of cultures: Selected essays*, 3-30. New York: Basic Books.

———. 1988. Being there: Anthropology and the scene of writing. In *Works and lives: The anthropologist as author*, 1-24. Palo Alto, CA: Stanford University Press.

Mead, Margaret. 1970. Research with human beings: A model derived from anthropological field practice. In *Experimentation with human subjects*, edited by Paul K. Freund, 152-77. New York: George Braziller.

———. 1976. *Letters from the field, 1925-1975.* New York: Harper and Row.

Whyte, William Foote. 1993. *Street corner society: The social structure of an Italian slum.* 4th ed. Chicago: University of Chicago Press.

Quick Read Synopsis

Being Here and Being There: Fieldwork Encounters and Ethnographic Discoveries

Special Editors: ELIJAH ANDERSON, SCOTT N. BROOKS, RAYMOND GUNN, and NIKKI JONES

Volume 595, September 2004

Prepared by Herb Fayer (Consultant)

Note:

To read the synopses for this volume, please go to the American Academy of Political and Social Science (AAPSS) website: http://www.aapss.org/. Under the "Programs and News" menu, find the September 2004 table of contents. Click on each article title to read the synopsis.